Language: A Righ

Thank you very much, Carol, for your inspiration, encouragement and enabling me to do something meaningful for the Hungarian Deaf Community and Culture:

István

Language: A Right and a Resource

Approaching Linguistic Human Rights

Edited by
MIKLÓS KONTRA
ROBERT PHILLIPSON
TOVE SKUTNABB-KANGAS
TIBOR VÁRADY

CEU PRESS

Central European University Press

Published by

Central European University Press
Október 6. utca 12
H–1051 Budapest
Hungary

400 West 59th Street
New York, NY 10019
USA

Distributed in the United Kingdom and Western Europe by
Plymbridge Distributors Ltd., Estover Road, Plymouth PL6 7PZ, United
Kingdom

ISBN 963-9116-63-7 cloth
ISBN 963-9116-64-5 paperback

Library of Congress Cataloging in Publication Data
A CIP catalog record for this book is available upon request

Printed in Hungary by Akadémiai Nyomda

Contents

vi

Market issues

Language planning issues

Education and ethnicity issues

List of Maps

List of Tables

List of Figures

List of Contributors

Bart Driessen is senior associate at the Brussels-based law firm *Vermulst & Waer Advocaten.*

Ina Druviete is Professor of General Linguistics at the University of Latvia, and head of the Department of Sociolinguistics at the Latvian Language Institute, Riga.

François Grin has held research and teaching positions at the universities of Montreal, Washington (Seattle), Geneva and Fribourg. He is currently Adjunct Director of the European Centre for Minority Issues (ECMI) in Flensburg (Germany), and interim Associate Professor at the Department of Economics of the University of Geneva. His research focuses on the economics of language, language policy and education, and he has widely published on these issues, including a theme issue of the *International Journal of the Sociology of Language* (no 121, 1996).

Amir Hassanpour is Assistant Professor at the Department of Near and Middle Eastern Civilizations, University of Toronto, Canada. He specializes in linguistics, communications and Middle Eastern studies, and is the author of *Nationalism and Language in Kurdistan, 1918–1985* (San Francisco: Mellen Research University Press, 1992).

Miklós Kontra is Professor of Linguistics at József Attila University, Szeged, and head of the Department of Sociolinguistics at the Linguistics Institute of the Hungarian Academy of Sciences, Budapest.

Angéline Martel is Professor of Sociolinguistics and Applied Linguistics at Télé-université, Montréal, Canada. She is editor-in-chief of the electronic journal *DiversCité Langues*. She has published widely on minority-majority power relations, on language rights, language teaching and technology.

István Muzsnai teaches at the Budapest School for the Deaf, and in the Theoretical Linguistics Program of Eötvös Loránd University, Budapest.

Uldis Ozolins is Lecturer in Politics at La Trobe University in Melbourne, Australia and has published widely on language policy and related issues in Australia, the Baltic States and elsewhere in the world.

Robert Phillipson is Associate Professor in English at the University of Roskilde, Denmark, where he has served as Dean of Humanities. He has written extensively on language pedagogy, linguistic imperialism, language policy and linguistic human rights. He serves on the board of the Danish Centre for Human Rights.

Mart Rannut has held leading positions in independent Estonia in language policy and human rights fields, and has recently completed a doctoral study of Estonian language policy.

Klára Sándor is Associate Professor of Hungarian Linguistics at Juhász Gyula Teacher Training College, Szeged, Hungary.

Tove Skutnabb-Kangas is Reader in Minority Education and Linguistic Human Rights, Åbo Akademi University, Vasa, Finland, and research associate at Roskilde University, Denmark. She has written and edited many books and articles in the areas of linguistic human rights, multilingual education, language and power, and linguistic imperialism (in twenty languages).

Andrea Szalai is a Ph.D. candidate in Applied Linguistics at Janus Pannonius University, Pécs, Hungary.

Tibor Várady is Professor of Law at the Legal Studies Department of the Central European University, Budapest. A former Minister of Justice in the government of Milan Panić in Yugoslavia (July 1992–March 1993), he has taught at universities in Yugoslavia, Hungary, and the USA. He is the author of many books and articles, and is editor in chief of the social science review *Létünk* (Yugoslavia).

Dr. Fernand de Varennes is Director of the Asia-Pacific Centre for Human Rights and the Prevention of Ethnic Conflict at Murdoch University, Australia. He is the author of numerous publications dealing with minority rights, international law and ethnic conflicts, which have appeared in Asia, Europe and North America in six languages.

Acknowledgments

This book grew out of the Linguistic Human Rights Conference and Workshop for NGO-Representatives, which took place at The Central European University Conference Center in Budapest, on 16–19 October, 1997. Special thanks are due to the Open Society Institute, Budapest, the Illyés Közalapítvány, and the MTA Stratégiai Kutatások Programiroda for their generous support which made the meeting possible. The event was hosted by the Linguistics Institute of the Hungarian Academy of Sciences, and the Human Rights Program of the Central European University. Overall planning for the conference, including the selection of plenary speakers and the screening of abstracts, was undertaken by Miklós Kontra, Gábor Halmai, Robert Phillipson and Tove Skutnabb-Kangas. The organizing committee comprised Gábor Halmai, Zoltán Kali, Miklós Kontra, Andrea Leitmann and Noémi Saly.

The editors thank the authors for delivering their revised manuscripts on time, and are grateful to Zoltán Kali for his help in the final phase of electronic manuscript preparation.

Conceptualising and Implementing Linguistic Human Rights

MIKLÓS KONTRA, ROBERT PHILLIPSON,
TOVE SKUTNABB-KANGAS,
TIBOR VÁRADY

This book grew out of a conference on Linguistic Human Rights held in Budapest in October 1997. In the post-Cold War years, language rights have appeared as one of the dimensions of the quest for a new society based on human rights. The emphasis and some arguments may be fresh, but the problem is certainly not a new one. The issue of language rights in Central and Eastern Europe (and not only in Central and Eastern Europe) has, time and again, prompted political action, legislation, and international treaties; it has also served both as a reason (or pretext) for brutal conflict, and as a touchstone of tolerance. Language can serve, in all spheres of social life, to bring people together or to divide them. Language rights can serve to unite societies, whereas violations of language rights can trigger and inflame conflict. There is, therefore, every reason to clarify the position of language rights in various states and in international human rights law, and to analyse the experience of the management of multilingualism in diverse societies.

This book has multiple goals. It brings together insights from a range of disciplines, in particular law, economics, and sociolinguistics. It also presents a rich variety of experiences drawn from many European states and from Canada so as to demonstrate how potentially conflictual situations are being handled. Granted the tension in many contemporary states in which minority groups feel that their linguistic human rights (hereafter LHRs) are being violated—from the Baltic States to Slovakia, Romania and Kurdistan—there is clearly a need for a careful scholarly analysis of the causes of conflict, the role played by language in these conflicts, and the paths that could be taken in order to build a more harmonious future. In addition to considered analysis of a wide range of contexts, including such matters as the rights of the Deaf community and of Gypsies (Roma or non-Roma[1]), the book seeks to clarify how principles of linguistic human rights can be approached in theoretically informed and valid ways.

Three Central Tasks for LHR Research

Why is this collection of articles important? One need that the book attempts to meet has to do with people from different professional fields talking at cross-purposes and misunderstanding each other. If sociolinguists, human rights lawyers, and politicians are to understand linguistic human rights in similar ways, multidisciplinary clarification of concepts is vital. We need to know more about whether our concepts are universally valid (for instance, whether a mother tongue has stable or fluid features) and about the relative importance given to specific rights (for instance, individual as opposed to collective rights, or rights versus duties). There may be Euro-centricity and Western-centricity in how language rights are conceptualized, and this need not be a blessing.

Secondly, a clarification of what LHRs are, and can—or cannot—do is also needed so as to show that a "language as a right"-oriented approach is not in contradiction to seeing "languages as a resource". The two are necessarily complementary. This means that there needs to be a shift from seeing the existence of linguistic minorities and of many languages as problems, to seeing them as resources, and that in this shift, LHRs are a necessary tool that can assist in the prevention of problems and in empowerment. South Africa seems to be one of the few countries where this has been understood at a policy level (e.g. Alexander 1995; Heugh 1995; LANGTAG 1996).

Thirdly, many approaches to languages in bilingual or multilingual contexts concentrate on one particular language, often to the exclusion of others. In much assimilation-oriented second-language discourse, the mother tongue of minorities is invisibilized or constructed as a handicap. In much assimilation-oriented majority discourse, the minority language can be seen as a necessary evil–but this demonizing can also happen to the majority language in some apartheid discourses and fundamentalistically self-segregation-oriented minority discourses.

Each of the three tasks will be explored in greater depth in what follows, firstly concept clarification, then what is involved in seeing LHRs as a matter of "both-and" rather than "either-or": language as both right and resource, and language rights in relation to more than one language, for instance rights to the mother tongue and a dominant language. These principles underlie many of the contributions to this book.

Cross-disciplinary Concept Clarification

Linguistic human rights are at the crossroads of several scientific disciplines. In most cases analyses and clarifications from various disciplines complement each other. However, one could often wish that researchers from various disciplines knew more about each other's work and accepted that the same issue can be legitimately approached through several disciplines.

Often lawyers take it for granted that some of the concepts used in international law, or various declarations and recommendations in relation to language in education, are clear and well-defined, whereas sociolinguists see them as problematic and in need of meticulous clarification. Even such basic concepts as language (see, e.g., Mühlhäusler 1996), mother tongue, first language, second language, foreign language, ethnolinguistic identity, learn a language, are unclear and in need of specification. Several recent charters and declarations on language rights have a section of definitions (e.g. The European Charter on Regional or Minority Languages) or specify in explanatory notes the restrictions and limitations, for instance on areas of implementation (e.g. The Hague Recommendations Regarding the Education Rights of Minorities from the OSCE, see Eide 1997, Packer 1997, Packer & Siemienski 1997, Szépe 1997, Thornberry & Gibbons 1997, and van der Stoel 1997; and most recently The Oslo Recommendations Regarding the Linguistic Rights of National Minorities & Explanatory Note). Most of these definitions and clarifications have been written by lawyers, for use by other lawyers. They do not necessarily correspond to definitions of the same concepts by researchers from other fields.

On the other hand, sociolinguists, sociologists, educationists, political scientists and others working with language rights often read human rights instruments in a much broader and more open way than human rights lawyers. There are dozens of examples of misunderstanding and cross-talk.

Fernand de Varennes (this volume) reminds us of one basic distinction, namely, the distinction

> between certain standards that are part of international law, and those principles that are morally or politically desirable, but not legally required.
>
> Moral or political principles, even if they are sometimes described as 'human rights', are not necessarily part of international law. They are things that governments 'should' do, if they are 'nice', not something they 'must' do. Being nice is not a very convincing argument

and is less persuasive than rights and freedoms that have the weight of the law behind them.

Often non-lawyers may think that a human rights instrument grants more rights than it in fact does; they are surprised when learning how much of what to them appear to be very clear rights in fact belongs to the "being nice" category, and is unenforceable in a court of law. Often non-lawyers may be shocked or at least disappointed at the result of a court case where what they see as legal hair-splitting may in their view make litigation about human rights a cynical farce, and lead them to reject the whole human rights system in despair.

But it works the other way round too: often lawyers and other people without specialist familiarity with sociolinguistics or education are surprised when hearing from the experts in these fields how complex and ambiguous matters are in these areas of expertise. Sometimes one can even discern a tendency of suspicion or even despair at the necessity of making all the distinctions that experts in various areas insist are necessary, as is the case, for instance, with the use of such terms as "mother tongue", "second language", and "foreign language", or when sociolinguists, for instance, question whether anybody yet knows what "a language" or "to learn a language" means.

As Ina Druviete shows in her study on Latvia, especially in the section on names, concepts that are assumed to be universally relevant may not be directly applicable in the states with a changed political order–in this case a post-communist state. Rannut's study on Estonia situates some of the fundamental language planning and language rights concepts in the ongoing resolution of potentially explosive conflicts.

Linguistic human rights is an area which urgently needs patient multidisciplinary clarification. What is needed is cross-disciplinary work where researchers really try to learn from each other and about each other's areas while pursuing a joint goal, to clarify and hopefully strengthen linguistic human rights. This collection is a step in that direction. It includes articles by lawyers, economists, sociolinguists, educationists, language planners, and political scientists. Such people regularly encounter profound problems in their professional lives because many social issues are inextricably linked to language issues. Thus lawyers, linguists and politicians (all of whom were numerically well represented at the Budapest conference) share an interest in addressing the dilemmas that they are increasingly aware of.

Language(s) as Problem, Right or Resource?

In a seminal article about minority education, Ruiz (1984) distinguished between three ways of seeing language: language as a *problem*, language as a *right*, and language as a *resource*. In several readings of Ruiz, the three have been seen as competing views, rather than the last two being complementary (and Ruiz himself does little to prevent this ambivalent interpretation). One result has been that some of those educationists and sociolinguists who emphasize that (minority) languages should be seen as resources, not as problems or handicaps, have dismissed "language as a right"-oriented approaches as being in contradiction to seeing languages as resources. This is to the detriment of both those seeking language rights and those who see languages as a resource, since it prevents those who are interested in making languages function as parts of positive cultural-linguistic capital from making use of the human rights system in the struggles of linguistic minorities for self-empowerment. It seems that the researchers who take this view do so partly because they lack adequate knowledge about linguistic human rights and cannot see the potential that a human-rights-oriented approach may offer.

A similar difficulty, probably for similar reasons, is encountered by those researchers, primarily in North America, who, in their eagerness to change terms which they see as negative and stigmatized, avoid the use of the term "minority". In the United States and elsewhere, many negative terms were in use about linguistic minority students that progressive teachers and researchers wanted to get rid of. These terms mostly defined minority students in a derogatory way and negatively, in terms of what they were *not* or could *not* do (instead of positively, in terms of who they *were* and what they *could* do), and with the linguistic majority as the norm. They were defined as deviant, deficient, the Other, subnormal or abnormal. Examples of these terms include USA LEP (Limited English Proficiency) or NEP (No English Proficiency), Australian speakers of LOTEs (Languages Other Than English), Canadian Heritage Language students, or British speakers of Community languages (as if the majorities did not have any heritage or community) and Danish "fremmedsprogede elever" (literally "foreign-languaged students"—foreign to whom?). Starting to employ alternative terms, seen as more positive, like "linguistically diverse students" and other nice euphemisms, used in the United States about minority students, actually (still) robs these children of the only protection they have in international human rights law. Objectively they ARE minority students, and progressive educators are harming them by refusing to use the term. "Linguistically diverse students" have no protection in international law; minority students do.

Most of the authors in this volume have distanced themselves from the "language as a problem" approach: the problem in connection with language is rather that many state institutions (the educational system, social services, etc.) do not see the existence of linguistic diversity and ALL languages as resources to be cherished, maintained and developed, or, at the very least, as something that should not be destroyed. Instead, many of them *construct* linguistic diversity and the presence of many languages and minority language speakers as a problem, both for the speakers themselves (who are constructed as deficient, suffering from lack of knowledge of the dominant language, rather than as owning a positive resource, another language, or multilingual skills) and for the state (which has to cater for them, offer them "extra" services, "help" them, etc.).

After all, a "minority" person is a normal human being who just happens to be in the "wrong" place in the sense that her/his first language (L1) is not the L1 of the majority in the state where s/he lives (or, possibly, in any state–some 80% of the world's languages are endemic to one state, according to Harmon, 1995). But this is only to be expected in a world where the number of States is around 200 while the number of languages is over 10,000 (at least some 6,500 oral languages and probably equally many sign languages).

"Linguistic human rights" can in the framework of "problem or resource" be understood in two ways, which have superficially opposing but in fact complementary goals–and this seems to be the understanding that underlies the views of most of the authors in this volume. Firstly, people need linguistic human rights in order to prevent their linguistic repertoire from *becoming a problem* or from *causing them problems*. Secondly, people need to be able to exercise language rights in order for their linguistic repertoire to be treated as, or to become, *a positive, empowering resource*. A combination of these approaches is clearly visible in, for instance, the two paradigms described in articles by István Muzsnai about the Deaf and the use or lack of use of Sign languages, by Andrea Szalai, on how the Gypsies are being treated in Hungary, and by Klára Sándor, on one of Europe's most enigmatic and least known minorities, the Hungarian-speaking *Csángós* living in Moldavia, Romania.

Access to Minimally Two Languages is a Right

Access to linguistic human rights generally means, in the case of minorities, access to at least two languages, the mother tongue and an official language. Some researchers, often those who want to prevent language from becoming/causing a problem, place greater emphasis on access to the dominant language by minorities/dominated groups. Others, often those who want to promote the "language as resource" aspect of the two-pronged approach, put greater emphasis on access to the first language/mother tongue of the dominated group. There has been too little contact between the two groups. One of the additional endeavors of this book is to bring them together, even if there are more authors emphasizing the mother tongue/first language aspect—but never to the exclusion of the dominant language.

What is needed is an emphasis on access to both, or in some cases several important languages. Dominant groups can also benefit from bi- and multilingualism. Dominated ethnolinguistic groups need access to learning and using both their own language and the dominant language and other additional languages. Dominant ethnolinguistic groups need access not only to their own (dominant) language, but to other languages in addition, including minority languages in their own countries. Dominated groups need protection from forced assimilation or segregation. Dominant groups need protection from forced monolingual reductionism. All of this "access to language" (or rather: "languages", in the plural) presupposes access to and implementation of language rights.

Access to Languages

South Africa is linguistically diverse, but "South Africa does not have a 'national language', nor has it ever had one", according to the LANGTAG Report (*Towards a national language plan for South Africa*, 1996, Language Plan Task Group, in the section clarifying essential terms). South Africa is moving from a system of institutionalized injustice to one which recognizes diversity and attempts to build on it, in order to achieve basic social justice. Language policy has a major role to play in this process. In the current Constitution the number of official languages is 11. A key question when seeking to valorize the African languages is whether English can be "reduced to equality", a vivid expression used earlier in relation to Afrikaans by Neville Alexander, a key figure in South African language planning, and chair of the group which produced the LANGTAG Report.

If all 11 official languages are to be strengthened, policies have to be evolved that allocate resources to each of them, that elaborate strategies appropriate for each region, and that promote multilingualism and language rights in all spheres of public life, including education and the media. Campaigns are under way to raise consciousness about many aspects of language policy. The tendency for English to assert itself as a sole hegemonic language is being resisted, for which the experience of successful measures elsewhere in strengthening other languages (e.g. French in Canada, Swahili in Tanzania) is relevant, but the implementation of rights for all languages will need constant vigilance. Whether the political will to achieve this is present will be decisive. In the work of the Truth and Reconciliation Commission, a key body in the process of bringing together the various communities of South Africa which heard evidence from South Africans from all walks of life, interpretation facilities were provided so as to ensure that people could exercise their democratic right to participate in civil society in the language of their choice.

The complexity of language policy issues can be seen in relation to Afrikaans, which is generally associated with "whites" of Dutch origin and discredited as the language of apartheid, although it is in fact also the mother tongue of large numbers of people who under apartheid were classified as "Coloured", and whose political and cultural rights were minimal. Groups with very different interests can therefore identify with Afrikaans, just as they can with English.

There are comparable but different problems in relation to African languages. The difficulties in assuring them greater status and influence relate to their marginal status in the past and inadequate teaching of them as second or foreign languages (often by non-native speakers with little competence in the languages) and the fact that little use is made of them on television or in public by influential politicians. This may be linked to a wish on the part of national leaders to avoid being perceived as identifying with or favouring any one ethnic group (for instance speakers of Sotho or Xhosa).

In the new South Africa the word "ethnic" is avoided. In the language policy report referred to earlier the only use of "ethnic" is in a section devoted to "depoliticising language": "Speakers of some languages, notably Afrikaans and Zulu, feel that their languages may receive inequitable treatment because of their association with ethnic politics which are unacceptable to the present government" (LANGTAG Report 1996, 57). Ethnicity is here seen as divisive, in conflict with goals of national reconciliation and unity. The authors of the report therefore regard the term ethnicity as inappropriate when devising strategies for improving the rights, status and use of all languages, including the "previously marginalised languages" and sign languages.

Language policy should aim to ensure equity for all language groups. The power of English is such that all groups can see the value of proficiency in the language. The challenge of reducing English to equality involves ensuring that English is learned as an additional language, perhaps in much the same way as it is learned in countries like Sweden or the Netherlands, where thus far the expansion of English has not been at the expense of Swedish or Dutch—although the forces of McDonaldization, and of cultural and linguistic imperialism are pushing in this direction. Speakers of African languages must be able to learn and use these languages for the full range of social, commercial and political purposes. Education must necessarily involve consolidating the multilingualism that is a feature of social life for most South Africans.

Choice in education must attempt to ensure that the use of a particular language as the medium of instruction does not imply condemnation to a low position in a hierarchical linguistic ordering or the exclusion of particular groups from access to power and resources. A first step might be to break with the pattern of schools being defined as educating children through the medium of language X or Y (Afrikaans, English, Zulu, ...), when the goal for such learners must be high levels of competence in languages X, Y and Z. A choice between X or Y is unfair when one language has a much higher status than all others and when parents cannot be expected to know what consequences will follow from an uninformed assumption that greater use of English will necessarily bring success. The evidence from both the post-colonial world and immigrant education in the west is that this will only be the case for the few.

There is a tendency for both elite and marginal groups in many states worldwide to desire competence in English for the obvious reason that English is seen to open doors. The appeal of English should not obscure the fact that in Africa as a whole 90% of the population speak only African languages. Likewise in India figures for the number of speakers of English are 3–5%. If the citizens of countries worldwide are to contribute to the solution of local problems, to use the local environment for locally appropriate purposes, cultural, economic and political, this must involve local languages. Language policy must reconcile these dimensions of language ecology with the pressures of globalisation and supra-nationalisation that are propelling English forward. Language policy must be made explicit, and must embrace equitable conditions for all people and all languages. This is a challenge for politicians and other policy-makers. There is enough scientific documentation of the issues to ensure that more visionary and democratic policies could be evolved globally and locally.

But are all *language* rights at the same time linguistic *human* rights protected by international law? No. Much of what is discussed in this book belongs so far to the categories (see de Varennes above) where a state can choose to be "nice"–or not. Education, for instance, is one of the fields where a State has several ways to be "nice" or not.[2]

Three Ways to Restrict Language-in-education Rights

The prevailing concepts of education on the one hand, and linguistic rights on the other hand, especially the right of access to education, often seem to come into conflict.

There are several ways of restricting the language-in-education rights of minorities. States can (1) restrict the age-groups and the range of school subjects for which minority-medium education is provided, (2) restrict the number of languages through which minority education in general is made available, and (3) reduce the number of people entitled to minority-medium education by obfuscating who the rightholders/beneficiaries are.

The first kind of restriction typically concerns national minorities, whose grievances often revolve around the duration of education made available through the medium of the minority mother tongue. Sometimes what is at issue is which school subjects should be taught in which language.

Ideally, minority-medium education can last from kindergarten through university. Accordingly, restriction of educational avenues can affect all phases of education from kindergarten through to, say, a university degree in physics. In the Central European countries of Slovakia and Romania, denying to the large indigenous Hungarian minorities the right to establish or reestablish Hungarian-language universities (see Ankerl 1994) is a manifestation of such language-in-education policy.

There is often an inverse relationship between the level of minority education and the state's toleration of it. Minority elementary schools are relatively safe in today's Romania and Slovakia, secondary schools are subject to more government interference and repression (see Kontra 1996), and the right to tertiary education, e.g. to the reestablishment of the Hungarian university in Cluj, Romania[3] or the establishment of a Hungarian-language university in Slovakia, is denied by the states. On the other hand, very few labor migrant minority groups in the world are offered anything other than submersion programs through the medium of the majority languages or, at the most, transitional early-exit programs where their own language is used as a medium for part of the time during the first years of elementary education. This situation is comparable for most language groups in Africa, who receive education in their own language in the early years. The very few minority-medium schools for immigrant minorities (e.g. 11 Finnish-medium schools in Sweden) suffer from great uncertainty, despite being able to show positive results.[4]

The language of instruction can also be a battlefield within a particular school type, that is for the same age-group. In Czecho-slovakia, for instance in vocational secondary schools for the Hungarian minority, science classes were taught in Slovak only, while the "humanities" subjects could be taught in Hungarian (Lanstyák 1991, 45). In February 1996 the Slovak Ministry of Education refused to issue a license to a private Hungarian school of trading because certain subjects, e.g. bookkeeping, would not be taught in Slovak only–but in Hungarian and Slovak (Kontra 1996, 2). The current coalition government in Romania[5] has experienced periodic crises over the proposal of Romanian nationalists that geography and history be mandatorily taught in Romanian only in all minority schools in the country.

The second kind of restriction mentioned above affects the range of languages or language varieties through which education is provided. In the Anglo-American context the 1979 Black English Trial in Ann Arbor, Michigan involved students who were mislabeled as linguistically handicapped because they spoke vernacular African American English (see Labov 1982 and Baugh 1996). The Ebonics controversy in Oakland, California in December 1996 (see Nunberg 1997) revolved around the same issue: to what extent is it legitimate to regard African American Vernacular English (AAVE) as a separate variety from Standard English and what are the educational consequences of the differences? To put it simply, the question is this: Is AAVE a degenerate variety of English which should never be used as the medium of instruction, or is it a variety different enough from Standard English to cause educational deprivation to its users if they are taught exclusively through Standard English? What is being contested in the US is what languages or language varieties should be recognized as fit for being media of instruction.

In Hungary some linguists have argued that one of the reasons why the Gypsy language is unfit for use as the medium of instruction (Vekerdi 1983, 116), is that, according to Vekerdi's claim (1988, 14,) it has an "astonishingly poor vocabulary" of no more than 1200–2000 words. This argument is similar to those floating around in the US "Head Start" debates in the 1970s. It was claimed that Black children had a vocabulary of 400 words, half of them four-letter words. Such arguments typically belong to the "language as problem" approach where minority children are to be saved from themselves (their linguistic heritage) via majority-medium instruction.

The third kind of restriction of language-in-education rights operates through the obfuscation of who is entitled to receive minority-language education. Two examples from the current Hungarian educational scene illustrate such practices. The first example concerns the Deaf in Hungary (see Muzsnai's paper in this volume) and the second the Gypsies (see Szalai, this volume).

An influential educator of the Deaf in Hungary, Csányi has recently argued that

> Sign Language should be used in education when a child needs it as the medium for a better acquisition of the syllabus, if the child's only means of communication in class is Sign Language, if its use plays an unequivocal role in the optimal development of the child.(1995, 105; our translation)

According to the author the use of Sign Language (SL) hinders the efficiency of teaching the hard-of-hearing because they often prefer to use SL rather than spoken Hungarian.[6] Sign Language, so the claim goes, is an easy way out and its users do not integrate into mainstream Hungarian society optimally. Most people with a hearing problem are not medically deaf but are hard-of-hearing, and because at an early age it is not possible to medically diagnose medically deaf children who will never learn to hear, it is only fair, so Csányi claims, to provide education for all through the acoustic channel.

What Csányi does here is to obscure the difference between medically deaf children who will never hear, and the hard-of-hearing who may learn to hear and speak to some extent, as a result of special education and by means of hearing aids. She seems to be taking an "equal educational opportunity for all" position, but in actual fact the implementation of her policy deprives the medically deaf children of their right to develop a linguistic competence by age three, and it deprives the Deaf or hearing children born to Deaf parents of their right to a mother tongue.[7] (For a brilliant analysis of the question of linguistic imperialism and the rights of the Deaf, see Branson and Miller 1998.)

While in the case of the hearing impaired in Hungary one of the problems is the identification of minority beneficiaries on the basis of sound medical diagnosis, in the case of the Gypsies of Hungary the rightholders' identification on the basis of their mother tongue is one of the causes of a violation of their LHRs. In both cases, the main problems, as Muzsnai and Szalai show in their articles, are reflections of linguicism: unequal access to power and material resources on the basis of language.

Under communism the Gypsies of Hungary were not regarded as a national or ethnic minority but as a socially handicapped group which needed to be integrated into mainstream Hungarian society. According to a 1961 Communist party resolution (quoted by Vekerdi 1988, 21)

> Concerning the Gypsy question, a number of erroneous views are to be met with. Some persons consider it to be a national question and propose promotion of Gypsy language, establishing Gypsy-language schools, Gypsy schoolboys' homes, Gypsy cooperative farms, etc. These views are not only erroneous but also harmful because they help to preserve the Gypsies' segregation and slow down the process of their integration.

If Gypsies are a socially disadvantaged group and not a people with a distinct language and culture, then they should not have Gypsy-language schools. In the Communist party resolution of 1961, as well as in the National Core Curriculum in force since 1995 in Hungary, there is not even an implicit reference to the banning of Romany or other Gypsy languages as media of instruction. Yet both the Communists in their time and the current government in post-Communist Hungary blatantly violate the LHRs of some Gypsies. The violation is based on the mythical Hungarian-dominant bilingualism of all bilingual Gypsies in the country.

According to a widely cited but linguistically unsophisticated sociological study conducted by István Kemény in the early 1970s, Gypsy-Hungarian bilinguals comprise about 21% of the entire Gypsy population of Hungary. A distinguished scholar of the Gypsy language and culture, Vekerdi (see, e.g., Vekerdi and Mészáros 1978, 13) made straightforward claims such as, "There is not a single Gypsy in Hungary who can only speak Gypsy" and "Our bilingual Gypsies have two mother tongues, and of the two (i.e. Gypsy and Hungarian) they invariably speak Hungarian better than Gypsy." Vekerdi's claims are linguistically naive and empirically unproven.

While the majority of Hungarian Gypsies speak Hungarian as their mother tongue, not all of them do. According to the 1990 census, there are 48,072 Gypsies who claim that their mother tongue is Gypsy. Most of the children born to such parents are educated in the state language, Hungarian, contrary to The Hague Recommendations Regarding the Education Rights of National Minorities (1996, 6), which condemn submersion-type approaches and state that the medium of teaching in kindergarten and primary school should ideally be the child's language.[8]

This pattern of linguistic discrimination is similar to that used in the case of the Deaf of Hungary: what is deemed to be good for the majority of the minority is presented as good for all of the minority by obfuscating the heterogeneity of the minority rightholders. In the case of Hungary's Gypsies whose mother tongue is Gypsy, such denial of their right to begin school in their mother tongue results in their dramatic overrepresentation among the unemployed. Discrimination based on the language of instruction gives rise to lifelong unemployment for many of them (see Kemény 1996 and Kontra 1997 for details).

All three types of restriction characterize the Californian Proposition 227, passed on 2nd June 1998. It was an Initiative Statute introduced by the multimillionaire Ron K. Unz, a high-technology entrepreneur who does not have children himself and has no expertise in education or languages. Unz ran for governor in the 1994 Republican primary and lost to Pete Wilson, a candidate he called "too moderate". Unz's positions on other issues are extreme right wing, from "eliminating workers compensation to cutting taxes for the wealthy to cracking down on welfare mothers" (NABE News 21:4, 11). The co-signer of the initiative, Gloria Matta Tuchman, is a former director of U.S. English, the leading English Only lobby in the USA. This is the organisation which proclaimed that "California was being taken over by 'fast-breeding' Mexican-Americans ('Perhaps this is the first instance in which those with their pants up are going to get caught by those with their pants down!')" and which questioned the "educability" of Latino children (ibid.). The Proposition takes California back to the period between 1872 and 1967 when California law required all instruction to be in English and when the Hispanic high school drop-out rate was close to 75%.

In 1960 the census found that only 50% of the state's Hispanic 18–24 year olds had even completed the 8th grade, one of the many negative results of this English-only educational policy.

The blanket directive is that "All children [shall] be placed in English language classrooms". If children know no English, they are allowed to have 180 days of English teaching (according to Unz "young children can easily learn a new language in a matter of months...", ibid., 6). After those 180 days schools are forbidden to use the native language of the students to facilitate subject-matter teaching, and all teachers can be threatened with lawsuits and personal liability for speaking even a few words of a language other than English in class. No professional standards or special ESL or other training is required by those who teach minority children; this has already led to some universities considering scrapping this kind of teacher training. It is proposed that schools are reorganized on the basis of student's English proficiency, across age and grade levels, completely ignoring the academic knowledge of students in other subjects. Parent choice is out. Waivers from the English-only instructional mandate may be obtained by some parents, but the procedures are cumbersome and for children under the age of 10 the circumstances in which a waiver is allowed are very limited.

The whole campaign which led to the passing of Proposition 227 was characterized by outright lies and false threats. These have been carefully documented and analysed by many responsible research and educational organizations, both Californian and countrywide.[9] Even before the initiative, only 30% of those minority students in California who were not yet fully competent in English had any type of bilingual education. In the overwhelming majority of cases this was of the early-exit transitional type. Now the restrictions mean that California is blatantly violating children's linguistic human rights, as these are interpreted in The Hague Recommendations from the OSCE High Commissioner (see Skutnabb-Kangas, this volume)—and the USA is a member of the OSCE.

Multidisciplinarity in LHRs

This excursus into education and LHRs illustrates the multidisciplinary contacts of language rights. LHRs can be inextricably interwoven with education (as demonstrated by the age of learners, the subjects taught in L1 and educational models for multilingualism in general), linguistics (as exemplified by determining what

language or language variety is fit to be the medium of instruction), or medical diagnosis (the identification of the hearing-
impaired as minority rightholders). The misidentification of the
mother tongue of some of the Gypsies of Hungary (a misuse or
abuse of socio- and psycholinguistics) results in the violation of
those people's LHRs.

But there are other important fields related to LHRs as well. Bart
Driessen, for example (this volume), looks at language rights from
a rare and neglected angle: the implications of international trade
law on language legislation in Slovakia. He demonstrates how a
European Union directive links the free movement of broadcasting
(an economic right) and the freedom of expression (a human
right). While Driessen speculates about the impact that the European Convention on Transfrontier Television may have on Slovak
language legislation in the near future, Amir Hassanpour looks at
the recent past by giving a detailed analysis of the operation of a
Kurdish satellite television channel founded by Kurds in Europe
and broadcasting since 1994. Among other things Hassanpour
demonstrates the important role that the market is playing in the
world of satellite television and thus in enabling the Kurdish satellite channel to let its millions of viewers "experience the citizenship of a borderless state with its national flag, national anthem,
national television and national news agency."

The way in which economic forces shape our linguistic environment is the major question adderessed by François Grin. Do
market forces exert a positive or a negative influence on linguistic
diversity? Grin and Tove Skutnabb-Kangas investigate the interactions of what they call the "free market" (their quotation marks)
and the survival or death (often the killing) of many of the world's
languages.

It is going to be important to monitor carefully how the forces
of globalisation associated with the WTO (World Trade Organization) and the proposed MAI (Multilateral Agreement on Investment) impact on the global linguistic ecology. There are indica-
tions that regional trade within the NAFTA (North American Free
Trade Agreement) and the European Union is strengthening "big"
languages at the expense of the "small". Even the limited protection of language rights that exists may disappear along with the
other types of protection that transnationals, with the help of WTO
and MAI, can force states to abandon in the name of "fair competition" (Mander and Goldsmith 1996, Pilger 1998).

While an alarmingly large number of the world's languages are
facing extinction, a few are becoming more widespread than ever.

Robert Phillipson addresses the issue of international languages and international human rights. For him, as well as for all the other contributors to this book, there is no doubt about the utmost importance of preserving the languages of the world. In this the authors all oppose what Brookes and Heath (1997, 206) say in a recent review of a book on LHRs: "Finally, a nearly taboo topic must be raised with regard to this book and indeed most academic studies concerned with language policy: language cannot universally be seen as a cultural whole nor value that either can or must be preserved. Nostalgia and unidimensional views of language and its role in cultural retention often account for these claims." Brookes and Heath identify what they call a taboo but offer little in support of their views. The lawyers, linguists, educators and other social scientists in this volume provide many an argument in favor of linguistic diversity and human rights, with language rights among them.

This collection advances arguments to the effect that minimally two languages (bilingualism) or all languages (in multilingual situations) are necessary and needed, for ALL groups. Since the implementation of LHRs, just like all other human rights, depends on negotiations between often unequal parties, it might be wise for minorities (who need LHRs for mere survival, psychologically, spiritually, economically, etc) to share the joys of high-level multilingualism with those majority populations whose monolingualism needs to be cured.

The relationships between social movements, social change, discourses, and the institutions that facilitate parliamentary democracy (for instance via the media and political parties) are explored in a historical account of the extensive experience of legislation on language rights in Canada, litigation in the wake of such rights being made available, and the consequences for the group and the nation as a whole. Martel explains how dominant hegemonic forces arise, how they can be influenced and changed, and the role of grassroots activism. She also raises questions as to how the forces that are unleashed in such struggles can be channeled in non-adversarial ways.

A number of articles represent surveys: for instance, de Varennes summarizes what rights minorities have under international law to use their language and to expect public services in their language (he covers such areas as language use in private and in public life, in the media, in education and in the political sphere). Skutnabb-Kangas goes through a large number of conventions in order to explore their potential for advancing LHRs, and Kontra reports on folk beliefs concerning language rights in six Central European countries.

Other papers are case studies, for instance, Ozolins' article covers the case of the Baltic states and their post-Soviet language policies. His chronological survey draws on the available scholarship and firsthand experience of the use of language issues in political discourse.

In this book linguists, lawyers, educators and other social scientists undertook to rethink the making of linguistic diversity and its consequences. A recurring focus shows—and tends to liberate from blurring or stifling contexts—various angles of a very simple truth: Languages are different. Therefore, in the realm of languages, the right to be equal cannot be implemented, cannot even be understood, without insistence on the right to be different.

Notes

1 See Szalai, this volume, for the Gypsy–Roma distinction.
2 See Skutnabb-Kangas 1998a for an analysis of existing linguistic human rights in education.
3 The Hungarian Bolyai University and the Romanian Babeş University were merged by the Romanian government in 1959, with the result that the Hungarian academic staff was rapidly phased out. The reestablishment of the Hungarian University in Cluj has been a bone of contention since 1990 and is a source of considerable conflict between the current (Fall 1999) coalition government and its opposition in Romania, but also within the coalition itself.
4 See Skutnabb-Kangas 1998b.
5 For the first time in their 75-year history as a minority, the Hungarians in Romania enjoy unprecedented political power. The Democratic Alliance of Hungarians in Romania (RMDSZ) is part of the ruling coalition which came into power in 1996.
6 A Sign Language is a concept-based system that has developed naturally among the members of a Deaf community, e.g. British Sign Language developed in Britain and American Sign Language developed in the USA. The two are not mutually intelligible. Signed English, on the other hand, closely follows the structure of English speech.
7 A Deaf or a hearing child born to Deaf parents learns SL as a mother tongue and for such native signers "signing is not a handicap but a natural means of expression quite comparable to the expressive potential of spoken language" (Crystal 1987, 267).
8 *The Hague Recommendations* refer to *national minorities*, or groups who constitute the numerical majority in one state but the numerical minority in another state. Thus their relevance to the Gypsies of Hungary might be questioned. However, because LHRs are meaningless if they do

not refer to all people, we would find it hard to deny the right to education through the mother tongue for Gypsies. In addition, all types of minorities, including immigrant minorities, were discussed as rightholders in the expert group drafting *The Hague Recommendations* (of which Tove Skutnabb-Kangas was a member).

9 For more information on the Unz Initiative, see the following web sites: <http://www.noonunz.org> (Citizens for an Educated America: No on Unz)

<http://www.nabe.org> (National Association for Bilingual Education)

<http://www.smartnation.org> (Smartnation)

<http://ourworld.compuserve.com/homepages/jwcrawford> (James Crawford's Language Policy homepage)

<http://www.onenation.org> (Ron Unz's Pro-Initiative Organization) *NABE News* 21:4, February 1, 1998 is a Special Issue on Unz.

References

Alexander, Neville. "Multilingualism for empowerment." In Heugh et al., eds. (1995), 37–41.

Ankerl, Géza. "The native right to speak Hungarian in the Carpathian Basin." *Hungarian Quarterly.* Vol. 35, no. 133 (1994): 7–23.

Baugh, John. "Linguistic discrimination." In Hans Goebl et al., eds., *Kontaktlinguistik,* 709–714. Berlin and New York: Mouton de Gruyter, 1996.

Benson, Phil, Peter Grundy, and Tove Skutnabb-Kangas, eds. *Language rights. Language Sciences.* Special issue, vol. 20, no.1 (1998).

Branson, Jan, and Don Miller. "Nationalism and the linguistic rights of Deaf communities: Linguistic imperialism and the recognition and development of sign languages." *Journal of Sociolinguistics.* vol. 2, no 1 (1998): 3–34.

Brookes, Heather and Shirley Brice Heath. Review of Tove Skutnabb-Kangas and Robert Phillipson, eds., *Linguistic Human Rights: Overcoming Linguistic Discrimination.* In *International Journal of the Sociology of Language.* No. 127 (1997): 197–208.

Crystal, David. *The Cambridge Encyclopedia of Language.* Cambridge: Cambridge University Press, 1987.

Csányi, Yvonne. "Gondolatok a jelnyelv alkalmazási lehetőségeiről a súlyos fokban hallássérült gyermekek és a fiatalok nevelése során" (Thoughts on using sign language in the education of children and youngsters with severe hearing problems). *Gyógypedagógiai Szemle.* Vol. 23, no. 2 (1995): 105–115.

Eide, Asbjørn. "The Hague Recommendations Regarding the Education Rights of Minorities: Their Objective." *International Journal on Minority and Group Rights.* Special Issue on the Education Rights of National Minorities. Vol. 4, no. 2 (1996/1997): 163–170.

The Hague Recommendations Regarding the Education Rights of National Minorities, & Explanatory Note. The Hague: Foundation on Inter-Ethnic Relations, 1996.

Harmon, David. "The status of the world's languages as reported in the Ethnologue." *Southwest Journal of Linguistics* 14 (1995): 1–33.

Heugh, Kathleen. "From unequal education to the real thing." In Heugh et al., eds. (1995), 42–51.

Heugh, Kathleen, Amanda Siegrühn, and Peter Plüddemann, eds., *Multilingual Education for South Africa.* Johannesburg: Heinemann, 1995.

Kemény, István. "A romák és az iskola" (The Roma and school). *Educatio* 1 (1996): 71–83.

Kontra, Miklós. "Assimilation through vocational training: Hungarian minorities in Slovakia and Romania." *New Language Planning Newsletter.* Vol. 11, no. 1 (1996): 1–2.

——. "Tannyelvi diszkrimináció és cigány munkanélküliség" (Discrimination based on the language of instruction and Gypsy unemployment). *Fundamentum.* Vol. 1, no. 2 (1997): 139–140.

Labov, William. "Objectivity and commitment in linguistic science: The case of the Black English trial in Ann Arbor." *Language in Society* 11 (1982): 165–201.

LANGTAG (Language Plan Task Group). *Towards a National Language Plan for South Africa.* Summary of the Final Report of the Language Plan Task Group (LANGTAG), 1996, Presented to the Minister of Arts, Culture, Science and Technology, Dr B.S.Ngubane, 8 August 1996. Summary available at <http://www.sacs.org.za/gov/arts&cul/docs/langrep.htm>.

Lanstyák, István. "A szlovák nyelv árnyékában (a magyar nyelv helyzete Csehszlovákiában, 1918–1991)" (In the shadow of Slovak: The Hungarian language in Czechoslovakia from 1918 through 1991). In Miklós Kontra, ed., *Tanulmányok a határainkon túli kétnyelvűségről,* 11–72. Budapest: Magyarságkutató Intézet, 1991.

Mander, Jerry, and Edward Goldsmith, eds. *The case against the global economy and for a turn toward the local.* San Francisco: Sierra Club, 1996.

Nunberg, Geoffrey. "Double Standards." *Natural Language and Linguistic Theory* 15 (1997): 667–675.

The Oslo Recommendations Regarding the Linguistic Rights of National Minorities, & Explanatory Note. The Hague: Foundation on Inter-Ethnic Relations, February 1998.

Packer, John. "The Content and Aim of Minority Education from the Perspective of International Instruments." *International Journal on Minority and Group Rights.* Special Issue on the Education Rights of National Minorities. Vol. 4, no. 2 (1996/1997): 171–174.

Packer, John, and Guillaume Siemienski. "Integration Through Education: The Origin and Development of The Hague Recommendations." *International Journal on Minority and Group Rights.* Special Issue on the Education Rights of National Minorities. Vol. 4, no. 2 (1996/1997): 187–198.

Pilger, John. *Hidden Agendas.* London: Vintage, 1998.

Ruiz, Richard. "Orientations in language planning." *NABE Journal* 8, 2 (1984): 15–34.

Siemienski, Guillaume. "Report on the Vienna Seminar on Minority Education Issues, 22–23 November 1996." *International Journal on Minority and Group Rights*. Special Issue on the Education Rights of National Minorities. Vol. 4, no. 2 (1996/1997): 175–185.

Skutnabb-Kangas, Tove. "Human rights and language wrongs–a future for diversity." In Benson et al., eds. (1998a), 5–27.

——. "Bilingual Education for Finnish Minority Students in Sweden." In Jim Cummins & Corson, David, eds., *The Encyclopedia of Language and Education*. Volume Bilingual Education, 217–227. Dordrecht: Kluwer Academic, 1998b.

Stobart, Maitland. "The Importance of Minority Education Rights in the New Europe." *International Journal on Minority and Group Rights*. Special Issue on the Education Rights of National Minorities. vol. 4, no. 2 (1996/1997): 156–162.

Szépe, György. "Some Remarks on the Education Rights of National Minorities." *International Journal on Minority and Group Rights*. Special Issue on the Education Rights of National Minorities. vol. 4, no. 2 (1996/1997): 105–113.

Thornberry, Patrick, and Dianna Gibbons. "Education and Minority Rights: A Short Survey of International Standards." *International Journal on Minority and Group Rights*. Special Issue on the Education Rights of National Minorities. vol. 4, no.2 (1996/1997): 115–152.

van der Stoel, Max. "Introduction to the Seminar." *International Journal on Minority and Group Rights*. Special Issue on the Education Rights of National Minorities. Vol. 4, no. 2 (1996/1997): 153–155.

Vekerdi, József. "Nemzetiség, etnikum, identitás" (Nationality, ethnicity and identity). *Látóhatár* (September 1983): 113–127.

——. "The Gypsies and the Gypsy Problem in Hungary." *Hungarian Studies Review*. vol. 15, No. 2 (1988): 13–26.

Vekerdi, József, and György Mészáros. *A cigányság a felemelkedés útján* (Towards the social rise of Gypsies). Budapest: Hazafias Népfront Országos Tanácsa, 1978.

GENERAL ISSUES

International Languages and International Human Rights

ROBERT PHILLIPSON

This article assesses how some languages have become "international" and cites examples of the promotion and legitimation of the most widespread one, English. The issue of equitable language rights is considered in relation to the management of multilingualism in supra-state organizations, the League of Nations and the United Nations, and in the most ambitious and comprehensive amalgamation of states, the European Union. There is a case for considering alternatives to a system involving use of a small number of official languages when this effectively accords rights to speakers of different language backgrounds on an inequitable basis. The paper also suggests that international languages are impacting on national languages in ways that conflict with human rights principles.

International Languages

> Language has always been the consort of
> empire, and forever shall remain its mate.
> (Nebrija 1492, cited in Illich 1981, 34)

The common-sense understanding of the term "international language" is as a language that people from different backgrounds or nations use with each other. In this sense there are many international languages in use on all continents, ranging from Portuguese and Hindi to Latin and Classical Arabic, as well as more locally restricted lingua francas and pidgins.

The term "international language" has also been used to refer to artificial or planned languages such as Esperanto, languages that were created specifically in order to facilitate international links and understanding, sometimes termed international auxiliary languages. Users of these languages do not have the backing of any nation or state, in marked contrast to languages that have been transplanted world-wide such as English, French and Spanish.

Linguistic dominance has its origins in conquest, military and political subjugation, and economic exploitation. The role of language in imperial expansion has been a central element of the europeanisation of the world. The underlying language policy was articulated in a pioneer language-planning document presented to the Spanish court in 1492 (see the citation from Nebrija above). At that time the dominant languages in Europe were spoken by only a few million people and had no international currency. The contemporary status of English, French, Spanish and Portuguese indicates how successfully and ruthlessly the principle of language imposition was applied.

Colonising powers were seldom prepared to recognize that languages and cultures other than their own had intrinsic values and rights. Linguists have followed in Nebrija's footsteps in legitimating colonial linguistic hierarchies (Calvet 1974; Crowley 1991). International linguistic hegemonies draw on beliefs and attitudes to linguistic hierarchies and interlock with the allocation of more resources to the dominant language.

The imaginative project in the inter-war period to devise a restricted form of English as an "international auxiliary language", BASIC English (BASIC = British American Scientific International Commercial), was promoted in the hope that lesser languages would be eliminated: "What the world needs is about 1000 more dead languages—and one more alive" (Ogden, 1934, cited in Bailey, 1991, 210). Here "international understanding" was seen as uni-directional, with other languages to be abandoned in favour of the dominant language, English, this having been made more accessible through simplification.

Linguistic imperialism has invariably presupposed the superiority of the dominant language, in both the colonial and postcolonial worlds (Mühlhäusler 1996; Phillipson 1992). The British and Americans created a substantial academic infrastructure to serve the promotion of English worldwide.[1]

Notions of the superiority of English and its suitability as the international language *par excellence* have a long pedigree. A detailed study of images of English through history concludes that "the linguistic ideas that evolved at the acme of empires led by Britain and the United States have not changed as economic colonialism has replaced the direct, political management of third world nations. English is still believed to be the inevitable world language; reasons for the prominent place of English in global affairs are the same ones that were first elaborated in the nineteenth century" (Bailey 1991, 121).[2]

A recent example of jingoist triumphalism is provided by a front page campaign in a London tabloid in November 1991, at a time when the British Government's commitment to the European Union was lukewarm and British influence on European integration minimal: "If Europe is to have a future, it needs more than a common currency, a common foreign policy and a common set of laws. It must have a common language. That language can only be English" (Daily Mail, 29 November 1991).

States that resist the advance of English and claim equal rights for their languages are branded as "chauvinist", suffering from "obsolescent national pride". The underlying belief seems to be that if English has been successfully imposed as the dominant language in states such as the UK and the USA, the same processes could apply at the continental, European level and globally. If monolingualism can triumph nationally (so it is seen), why not internationally too?

Whose Interests Do International Languages Serve?

> What has been happening in my lifetime
> is the Americanization of the world.
> (George Bernard Shaw, born 1856, writing in 1912)

The British government is well aware of the political benefits that accrue to Britain as a result of the privileged position of English,[3] and the resulting economic impact.[4] The media applaud in the same spirit.[5] There is a steady stream of books on various aspects of English worldwide, not all of which are naively celebratory.[6] A recent publication commissioned by the British Council on the future of English (Graddol, 1997) is a reflective, multi-dimensional analysis that assesses the role of various factors, economic, technological and political, that might in future propel other languages forward as dominant international languages.

The present context is one of McDonaldization, of structural asymmetry due to economic might, symbolized by the fact that

80% of films shown in western Europe are of Californian origin, whereas 2% of films shown in North America are of European origin. McDonaldization can be seen as creating global customers, services and suppliers; "aggressive round-the-clock marketing, the controlled information flows that do not confront people with the long-term effects of an ecologically detrimental lifestyle, the competitive advantage against local cultural providers, the obstruction of local initiative, all converge into a reduction of local cultural space" (Hamelink, 1994). A number of measures have been taken so as to attempt to counteract this influence at the European Union level and at the national level, particularly by France, the goal being to protect cultural and linguistic diversity: this is an area in which the relationship between economic factors, culture and language policy is being explored, but needs further elaboration (Grin & Hennis-Pierre, 1997).

Commercial and media globalizing pressures dovetail with the work of educationalists who are promoting "global education". There are scholars who foresee a global core curriculum in a globalized education system, complete with a global qualifications system and global arrangements for quality assurance in education and training.[7] The proposed global core curriculum names seven key domains of learning, one of which is the "world-language", which is imperative for all, i.e. English; a second relates to other languages, which those unhappy enough to be born without English as their mother tongue need to learn.[8] Effectively, this educational vision posits two human types: monolingual English-speakers, and bilingual others. It is a recipe for a return to an ante-diluvian pre-Babel world where everything of value is generated in a single language.

The Diffusion of English, or the Ecology of Language?

Globalization is not a phenomenon that has emerged recently, though fashions in academia might create this impression. What is novel is the extent and depth of the penetration of cultures worldwide. Many of the dimensions of contemporary language policy are insightfully brought together in two competing paradigms by the Japanese communications scholar, Yukio Tsuda.

Diffusion of English Paradigm
A. - capitalism
B. - science and technology
C. - modernization
D. - monolingualism
E. - ideological globalization and internationalization
F. - transnationalization
G. - Americanization and homogenization of world culture
H. - linguistic, cultural and media imperialism

Ecology of Language Paradigm
1. - a human rights perspective
2. - equality in communication
3. - multilingualism
4. - maintenance of languages and cultures
5. - protection of national sovereignties
6. - promotion of foreign language education.

(Tsuda, 1994, our lettering and numbering, for elaboration see Phillipson & Skutnabb-Kangas, 1996; Skutnabb-Kangas, 1999).

The two contrasting perceptions of what is at stake can be seen in relation to language policy in Africa, where some forces are strengthening the diffusion of English, others local language ecologies. Mazrui (1997) assesses how it is that the linguistic hierarchies of the colonial period continue to underpin World Bank and IMF education policies, currently setting the tone for "aid" alongside notoriously anti-social, poverty-inducing structural adjustment policies: "the World Bank's real position ... encourages the consolidation of the imperial languages in Africa... the World Bank does not seem to regard the linguistic Africanisation of the whole of primary education and beyond as an effort that is worth its consideration. Its publication on strategies for stabilising and revitalising universities, for example makes absolutely no mention of the place of language at this tertiary level of African education. ... under World Bank-IMF structural adjustment programmes, the only path open to African nations is the adoption of the imperial languages from the very outset of a child's education". (Mazrui, 1997, 39–40)

Educational "aid" reflects the linguicist[9] belief that only "international" (meaning European) languages are suited to the task of developing African economies and minds. The falsity of this position has been exposed by many African scholars, including Ansre, Bamgbose, Kashoki, Mateene, and Ngũgĩ (references in

Phillipson 1992; see also Djité 1993; and especially on language rights in Africa, Akinnaso 1994; and Phillipson & Skutnabb-Kangas, 1994).

An alternative approach, based on strengthening African languages, can be seen in a succession of policy documents approved by African governments over the past 15 years, culminating in "The Harare Declaration", agreed at the Intergovernmental Conference of Ministers on Language Policies in Africa, 20-21 March 1997 (reproduced in the New Language Planning Newsletter, 11/4, June 1997). It affirms that appropriate policies that build on African languages have not been implemented, and outlines many strategies for strengthening the local language ecology. It sees the promotion of African languages as central to processes of democratization and peaceful coexistence: "... the optimal use of African languages is a prerequisite for maximizing African creativity and resourcefulness in development activities.

... Africa where scientific and technological discourse is conducted in the national languages as part of our cognitive preparation for facing the challenges of the next millennium.

... (African governments) appeal to all concerned in Africa and throughout the world to engage in a clear and forthright cooperation, with respect for the integrity of African identity and the harmonious promotion of human values and dignity as given expression in African languages."

World Bank policies, and donor activities in harmony with them, consolidate the diffusion of English. The Harare Declaration by contrast seeks to strengthen African language ecologies, to build on the existing multilingualism, and to harness local languages for the solution of local problems. English can still be learned as a foreign language but would not be learned subtractively or used intrusively.

These samples of discourse on language policy need to be situated in political realities. To assess linguistic hierarchies globally, in postcolonial, postcommunist or European Union contexts, one needs to look at economic and political factors, at how resources are allocated to one or some languages rather than others, at ideologies that legitimate such preferences and which tend to glorify some languages and stigmatize others. Theories of language and power, of language policy or social structuring, of language in educational reproduction, need anchoring in the complex real world of cash and hegemonic negotiation. It is a world in which inequality is structured and legitimated by linguicism. The "international" language English is regarded as univerally relevant, despite the abundant evidence that its widespread use in post-colonial contexts has served western interests well (which is what globalization seeks to achieve) and not met the needs of the mass of the population in such countries.

An ecology of language paradigm has a different starting-point. It assumes that speakers of different languages have an equal right to communicate, that multilingualism is desirable and worth encouraging and facilitating, and that language policy should be guided by principles of equity and human rights.

A Utopian Intermezzo: Proposals for a Genuinely Neutral International Language, Esperanto, in the League of Nations and the European Parliament

> Remember that the sole means of achieving peace
> is to abolish for ever the main cause of
> wars, the survival since the most distant
> pre-civilization world of antiquity of the
> domination by one people of other peoples.
> (Zamenhof, 1915, cited in Centassi & Masson, 1995)

The League of Nations was created as a forum to work for the avoidance of military conflagrations like World War I. Membership fluctuated at between forty and fifty states, whereas in the United Nations at present there are roughly 200. The United States remained outside the League of Nations, despite the key role played by President Wilson in the founding of the organization.

The League of Nations had to consider what languages its deliberations should be conducted in. French had hitherto served as the primary diplomatic language (at least in the western world), though not at all "international" conferences. At the Universal Esperanto Association conferences prior to 1914 some governments were officially represented, no fewer than 11 at the conference in 1910 (Centassi & Masson, 1995).

Serious consideration is seldom given by international organizations to the use of a planned language, a neutral one that is not associated with a particular power, a language that is easy for anyone to learn. Esperanto tends to be rejected without serious consideration of why it could represent an alternative to a "natural" language.[10]

The possibility of the League of Nations encouraging Esperanto and even adopting it as a working language was considered seriously, but met fierce resistance on the part of France. Esperanto was discussed several times between 1920 and 1924, and consideration was given to reports of the experience of learning the language in 26 countries. Delegates of eleven states (Belgium, Brazil, Chile, China, Columbia, Czechoslovakia, Haiti, India, Italy, Persia, South Africa) recommended in 1920 that Esperanto should be learned in schools "as an easy means of international understanding" (Lins, 1988, 49–61). Smaller states, including some Asian ones, favoured a neutral international language. But the forces behind the languages of the big member states had their way. The existing world order might have been threatened not only by a neutral language but also by the pacifist utopian political beliefs embraced by some Esperantists.[11] The Esperanto option was rejected, a pattern that holds to this day, apart from some nominal recognition and consultative status at the UN and UNESCO and the International PEN Club.

There is a copious literature on Esperanto. Among the most relevant sociolinguistic facts are that several thousand children worldwide are growing up (in over 2000 families) with Esperanto as one of their mother tongues; that fiction flourishes, novels and poetry in the original as well as in translation; that it is used as the medium for frequent scientific conferences on many topics; that the language can be learned much faster than other languages because of the regular, productive rules underlying it; that although it mainly draws on European basic vocabulary, its systematicity makes it easier for non-Europeans to learn than European languages; that proficiency in Esperanto enables its speakers to meet people from a wide range of cultural and linguistic backgrounds.

In inter-personal communication, the absence of links between Esperanto and any nation-state may facilitate symmetrical communication, irrespective of the mother tongue of the speakers. At the inter-state level, in political institutions which debate the fate of the world's population, lack of political clout is of course the primary weakness of the language. It is the powerful states that can require that their languages have "official" status.

The concept of an official language in supra-state organizations dates from the early years of the League of Nations, when French and English were granted equal status, and in so doing established "the fiction–that a text written in 'language' can be rendered into any number of 'languages' and that the resultant renderings are entirely equal as to meaning" (Tonkin, 1996, 14).

The same principle of textual equivalence applies in the European Union with its 11 official languages, with in theory the "same" semantic content being expressed in each. Anyone familiar with translation processes and products knows that squaring the circle of conceptual, cultural and linguistic difference is a utopian ideal that is remote from how different realities operate. For instance, the legal systems in each of the 15 member states of the European Union have evolved in uniquely distinct ways and texts can never mean precisely "the same" in each language and culture.

There are, however, forces attempting to persuade the European Parliament to consider the Esperanto option seriously, and an increasing number of Members of the European Parliament (MEPs) are reportedly interested in debate on such matters. A hearing was held in 1993, and one on broader issues of language policy is planned.[12] This ultimately reflects the fact that supra-national EU institutions are, in principle, committed to multilingualism and linguistic equality, though the current linguistic hierarchy militates against this: some languages are more equal than others, especially French and English in EU fora.

The Universal Esperanto Association is attempting to influence language policy in international organizations. The Manifesto approved at its 81st World Congress in Prague in 1996 enumerates a number of principles that the movement for the "international language Esperanto" stands for. These cover democracy, global education (ethnic inclusiveness), effective education (better foreign-language learning), multilingualism, language rights, language diversity and human emancipation. The two most relevant principles in the present connection are:

Democracy. Any system of communication which confers lifelong privileges on some while requiring others to devote years of effort to achieving a lesser degree of competence is fundamentally antidemocratic. While Esperanto, like any language, is not perfect, it far outstrips other languages as a means of egalitarian communication on a world scale. We maintain that language inequality gives rise to communicative inequality at all levels, including the international level. *We are a movement for democratic communication.*

Language Rights. The unequal distribution of power among languages is a recipe for permanent language insecurity, or outright language oppression, for a large part of the world's population. In the Esperanto community the speakers of languages large and small, official and unofficial, meet on equal terms through a mutual willingness to compromise. This balance of language rights and responsibilities provides a benchmark for developing and judging other solutions to language inequality and conflict. We maintain that the wide variations in power among languages undermine the guarantees, expressed in many international instruments, of equal treatment regardless of language. *We are a movement for language rights.*

It is only fair to add that I have only become aware of the potential of Esperanto quite recently, meaning that like most sociolinguists I have not taken it seriously hitherto. In addition to the intellectual arguments summarized here, I had the experience of attending two "international" conferences in the summer of 1996. At the Language Rights conference held in Hong Kong, English was virtually the sole means of communication. A South African participant expressed surprise that those whose competence in English was less than ideal, particularly Asians who had great difficulty in expressing themselves in English, accepted the unequal communication rights imposed on them by the conference organizers. At the Universal Esperanto Association's 81st World Congress in Prague a few weeks later, it was amazing to experience several thousand participants from all over the world communicating confidently in a shared international language, among them a number of Asians who were manifestly at no disadvantage.

Language Rights in Supra-statal Organizations

Certain languages are assigned preferential rights in international fora, such as the UN, military or trading alliances, bodies that control such international concerns as shipping and air traffic, and professional associations. These typically operate in one or more official languages. The language that has increasingly imposed itself this century is English, accompanying technological and communication revolutions, and reflecting political, economic and military power. While the hierarchies of language in postcolonial contexts have been subjected to much analysis, international language policy in the sense of the functioning of languages in international organizations is "little studied and little understood" (Tonkin 1996, 9; see also Coulmas 1996; Fettes, 1996).[13]

Studies of the operation of the UN language system over a period of years by Tonkin (1996) and Fettes (1996) indicate that the present language regime reflects political power rather than any principle of equity (e.g. those languages with most speakers, or a representative selection from the global language ecology) or efficiency. Thus four languages, all of European origin (English, French, Russian, Spanish), were accepted as the official languages of the UN in 1945, since which time there has been sufficient weight behind Arabic (after the oil crisis of 1973) and Chinese (of major demographic and geopolitical importance) to ensure their addition.

In theory there are six official languages with equal rights at the United Nations, and a huge amount of documentation is produced in these languages by an expensive translation service. In practice, English is the *de facto* dominant working language, and this is covertly accepted at the UN. Dissatisfaction has been expressed by the French-speaking powers at the UN, but to no avail, and their protest has little to do with equity or the rights of languages other than French.[14] There is major resistance to reform of the system, as it reflects a set of political compromises, attachment to the system by those who operate it, and a reluctance to consider alternatives.

Possible alternatives suggested by Tonkin (1996, 22–24) might involve more overt acceptance of the use of a single language, either English or Esperanto, or a greater focus on language learning and receptive multilingualism, or a system by which language services could be available on demand and for payment. At present there is no indication that there is any willingness to alter the system, despite the fact that the UN is looking to cut costs and as much as a quarter of the UN working budget is spent on the interpretation and translation services (Fettes 1996, 119). The system is inefficient because many speakers are less than fluent and comprehensible in one of the official languages, because of logistic problems in providing interpretation into the designated official languages, and because of waste when texts are translated into all the official languages without extensive use being made of them. As a former interpreter in the UN system notes, it is paradoxical to devote substantial funds to such matters when the UN's primary activities such as peace-keeping, health care, and the promotion of human rights are under-funded (Piron 1994).

It seems fair to conclude that the present system of assigning rights to certain languages effectively deprives speakers of other languages of equal access to the system. In addition, selecting a certain number of languages does not mean that there is no hierarchy among those selected—quite the opposite.

In the European Union, language policy is such a political hot potato that few concerted high-level initiatives have been taken. Language policy does not have a high profile. Most language policies are covert rather than overt. As the editor of an issue of the International Political Science Review on "The emergent world language system" notes: "The subject of languages has been the great *non-dit* of European integration. There was much talk of milk pools and butter mountains, of a unitary currency, of liberalizing movements for EC citizens and restricting access for outsiders, but the language in which these issues were dealt with remained itself a non-issue (de Swaan, 1993, 244).

There have been few systematic studies of language policy in the EU, and none within an elaborate multi-disciplinary framework. What is currently available is fragmentary, and largely impressionistic. Books on European integration in political science neglect the language issue (e.g. Richardson, 1996). Studies of EU language policy contain analysis of the regulations governing language policy, empirical studies of the use made of particular languages, and attitudes to language use. The pioneer works are by a French Canadian (Labrie 1993), a German (Schlossmacher 1996), and a Norwegian (Simonsen 1996), and it is doubtless not fortuitous that the first studies are by scholars who come from states who feel that their languages are threatened, in all cases by the advance of English. The books are in French, German and Norwegian, respectively, which may restrict their readership. Many of the issues have, however, been dealt with in English (see the annual *Sociolinguistica;* Phillipson & Skutnabb-Kangas, 1997).

In theory language policy is, like culture, a matter for each member state, but globalization and Europeanization processes, and the intensity of links in so many fields across national borders, many of them encouraged by measures adopted in the EU, make national autonomy in some measure illusory. For EU institutions the most significant language legislation is the 1958 granting the four dominant languages of the founding states (Dutch, French, German and Italian) equal rights as official and working languages. When new states acceded progressively, their languages were added (Danish and English in 1972, Greek, Portuguese and Spanish a decade later, Finnish and Swedish from 1994). The preamble to the initial decision explains that it is those languages that are official throughout the territory of a state that are eligible as EU languages. This therefore excludes regional languages such as Catalan in Spain, even though it has more speakers than some of the official languages.

Membership of the European "Union" involves a pooling of sovereignty with the other member states. There is therefore a manifest need for written documents that are the outcome of negotiations between the member states (for instance in the Council of Ministers) to be disseminated in each state in the dominant language, since texts (treaties, regulations, etc.) with the force of EU law over-ride national law. Here there is a clear need for optimally close textual equivalence in 11 official languages.

The present system of interpreting into the 11 official languages (11 × 10 possible combinations) is cumbersome, and a system of relay interpretation, e.g. from Danish to Greek via French or English, is often in operation (Dollerup, 1996). In principle each of the 11 languages has the same right to be used as a working language: in practice speakers of "small" languages often waive their rights and operate in one of the "big" languages. Often draft texts are only available in French or English.

It is probable that the equality of official languages has always been a fiction. French was in the early years the dominant language of the EU Commission in Brussels, and still is so in some domains. The Germans accepted this, even though political and business leaders periodically complain that German interests suffer as a consequence of German not enjoying *de facto* the same rights.

Most of the explicit language policy agendas are minimalist, aiming at some kind of equity among the 11 official languages. EU schemes for promoting student mobility aim to strengthen competence in foreign languages in the member countries and the formation of "European" identity. In theory, the architects of Europeanization proclaim that cultural and linguistic diversity are to be maintained. However, the reality is more complex, as regards both the use of all national languages at the supra-national level and the status and rights of minority languages in each state. In addition, English is impacting on national languages. In EU institutions English is expanding at the expense of other potential lingua francas, French and German in particular. The less "international" languages of the other member states have few rights in practice. There is, in other words, tacit acceptance of a hierarchy of EU languages.

How EU language policy will evolve is difficult to predict. There are many unanswered questions: is the EU moving towards diglossia, with English as a second language for elites other than the Brits and the Irish who will remain mostly monolingual? Or can a more substantial degree of multi-directional and reciprocal multilingualism be established? Will EU institutions continue with a cumbersome system of translation and interpretation, or will they re-think their policy for working languages and the drafting of texts? This is likely when the EU expands to take in new members. Are current schemes that fund student mobility (Erasmus, Socrates etc) achieving their declared goal of strengthening the less widely used EU languages, or are they in fact boosting English?[15] Is there any informed discussion of the viability of alternatives such as Esperanto? Which constituencies exercise most influence on language policy formation, national or supra-national elites, professional bodies, or mythology generated in the media world and political discourse? Is it fair to assume that the political sensitivity of the issues, coupled with the fragility of the infrastructure, nationally and supra-nationally, for guaranteeing informed public debate about those issues, means that market forces will progressively strengthen English? And if this happens will it necessarily be at the expense of (speakers of) other languages?

Much is at stake, at multiple levels (individual, regional, societal, global) and in many domains (cultural, economic, political, etc.), both in local linguistic ecologies and at a macro, European level.

Empirical studies indicate that it is only French and English that effectively function as official and working languages in internal EU affairs (Schlossmacher 1996, data collected in 1992). Northern Europeans tend to use English, southern Europeans French. English predominates as the means of communication externally (e.g. with EFTA countries, and even with post-communist states, where German has traditionally been strong). Quell's more recent study (1997) confirms this picture. Competence in French and English is a condition for adequate participation in political decision-making, even in the European Parliament, where interpretation services are more widely available, and greater use is made of many languages, at least in plenary sessions of the Parliament.

When asked whether regulations on a new system of working languages were needed, a large proportion of the bureaucrats employed by the EU indicated that they would welcome this (78%), whereas far fewer MEPs would (41%, Schlossmacher 1996, 98). It is typically those from "small" language groups (e.g. Danish and Portuguese) who do not wish for change, presumably because of the risk of their language being marginalized even further than is already the case.

The same study also shows a large proportion wishing German to be used as a language with top priority and status, rather than a system with only English, or only French and English, as working languages, even if this is not currently the case (ibid. 103). Quell's informants were also asked whether a possible formalized resolution of the issue of working languages in the EU would be a one-, two- or three-language system, and if so, which of the 11 languages should be granted this status. The results show a marked preference for a bilingual (French and English) or a trilingual (English, French and German) system rather than a monolingual one. They also suggest that there is more support for an English-only system among users of English as a second language than among native speakers.[16]

Schlossmacher's study also reveals a wide range of views on whether new member states should necessarily have the same language rights as do member states under the present scheme of things. Again, the pattern is that fewer bureaucrats than MEPs seem to believe incoming languages/states should have the same rights.[17] It is more than likely that decisions on language policy will be taken when new states are added, if only because additional languages will complicate immensely the logistics of simultaneous interpretation. Does this mean that in the EU of the future, at meetings attended by heads of state, senior and middle-level bureaucrats, politicians and experts, there will be no right to operate in the mother tongue? When admitted to the European club (a club whose rules have the force of law in each member state), will speakers of Czech, Estonian, Hungarian and Polish only be heard speaking English and French? Answers to these questions are anyone's guess at present, but they raise a fundamental issue: is the EU really a democratic partnership of member states with equal rights?

As the present policy is one of inaction, "regulation by default... the only language which stands to gain is English. Considering the fact that most people do not wish to see English gain more ground, it is curious that it is, nonetheless, establishing itself as the dominant language of the European bureaucracy" (Quell 1997, 71).

English has, over the past quarter century, acquired the status of a supra-national language in the EU comparable to its position in the UN and many postcolonial states, and reflecting its position as the language of Americanization and McDonaldization. This has consequences for the ecology of the languages of the EU that are likely to become increasingly visible over the coming decades. English has a hegemonic position as an international language that international law, including human rights law, has no means of counteracting, whatever is stated in covenants about the unacceptability of discrimination on the grounds of language (for the limitations of these see Skutnabb-Kangas & Phillipson, 1994b).

International Linguistic Hegemony

English linguistic hegemony is asserted in multiple ways. Some of them reflect economic strength. The diffusion of English depends less on military force (though "peace-keeping" in Bosnia strengthens and diversifies English) than on commercial pressures, not least those of transnational corporations and global and regional organizations such as the EU.

Clearly linguistic hierarchies at the international level do not correlate in a straightforward way with national demographic or economic strength. German has the most native speakers of any language group in the EU, the largest internal market and the strongest economy, as well as some extra-national functioning, but there is little sign that German will be able to compete with English.

English also benefits through foreign-language learning confirming the international linguistic hierarchy. So as to be able to compete in the global market-place, states whose languages are competing lingua francas—France, Germany and Spain—invest heavily in the learning of English in state education, even though the language is regarded as a threat to local cultural and linguistic values.[18]

International scientific collaboration is also increasingly dominated by English. Peripheral areas are vulnerable to collaborative ventures underpinned by scientific and linguistic imperialism:[19] there are asymmetrical relations in academic discourse that the status of English consolidates, and a hierarchy of research paradigms that is often legitimated and internalized unquestioningly.

The top language benefits through the image-making of the ads of transnational corporations and the connotations of English with success and hedonism. These symbols are reinforced by an ideology that glorifies the dominant language and serves to stigmatize others, this hierarchy being rationalized and internalized as normal and natural, rather than as expression of hegemonic values and interests.[20]

The diffusion of English is clearly visible in post-colonial language policies that ignore the local language ecology. Western scholarly studies of the sociology of language often reflect an asymmetrical relationship, as a review of a book by a North American on language policy indicates: "This is a typical specimen of Indian and Western collaboration: superficial and patronizing... By ignoring scholarship in India's regional languages on India's language issues, we are missing vital insights. The English language provides us just one dimension, one perspective and one window." (Kachru 1996, 138, 140).

Globally these trends and many others that are an integral part of McDonaldization, have led to a tendency for both elite and marginal groups to desire competence in English for the obvious reason that English is seen to open doors. The appeal of English should not obscure the fact that in Africa as a whole 90% of the population speak only African languages. Likewise in India figures for the number of speakers of English are 3–5%. If the citizens of countries worldwide are to contribute to the solution of local problems, to use the local environment for locally appropriate purposes, cultural, economic and political, this must involve local languages. Language policy must reconcile these dimensions of language ecology with the pressures of globalization and supranationalization that are propelling English forward. Language policy must be made explicit, and must embrace equitable conditions for all people and all languages. There is a case for international human rights law to be extended so as to control the invasion of dominant international languages.

Notes

1 A key policy document, "The diffusion of English culture outside England. A problem of post-war reconstruction" (Routh, 1941), was produced by an adviser to the British Council, a body established in the 1930s to promote English and to counteract the successful promotion of their languages by fascist governments. This was a blueprint for the creation of the global English-teaching profession that came into being in the late 1950s and has expanded dramatically since.

The Americans poured money into education systems in "Third World" countries, and not least the English as a Second Language profession: "... the expenditure of large amounts of government and private foundation funds in the period 1950–1970, perhaps the most ever spent in history in the propagation of a language" (Troike, a director of the Center for Applied Linguistics, Washington, DC, 1977).

2 These notions relate to its form (an amalgam of several, primarily European languages) and its role as a medium for Christianity, literature, wealth, technology, science, progress, etc. "Dissent from the imperial theme is rare even today" (Bailey, 1991, p. 116). There is a long and still vibrant tradition of pretending "to offer evidence for anglophone superiority in all fields of human endeavor. Many have justified the most pernicious forms of injustice. Few withstand rigorous and dispassionate scrutiny" (ibid, 287).

3 Malcom Rifkind, when British Foreign Secretary: Britain is a "global power with worldwide interests thanks to the Commonwealth, the Atlantic relationship and the growing use of the English language" (reported in *The Observer*, 24.9.1995).

4 The British Council's "English 2000" project, launched in 1995, reports in its publicity material that it aims to "exploit the position of English to further British interests, as one aspect of maintaining and expanding the role of English as the world language into the next century... Speaking English makes people open to Britain's cultural achievements, social values and business aims."

5 *The Sunday Times*, London, 10.7.1994: The way of salvation for the French language is for English to be taught as vigorously as possible as the second language in all its schools... Only when the French recognize the dominance of AngloAmerican English as the universal language in a shrinking world can they effectively defend their own distinctive culture... Britain must press ahead with the propagation of English and the British values which stand behind it.

6 The flood of recent books on globalization and English can be broadly classified as:

regional (e.g. *Linguistic ecology. Language change and linguistic imperialism in the Pacific region*. Mühlhäusler, Routledge; *South Asian English*, ed. Baumgardner, Illinois UP)

comparative (*Post-imperial English: Status change in former British and American colonies, 1940–1990*, ed. Fishman, Conrad & Rubal-Lopez, Mouton de Gruyter; *Language policies in English-dominant countries*, Herriman/Burnaby, Multilingual Matters)

triumphalist (*English as a global language*, Crystal, Cambridge UP)

analytical (*The politics of English as an international language*, Pennycook, Longman; *Problematizing English in India*, Agnihotra & Khanna, Sage; *Linguistic imperialism*, Phillipson, Oxford)

radical-critical (*The otherness of English. India's auntie tongue syndrome*, Dasgupta, Sage; *De-hegemonizing language standards. Learning from (post)colonial Englishes about 'English'*, Parakrama, Macmillan)

predictive (*The future of English*, Graddol, British Council).

7 These are the highlights of the abstract of the paper given by the President of the British Association for International and Comparative Education, Sir Christopher Ball, at the Third Oxford Conference on Education and Development, 1995.

8 The domains of learning are
   (i) learning how to learn
   (ii) the world-language
   (iii) the mother-tongue (if different from ii)
   (iv) numeracy
   (v) cultural literacy
   (vi) social skills
   (vii) religion, ethics and values.
9 Linguicism is defined as "ideologies, structures and practices which are used to legitimate, effectuate and reproduce an unequal division of power and resources (material and immaterial) between groups which are defined on the basis of language" (Skutnabb-Kangas 1988).
10 Zamenhof himself quoted Ovid with reference to people who reject Esperanto without being familiar with its potential or reality: "Ignoti nulla cupido" = One does not wish for what one is ignorant of (quoted in Centassi & Masson 1995).
11 In the autumn of 1915 Zamenhof wrote an article entitled "After the Great War—an appeal to diplomats", a kind of political testament. He propounded four principles (Centassi & Masson 1995, 329–331):

All countries belong to their inhabitants and those who have settled there (naturalized). No people should, within a country, exercise rights or have duties which are superior or inferior to those of other peoples.

Everyone has the inalienable right to use the language of his/her choice and to practice whatever religion they prefer.

The government of each country is responsible for all injustices committed (by it/in its name) before a permanent European Tribunal constituted with the consent of all the European countries.

No country and no province should bear the name of a people but rather a name which is geographically neutral and freely accepted by all the other peoples.
12 "Das Kommunikations- und Sprachenproblem in der Europäischen Gemeinschaft—in wie weit könnte eine Plansprache zu seiner Lösung beitragen?", European Parliament, Brussels, 29 September 1993, organized by the Hanns Seidel Foundation. A second hearing has been planned by the Working Group on the Language Problems of the European Union. Details can be obtained from the Universala Esperanto-Asocio, Nieuwe Binnenweg 176, 3015 BJ Rotterdam, the Netherlands.
13 The Center for Research and Documentation on World Language Problems, based at the University of Hartford, USA and associated with the journal *Language problems and language planning*, has organized a series of conferences at the UN on language policy (for references see Tonkin, 1996).
14 See the General Assembly resolution of 2 November 1995 reported in Fettes, 1996, 130.
15 For decades the Council of Europe has advocated the learning of two foreign languages. The EU Commission in its White Paper on Education and Training (COM(95) 590 of 29.11.1995) recommends the learning of at least two Community foreign languages by all young people, and a variety of measures

to strengthen foreign language learning. Many schoolchildren in Europe are already doing so, and most EU governments other than the British are willing to endorse the principle of learning two foreign languages.

16 While meticulous and cautious in his analysis, Quell inclines to the view that L2 speakers are "ideal agents of change because not only are they highly motivated but as they are supporting a language to which they are not tied in a primary national and cultural sense, they are unlikely to be perceived to be supporting a policy for selfish nationalistic reasons." (Quell, 1997, 70)

While this may be a valid conclusion for this investigation, putting it in a broader context may reduce its generalizability. Schlossmacher's research indicates that EU bureaucrats are much less insistent than MEPs on maintaining their right to use the L1 in EU institutions.

17 To some extent this "result" might be an artefact of the questionnaire exercise, since informants inevitably had to interpret statements that can be understood in various ways, however carefully drafted. And is "Amtssprache" an exact equivalent of "official" language?

18 For details of change in foreign language learning in EU countries over the past half century, and analysis of the implications for choice of language in interpersonal communication see Labrie & Quell, 1997.

19 There are lively debates in Hungarian social science journals about the unequal relationship between North American researchers and their Hungarian "partners": see the special issue of *replika* "Colonisation or partnership? Eastern Europe and western social sciences", 1996. I am grateful to Miklós Kontra for drawing my attention to this.

20 A recent example of this: a senior British Council officer regards the contemporary dominance of English in key domains of globalization as comparable to water running downhill and the sun rising in the East, and that granted this social reality, it "is legitimate and inevitable that native English-speaking countries will seek to turn this reality to national advantage..." (Seaton, 1997, 381).

References

Abou, Sélim and Katia Haddad, eds. *La diversité linguistique et culturelle et les enjeux du développement*. Montréal: AUPELF–UREF, 1997.

Akinnaso, F. Niyi. "Linguistic unification and language rights." *Applied Linguistics* 15, no. 2 (1994): 139–168.

Bailey, Richard W. *Images of English: A cultural history of the language*. Cambridge: Cambridge University Press, 1991.

Calvet, Louis-Jean. *Linguistique et colonialisme: petit traité de glottophagie*. Paris: Payot, 1974.

Centassi, René and Henri Masson. *L'homme qui a défié Babel*. Paris: Ramsay, 1995.

Coulmas, Florian. "Language contact in multinational organizations." In Hans Goebl, Peter H. Nelde, Zdeněk Starý, and Wolfgang Wölck, eds., *Kontaktlinguistik/Contact Linguistics/Linguistique de contact: An international handbook of contemporary research*, 858-864. Berlin and New York: de Gruyter, 1996.

Crowley, Tony. *Proper English? Readings in language, history and cultural identity*. London: Routledge, 1991.

de Swaan, Abram. "The emergent world language system: an introduction." *International Political Science Review* 14, no. 3 (1993): 219-226.

——. "The evolving European language system: a theory of communication potential and language competition." *International Political Science Review* 14, no. 3 (1993): 241-256.

Djité, Paulin. "Language and development in Africa." *International Journal of the Sociology of Language* 100/101 (1993): 149-166.

Dollerup, Cay. "English in the European Union." In Reinhard Hartmann, ed., *English language in Europe*, 24-36. Exeter: Intellect, 1996.

Fettes, Mark. "Inside the tower of words: the institutional functions of language at the United Nations." In Léger, ed. (1996), 115-134.

Graddol, David. *The Future of English?* A guide to forecasting the popularity of the English language in the 21st century. London: British Council, 1997.

Grin, François and Catherine Hennis-Pierre. "La diversité linguistique et culturelle face aux règles du commerce: le cas du film et des émissions de télévision." In Abou and Haddad, eds. (1997), 265-286.

Hamelink, Cees J. *Trends in world communication: on disempowerment and self-empowerment*. Penang: Southbound & Third World Network, 1994.

Illich, Ivan. *Shadow work*. Boston & London: Marion Boyars, 1981.

Kachru, Braj B. Review of Grant D. McDonnell's "A macro-sociolinguistic analysis of language vitality: Geolinguistic profiles and scenarios of language contact in India." *Language in Society* 25, no. 1 (1996): 137-140.

Labrie, Normand. *La construction linguistique de la Communauté européenne*. Paris: Henri Champion, 1993.

Labrie, Normand and Quell, Carsten. "Your language, my language or English? The potential language choice in communication among nationals of the European Union." *World Englishes* 16:1 (1997): 3-26.

Léger, Sylvie, ed. *Vers un agenda linguistique: regard futuriste sur les nations unies (Towards a language agenda: futurist outlook on the United Nations)*. Ottawa: Canadian Centre for Linguistic Rights, University of Ottawa, 1996.

Lins, Ulrich. *Die gefährliche Sprache. Die Verfolgung der Esperantisten unter Hitler und Stalin*. Gerlingen: Bleicher, 1988.

Mazrui, Alamin. "The World Bank, the language question and the future of African education." *Race and class* 38, no. 3 (1997): 35-48.

Mühlhäusler, Peter. *Linguistic ecology. Language change and linguistic imperialism in the Pacific region*. London: Routledge, 1996.

Phillipson, Robert. *Linguistic imperialism*. Oxford: Oxford University Press, 1992.

Phillipson, Robert and Tove Skutnabb-Kangas. "Language rights in postcolonial Africa." In Skutnabb-Kangas and Phillipson, eds. (1994), 335–345.

Phillipson, Robert and Tove Skutnabb-Kangas. "English only worldwide, or language ecology." *TESOL Quarterly*, special issue on language policy, 30, no. 3 (1996): 429–452.

Phillipson, Robert and Tove Skutnabb-Kangas. "Lessons for Europe from language policy in Australia." In Pütz (1997), 115–159.

Piron, Claude. *Le défi des langues: du gâchis au bon sens* (The languages challenge: from waste to common sense). Paris: L'Harmattan, 1994.

Pütz, Martin, ed. *Language choices: Conditions, constraints and consequences.* Amsterdam: John Benjamins, 1997.

Quell, Carsten. "Language choice in multilingual institutions: A case study at the European Commission with particular reference to the role of English, French and German as working languages." *Multilingua* 16, no. 1 (1997): 57–76.

Richardson, Jeremy, ed. *European Union: power and policy-making.* London: Routledge, 1996.

Routh, H. V. *The diffusion of English culture outside England. A problem of post-war reconstruction.* Cambridge: Cambridge University Press, 1941.

Schlossmacher, Michael. *Die Amtssprachen in den Organen der Europäischen Gemeinschaft.* Frankfurt am Main: Peter Lang, 1996.

Seaton, Ian. "Linguistic non-imperialism." *ELT Journal* 51, no. 4 (1997): 381–382.

Simonsen, Dag. *Nordens språk i EUs Europa. Språkplanlegging og språkpolitikk motår 2000* (The Nordic languages in the Europe of the EU. Language planning and language policy towards the year 2000). Oslo: Nordisk Språksekretariat, 1996.

Skutnabb-Kangas, Tove. "Multilingualism and the education of Minority Children." In Tove Skutnabb-Kangas and Jim Cummins, eds., *Minority education. From shame to struggle*, 9-44. Clevedon: Multilingual Matters, 1988.

Skutnabb-Kangas, Tove and Robert Phillipson, eds. *Linguistic human rights: overcoming linguistic discrimination.* Berlin: Mouton de Gruyter (paperback version 1995), 1994a.

Skutnabb-Kangas, Tove and Robert Phillipson. "Linguistic human rights, past and present." In Skutnabb-Kangas and Phillipson 1994a, 71–110; 1994b.

Skutnabb-Kangas, Tove and Robert Phillipson. "Language rights in postcolonial Africa." In Skutnabb-Kangas and Phillipson 1994a, 335–345; 1994c.

Tonkin, Humphrey. "Language hierarchy at the United Nations." In Léger (1996), 3–28.

Troike, Rudolf. "The future of English". Editorial, *The Linguistic Reporter* 19/8 (1977): 2.

Tsuda, Yukio. "The diffusion of English: its impact on culture and communication." *Keio Communication Review* 16 (1994): 49–61.

Heroes, Rebels, Communities and States in Language Rights Activism and Litigation

ANGÉLINE MARTEL

It is a sign of the times when a search for the single word *activism*, via a single search engine on the Internet, should produce 48,120 hits. The phenomenon is as diverse as it is pervasive: citizen activism, social and environmental activism, student activism, blue ribbon activism against censorship on the Net, gay/lesbian activism, even shareholders activism. Some activist movements are regional, others national or international. They signal sociopolitical mutations: unprecedented demands for participation and influence in political life; the increasing powers that groups can gain by their discourse and actions; the longing to effect social change around the world; the collective bonding of individuals in order to make their voices heard.

As sociopolitical practices and structures are being pressured to change, the activist phenomenon raises issues that need to be reflected on:

- its *societal and ethical significance*: the vision of justice, of emancipation or of local interests that it nurtures;
- the *instruments* used for advocating change: litigation, lobbying, research, community mobilization, media coverage, even violence;
- its *sphere of activity*: beyond/within/against state boundaries, interrogating a new geographical dynamics in an age of globalization;
- its *results*: efficiency in effecting change.

These issues need to be addressed when analyzing language rights activism. Others must also be included. An activist movement brings its own linguistic objectives, its particular regional/national/international dynamic, its use of law as an instrument of change and its (partial) ability or inability to neutralize unequal power relations and domination. As a rights-oriented process, it also raises issues of interaction between actors (individuals, communities, states) in the process of elaborating legal statutes, of interpreting these statutes through the courts, and of implementing legal measures through appropriate social and political structures.

This paper looks at all these perspectives. It is set against the backdrop created by activist movements and law in a world of increasing democratization and globalization, of enlarging educational and political consciousness, of multiplying informational and communicational channels. Through an analysis of Canadian language laws for Francophone minorities it examines the influence of language rights activism and litigation on social and political relations. Heroes, rebels, communities and states are all actors who work through/against language rights and litigation to impact on the social practices, ideologies and structures influencing the preservation and development of language communities.

First, the paper summarizes some sociopolitical issues that influence language rights activism by considering the social/ethical meaning of activism as a general phenomenon. It also examines the role and the sphere of influence of law as an instrument for change. Secondly, through a Canadian example, it deals with the processes of elaborating rights, of interpreting them through litigation with the actors involved. Thirdly, it examines positive and negative results of this process with regard to (minority) community development and social organization. Finally, using these experiences, it suggests strategies for social change and minority community development through language rights activism.

Its main thesis is that litigation and language rights activism are necessary and inevitable processes that can successfully guide language community development. However, they also deepen an adversarial sociopolitical climate borne by litigation. Such a climate may be counterproductive, particularly in view of the development of a sociopolitical organization based on complementarity and solidarity.

Language Rights Activism and Litigation:
A Global Environment

Activism Today. Why?

A cornerstone of today's ideological clashes and discourses on sociopolitical organization is the dialectic between domination and autonomy. From different perspectives emerge different vocabularies to label one or both of its poles. From a sociocultural point of view, we speak of submission/oppression, or of emancipation/ empowerment. From a political perspective, key words are control/domination/authority or independence/self-determination/ sovereignty/revitalization. From an economic perspective, one speaks of centralization/monopoly or decentralization/self-management. Undercutting this dialectic are contiguous modes of relating that could be placed on a continuum between competition/conflict/rivalry (fostering oppression) and solidarity/ harmony/ cooperation (fostering emancipation).

In life, however, the dialectic is never so limpid. For example, political demands for independence/self-determination/sovereignty are seen less in terms of total independence in an increasingly interconnected and networked world than in terms of claims by social groups, such as ethnic and minority communities, towards a middle ground of devolution of power, of effective control of a community for revitalization, and of participation in the life of the larger entity (state, city or international organization) (Hannum 1993).

In this context, activism can be seen as a manifestation of a rising consciousness, and rejection, of conditions of submission/ oppression/control/domination/authority/centralization/monopoly. It can be a challenge to sociopolitical structures that reproduce non-equitable power relations. It can also be a symptom that a culture of individualism, in the political sphere, is not necessarily compatible with collective well-being and development; the paradox being that an individual's well-being depends on that of the collectivity.

Activism and Democracy

In a relations-oriented process from oppression to emancipation, activism also raises important issues with respect to democratic values. On the one hand, activism can be seen as challenging the tradition of elective democracy. Interest groups (and individuals) attempt, and depending on the circumstances and the political systems do, influence the decision-making process. These actors can be seen to bypass representation, a basic principle of democracy. By so doing, the argument goes, interest groups insert their particular interests in a process that should take into account the better interests of all. This argument can be seen to articulate a majoritarian perspective. It does have a valid argument in that interest groups, by definition, look after their own interests, which could be an Achilles heel of activism.

From a minoritarian (dominated) perspective, however, the "challenge to democracy" argument can be critiqued as an attempt to protect the effective power position of dominating groups. And democracy can be deemed a fiction, an ideal unrealized where, traditionally, activism and lobbying have been the almost exclusive domain of the major economic interests in society (Brickey and Cormack 1987).

On the other hand, the voicing of demands by minority communities and disadvantaged groups through activism can also be seen as the very condition of democracy. Two reasons underlie this claim. First, activism puts forward the point of view of people who are not in power, thereby giving substance to the expression of social pluralism and guarding against status quo through consensus (or the silent majority). This excludes from our perspective on activism such movements as skinheads or extreme right-wing movements whose interests are to maintain a status quo of inequality and injustice and to exclude groups from social power bases.

Secondly, minorities are structurally disadvantaged by most elective democracies to the extent that they cannot usually expect to be in opposition today and in power tomorrow. Unless measures (affirmative action, rights and protection measures) are taken to correct this structural non-representation, disadvantaged groups have to voice their concerns through alternative channels, namely activism.

Activism can also be a sphere of innovation. The inventiveness of groups who create their collective spheres at the margins of power has been documented (Soulier 1989). Activist groups are political, but usually do not seek power through politics and, as such, they may come to offer new sociopolitical models on the solidarity/harmony/cooperation side of the relations continuum.

A Test for Activism: Empowerment, Justice and Larger-than-Local Interests

Although activism is today a pervasive sociopolitical phenomenon, and although it raises questions on the nature and the development of democracies, the test that it must pass, from an ethical point of view, is its capacity to lead to the empowerment of communities within a larger vision than (their) local interests. In other words, does activism provide the possibility to be politically active on alternative grounds, to chart courses of conciliation between harmony and competition? Does it remind us that democracy, as we know it now as the winner of the Cold War, is a Western-centric device of social regulation whose further evolution and transformation are inevitable? And does it lead to structures for a more equitable world, which is, in substance, the fundamental demand that activism brings to the foreground?

Law as an Instrument of Change

Another question needs to be considered: Can law be an instru-ment that activism can use in order to *effect* social change? An-swers here are either cynical or enthusiastic. This is so because rights activism is set against the perceived nature and effectiveness of legal systems.

Generalized Criticisms of Legal Systems

Generally, legal systems are the subject of much criticism for their inadequacies and their inability to achieve justice for individuals and groups. Detective stories are good places to probe the degree of confidence that citizens and legal actors have in the law. Here is an example from Sweden: "But how many transgressors of the law get away without ever appearing before a court–quite apart from the fact that the law has been designed to protect certain social classes and their dubious interests, and otherwise seems mostly to consist of loopholes?" (Sjöwall and Wahlöö 1992, 158).

More than fiction, however, are the conclusions of Mandel's analysis of the effects of the Canadian Charter of Rights and Free-doms since 1982: "Where the Charter has had an effect, that effect has been to strengthen the already great inequalities in Canada. It has weighed in on the side of power and, in both crude and subtle ways, has undermined popular movements as varied as the anti-nuclear movement, the labour movement, the nationalist move-ment in Quebec, the aboriginal people's movement and the women's movement. Filtering democratic opposition through the legal system has not only failed to reduce Canada's already great social inequalities but has actually strengthened them." (1989, 4).

Does this mean that the law is inadequate as an instrument for justice and social transformation? In this paper I answer both in the negative and the positive. Law can be a blunt instrument for effecting change, much less efficient than, for example, economic power or political mobilization (Livingston and Morrison 1990, 1). Nor is it synonymous with justice.

The relationship between law and social change is complex, even contradictory, and the perspective adopted matters a great deal. Law can be seen as one of the tools of domination by the ruling class which, by virtue of its economic power (ownership and control of the means of production), is able to manipulate institutions within the state, including the police, the courts and prison system. Institutions within the state can also be seen as a means of reproducing class relations and class domination under capitalism. From these perspectives, in order to effect change a system would either have to eradicate its social class system and/or change its political structure. And law would remain a servant of both social classes and political structure.

Although these perspectives are not improper, lived experience tells us that changes in laws *do* change things in our lives. We adapt to new legal norms, we lobby for others. Legal statutes constitute landmarks in our societies. Whether law effects change in the direction of justice and equity is, however, a more important question. This question requires an ethics of law as an agent of social change. In the process both of constructing this ethics and seeking its realization, the legal sphere is an arena of struggle which engages individuals and groups of different classes and political positions (Brickey and Cormack 1987) in actions toward the recognition and operationalization of their ideals and interests.

Law as Ideology

The law as ideology perspective is fruitful when it comes to understanding and acting towards social change. It allows for the paradox that an instrument of oppression can also serve as an instrument of emancipation. A legal text can be seen as a reified ideology if we take it that ideologies are systems of more or less coherent ideas, networks of given ideas, of ethical principles, of holistic representations that rule the relationships that individuals and groups entertain amongst themselves, with strangers, with nature, etc. Even if they do not determine behavior, ideologies largely reflect the interests of the agents (individuals or groups) that share them (Martel 1996; Tollefson 1991). As ideology, law is a source of common sense and of the manufacturing of consent to the extent that it crystallizes a series of values and sociopolitical compromises and takes them as quasi-unquestionable (Kevelson 1988). In this manner, law is more properly viewed as a dynamic entity. Far from being a set of abstract rules largely impervious to the changing social climate, law is directly implicated in both changing and being changed by social events.

Law as a Sphere of Action

These considerations lead us to focus on the workings of lived law. First, lived law includes not only the law as a system of normative rules, that is, what is done in its name and on its margins, but also its appropriation by actors: their rights. Secondly, law can be conceived as an amalgam of discourses or concrete social practices through which a network of institutions and agents act and transform social rules based on ideological struggles of inclusion and exclusion, of dominance and domination (Landowski 1988). Finally, it encourages an emphasis on the role of social actors in the constitution and reproduction of legal order. In effect, it assumes that states do not have the monopoly of the production of law. It also allows consideration of the degree of confidence the less powerful gain from the sociopolitical system that harbors them, and from the law.

This degree of confidence is highlighted by the contemporary pervasive appeal to rights. Hunt (1981) notes the objection to the discourse of rights as an inappropriate form for generating liberating practices. The fact remains that the very terms of political argument and debate in advanced capitalist societies are unavoidably legalistic. In consequence, so persistent is this appeal to rights that it makes little or no sense to dismiss this reality by arguing that rights are merely ideological masks disguising naked interests. Rights discourse, at the very least, offers the potential to facilitate activism by mobilizing political action among subordinate groups.

A growing importance is accorded to law, particularly to international statutes and constitutional measures. This is also true for languages since, by 1992, the constitutions of 120 sovereign states (approximately 75 percent of the states then recognized by the United Nations) contained one or more linguistic measures pertaining to language status, usage in courts and public administration, national education, and rights for linguistic minorities (Gauthier *et al.* 1993). Consequently, the law, and particularly litigation and rights activism, are prominently effecting a legalization and judiciarization of the political sphere around the world. A new dynamic is at work between the political sphere and civil societies where the law is used as a tool for community development.

A Rights-Oriented Process: Promulgation and Litigation

The Canadian experience is interesting for our analysis of the relationship between language rights activism, litigation, and social change. First, pursuant to the promulgation in 1982 of the Canadian Charter of Rights and Freedoms and its section 23, "Minority Language Instructional Rights", important changes have been effected in the educational situation of the Francophone minorities living outside of Quebec in the English-speaking majority provinces and territories. Secondly, an analysis of issues of self-governance for language communities enables a study of the workings of emancipation through activism and litigation. Thirdly, even though Francophone minorities are well positioned in that they have the status of official minorities, their situation and development serve as precedents for the revitalization of native peoples and for communities emerging from immigration, particularly in the type of schools and community centers established and the school management structures designed for minorities.

This section begins with demographic information and a description of section 23. It then describes the historical processes that led to the promulgation of section 23 (ideological bases and negotiation of consensus), the litigation process that followed its promulgation (intense and fueled by federal state support), and the actors involved (unified voices and dissension in communities).

Language Rights in Canada: A Background

Francophone minorities are established in nine provinces and two territories of Canada where in 1991, according to *Statistics Canada* (Harrison and Marmen 1994), they represented a national average of 4.8 percent out of an overall population of 20,183,735. In total, 976,415 persons declared French as their mother tongue (first language learnt and still spoken). This proportion varies con-

siderably from province to province (table 3.1): from 34 percent in
New Brunswick to 0.5 percent in Newfoundland.

Table 3.1

Official language minorities in provinces and
territories of Canada

Minority populations and percentages of
total population 1951 and 1991

Proportion*		1951			1991	
	Province/ Territory	Minority population	Minority/ Total	Province/ Territory	Minority population	Minority/ Total
Considerable (>1/3)	New Brunswick	185,110	35.9%	New Brunswick	243,690	34.0%
Important (10 to 33%)	Quebec	558,256	13.8%			
Intermediate (4 to 10%)	Prince Edward Island	8,477	8.6%	Quebec	666,923	9.4%
	Ontario	341,502	7.4%	Ontario	503,345	5.0%
	Manitoba	54,199	7.0%	Manitoba	50,775	4.7%
	Nova Scotia	38,945	6.1%	Prince Edward Island	5,750	4.5%
	Saskatchewan	36,815	4.4%	Nova Scotia	37,525	4.2%
	Alberta	34,196	3.6%	Yukon**	905	3.3%
Low (1 to 3%)	British Columbia	19,366	1.7%	North West Territories**		
				Alberta	1,455	2.5%
				Saskatchewan	56,730	2.3%
				British	21,795	2.2%
				Columbia	51,585	1.6%
Minimal (<1%)	Newfoundland	2,321	0.6%	Newfoundland	2,855	0.5%

Sources: Harrison and Marmen (1994)
*   Model in Martel (modified 1991, 64)
**   No data for 1951

But the French mother-tongue population is decreasing in relation to the overall population. It constituted 7.3 percent of the
total population of English-speaking majority provinces and territories in 1951, but constituted only 4.8 percent in 1991 (table 3.2).
Two of the main reasons are assimilation and the increase of provincial and territorial populations through immigration. The population of English-speaking majority provinces and territories
increased by more than ten million (102.8 percent) in forty years,

Table 3.2

Evolution of Francophone minorities in English-speaking majority
provinces and territories in Canada (excluding Quebec)
1951 to 1991

	1951	1961	1971	1981	1991	% Change 1951–1991
French mother tongue	721,820	853,462	926,400	923,600	976,415	+35,27
Total provin-cial/territorial population	9,953,748	12,979,036	15,540,545	17,714,450	20,183,735	+102,78
% French/total population	7.25%	6.58%	5.95%	5.21%	4.84%	

Source: Harrison and Marmen (1994).

while the increase in the French-speaking population was 35.3 percent (254,595 persons). Consequently, the demographic strength of
Francophone minorities suffered a net decrease, although this has
been partly compensated by the ideological shift in government
policies that tended to favor their protection and development.

Section 23: Linchpin of the Canadian Duality Ideology

Section 23 of the Canadian Charter of Rights and Freedoms (1982)
is a "non-derogatory" disposition; provincial and territorial governments cannot withdraw from it as they can from fundamental
freedoms (section 2) and from legal and equality rights (7 to 15).
This confirms state responsibility towards official-language-
minority communities, both French and English. It is a positive,
affirmative action of protection to the extent that it affords rights
that are superior to non-discrimination rights.

Three Types of Rights Conferred

In effect, section 23 confers three types of rights on Canadian citizens with French or English as their mother tongue and who are
residing in a minority situation. They apply to primary and secon-

dary schooling, are provided through public funds, and are subject to the proviso of "sufficient numbers". The first proclaims the right of access, of official-language minorities, to instruction through the medium of their own language. This is a general right which applies to language and culture.

The second right (paragraph 23(3)b) specifies the type of educational facilities in which education is to be provided: "minority language educational facilities", where numbers warrant. Should such facilities be exclusively reserved for minorities, or can they be administered to include a mixed population (majority and minority)? Several courts have confirmed the point of view that mixed schools (serving the majority and minority) do not ensure the cultural growth of linguistic minorities but serve, on the contrary, to assimilate them. According to the courts, homogeneous schools expressly reserved for members of the linguistic minority are to be set up where numbers warrant. The language of administration used, and the values transmitted in these schools should be those of the minority.

The third and most substantive right conferred by paragraph 23(3)b) gives official-language minorities the right to manage their educational facilities. Most court interpretations have accepted the principle that, in order to maintain and develop their educational systems, minorities must manage and control them. However, they have also been attentive to state prerogatives; provincial governments are to determine the forms of school management appropriate to a given situation, thus preserving their exclusive power of legislation. The Supreme Court deemed in 1990 (*Mahé et al.*) that section 23 intended to give minorities the management and control of their educational facilities. This control might take various forms, but wherever instruction is provided there must be management of those aspects ensuring the vitality of the language and culture. At the very least, representatives of the minority must have exclusive decision-making authority over the expenditure of funds, the appointment and direction of the administration, instructional programs, the recruitment of teachers and personnel, and the making of agreements for education and services. The type of institutional structure needed to implement rights will depend on local circumstances and on the numbers involved. An independent school board may be required, or there may be a minimum proportional representation of the minority on the majority school board.

Section 23 as a Double Anomaly: More Precise and Programmatic

In the Canadian charter, section 23 is a double anomaly. First, it is more precise than the other articles that, for the most part, spell out internationally recognized fundamental liberties and rights. However, the preciseness of expression does not, for all that, mean that section 23 is clear and unambiguous. *On the contrary*, I have analyzed numerous instances of polysemy contained in section 23 (Martel 1995): polysemy in the definition of terms (the beneficiaries of rights–Canadian citizens, residents of other provinces or territories, parents, members of the linguistic community, persons who received primary schooling); polysemy in the area of implementation (type of instruction, modes of instruction, minority language facilities, public funding, sufficient numbers); and contextual polysemy (the role and determination of the actors, political compromise, coincidence between rights and reality). In this perspective, litigation in order to clarify meaning was to be expected.

Section 23 is also an anomaly because it is programmatic; it encourages the elaboration of new educational systems that are more conducive to the preservation and development of minority communities. It was deemed to be a remedial clause both by the constituents and by the courts, that is, as something to remedy the defects of the educational systems in place before 1982. That is why, in 1982 and thereafter, section 23 was seen as a promise of institutional and structural emancipation by Francophone communities. And, as such, it raised a tidal wave of demands, community actions and litigation.

In 1990, the Supreme Court of Canada deemed that section 23 was "a linchpin in this nation's commitment to the values of bilingualism and biculturalism".[1] In this perspective, giving official-language minorities such extensive and programmatic rights was a way of guaranteeing their maintenance and development across the country. In order to understand this ideological position, we need to look back at the history of Canadian ideologies and at the elaboration process of the charter.

Elaboration and Promulgation: Processes Based on Ideology

In the first part of this paper the premise has been that law and ideology are intimately tied. Through an analysis of the elaboration and promulgation process of section 23, it will now be shown that rights enshrined in the law are not simply handed down by benevolent states–they are negotiated and are only implemented if supported by a dominant ideology. Three issues will be considered in the analysis: autonomy/domination, the clash between homogenizing and duality ideologies, and the role of out-of-state allies.

Rise of States, Loss of Community Autonomy

Historically, Francophone communities were autonomous (Martel 1996). During the seventeenth and eighteenth centuries, French-language educational services were set up as Francophone communities were established, in accordance with the needs of each community. Instruction, and the financing and administration of these rudimentary educational services, were the responsibility of the community in collaboration with the religious authorities. Francophone minorities at this time had full autonomy in educational matters.

After the British North America (BNA) Act of 1867, this autonomy was gradually lost as states built up their authority. Canada was gradually consolidated under provincial governments, each of which constitutionally received, and consequently took, responsibility for education within its own boundaries. Provincial governments, largely through public funding, gradually took over an area of jurisdiction formerly handled by local authorities.

Within the new confederation, the dominant majority saw things in terms of homogeneity (Martel 1995); it was considered that each minority group, be it a historic minority such as the Francophones, or an immigrant minority such as the Ukrainians or Japanese, should surrender its own language and culture and adopt the language and culture of English speakers. Furthermore, section 93 of the BNA Act accorded each provincial government exclusive jurisdiction over educational legislation. Provincial governments subsequently adopted laws and regulations which directly and unilaterally regulated such matters as the use of English as a language of instruction, certification of teaching staff, subjects taught, textbooks, and the geographic boundaries of school districts. Each provincial government, eager to consolidate its power and to satisfy the linguistic majority, subsequently tried to set up a uniform province-wide education system. A considerable amount of legislation blatantly restricted, repealed or prohibited, in whole or in part, the provisions which had previously permitted instruction in French, and gradually imposed English as the only authorized language of instruction.

The Courts Enshrine the State Ideology

At the request of Anglo-Quebecers, section 93 of the BNA Act also provided protection for religious minorities (Catholics and Protestants). This was seen, at a time when religious and linguistic identities coincided, as an efficient way to protect the Anglophone-Protestant minority in Lower-Canada (Quebec), and was clearly extended in the text of the constitution to the Francophone-Catholic minority of Ontario. However, section 93 is ambiguous; it bears the imprint of the tumultuous negotiations that gave birth to the new confederation. In the case of the Francophone minorities, three court cases between 1870 and 1917 concluded that Francophones had no constitutional rights under section 93. Through their literal interpretation of the religious criterion, the courts gave their consent to this dominant ideology represented by the provincial states. Despite their numerous representations, litigation bore little fruit for the Francophone minorities.

The Beginnings of Activism

Between 1910 and 1920, Francophone activism emerged and the evolution of French-language education took a slightly different direction. Francophone minorities gradually formed associations, thereby increasing their pressure-group leverage with respect to their provincial or territorial government. Most provinces came to adopt a more open attitude to their Francophone communities and gradually began to modify some of their legislation so as to reinstate instruction in French. The original uniformity of the province-wide educational system began to make room for the presence of the French-language minority. But this more liberal attitude was limited to specific grades (years of instruction) and usually covered only a portion of the school day.

The Rise of the Duality Ideology: Countering the Homogenizing Ideology

A new ideology was emerging with the turn-of-the-century litigation surrounding the Franco-Catholic rights inscribed in section 93—that of a *compact* between two nations (Cook 1969). Franco-Canadians, including Quebecers, interpreted the confederation as a negotiated pact between the two founding nations of Canada.

Consequently, the French nation requested equality with the English nation. This ideology influenced the role that Francophone minorities were to play in the new nation, since they were to be protected coast to coast as part and parcel of one of the founding nations. In fact, they were seen as the very cement that united the country. However, a large proportion of the majority, represented by the provincial governments of English-majority provinces, refuted the compact theory, assuming that making a concession to a bilingual "preserve" in Quebec was sufficient, and that French minorities in the rest of Canada were no different from the immigrant minorities.

Although these ideologies clashed for decades, each was influenced by the events that led to the predominance of the duality (compact) ideology. This change was brought about by three main factors: (1) an increased mobility which led both groups, Francophones and Anglophones, to acquire a greater knowledge of one another, particularly during the two World Wars; (2) a worldwide movement towards the recognition and valuing of pluralism, consecrated in article 27 of the 1966 International Pact Relative to Civil and Political Rights; and (3) the nationalist movement in Quebec, which forced the rest of Canada to change its strategies towards Francophones.

This change of ideology became more prominent during the 1960s when a new national vision began to influence provincial and territorial governments, and Pierre Elliot Trudeau came to power at the federal level. At this time the federal government officially recognized the linguistic duality of Canada and undertook to establish national policies that respected it. The Royal Commission on Bilingualism and Biculturalism was set up in 1963. It raised the question of official-language-minority education rights to the level of nationwide public debate. The demands of French-language communities concerning education rights found widespread recognition. The federal Official Languages Act, proclaiming the bilingual character of Canada, was adopted in 1969. These events concretely confirmed that the power stronghold had changed. The languages of both of the founding peoples were, at least theoretically, reaching a point of equilibrium and Francophone minorities were no longer left alone with their provincial governments.

Negotiating Consent for the Duality Ideology

With the adoption of the duality ideology by the federal government, minority education, although exclusively a provincial matter, was raised to the level of a national concern. In the 1970s, official-language-minority education rights became a focus for intergovernmental negotiations. In parallel, Francophone minorities made significant gains at the level of provincial education.

However, the process of institutionalizing minority rights was not an easy, linear task. It necessitated numerous negotiations between the federal and the provincial governments. It required considerable resources in terms of constitutional discussions: a second commission (the Commission on Canadian Unity), two special mixed committees of the Senate and the House of Commons (1972 and 1980), nineteen federal-provincial conferences on the constitution, eleven of which dealt specifically with the linguistic or educational rights of minorities, and four inter-provincial conferences.

In 1978, the Premiers of the nine provinces with English-speaking majorities published a common statement which formally recognized education as an indispensable tool to ensure the vitality of minority language and culture, stating that the children of official-language minorities have the right to receive instruction in their own language within elementary and secondary schools, wherever numbers warrant. However, these Premiers were also, and perhaps primarily, concerned with the English-language minority in Quebec. Adherence to the duality ideology would not only, so they thought, serve their Francophone minority, but would also serve to protect the English-speaking minority in Quebec.

The inclusion of minority educational rights was even the subject of last minute bargaining. In a marathon negotiation session on 5 November 1981, the provinces reluctantly agreed to section 23: "After breakfast, the first ministers met once more in closed session. Trudeau [then prime minister of Canada] still had reservations... He then asked for a stiffer opting-out clause, making it less easy for a province to exempt itself from a constitutional amendment. The provinces refused. *Trudeau's final request was for the inclusion of minority language education rights*. Accepted. The agreement was in place". (Cohen et al. 1987, 73. Emphasis added). Such is, in brief, the sinuous road that served as the foundation for the nationwide recognition of the education rights of Francophone minorities, conferred by section 23 of the Charter.

This process shows that law and ideology are intimately tied; the courts interpret the law in light of the dominant ideology, and laws are promulgated in accordance with this ideology. Secondly, this process has also shown that activism is part and parcel of the emancipation process of minority communities. Thirdly, and perhaps most importantly, it has shown that, in order to gain rights, minority communities need political allies who are situated in out-of-state positions. For Francophone minorities, this was the federal government; for other national minorities it might be international instances.

The Litigation Process: Negotiating Grounds between State Powers and Community Autonomy

In 1982, an evaluation of the perceived discrepancy between the rights conferred by section 23 and the prevailing situation gave rise to a renewed militancy on the part of the Francophone minorities. Pressing demands were addressed to provincial governments calling for them to provide a treatment comparable to that given to the Anglophone minority in Quebec. Lukewarm, if not negative responses by provincial governments, and dissent over the interpretation of the nature and extent of the rights conferred became evident. Faced with inaction or outright refusal, Francophone minorities went to court across the country.

Financial Support for Litigation

The federal government, attempting to fulfill the role of guardian of the Charter, provided the financial means by which a wave of litigation was set in motion. In December 1982, the federal government ratified a "Court Challenges Program" in order to assist, among others, the implementation and interpretation of section 23. Over fourteen years, this program subsidized test cases in order to ensure that official-language minorities might benefit from section 23.

A Tidal Wave of Litigation

After 1982, official-language minorities began to assert their rights through the courts. Between this date and 1997, twenty decisions were handed down in cases related to section 23. In keeping with the more immediate concerns at the time of promulgation, and with the political context in 1982, Quebec's Anglophone minority was the first to avail itself of the courts. It won its case against the *Quebec clause* of the *Charte de la langue française* (the Charter of

the French Language, known as Bill 101) before the Supreme
Court of Canada. The French-language minorities were quick to
follow suit, using the judiciary system both as a negotiation strategy and as an intermediary between themselves and their respective government. First in New Brunswick (1983), then in Ontario
(1984) and Alberta (1985), then in Ontario again (1986), they took
their cases to court and obtained favorable judgments. In 1987
alone, three judgments were delivered: in British Columbia, Alberta and Nova Scotia; in 1988, judgments were handed down in
Saskatchewan and Prince Edward Island, and again in Nova Scotia
in 1989. In 1990, two more judgments were handed down: in
Manitoba and in the Supreme Court of Canada in the *Mahé et al. v.
the Queen* case (Alberta). Lastly came a second Supreme Court
judgment in 1993 (Manitoba). In 1996, it was the turn of British
Columbia and Prince Edward Island. These actions are only the tip
of the iceberg. Francophone minorities have also engaged in research, meetings, negotiations, agreements, social animation and
information campaigns (Martel 1993).

*Courts Weaving Grounds Between Minority Development and
State Powers*

The general interpretation of section 23 adopted by the various
courts indicates an attempt to reconcile three issues: national protection, provincial state obligations and Francophone-minority
community development. As a rule, judgments are favorable to
Francophone minorities. The courts accept the objectives of section 23, and recognize its legitimacy and its importance in the context of the development of Francophone minorities. In so doing,
the courts side with the dominant national ideology, or do not dare
to oppose it. First-level-court judgments are more generally in favor
of provincial autonomy, refusing to *impose* on provincial governments the means of remedying the situation. Appeal courts are
more generous towards minorities. As for the Supreme Court, it
confirms outright the duality ideology and, while recognizing provincial autonomy, urges provincial governments to act.

Judges were, however, cautious in at least two respects. First, the
courts were anxious to preserve the full autonomy and decision-
making authority of the provinces with respect to education. This
limited the Francophone minorities' development to the extent
that the courts refused to intervene directly in the legislative process, laying down guiding principles without prescribing the meth-

ods by which governments should meet the demands arising from the rights conferred. This situation brought about a vicious circle: the methods for implementing section 23 being generally unclear, provincial and territorial governments had difficulty implementing them; minorities then continued the judicial process in order to obtain clarifications which were not necessarily forthcoming; and so on.

Secondly, the courts also dealt cautiously with the question of linguistic equality between (Francophone) minorities and the (Anglophone) majority, an issue which carries the duality ideology from the two official languages to the two official-language communities. Some reject on principle the possibility of equality between minority and majority, while others accept it but fail to carry it to its logical conclusion in the application that it warrants.

Litigation: Winning the Battles Lost Elsewhere

Activism before the courts is a continuation of battles that have been lost elsewhere, particularly in the political arena. When minorities demanded services from their provincial and territorial government, lobbying, community solidarity actions, research, and media interventions had limited impact. Governments were more responsive to the opinions of their majority electorate than to the demands for justice and equality for minorities. In effect, litigation remained a final strategy and a sword of Damocles in negotiations with the state.

Rebels and Heroes: Confronting the State and the Communities

Section 23 played a determining role in giving communities a new impetus. A review of the media coverage of the educational question shows the extent to which it has provided ground for a new discourse: "our rights, our communities, our schools, our school boards." In effect, the school issue came to dominate minority communities' concerns. This social movement discourse is in strong contrast to market discourse and to state discourse. It is based on an ethical logic of the right to equality and the right to dignity and respect that is voiced through demands for services: schools and their control and management. Law and language rights were a way of establishing meaning and constituting communities in and through language. In effect, section 23 provided a new discursive power that allowed a redefinition of self and of community by drawing upon the symbols, the rituals, and the language of the law to further their vision and their interests.

Labeling and Identity

Historically, Francophone communities have been defined, and have identified themselves, as minorities. However, they now reject the minority label and identity, calling themselves "Canadian Francophone and Acadian Communities." The rejection of the minority label and the consequent adoption of the more dynamic self-description of community, indicate the rejection of the power structures that underlie the concept of minority.

This evolution can be explained by sociopolitical factors such as the promulgation of linguistic and educational rights (the Official Languages Act of 1969, the Charter of 1982, and the Official Languages Act of 1988) that have given official political and legal status to Francophone minorities; the example of the nationalist movement in Quebec, which set a precedent in the French-Canadian family; the construction of regional Francophone identities, which led to the fragmentation of the French-Canadian identity coast to coast, and thence to local affirmation; and the availability of important grants from governments (mostly federal) and agencies, which contributed to the construction of intra- and inter-community networks.

The Impetus for Litigation

In interviews, persons who brought cases before the courts expressed their initial reactions to the promulgation of section 23 through a number of emotional concerns. They evaluated the "poverty" of Francophone educational services in comparison to the majority system: lack of homogeneous schools, of rooms, of resources, of qualified personnel, of equipment, of programs, of control and management. They realized the slowness of the improvement process. They described with emphasis their frustrations with the inaction of the provincial and territorial governments, and of school boards in taking heed of their demands. They strongly expressed the sense of urgency that they felt at seeing their children lose their mother tongue. And they were most of all relieved that the law had given words and weight to their concerns.

Language rights were lived profoundly and emotionally. Section 23 became a filter that guided action. Not only did things have to change, they said, but things had to change for their children and for those of the community. The shortcomings of the system, coupled with impatience at the apparent good will but inaction of the government, incited them to action. Through litigation, they hoped for a redistribution of resources.

The Litigation Process

Once conscious of the injustice in the educational system, these persons who eventually brought actions through the courts began community mobilization. Actions carried out included door-to-door canvassing, kitchen meetings, telephone campaigns, workshops, conferences, consultation of experts, surveys, use of the media, publication of brochures, political lobbying, even Christmas cards. The process was one of moving community opinion towards militancy.

Reactions were mixed. Some local Francophone associations were lukewarm, or even hostile. Others provided support or took charge of part of the process. The community itself was not always supportive. Some communities were even torn apart (and still are) by the process. Others evolved and, with time, came to fully support the process and even claim the benefits arising from it. As for families, many individuals, particularly those who had a non-Francophone partner, indicated the stress that it brought into the home: less time with their children, conflicts with their partner. Many individuals indicated that the process put a severe strain on their marriage.

There was, however, unanimity on one point: the importance of out-of-community and out-of-state allies. Many mentioned the invaluable support of some provincial, but mostly federal, government officials or bureaucrats, and of experts and lawyers.

Individuals and Organizations as Beneficiaries of Litigation

In the majority of cases brought before the courts individuals initiated the legal actions. As time progressed, however, an increasing number of associations became parties to the process. Today, a national association joining parents across the country (Commission nationale des parents Francophones) is taking the initiative in coordinating test cases and collective legal actions.

This evolution indicates that litigation is profitable. In spite of the angst, the fatigue and the discouragement, individuals have indicated that they have personally gained a great deal from the litigation process: an enriching leadership experience, a new political, judicial and educational knowledge, contacts across Canada, the opportunity to provide an example of courage and determination for their children, and eventual community bonding. They became a local, provincial, and even national *élite*.

Their were also benefits for associations. Funding for educational projects was more easily available despite budget cuts. In effect, some associations consolidated their bureaucracy through section 23 projects and identified its potential for positioning themselves politically.

Through the judicial process, typical characteristics of community action—particularism, localism, irrationalism, non-professionalism (De Sousa Santos 1992)—were transformed. Community action was no longer local or provincial, but also national. It was no longer particular, but represented the plight of minorities across the country, particularly that of the autochthonous peoples with whom strategic alliances were established. They remained, however, in a favored position, being an official minority. The actions became rational and professional via the law. However, one feature of community action remained: closeness to local people's practice and discourses. Activism through litigation took on a distinctly professional flavor.

Language Rights, Litigation and Community Development: Results

What changes were brought about by this process of litigation and the consequent political struggles for Francophone community development? Two types of results are described here: community development and the side effects of litigation.

Community Development
The Choices at Hand

What models of education are available pursuant to the rights granted by section 23 of the Charter? Figure 3.1 provides an overview of the options that have been suggested or put into effect throughout Canada since 1980. Seven types of measures are placed on a spectrum from individual to community development.

1. Bussing	4. Mixed schools	6.Homogeneous schools
2. Distance education	5. Separate classes	7. School & community
3. Boarding		centers

← More individual importance given   ←→   More community importance given →

Figure 3.1. Available educational measures:
French minority language

The first three (on the left of the spectrum)—bussing, distance education and boarding—are measures that answer individual needs. They do not tend to strengthen identification with the individual's community of origin. Two intermediate and usually transitory measures are mixed schools and separate classes. In Francophone educational services, the expression "mixed schools" refers to cases where education using French as a first language is offered (and often administered) on the same premises as other types of educational programs serving different clienteles (French immersion for Anglophones or education for those with English as a first language). As for separate classes, these are classes in which instruction in French as a first language is offered to minority students as a group/class within an English environment. The latter two measures are usually temporary. Mixed schools have been seen as assimilation situations for Francophones. The implementation of separate classes is usually a measure taken by school authorities while waiting for a Francophone school to be established. These mixed schools and separate classes then become homogeneous schools or cease to offer partial services.

As for the two measures on the right of the spectrum—homogeneous schools and school-community centers–these have been identified by Francophone communities in Canada as institutions which are fundamental for their development. Homogeneous schools are so called because they offer instruction in French as a first language to Francophones, mostly to section 23 beneficiaries. Both of these types of school provide instruction to individuals but are also seen to sustain community development. They have been chosen by communities and the courts as the best educational measures available to preserve and develop the French language in a minority situation. These schools are seen to function as microlinguistic communities in which students come to identify with their ethnolinguistic group and to value their origins. The language competition is here reduced to the advantage of the minority language, since, in situations of competition, the dominant language normally has a decided advantage.

Opting for Homogeneous Schools

The promulgation of section 23 favored the creation of homogeneous schools. Table 3.3 shows their substantial increase–fifty-nine schools (+12 percent) between 1986 and 1995. Inversely, other types of educational structures, that is, mixed schools, separate classes, distance education, etc. (see figure 3.1) have diminished. The result is that in 1995, a total of 85 percent of all schools offering educational services ("all programs" in table 3.3) to Francophone minorities are homogeneous schools, while such schools constituted 79 percent in 1986.

Table 3.3

Schools offering services to Francophone minorities in English-speaking majority provinces and territories in Canada (excluding Quebec) 1971-72 to 1995-96*

	1971	1981	1986	1988	1989	1990	1991	1992	1993	1994	1995	%Change 1986–1995
Homogeneous schools**			499	522	531	547	555	556	554	552	558	+11.8%
All Schools ***	678	655	630	647	643	664	668	669	668	665	658	+ 4.4%
% Homogeneous schools/All			79.2	80.7	82.6	82.4	83.1	83.1	82.9	83.0	84.8	

*School year: September to June

Sources: ** Ministries of Education of the provinces and territories
*** Official Language Commissioner's Reports (1971, 1981). For the other years, Ministries of Education of the provinces and territories. Includes all types–homogeneous and mixed schools, separate classes, distance education.

School Enrollments: Initial Increase and Stability

A statistical evaluation of the aftereffects of section 23 can also be provided by comparing enrollments in French-language minority education in all services and in homogeneous schools between 1981 and 1995. In general, the decline in total French-language minority enrollment has been halted, falling by 13.2 percent between 1981 and 1986 (from 157,734 to 136,903), to become relatively stable since 1986 (table 3.4).

Table 3.4

Enrollments in schools offering services to Francophone minorities in English-speaking majority provinces and territories in Canada 1971–72 to 1995–96

	1971	1981	1986	1990	1991	1994	1995	% Change 1986–95
Homogeneous schools **			123,027	129,461	129,778	129,526	132,794	+7.9%
All schools ***	196,087	157,734	136,903	137,500	137,175	136,880	137,806	+0.7%
Total: provincial and territorial***	4,066,643	3,670,993	3,624,158	3,714,211	3,934,660	4,077,388	4,123,444	+13.8%
All programs/ Total provincial	4.82%	4.30%	3.78%	3.70%	3.49%	3.36%	3.34%	

School year: September to June
Sources: ** 1986 to 1994, Ministries of Education of the provinces and territories.
*** Official Language Commissioner's Reports (1971, 1981). For other years, Ministries of Education of the provinces and territories. Includes all types–homogeneous and mixed schools, separate classes, distance education.

The Establishment of School Management Systems: a Degree of Self-determination

The right of minorities to control and manage their schools is the third right conferred by section 23. It was the most difficult to implement for it required changes in the administrative structures of education at the provincial level: the decentralization of decision making and an increase in responsibility for the Francophone communities themselves.

Historically, Francophone minorities lost their autonomy in school management when small school boards were consolidated to form larger administrative units. The changes to school boundaries made by provincial governments removed some *de facto* local school management from the Francophone minority (with the exception of New Brunswick, where concentrations of Francophone minority population were great enough in 1966 for the large school districts to include significant numbers of Francophones in the majority groups). As the geographic areas governed by the school boards grew, fewer and fewer Francophones were elected to school boards, and those elected were further and further removed from their communities and their communities' interests.

Most of the active claims for the control of school management by Francophone minorities have appeared since 1982. Various models have been proposed to this end: advisory committees, contracts, proportional and guaranteed representation, and provincial Francophone school boards. Because of their proven efficiency, the models most sought after are those which parallel the majority structure.

These models have been implemented in Ontario since 1988, in Toronto and Ottawa-Carleton where French-language homogeneous school boards were set up. A generalization of this model is in process in Ontario. In Prince Edward Island, a provincial school board has been responsible for the management of French-language instruction since 1990. In Saskatchewan, a management model, wherein school boards are associated with a Francophone provincial general council, has been established. In Manitoba, a provincial board has been established with regional advisory councils. In Alberta, regional minority school boards have been in effect since 1991, and others are being implemented in Newfoundland and British Columbia.

The provision of educational rights and services for Canada's Francophone minorities is part of the trend towards self-management and self-determination. The right to school management granted to Francophone minorities by section 23 has forced provincial governments to make structural changes to the process of decision making in education—or at any rate to propose them.

New Institutions: Community Centers and Associations

Section 23 has also favored the rise of new institutions other than the school board structures established to respond to the letter and spirit of the law. The most prominent is the community center. In these centers, school and community contribute jointly, each in their own sphere, to the preservation and creation of linguistic and cultural values. Such centers offer a diversity of services according to the needs of the (emerging) community, and may group many institutions: school, kindergarten, continuing education and literacy programs, library, bookstore, community meeting spaces and cafeteria, artistic and social clubs, etc. There are seven such centers in the Atlantic Provinces, one is emerging in Alberta, and four others in Ontario.

Table 3.5

Example of enrollment change with the creation of a
school in a community center,
École François-Buote: Charlottetown[a] 1980–1995[b]

	1980[c]	81	82[d]	83	84	85	86[e]	87[e]	88[e]	89	90	91[f]	92	93	94	95
Enrollment	3	22	21	31	36	49				51	81	115	102	140	169	185

a. Source: Ministry of Education of Prince Edward Island.
b. School year: September to June.
c. In September 1980, 3 students. In June of the same year, 11 students.
d. Official opening of the school: September 1982.
e. No data.
f. September 1991: the school moved into a new community center, the
"Carrefour de l'Île-Saint-Jean".

One example of the influence of such a center on school enrollment can be found in Prince Edward Island. Table 3.5 describes the statistical and historical progression of a community center established in 1991. It shows how school enrollment was not only consolidated, but gradually increased after it became part of the school community center. When such a school is established parents naturally buy property close by. With time, businesses move into the area to serve this new clientele, bringing new students to the school. A sense of belonging and involvement develops among the school, the community, the students, the parents and other members of the minority. School projects come to involve community members. In some instances, where space is available in the school, community groups ask to use it after school hours. And thus the school develops as the center of the community. A synergetic relationship is established. The school grows with the community and the community grows with the school. Such was the process through which the François Buotte school went until, in 1991, a new building was opened housing community center and school.

Other associations have been founded. A network of parents' associations has been created in all provinces and territories. These are brought together in a national association which carries out research and lobbying, and offers support to parents' groups.

Pedagogy and Litigation: States Listening and Hearing

The advent of rights changed the way of doing minority politics. For minorities, law remains an essential tool for two reasons. First, to the extent that law is founded on a *fiction* that places it, in appearance, outside of social relations, it contains considerable power in terms of legitimization—a power that minorities and disadvantaged groups can claim to their profit. This power, inherent in law, is used by actors as a reference, and is invoked by them in their discourse during negotiations for services and structures. It is also because of this power that parties together before the court, minorities and majorities, disadvantaged groups and governments, each attempt to interpret the law in its favor. Thus, Francophone communities call on the law to legitimize their demands. They effect community mobilization in its name. For, contextually, in Western societies, rational and legal power constitute the major sources of legitimized domination. Law and litigation construct, in a pedagogical manner, the ideologies that guide community perceptions and decisions. In the processes that surround litigation, minorities also gain confidence in their actions and demands in the belief that they are more legitimate since they are found in the law.

Secondly, the law constitutes an effective third symbolic party capable of grounding communication between groups. Although it is the object of major confrontations, judicial discourse is also a remarkable means of social communication. Paradoxically, conflicts over rights constitute many occasions where all parties are obliged to negotiate and, in the process, where ideologies clash and influence one another. Interacting through the law and the judiciary, social actors agree to meet the other, and gradually learn to listen and understand. In democracies, founded by definition on the presupposed majority consensus, law acts as an intervenor, capable eventually of counterbalancing the tendencies of majorities to impose their hegemony in political and institutional spaces. In this sense, law contains important pedagogical power.

Processes of Emancipation

Perhaps most important, however, have been the processes of emancipation brought to Francophone communities by language rights activism and litigation pertaining to section 23. As a result of litigation and lobbying, these communities have become familiar with the corridors of power. To state powers, activism and litigation have brought counter powers. Furthermore, the very act of subordinated groups approaching the law as a collective is of value, to the extent that it politicizes the manner in which the problem is defined. This may result in the individual or group losing the sense of inferiority that is often inherent in a minority situation. It can be understood as a political situation.

Some Side Effects

"Sometimes, law works to bring change in the expected way but often it miscarries, fails to engage, has undesirable side effects or in some other way introduces unexpected results" (Livingstone and Morison 1990, 1). Section 23 has, indeed, produced side effects in Canadian society, in community identity and relations, and in state governments.

The Judiciarization of Social and Political Relations

If language rights bring the advantage of systematically avoiding violence by managing disagreements on the basis of known rules, they also bring the disadvantage of displacing the arena of problem solving beyond the individuals and communities who should be solving the problems. Decisions are taken in a sphere other than the everyday sphere, one in which the appearance of neutrality hides real power games that tend to perpetuate the stronghold of the dominating groups. Law *is* infused with power relations. Beyond its visible structure which takes the form of a legal text, law hides a power structure reflecting social relations.

This does not prevent communities from invoking the law and proceeding with litigation. In the process, relations between the majority, the state and the Francophone communities become not only politicized, but also judiciarized. The courts are invoked on every possible occasion. Ultimately, this process allows a third party to decide for the actors involved.

The Spread of Ideologies of Conflict

Consequently, minority Francophone communities exist in attitudes of conflict. So do states when it comes to examining minority-language issues. One good example of the interiorization of this
attitude was provided in 1996, when minority Francophone communities considered using section 24 of the charter to claim dam-
ages and interests for the inaction of provincial states between
1982 and 1996. Based on tort law (the law of private or civil wrong
by act or omission), this article can lead to the transformation of
demands into vindications. Although the impatience of minority
communities is understandable, such projects show to what extent
the rule of law and its letter can produce conflictual and vindictive
relations.

Although the law provides for a beneficial third party intervention, even if this intervention is ideological and not neutral, it does
not, in essence, teach communities and states to build compromises together. And, in the end, one party has to lose and the other
win. Based on adversarial practices, the law does not foster ideologies of solidarity/harmony/cooperation. On the contrary, it reinforces those of competition/conflict/rivalry. If the rule of law is to
invade every sphere of life, this aspect of its nature must be attended to.

The Constitutionalization of Identities

Relations between groups also tend to become legalized. I have
called this the constitutionalization of identities. Having rights
becomes part of the minority identity. To invoke these rights becomes a daily reflex. One good example of this is the way in which
Francophone minorities in Canada's nine provinces and Quebec
Francophones have come to see each other through charters.

The Boomerang Effect: State Obligations

A final question must be considered. If provincial governments
were not willing to implement the rights conferred, why did they
sign a charter which included section 23? To answer the question,
one needs to recall the conditions that encouraged provincial governments to deal with litigation rather than provide a pro-active
remedial battery of services upon demand. First, governments ac-

cepted section 23 under duress during negotiation, feeling that they were obliged to accept section 23 in order to gain other provisions. Secondly, their interests at the time of signing the agreement lay mostly in protecting the English-speaking minority in Quebec whom they saw as oppressed by Quebec's Bill 101. Thirdly, when the time came to implement section 23, it became evident that the duality ideology did not have a dominant stronghold in their electorate. On the contrary, the homogenizing ideology was still very much alive in the majority, who considered the duality ideology as "made in Ottawa".

Under these conditions, the provincial governments preferred to have the courts impose the new provisions. Litigation was an unavoidable process for Francophone communities. However, provinces and territories had not counted on litigation funding being available from the federal government, nor had they foreseen the vigor with which Francophone communities would appropriate section 23. In the end, Francophone communities forced modifications to the educational legislation of all nine provinces and territories. Furthermore, section 23 obliged them, reluctantly, to accept and adopt structures of control and management for Francophones, while other minority communities viewed the process with interest as a precedent for their own education. This is the kind of boomerang effect of language rights promulgation and activism with which state governments had to contend.

Strategies for Thought

These experiences from the Canadian context and from the law as it applies to minority Francophone communities in Canada can be summed up in a few strategies that are proposed for other rebels, heroes and communities. They are presented here as a résumé of this paper:

- Adopt a systematic approach to litigation. This means:
  - selecting winnable cases;
  - consolidating cluster of cases to build jurisprudence;
  - increasing the chances of being heard before the courts by representing the collective interest of the group (class action suits);
  - seeking intervenors for the judicial proceedings (amicus curiae).

- Be realistic in the hopes that are placed in language rights and litigation.
- Complement litigation actions. An array of consolidating activities can provide a background for litigation:
  . survey actual and potential community members, analyze data and reports;
  . have particularly contentious points proven by original research;
  . participate in media forums;
  . lobby groups and individuals that can help;
  . make demands at every level of competence;
  . do not be afraid to take no for an answer. It later becomes a piece in the puzzle that can convince the courts.
- Understand the role of ideologies and discourses, yours as well as that of the opposing party. Arguments are better formulated when ideologies are understood.
- Take into consideration the interests of other groups.
- See the process of activism and litigation as educational processes in which you are the mentor. There is a need to educate governments and lawyers.
- Above all, do not attempt to replicate the adversarial climate that can surround language rights activism and litigation. Remember that these are part of a larger process towards constructing a more harmonious and just social space.

Conclusion

One might argue that the minority Francophone communities of Canada are not a typical minority, should such a condition exist. That is true, since they are an official-language minority. However, the situation of Francophone minorities in Canada constitutes an interesting laboratory with regard to the upper spectrum of minority provisions. Their application provides enlightenment as to the possible conditions for survival and development with measures short of complete self-determination and in opposition to submission, submersion and oppression.

The Fragility of Language Rights

However, as in the case of all social action, activism and litigation are forever unfinished agendas; they do not solve all problems.

Indeed, language rights are fragile. They run the risk of being rescinded or abrogated in the event of the change of a supporting ideology or government: "The foundation for rights is *power* and constant *struggle* is necessary to sustain language rights... Language rights are a fragile basis for language policy, and [...] constant struggle is necessary to protect rights, even in a country with a long historical commitment to—and a federal structure which supports it—a pluralist language policy" (Tollefson 1991, 167 and 197).

Despite the fragility of rights, I would nevertheless conclude that the legal system is a very powerful language planning tool for minorities. However, in accordance with our basic premise, such planning must be supported by a dualistic or pluralistic type of ideology at all levels of government. Otherwise, the law will remain non-operational; one level of government will be in disagreement with another and the courts will judge in favor of the dominant ideology.

Activism and Litigation as Never-Ending Agendas

When a structure is created, as was the case for educational management and control measures for Francophone minorities, other issues that cannot be solved by rights and litigation have to be envisaged. However, the larger issues that activism and litigation help to construct are crucial. Activism and litigation contribute to the new dynamic of social action that attempts to transform the status quo into more just and equitable spheres of self-respect and solidarity. They must attempt to innovate and guard against ideologies favoring competition/conflict/rivalry.

Note

1 *Mahé et al. vs. The Queen* (Alberta,1990) 1 R.C.S. 342, 68 D.L.R. (4d.), 69 (C.S.C.).

References

Brickey, S., and E. Cormack. "The Role of Law in Social Transformation." *Canadian Journal of Law and Society*, 2, (1987): 97-119.

Cohen, L., et al. *The Vision and the Game*. Calgary: Detslig Enterprises Ltd. (1987): 197.

Cook, R. *Provincial Autonomy, Minority Rights and the Compact Theory 1867-1921*. Ottawa: Studies of the Royal Commission on Bilingualism and Biculturalism, (1969): 310.

Gauthier, F., et al. *Langues & constitutions* (Languages and constitutions). Québec: Les Publications du Québec, (1993): 132.

Hannum, H. *Documents on Autonomy and Minority Rights*. Dordrecht/Boston/London: Martinus Nijhoff Publishers, (1993): 729.

Harrison, B. and L. Marmen. *Languages in Canada*. Ottawa: Statistics Canada, (1994): 42.

Hunt, A. "The Politics of Law and Justice". In A. Hunt, ed., *Politics and Power IV*. London: Routledge and Keagan Paul, (1981): 280.

Kevelson, R. *The Law as a System of Signs*, New York: Plenum Press, (1988): 326.

Landowski, É. "Toward a Semiotic and Narrative Approach to Law". *Revue internationale de sémiotique juridique* (International Journal of Judicial Semiotics) 1 (1), (1988): 79-104.

Livingstone, S. and J. Morison. *Law, Society and Change*. Vermont: Dartmouth Publishing Company, (1990): 320.

Mandel, M. *The Charter of Rights and the Legalization of Politics in Canada*. Toronto: Wall & Thompson, (1989): 368.

Martel, A. Compétition idéologiques et les droits scolaires Francophones en milieu minoritaire au Canada (Ideological competition and educational rights of Francophone minority communities). *Canadian Modern Language Review*, 49 (4), (1993): 734-75.

Martel, A. & D. Villeneuve. "Droit constitutionnel et rapports de pouvoir: les droits scolaires des Francophones minoritaires du Canada avant 1960" (Constitutional law and power relations: educational rights of Francophones in Canada before 1960). *Canadian Journal of Law and Society*, 10 (1), (1995): 25-63.

Martel, A. "Language Planning, Ideology and Constitutional Law: Francophone Minority Education in Canada". *Language Problems & Language Planning*, 20, (2), (1996): 127-145.

Sjöwall, M. and P. Wahlöö. *The Locked Room*, Vintage Crime/Black Lizard Edition. First publication, 1972: P.A. Norstedt & Söners Förlag. Translated from the Swedish *Det Slutna Rummet* by Paul Britten Austin, (1992): 312.

Soulier, G. "Minorités, État et société" (Minorities, State and Society). In G. Soulier, ed., *Les minorités et leurs droits depuis 1789* (Minorities and their rights since 1789). Paris: Éditions de l'Harmattan, (1989): 75-109.

Tollefson, J. *Planning language, planning inequality: Language policy in the community*. London: Longman, (1991): 236.

"Don't Speak Hungarian in Public!"— A Documentation and Analysis of Folk Linguistic Rights

MIKLÓS KONTRA

In a park someone asked me why I spoke Hungarian to my grandchildren once they were born in Austria. I asked back: "How would
you speak to your grandchildren in Brazil?" He said: "In German."
I said: "I speak Hungarian to them for the very same reason."
(Hungarian woman living in Vienna)[1]

Introduction

Traditionally, linguistics has been an enterprise in which professional linguists study language as it is used by non-linguists. In folk
linguistics (see, e.g., Hoenigswald 1966; Preston 1989) professional
linguists study what non-linguists think about language, or to quote
Preston (1993, 181), "Folk linguistics seeks to discover non-
linguists' beliefs about language in general". One of Preston's arguments for the study of folk perceptions of language is related to
the broader issue of scholarship and science and their social usefulness. He says:

> A great deal of money and energy is spent trying to bring about ef-
> fective, standard language use in both non-native and nonstandard
> speakers. To be ignorant of how the nonlinguistic community char-
> acterizes linguistic facts is to hamper our own usefulness in talking
> with that very community about the subjects we know most about.
> (Preston 1989, xi–xii)

The study of linguistic human rights (LHRs) is a new field of inquiry, cultivated mainly by sociolinguists, for example, Skutnabb-
Kangas and Phillipson (1994) and lawyers, for instance Driessen
(1997), Thornberry (1991), Várady (1997) and de Varennes
(1995/96). As in linguistics, most research into LHRs is carried out

by professionals who investigate by probing into the well-
established fields of linguistic science and legal studies. This is
commendable but not enough. In this paper I wish to suggest that,
in order to successfully implement linguistic human rights, we
need to study folk linguistic rights as well. Exactly like in the Preston argument above, unless we know how "normal people" (i.e.
non-linguists and non-lawyers) characterize language rights, we
hamper our own usefulness in talking with the communities about
the subjects we know most about.

This paper is a modest attempt to investigate some folk beliefs
about linguistic rights in Central Europe.[2] I will first look at some
(press) reports about various cases involving an imperative "Don't
use language X!" Then I will present some data on folk perceptions
of language rights as revealed in a sociolinguistic study of the Hungarian minorities in Slovakia, Ukraine, Romania, Yugoslavia, Slovenia and Austria.[3] Folk beliefs about language rights will be demonstrated by analyzing 250 instances in which people were told not
to speak Hungarian in public. A preliminary taxonomy will be offered of the communicative acts in which the negative imperatives
not to use Hungarian were communicated either verbally or non-
verbally. Finally, it will be argued that the study of folk linguistic
rights is an important prerequisite for the successful implementation of LHRs in all states.

(Press) Reports

Prohibitions on the use of language X abound all over the world,
occurring in very diverse situations and a multitude of forms. In
the United States the prohibition on the use of minority languages
in the workplace is common practice (Hernández–Chávez 1994,
154). In Latin America legal prescriptions often prohibit the use of
the Indian languages at school (Hamel 1994, 27). In Turkey Kurds
are not allowed to speak Kurdish in public places (Skutnabb–
Kangas and Bucak 1994, 347). In Quebec, Canada, under Bill 101
penalties would be imposed where merchants advertised their
products in languages other than French (Lemco 1992, 431). In
1918 the state of Texas enacted criminal penalties for teachers
speaking anything but English in the classroom, except to teach
foreign languages in the upper grades (Crawford 1992, 72).

In Slovakia the war on personal names (see Kontra 1996b) has
not really ended: government officials coerce some Hungarian
women into using their family names with the Slovak suffix -ová,

which is in violation of a current Slovak law (see Pazonyi 1997). Also in Slovakia, in the latest telephone directories some Hungarian surnames which were earlier listed with Hungarian spelling are now respelled according to Slovak orthography (bodzsár 1997). For the first time in the seventy-seven-year history of the Hungarian minority in (Czecho)Slovakia, Hungarian schoolchildren were denied the right to receive bilingual school reports. Those teachers who issued bilingual reports despite the government coercion received various forms of punishment–a certain Mr. Agócs, for example, lost his 1,000 crown monthly bonus (see Vojtek 1997a) and the principal of the Hungarian *gymnasium* in Bratislava was fired (see Vojtek 1997b). In the city of Nitra skinheads recently brutalized Hungarian university students and soldiers simply for speaking Hungarian (Tóth 1997; vrabec 1997).[4] In another case two high school pupils spoke Hungarian to each other in a public building and a Slovak man warned them to speak the state language. The girls ignored his demand and the man slapped one of them in the face. None of the bystanders present found this strange (Mojzes 1997, 61).

The prohibition on speaking language X is often just a part of a larger prohibition "Don't use language X". In recent years the Romanian city of Cluj (Hungarian: Kolozsvár), where the population is about 20 percent Hungarian, has been the scene of many such prohibitions and conflicts. A selection of press reports published between 1992 and 1996 (Balázs–Schwartz 1997) contains a plethora of such conflicts. Attempts to make Hungarian invisible have included:

- a prohibition on the posting of a Hungarian sign *Bartók Béla Emléknapok* (Béla Bartók Memorial Days) on the Hungarian Opera in the city (1652);[5]
- a plan to change street names bearing the names of Hungarian, Jewish or Communist persons and name them after Romanian historical heroes (1798);
- the practice of writing *Inform the sender that Romanian is the official language* on envelopes addressed correctly in Romanian but with the city name written in Hungarian (1465);
- criticizing the Hungarian Student Association, KMDSz, for using Hungarian city names like *Kolozsvár* in their English correspondence instead of the Romanian name *Cluj* (1853);
- urging extremely heavy fines for singing the Hungarian national anthem or flying the Hungarian flag (1366); and

- a request to discontinue the broadcasting of Hungarian programs on Romanian Television (1362).

In promoting Romanian as the official language of Romania, the
mayor of Cluj/Kolozsvár has said that even foreign tourists who
buy bread in a store should ask for it in Romanian (585). I will return to the bread theme below.

Our Data

In 1996, a sociolinguistic questionnaire was administered to ethnic
Hungarians in all neighboring countries of the Hungarian Republic
with the exception of Croatia.[6] The questionnaire included well
over 100 questions on the sociological context of language use by
minority Hungarians, as well as a great number of linguistic tasks
proper. One of the questions asked reads: *Előfordult-e már, hogy
valaki rászólt Önre, hogy ne beszéljen magyarul? Ha igen, az
utóbbi két évből hány ilyen esetre emlékszik? Mesélje el valamely-
iket!* (Have you ever been told by anybody not to speak Hungarian?
If so, how many times has it happened in the last two years? Please
give an example.) Table 4.1 shows the total number of informants
in each country and the number of those who described such an
incident.

Table 4.1

Hungarian informants in six countries and the number of those
who related they had been told not to speak Hungarian

Country	No. of informants	Those told not to speak Hungarian
Slovakia	108	42 (39%)
Ukraine	144	65 (45%)
Romania	216	81 (38%)
Yugoslavia	144	20 (14%)
Slovenia	66	17 (25%)
Austria	60	25 (41%)
Total	738	250 (33%)

As can be seen, in the case of Yugoslavia (Serbia) there are very
few reports, which is quite probably due to the fact that most
Hungarians in Voivodina are afraid to speak about inter-ethnic
strife so soon after (?) the ethnic cleansing in the former Yugoslav
federation.

On the Context of the Prohibitions

The question of who, typically, issues prohibitions on the use of a language, and in what settings or speech situations, merits investigation if we are to learn more about such speech acts. In this section I will enumerate the typical contexts as revealed in our six-country study.

Means of *public transportation* such as streetcars, buses or trains are often the scene of such prohibitions. Thirty-four such instances have been reported in five of the six countries. Informants in Ukraine, for instance, reported that they had been told not to speak Hungarian to a cab driver, or to fellow travelers on a train. Sometimes the prohibitions are directed at private conversations, such as in the case of a woman in Slovakia who was asked why she and her husband spoke Hungarian to each other.

The *workplace* has been mentioned in twenty-nine cases by informants in five countries. A Hungarian woman in a shoe factory was counting something in Hungarian and a colleague told her to speak Romanian. Somebody in Yugoslavia was told that speaking Hungarian in the workplace was "a provocation". Another person, in Slovenia, was told not to listen to Hungarian radio. In the dressing room of the Vienna Opera two Hungarian women were talking Hungarian under their breath and a colleague rebuked them.

In over a dozen cases informants reported being told not to speak Hungarian in a store or a farmers' market. Other situations include local government offices, hospitals and doctor's offices, restaurants, the army, schools and universities (including dormitories), and the street. Examples include a resort at the Black Sea in Romania where a group of friends lining up for bread were told not to speak Hungarian among themselves. A class of schoolchildren went to see an international exhibition in Bucharest and were told to speak Romanian among themselves. A student translated a given text into Hungarian in his German class, and Ukrainian fellow students criticized him.

Sometimes the prohibitions are accentuated by physical violence or the threat of violence: a few days after being drafted into the Romanian Army, an ethnic Hungarian soldier was told not to speak Hungarian, and not to use Hungarian for writing letters. He was beaten up for doing so. A woman in Austria reported that she was talking to her friend quietly in a metro station and an old man threatened to throw them in front of the train, shouting *Ausländer!* "Foreigners!"

Having surveyed the places where the prohibitions occurred, let us turn to the people who issued them. They range from very close family members such as a spouse or parent, to complete strangers. One person's spouse told them not to speak Hungarian to their children in the presence of Slovaks. Another informant reported that she had been told to speak Slovenian to her mother on the phone. When the same woman spoke Hungarian to her son in the company of Slovenes, he warned her that it was bad manners to speak Hungarian. In a group of Hungarian and Romanian friends a Hungarian spoke his mother tongue to a fellow Hungarian and a Romanian told them that he did not understand them. A man in Ukraine reported that he had not been allowed to swear in Hungarian when he was in the army. Finally, a command not to speak Hungarian in the street can be issued by complete strangers. What can be generalized from these reports is that the prohibitions seem to occur without regard to the degree of familiarity between the interlocutors who issue and receive them.

In the countries surveyed, where Hungarians form minorities subject to attempts to make their language invisible, a switch from Hungarian to the state language often occurs voluntarily, as when five Hungarians are joined by one Serb while at work. However, the switch can also be involuntary: a Slovenian colleague entered an office where all the workers were Hungarian and demanded that they stop speaking Hungarian. As for the reasons offered for not speaking Hungarian, perhaps the most typical one is a reference to observing "a basic rule of conduct", according to which one should not speak Hungarian in the company of a person who does not understand it.

Three Major Reasons Not to Speak Hungarian

There are three frequent reasons reported for rationalizing the prohibitions. I will call them (1) the intelligibility reason; (2) the speak-X-in-X-land reason; and (3) the "bread reason".

Informants in all the six countries reported a large number of cases in which majority speakers demanded that Hungarians speak the majority language so that the majority speakers too could understand what was being talked about. Frequently the demand is supported by a suspicion that Hungarians may be mocking the majority population. Such a suspicion can be very widespread, as shown by a newspaper report about events before the March 1990 language-related pogrom in Tîrgu Mureş/Marosvásárhely, Romania:

The fights were still going on in Bucharest in December 1989 when in Tîrgu Mureş about a score of us drafted a declaration in which we pledged to stop inter-ethnic hatred. ... I remember the embarrassment of the Romanian writers and journalists when Előd Kincses, a prominent figure in the events three months later, dared to say that Romanians in Transylvania should be obliged to understand Hungarian. If this were the case, their constant suspicion about what the Hungarians might be talking about would disappear.

(Máthé 1997)

The second very widespread reason, reported in all the countries, can be generalized as "This is X-land, you must speak X-ish." An informant reported that he was warned in Bratislava that "the language law had been passed, so he should speak Slovak." One person was questioned as to why he was buying a Hungarian newspaper in Slovakia. A Hungarian conversation in a streetcar in Bratislava provoked the remark, "Gee, they think they are in Budapest!" A Slovak colleague visited a Hungarian in her home and demanded that the Hungarians speak Slovak everywhere in their apartment, regardless of the presence of Slovaks. One person who needed an injection on the Ukrainian side of the Hungarian border, and who could only speak Hungarian in the doctor's office, was told to go to Budapest. Under Communism, the president of a kolkhoz went into an office and spoke Hungarian, and he was told to speak Romanian since he lived in Romania. Two Hungarians speaking Hungarian in a laundry were told to speak German since they were in Austria. In a store a policeman told a Hungarian to speak Serbian because Serbia was not Hungary. A Hungarian who was told to speak Slovenian in Slovenia countered that where he lived had, originally, been Hungary.

When speakers of different languages live together there can be two expectations about language learning. In the one case, speakers of X expect the speakers of Y to learn X, but they themselves do not learn Y. Bordás et al. (1995, 100) call this "linguistic fundamentalism". In the other case, there is a mutual expectation that people will learn each other's language. The Austrian quoted at the beginning of this article illustrates linguistic fundamentalism: he expects others to speak German in Austria, but he himself would also speak German in a non-German-speaking country such as Brazil. Linguistic fundamentalism seems to be the rule in southern Slovakia, where 80 percent of Slovaks are unwilling to learn Hungarian even though they expect Hungarians to learn Slovak.[7] Bordás et al. (1995, 101) claim that the sources of this Slovak fundamentalism are twofold: a fear of assimilating to the Hungarians,

and the hegemonic ambition that "Slovakia should be ruled by Slovaks".

The third reason often given by majority speakers for issuing a
prohibition on the use of a minority language is what I will call
"the bread argument". In a study of ethnic Romanians in Hungary,
Borbély (1995, 38–9) describes it as follows:

> Another remarkable difference between the old and the young is
> their attitude to the stereotype "Speak Hungarian since you eat Hun-
> garian bread". When Hungarians made this remark to them, the older
> Romanians were offended. The young, however, often rationalize
> their more frequent use of Hungarian with this stereotype: "I speak
> Hungarian since I eat Hungarian bread and live in Hungary".[8]

Several informants in our study reported that they had encountered the same argument. A Hungarian in Ukraine was asked at
work why, if he ate Russian bread, did he not speak Russian? An
informant in Romania was speaking Hungarian to somebody when
a stranger in the street told him not to speak Hungarian since he
ate Romanian bread.

In a few cases we have reports of a rejection of this argument,
which may go "We are Hungarians and we eat our own Hungarian
bread". This bread argument seems to be widespread[9] not only
among majority speakers but also among minority speakers (such
as the above example of the younger, more assimilated Romanians
in Hungary shows), hence the counterargument may sometimes be
spelled out in quite some detail, as in the following newspaper
article (Hajnal 1997):

> Unfortunately even my own Hungarian relatives in Košice/Kassa
> [Slovakia] often say that Hungarians should speak the language of the
> state whose bread they eat. I believe this is where the fundamental
> difference in attitudes is rooted. Why? Because the Hungarians, the
> Czechs, the Ruthenians, the Poles, and the list could be continued,
> eat their own bread in the country beyond our northern borders, not
> the bread of the Slovaks, let alone that of the Slovak state. As taxpay-
> ers, they have rights and obligations. They have an obligation to be
> loyal to the Republic of Slovakia. They have a right to their homeland,
> to the use of their mother tongue at all levels of public education and
> some levels of public administration.

On the Usefulness of the Study of Folk Linguistic Rights

Rules of language reside in people's minds, but the codified rules of a language are written by (prescriptive) linguists and printed in books. Usually there is a considerable difference between people's rules and linguists' rules, which is one of several main sources of the conflicts surrounding language matters. Just as the rules of language in people's minds may be in conflict with the codified linguistic rules, so may the language rights in people's minds be in conflict with the codified linguistic rights. As Turi (1994, 114) has recently emphasized, the applicability of legal rules hinges on a respect for local customs: "legal rules, like socio-linguistic rules, are only applied and applicable if they respect local custom and usage and the behaviour of reasonable people ...".[10]

In order to reduce the conflicts between people's rules or rights and codified rules or rights, the gap between the two systems needs to be narrowed. For this to happen we should obviously know more about folk beliefs concerning language rights. I would like to show that the significance of custom and popular faith in regulating linguistic and legal matters may be greater than we might think and they should be considered carefully when attempts are made to change the law, as in the case of the drive to formulate and then implement linguistic human rights.

First, I will demonstrate the importance of understanding folk knowledge and beliefs about language for successful communication. Second, I will quote an example of folk beliefs concerning a recent language law.

I would like to illustrate the important role of language in creating, reproducing and maintaining inter-ethnic strife by summarizing an excellent analysis by the Hungarian linguist[11] Sándor N. Szilágyi (1996, 78–95) of Transylvania, Romania.

There is a fundamental distinction between the real world and the linguistic world. The former is what surrounds us, what we can experience, and what exists—without regard to whether or not we speak about it. When we speak about objects in the real world we name them, and by naming them we turn them into elements of the linguistic world. The elements of the linguistic world are linguistically categorized. Humankind perceives the objects of the real world and also makes them the objects of linguistic perception, that is, categorizes them linguistically as objects which have particular names. In a similar fashion to the way colors belong to objects in the real world (objects have color only when they are seen by somebody or something), names and hence linguistic categorizations belong to objects only when we speak about them. When objects in the real world are not being spoken about, they belong to the real world without belonging to the linguistic world. This is rather difficult to understand or believe, since people are prone to think that the color or name of an object is an inherent characteristic, whether or not we see or speak about it.

A true statement about two objects in the real world in one language may not correspond to a true statement about the same two objects in another language. If a Hungarian points to an apple tree, he calls it a *fa*. If he points to a locust tree, he calls that a *fa* as well. These are true statements in the Hungarian linguistic world. If a Romanian points to an apple tree, he says *Ăsta-i un pom*, which is a true statement in the Romanian linguistic world. But the same utterance used about a locust tree would be inadequate or false in the Romanian linguistic world because Romanian makes a lexical distinction between a fruit tree (=*pom*) and a non-fruit tree (=*copac*) which does not exist in Hungarian. Hence the true Romanian statement about a locust tree is *Ăsta-i un copac*. This example should serve to illustrate why it is necessary to distinguish the real world from various linguistic worlds.

The real world is subdivided into two regions: (1) the inanimate region; and (2) the animate region. The linguistic world also contains these two regions: the word *horse* belongs to the animate region when it means "a large animal which people ride on", but it belongs to the inanimate region when it means "a wooden apparatus which people can vault over for exercise." Both the animal and the wooden apparatus are objects of the real world, and when they are named they are objects of the linguistic world. When they are not named, they are objects of the real world alone; they exist and can be perceived in the real world, but they do not exist in the linguistic world.

However, the linguistic world has a region (3) as well, a secondary region which is created through language. This third linguistic region has nothing to correspond to it in the real world. English has the word *whiteness,* but there is no object whiteness in the real world. In the case of regions (1) and (2), the existence of real-world objects precedes their naming and hence also their becoming objects in the linguistic world, but in the case of region (3) the relationship is reversed. When we create a name like *whiteness,* this name is not the name of a real-world object. Through the name we create an object in the linguistic world. The cognitive trap here is that speakers believe that objects in region (3) in the linguistic world have a real existence since they believe that what can be spoken about exists in the real world.

Problems galore arise when we try to define objects belonging to region (3) in the linguistic world. Attempts to create definitions for objects in region (3) as if they were objects in regions (1) and (2) often result in a wild-goose chase. For instance, debates about "the nation" are doomed to failure. There is no nation in the real world, but it exists in the linguistic world when people use the name *nation* in English, *nemzet* in Hungarian or *națiune* in Romanian.

If we now recall that a true statement about two real-world objects in one language may not correspond to a true statement about the same two objects in another language it should come as no surprise that a true statement about an object belonging to region (3) in one language should be next to impossible to translate into another language. After all, region (3) of the linguistic world is created through people speaking, and the way people speak is culturally determined. Linguistic worlds and world views differ, hence Hungarian *nemzet* and Romanian *națiune* are mutually untranslatable.

The Hungarian word *nemzet* denotes the community of a people with the same language and cultural traditions, regardless of what state they live in; in other words it is an ethnonym. The Romanian word *națiune* denotes the community of those people who have the same citizenship; in other words it is a politonym. Problems arise when an ethnic Hungarian member of the Romanian Parliament needs to speak about "the nation" in Romanian in the Romanian Parliament. He can switch between languages, but cannot switch between concepts. He has no choice but to use the Romanian word *națiune* in trying to convince the Romanian politicians of the truth of his statements about the Hungarian concept of "the nation." He uses *națiune* "citizens of a state" to mean *nemzet* "people with the same language and culture in any state". Were he to use the Romanian word with its Romanian meaning (a perfectly sensible thing to do), it would not be advisable for him to walk the streets anymore. After all, who could afford to claim that Hungarians in Romania are an organic part of the Hungarian nation (when speaking Hungarian) and an organic part of the Romanian nation (when speaking Romanian)? It is for this reason, says Szilágyi, that every time Hungarian and Romanian politicians in the Bucharest Parliament debate a topic significantly related to "the nation", the result is invariably scandal. There is no chance for mu-

tual understanding because the truth of the statements in one linguistic world is lost in the other. Charges of Hungarian irreden-
tism, all too frequently made in Romania, thus have a linguistic
cause as well.

The *nemzet* vs. *naţiune* example demonstrates the linguistic
deep-rootedness of inter-ethnic conflicts. I would like to suggest
that *folk beliefs about language rights* can have an equally important influence. These folk beliefs fall into two broad categories: (1)
those beliefs which constitute the body of "general truths", such as
the imperative "speak-X-ish-in-X-land" or the bread argument; and
(2) those beliefs which concern the laws in a particular country at
a particular time.

Langman (1997, 125) offers an ethnographic analysis of folk beliefs with respect to the 1995 Slovak state language law.[12] She
writes:

> Two stories are repeatedly told and familiar to all my informants as
> well as many people in Slovakia and abroad with an interest in mi-
> nority issues in Slovakia: two Hungarian colleagues riding on a bus
> must speak Slovak to one another as they are in a public place; an old
> Hungarian woman who goes to the doctor (who is also Hungarian) is
> required to speak Slovak, leading to potentially dangerous outcomes,
> if the old woman doesn't understand the doctor's advice.

Both of these stories are believed to be part of the law, despite
the fact that they are not *explicitly* stated in it.[13] These two scenarios "have taken on almost mythic proportions and are part of
common knowledge among Hungarians in Slovakia" (Langman
1997, 125). This common knowledge creates an atmosphere of
distrust and resentment among members of the minority.

If lexical differences between languages can cause inevitable
scandals in parliaments, and if folk beliefs about a language law can
assume almost mythic proportions, then it should come as no surprise that there are no quick and easy solutions to language rights
conflicts. Péter Hunčík (1995, 232), leader of the team which has
studied the ethnopsychology of Hungarian-Slovak relations and
which conducts training sessions in Slovakia to teach people to
defuse crises, has this to say about certain attempts to find quick
and easy solutions:

> With all due respect to the self-denying researchers who are willing
> to travel several thousand kilometers in order to help to solve the
> problems in this region, it must be said very clearly that it is impossi-
> ble to become familiar with the major problems of the region in four

or five days. A one-week fact-finding mission can result in colorful articles in magazines, but it can contribute but little to the creation of an efficient ethnic crisis management program.

I would argue that a thorough understanding of the cultural and linguistic context of inter-ethnic conflicts seems to be indispensable for defusing conflicts and quick fixes are doomed to failure.

States occupy an entire continuum from prohibition to promotion of language rights (see Skutnabb-Kangas and Phillipson 1994, 80) or from assimilation-oriented policies to maintenance-oriented policies towards minorities. People also vary in their attitudes towards language rights. The impact of such social factors as education or urbanization is by no means constant across countries; for instance, Crowther (1997, 48) reports that in Moldova "hostile attitudes toward minorities are much more strongly associated with higher levels of education than in Romania."

Conclusion

In the process of implementing linguistic human rights, folk beliefs should be carefully studied and full use should be made of the research results in designing implementation strategies for each particular country or region. In this paper three extremely powerful folk beliefs have been identified which restrict the public use of minority languages in Central Europe: the intelligibility reason, the speak-X-in-X-land reason, and the bread reason. It has been demonstrated that language itself can be the cause of inter-ethnic miscommunication and can create and maintain inter-ethnic strife, without people realizing that they are victims of the languages they use. States vary in their tolerance or promotion of linguistic human rights. People vary in their attitudes to language rights within a state as well as between states. Codified language rights and folk beliefs about them can be so different as to make successful implementation difficult. With careful social planning which pays due respect to local legal, linguistic and cultural custom, linguistic human rights may take root in a country, but without such planning there seems to be little chance for the elimination of linguistic discrimination.

Notes

1 This quotation is taken from our six-country study conducted in 1996 and described in the section *Our Data*.

2 I am aware of the methodological limitations of this study, e.g. the inadequate contextual information obtained by means of the questionnaire and the lack of tape-recorded interviews. Nevertheless I believe the information obtained provides a useful basis for a study of linguistic rights which reaches beyond the offices of lawyers, linguists, political scientists and similar professionals.

3 Our work has been assisted by the Research Support Scheme of the Higher Education Support Programme, grant no. 582/1995. The team includes István Lanstyák (Slovakia), István Csernicskó (Ukraine), János Péntek and Sándor N. Szilágyi (Romania), Lajos Göncz (Yugoslavia), Ottó Vörös (Hungary), István Szépfalusi (Austria), Klára Sándor (Hungary) and myself. For a brief description of the research see Kontra (1996a).

4 In the years following 1945, when Hungarians and Germans in Czechoslovakia were deprived of all rights including their citizenship, in nearly all public places signs were put up with *Na Slovensku po slovensky!* (Speak Slovak in Slovakia!) This can be interpreted as saying no more than "Don't *speak* Hungarian in Slovakia!" But another public sign also frequently seen in those years, *Mad'ari za Dunaj!* (Hungarians, go beyond the Danube!), says "Don't *be* Hungarian in Slovakia!" or else you will be deported (Gyönyör 1990, 33).

5 Balázs–Schwartz (1997) contains 2,464 news reports, which are numbered. Rather than referring to page numbers here I will refer to the serial number of each particular news item.

6 The ongoing war in the former Yugoslavia made it impossible to include eastern Slavonia at the time the fieldwork was carried out. In each country a quota sample was used which was stratified according to age, educational level, and settlement type (city vs. village, and local majority vs. local minority). Further details are given in Kontra (1998).

7 The survey was conducted in March 1994 with a representative sample comprising 634 Hungarians and 582 Slovaks living in ethnically mixed southern Slovakia, and 624 Slovaks living in ethnically homogeneous northern Slovakia (Bordás et al. 1995, 27).

8 My translation from the Hungarian.

9 Tove Skutnabb-Kangas reports to me that the bread argument is also "proverbial" in Finland.

10 Over a century and a half ago the German jurist Friedrich Karl von Savigny proposed that the prescriptive content of the law must accord with the spirit of the people, the *Volksgeist.* "A law that was not in conformity with this was doomed" (The New Encyclopaedia Britannica, vol. 10 [1988], 482). Savigny's ideas had considerable influence on linguistics as well, see Austerlitz (1991).

11 S. N. Szilágyi is a citizen of Romania. His mother tongue is Hungarian and he identifies himself as a Hungarian born and living in Romania. According to the theory of "political nation" he is a Hungarian-Romanian. According to the theory of "cultural nation" he is a Hungarian in Romania. For this writer, as well as for all Hungarians, the appropriate English term is *Hungarian linguist in Romania*, but for American, English, French and other readers who tend to define people's national identity on the basis of citizenship rather than language and culture, Szilágyi is a Hungarian-Romanian (or simply: Romanian) linguist. Szilágyi belongs to the Hungarian ethnic/national community and to the Romanian political community. Using the concepts developed by the Soviet academician Yu. Bromley, Skutnabb-Kangas (personal communication) says that linguonymically Szilágyi is Hungarian, politonymically he is Romanian, ethnonymically he is Romania-Hungarian or simply Hungarian, and toponymically he is Romanian.

12 For the text of the Slovak State Language Law see Kontra 1995–1996 or Kontra 1997.

13 Section 8, paragraph 4 of the law says, "Health care institutions conduct all their administration in the State language. Contact between health care employees and patients takes place usually in the State language; if the patient is a citizen or foreigner unfamiliar with the State language, then also in such a language in which they can understand each other".

References

Austerlitz, Robert. "Gombocz Zoltán és a mai magyar nyelvtudomány" (Zoltán Gombocz and contemporary Hungarian linguistics). In Jenő Kiss and László Szűts, eds., *Tanulmányok a magyar nyelvtudomány történetének témaköréből*, 26–29. Budapest: Akadémiai Kiadó, 1991.

Balázs, Sándor and Róbert Schwartz. *Funar korszak Kolozsváron a helyi sajtó tükrében, 1992–1996.* (The Funar era in Cluj as reflected by the local press, 1992–1996). Kolozsvár: Erdélyi Híradó Könyv- és Lapkiadó, 1997.

bodzsár. "Szlovákosított nevek. Véletlen elírások a telefonkönyvben?" (Slovakized names. Inadvertent misspellings in the telephone directory?) In *Új Szó* (6 February 1997), 3.

Borbély, Anna. "A magyarországi románok nyelvhasználata a változások tükrében" (Changes in the language use of Romanians in Hungary). In *Regio* 6, no. 3 (1995): 34–43.

Bordás, Sándor, Pavol Frič, Katarína Haidová, Péter Hunčík, and Máthé Róbert. *Ellenpróbák: A szlovák-magyar viszony vizsgálata szociológiai és etnopszichológiai módszerekkel Szlovákiában* (Counter proofs: a sociological and ethnopsychological investigation of Slovak–Hungarian relations in Slovakia). Pozsony–Dunaszerdahely: Nap Kiadó, 1995.

Crawford, James. *Hold Your Tongue: Bilingualism and the Politics of "English Only."* Reading, Mass.: Addison-Wesley, 1992.

Crowther, William. "The Construction of Moldovan National Consciousness." In Kürti and Langman, eds. (1997), 39–62.

Driessen, Bart. "A new turn in Hungarian-Slovak relations? An overview of the Basic Treaty." *International Journal on Minority and Group Rights,* 4 (1997): 1–40.

Gyönyör, József. *Mi lesz velünk, magyarokkal? Fejezetek a csehszlovákiai magyarság történetéből 1918-tól napjainkig* (What will happen to us Hungarians? Chapters on the history of Hungarians in Czechoslovakia from 1918 to the present day). Pozsony: Madách, 1990.

Hajnal, László. "Anna néni magyarul beszél" (Aunt Anna speaks Hungarian). In *Magyar Hírlap* (9 September, 1997), 7.

Hamel, Rainer Enrique. "Indigenous education in Latin America: policies and legal frameworks." In Skutnabb-Kangas and Phillipson, eds. (1994), 271–287.

Hernández-Chávez, Eduardo. "Language policy in the United States: A history of cultural genocide." In Skutnabb-Kangas and Phillipson, eds. (1994), 141–158.

Hoenigswald, Henry M. "A proposal for the study of folk-linguistics." In William Bright, ed., *Sociolinguistics,* 16–26. The Hague: Mouton, 1966.

Hunčík, Péter. "Terveink" (Our plans). In Bordás et al. (1995), 231–235.

Kontra, Miklós. "English Only's Cousin: Slovak Only." *Acta Linguistica Hungarica* 43, nos. 3–4 (1995–1996): 345–372.

——. "Magyar nyelvhasználat határainkon túl" (Hungarian language use beyond Hungary's borders). In László Diószegi, ed., *Magyarságkutatás 1995–96,* 113–123. Budapest: Teleki László Alapítvány, 1996a.

——. "The Wars over Names in Slovakia." *Language Problems & Language Planning* 20, no. 2 (1996b): 160–167.

——. "On the right to use the language of one's choice in Slovakia." *Canadian Centre for Linguistic Rights Bulletin* 4, no. 1 (1997): 5–8.

——. "Final Report to the Research Support Scheme on *The Sociolinguistics of Hungarian Outside Hungary*" Manuscript. Budapest: Linguistics Institute of the Hungarian Academy of Sciences, 1998.

Kürti, László and Juliet Langman, eds. *Beyond Borders: Remaking Cultural Identities in the New East and Central Europe.* Boulder, Col: Westview Press, 1997.

Langman, Juliet. "Expressing identity in a changing society: Hungarian youth in Slovakia." In László Kürti and Juliet Langman, eds. (1997), 111–131.

Lemco, Jonathan. "Quebec's 'Distinctive Character' and the Question of Minority Rights." In James Crawford, ed., *Language Loyalties: A Source Book on the Official English Controversy,* 423–433. Chicago: The University of Chicago Press, 1992.

Máthé, Éva. "Kis séta a transzszilván labirintusban" (A small walk in the Transylvanian labyrinth). *Magyar Hírlap* (12 September 1997), 7.

Mojzes, Tímea. "Nyelvi kölcsönhatások vizsgálata egy 'vérbeli' alternatív iskolában" (A study of linguistic interactions in a 'genuine' alternative school). *Irodalmi Szemle,* 40, no. 5 (1997): 61–76.

The New Encyclopaedia Britannica, volume 10, Micropaedia. 15th Edition. Chicago: Encyclopaedia Britannica, Inc., 1988.

Pazonyi, Tibor. "Kedves Vadkerty Andrea!" (Dear Andrea Vadkerty). In *Új Szó* (21 February 1997), 2.

Preston, Dennis R. *Perceptual Dialectology: Nonlinguists' Views on Areal Linguistics*. Dordrecht: Foris Publications, 1989.

——. "The uses of folk linguistics." *International Journal of Applied Linguistics* 3, no. 2 (1993): 181–259.

Skutnabb-Kangas, Tove and Sertaç Bucak. "Killing a mother tongue–how the Kurds are deprived of linguistic human rights." In Skutnabb-Kangas and Phillipson, eds. (1994), 347–370.

Skutnabb-Kangas, Tove and Robert Phillipson, eds. *Linguistic Human Rights: Overcoming Linguistic Discrimination*. Berlin and New York: Mouton de Gruyter, 1994.

Skutnabb-Kangas, Tove and Robert Phillipson. "Linguistic human rights, past and present." In Skutnabb-Kangas and Phillipson, eds. (1994), 71–110.

Szilágyi, N. Sándor. *Hogyan teremtsünk világot? Rávezetés a nyelvi világ vizsgálatára* (How to create a world. An introduction to the study of language). Kolozsvár: Erdélyi Tankönyvtanács, 1996.

Thornberry, Patrick. *International Law and the Rights of Minorities*. Oxford: Clarendon Press, 1991.

Tóth, Gábor. "Mi történik Nyitrán?" (What is happening in Nitra?) In *Új Szó* (12 March 1997), 2.

Turi, Joseph-G. "Typology of language legislation." In Skutnabb-Kangas and Phillipson, eds. (1994), 111–119.

Várady, Tibor. "Minorities, Majorities, Law, and Ethnicity: Reflections of the Yugoslav Case." *Human Rights Quarterly*, 19 (1997): 9–54.

de Varennes, Fernand. "The Protection of Linguistic Minorities in Europe and Human Rights: Possible Solutions to Ethnic Conflicts?" *The Columbia Journal of European Law* 2, no. 1 (1995/96): 107–143.

Vojtek, Katalin. "Agócs Béla személyi pótlékot sem kapott" (Béla Agócs did not get his bonus either). In *Új Szó* (22 February 1997), 2.

Vojtek, Katalin. "Égetően szükséges egy pénzalap létrehozása" (Funds must be created immediately). In *Új Szó* (6 October 1997), 5.

vrabec. "Magyar sorkatonákat vertek meg bőrfejűek" (Skinheads beat Hungarian conscripts). In *Új Szó* (4 March 1997), 1.

The Common Language Problem

MART RANNUT

The aim of this article is to map how the power structure of society is reflected in language policies, and to trace the development from the idealistic notion of state-nation-language of two centuries ago through to its accommodation to the needs of contemporary society. The role of language as the cornerstone of nation building has been maintained, along with the role of a common language as the primary generator of linguistic homogenization. In analyzing the basis for the establishment of the common language we assess the roles of three groups that may influence policy–the emerging state bureaucracy, groups representing economic interests, and the ethnic majority–by considering their interests, instrumental and primordial, in language. The article comprises a presentation and analysis of various policy options and their implementation and the relationship between the common language and other languages through the prism of three language-policy models: language spread, nation building, and minority-language protection. As the legal aspects (linguistic human rights included) that regulate the relationships between various models are of greatest concern in minority-language protection, the issue of instrumental and collective rights is considered in more detail. Likewise, the interaction of the three language-policy models is discussed.

Societal Structure

The current political situation is significantly different from the Herderian times that produced the triad of *état-nation-langue,* idealized up to the beginning of the 20th century. It led to the generalization of nation-states in the wake of collapsed empires that were unable, among other things, to cope with linguistic diversity and implement integrative and cost-effective language policies. The solution for facilitating societal balance was found in the form of the nation-state, which in turn has shown itself to be a temporary one as well. With the birth of international organizations, transnational corporations and global media as well as information networks, a good deal of power has shifted away from states, save the most totalitarian ones. Simultaneously, the homogeneity of a state showed itself to be wishful thinking in most cases, as seen in the revival of hidden minorities and increasing migrational flows.

Therefore, in order to describe the current position with societal power as an integral element, a new paradigm is necessary. One component of this paradigm has to be *language*, which over time plays an even more central role, penetrating all domains of society and leaving less room for negotiations over language choice. The reason for the importance of language seems to be its transformation into a political object and resource similar to other politically negotiable objects and resources (Ozolins 1993, 34) in both the primordial and instrumental senses (Phillipson et al. 1994, 9). From the primordial point of view, language is seen as an integrative component of ethnicity and a natural symbol of inherent group rights, simultaneously being, due to the exclusive nature of language, one of the most common differentiating factors in human affairs. Any negative change that may be linked to language is thus a visible signal for those operating in defense of their ethnolinguistic interests. In this way language has maintained its role as an organizer of ethnic divisions within society. These divisions are sustained by boundary-maintenance mechanisms: "ideologies, rules, practices which serve to maintain ethnic group distinctiveness by maximizing close social relations between ethnic insiders and by strictly limiting and controlling social relations between insiders and outsiders" (Kallen 1996, 119).

Simultaneously, the increase of the instrumental value of language and its exclusive characteristics, rearranging society on a language domination axis, is inevitably connected to the economic and social well-being of its speakers. Thus language acts as a regulator of unequal access to power. Taken together, both primordial and instrumental values tend to produce a synergetic effect, making language one of the most important factors in the contemporary political scene.

Another component in our modernized triad seems to be *power*, which on a macro scale was earlier available only to states. Power, sufficient to reproduce nations with all their characteristics generation after generation, was traditionally controlled by states, based on principles of territoriality, sovereignty and exclusivity (Buzan 1993). Thus, states concentrated power, together with authority and identity. However, the current situation may be characterized by a different pattern of power distribution, influencing directly the security agenda of states and the behavior of nations. Thus, the principle of the territoriality of power will be just one among several principles. However, power itself stays as a cornerstone in the build-up of modern society, but in a substantially modified form. Power is qualitatively more transmitted through language as a channel, used as an instrument of manipulation in discourse. This means that beside resources and structural agents, ideological agents have come to the forefront of policy making (including language policy). Neither linguistic human rights nor language policy in general are the focus of interest of any state (although, together with diminishing power in other spheres, states have taken more interest in language matters, e.g. France). State interests are usually elsewhere rather than in language policy, for instance in the economy, security, social policies. The sort of language policy adopted is the consequence of decisions taken in other domains, for achieving goals that usually have little in common with language issues. Behind these domains, two opposite factors, called the market and market correctives (Tomaševski 1996, 104; Skutnabb-Kangas 1996), influence development, creating order and structure in the domain concerned. In this way, human rights—linguistic human rights included—act as correctives to the free market, they should guarantee that the basics needed for survival and for the sustenance of a dignified life overrule the law of supply and demand. Thus they should be outside market forces. A state is successful if these two factors are in balance. Among other non-tradable issues, McGarry and O'Leary (1993, 16) list other ethnicity-related matters, such as nationality, territorial homelands, and culture. When overridden, they tend to create zero-sum conflicts.

The third component in our paradigm is *society*—the subject that makes use of power and is simultaneously an agent of it. In contemporary times the term *society* need no longer denote a nation, or even any homogenous language group, but rather a group with common or similar (linguistic) interests. The inherent structure of a society is influenced by the power relations channeled through the instrumental functions of language, as well as by language directly, through its primordial aspect. In order to reveal the connections between these three components, we focus on the issues of power reflected through societal structures functioning in a language.

Underlying Power Structure

The role of language as the cornerstone of nation-building is maintained by states, together with the issue of the common language as the primary generator of linguistic homogenization, a form of homogenization of cultural practices. Various arguments in support of the common language, economic as well as political, are proposed. Stewart (1968, 541) observes that different languages are not competitive when they are used by different people for the same things, or by the same people for different things. Conflict arises when two or more languages are defined as appropriate for use in the same situation by the same people. Thus, the common language as a negotiated neutral code is seen as the best solution for avoiding conflicts and strengthening integrity and security. In analyzing the basis for the establishment of the common language, one has to assess the roles of three groups that may influence decisions—the emerging state bureaucracy, groups representing economic interests, and the ethnic majority—by comparing their respective instrumental and primordial interests in language.

The role of language in state bureaucracy has been constantly increasing. Though the sovereignty of a state in international terms has diminished, its role as a major purveyor of services, employment and economic opportunities has expanded. It provides a wide range of services and regulatory mechanisms for the society. Thus, states explicitly value instrumental aspects of language and claim to base their language policies on principles deriving from these instrumental values. However, language has been skillfully implemented on a major scale by states as a power instrument of the elite, though as a hidden agenda. A government may directly affect the political power structure of the state by making language knowledge a predominant factor in access to employment and education opportunities, as native speakers of the official language are more likely to reach the higher echelons of the state machinery. The central role of a language means professional and bureaucratic employment opportunities, linked with significant economic benefits. Thus, while the introduction of the common language may seem to promote instrumental value, it is, in fact, linked to primordial value, simultaneously producing inequality.

The interests of the state are usually complemented by the market economy, playing a major role in power structures. In this domain the two values surface again. Language is not used only as a neutral means of communication. Economic losses and gains are immediately reflected through the status of those beneficiaries, speakers of a certain language. In this way, language is viewed as a resource and knowledge of a particular language may provide a privileged position. The economic policy is usually based on a quite valid understanding that monolingualism in a monolingual state is economical. However, the other valid claim, that multilingualism in multilingual states is economical, is usually substituted by the false hybrids of the two claims (cf. Galtung 1988). The reason for this seems to stem from the primordial agenda, connected with linguistic groups. The same twofold scheme directing language interests in the common language policy seems to be true in other domains also.

The role of the ethnic majority seems to be crucial in the common language choice. If an ethnic majority is identified primarily with a particular language, and if it is powerful enough, its language choice is transferred to the emerging state bureaucracy and economy. If the ethnic majority lacks the necessary support within society, language choice is further negotiated (cf. India). If the ethnic majority is characterized primarily by other criteria than language, these other criteria may be taken as the basis for language choice. (Malay, as the language identified with Islam, was adopted in Malaysia instead of Javan, the language spoken by the majority.) Thus, in the case of the ethnic majority, the instrumental factor is secondary to the primordial.

Policies

Although in reality there may be linguistic conflict, the common language policy focuses on the aim of linguistic homogenization. The policy is based on three pillars: societal (it is usually based on majority), political (promoted by states) and economic (it is claimed to be cost-effective in business). For this purpose the state has chosen at least one language in the discharge of its duties, rejecting several others and constraining economic opportunities for their speakers. In this way language has become highly politicized, being intimately connected to economic and social mobility–as Lo Bianco (1987, 1) stipulates: "In a world which is becoming more dependent on language, its skilled and proficient use is a key factor in economic and social opportunities". Language policies affect the identity of communities living within the control of the state and their patterns of participation. And even if no official language

policies are declared, this is also a form of policy, negatively influencing linguistically dominated groups, as the state's liberal *laissez-
faire* policy benefits dominance.

The reasons for introducing the common language policy are
the following (Mazrui 1996, 115–116, my summary):

- to aid the consolidation of the national market (and the
  integrity of the state);
- to improve the characteristics of mass mobilization and
  organization of labor;
- to improve the dissemination of information;
- to contribute to effective social policies;
- to create counterhegemonies and transform foreign relations
  by establishing linguistic barriers against outside penetration;
- to retain national human resources and resist the outward
  flow of national expertise (brain drain).

However, in the context of modern government, one is
restricted in the available options. Laitin (1996, 56–57) names the
following constraints:

- the standard tasks performed by contemporary states involve
  significant contact with ordinary citizens, hence the need for
  effective communication along multilingual lines;
- international human rights standards are respected more than
  before;
- modern bureaucracies tend, in their own interest, to resist
  policies promoting any form of language change.

The list above proves that the common language decision is
inevitable, as de Varennes (1996) remarks: no government can
afford to provide services and official documents in every language
spoken on its territory, thus a state must necessarily restrict itself
to the use of a limited number of languages in its contacts with its
citizens. "Most countries provide constitutional or legislative
measures for an official language, or may proclaim a national
language. This does not necessarily imply exclusive use by a state:
there are sometimes, but not always, additional measures providing
for some use of other languages by government institutions. A few
states do not always clearly have a legislated or constitutional official
language, though in effect by tradition, omission or by other
measures, they recognize or permit the official use of only one
language" (de Varennes 1996, 9). Thus, the common language policy
is the underlying feature of the nation-building model.

There are usually powerful links between this model, the language-
spread model (so-called Languages of Wider Communication, LWCs)
and the minority-protection model. In relation to the former, the

nation-building model often has to play second fiddle; in relation to the latter, it can often do as it pleases. Thus, while perfectly well founded in law, the nation-building model, when combined with the common language principle, may easily veer towards illegal discrimination and violation of human rights standards (de Varennes 1996). The origins of the discrimination are often primordial, with reference to national unity and territorial integrity. There may be three variants of how this language policy functions:

A. the common language(s) with some other languages that enjoy some sort of functional freedom and legal protection;
B. the common language(s) with other languages that are not legally protected;
C. the common language used exclusively.

This last option, based on an assumed and false link between monolingual state policy and national unity, represents a die-hard phenomenon, as Phillipson et al. have shown (1994, 4–6).

The various possible language planning models are captured in the taxonomy, in Table 5.1.

Table 5.1

Various relationships of language planning models

LS	NB	MP	Examples
–	–	+	pre-statal situation
–	+	–	homogenizing state (Turkey, Slovakia, France, etc.)
–	+	+	multilingual state, national language and minority languages (Spain)
+	–	–	postcolonial Africa with former colonial language as lingua franca
+	–	+	powerful LS (South Africa), powerful MP (Switzerland)
+	+	–	competing dominant languages (Algeria)
+	+	+	multiple overlapping models (India)

LS = language spread of LWCs;
NB = nation building for the official and common language;
MP = minority language protection

Two relationships commonly occur and need further attention:

I. The relationship between language spread and nation building (LS-NB relationship). As this relationship is usually (but not always) reflected through the behavior of sovereign states, the language-spread model makes use of foreign policy instruments, ranging from informal penetration (including pedagogy) to diplomatic, economic and military measures. Most of the measures belong to the non-legal domain; (exceptions are the World Trade Organisation [WTO], and the proposed Multilateral Agreement for Investment [MAI], agreement on the free flow of goods, including cultural goods [films, videos, etc.], with France obstructing it), and some aspects of humanitarian law.

II. The relationship between nation building and minority protection (NB-MP relationship). Here language planning has to accommodate human rights standards most. It will be discussed further below.

One can also observe cases of the substitution of an LS-NB relationship by an NB-MP relationship in response to outside pressure, since the legal framework in the latter is much more powerful. It usually means that a state uses the situation of kindred minority in other states to increase its influence there, when the legal status of a formerly dominant language has changed from overdog to underdog. In this case the minority becomes a pawn in a wider political game (as is the case of the Baltic states vis-à-vis Russia; cf. the comparable situation of a regional majority language like French in Quebec, Maurais 1997).

Implementation Strategies

The relationship between the nation-building and minority-protection models can be seen in the implementation of specific strategies for action. There are two different, largely incompatible sets of strategies: one set introduces the exclusive use of the common language, and constrains and ousts other languages; the other set of strategies is based on managed cooperation between the state-promoted common language and minority languages. McGarry & O'Leary (1993, 4) present a taxonomy of the practical macro-political forms of ethnic conflict regulation (covering both conflict termination and conflict management) that we shall apply below to various related language situations deriving from NB-MP relationship. The political strategies which seek to introduce the common language usage pattern by eliminating ethnic differences, at least within a given state, are genocide, forced mass population transfers, partition, secession (external self-determination), integration and/or assimilation. Of these, there are moral justifications for partition/secession and arguments for integration. Such linguicidal methods as forced population transfers and genocide are explicitly prohibited in international law and thus fall outside our particular concerns. The methods for managing the coexistence of the official language and minority languages are hegemonic control, arbitration (third-party intervention), cantonisation or federalization, and consociationalism or power sharing (ibid.). Partition, secession, cantonisation and federalization may lead to the introduction of the principle of the territoriality of language, while the personal principle is manifested through assimilation/integration.

Democratic solutions of "getting rid" of minority languages, based on the territorial principle, are *partition, self-determination and secession* (cf. Czechoslovakia, Bangladesh). These are compatible with the standards of linguistic human rights. However, such outcomes may themselves derive from reactions to the absence of linguistic human rights and other civic freedoms, that is, from situations of linguistic or cultural discrimination where the implementation of the right to self-determination is the only way out (McGarry & O'Leary, ibid.).

Linguistic integration, concurrent with assimilation, is built upon the idea of rearranging the linguistic identity of the relevant ethnic communities into a new identity, along with proficiency in the common language. This follows the personal principle. Depending on the methods used with the identity the immersion or submersion in the majoritarian language may lead to either integration or assimilation, the latter being definitely in conflict with linguistic human rights standards. The other differentiating factor may be the functional allocation of languages, which is denied in assimilation. Linguistic assimilation in the homelands of indigenous speakers implies the destruction of a local culture, language, and sometimes religion. By contrast, integration is in full accord with linguistic human rights, although achieving this may be accompanied by some coercive measures such as compulsory education. De Varennes (1996, 297) has clarified this issue: "...A state has an obligation to ensure that teaching of a national language is always provided, at least as a second language, in all schools, if it is to respect the non-discrimination principle. This has been shown and acknowledged to be necessary in order not to create a de facto segregation between members of various language communities within a country, as well as being confirmed in the Belgian Linguistic Case. The dangers of state education confining individuals in a linguistic ghetto, unable to accede high echelons of activities in the greater national community because of their never having been granted the possibility of learning the national language, has occurred in the past and would in every situation constitute discrimination on the basis of language".

The main problem seems to be in the actual and timely differentiation between integration and assimilation. The same educational system that produced the benefits of integration to parents may bring along assimilation to their children. Thus, it may be necessary to introduce methods of partial physical segregation in education (e.g. language shelter programs) and neighborhood, in order to avoid complete assimilation.

Of the coexistence strategies for the official and minority languages the most common system practiced in multilingual states (cf. the ex-Soviet Union) is the concept of *hegemonic control* (see Lustick 1979), based on coercive domination and elite co-option. Lustick provides the following criteria: resources are allocated according to the dominant group's interest as perceived and articulated by its elite. Thus, the dominant group extracts what it needs and delivers what it sees fit, with no hard bargaining taking place, since the official regime, or state apparatus, acts as the administrative instrument of the dominant group. The existing political order is legitimated by the ideology of the dominant group. Hegemonic control need not rest, although it often does, on the support of the largest or most powerful ethnic community, as it is sufficient to control the relevant coercive apparatuses. In multilingual states, hegemonic control also prescribes the form of language policy. However, hegemonic control itself need not require any assimilationist steps to be taken toward other languages, as the main goal is in the maintenance of stability through hegemony.

Arbitration and mediation in ethnic and linguistic issues are more common in international relations. Usually it is a matter of conflict regulation where a neutral third-party intervention is necessary. Arbitration is distinguishable from mediation because the arbiter makes the relevant decisions, whereas mediators merely facilitate them. Arbitration and mediation are of two broad types: the internal (various types of Ombudsman and tribunals in addition to the Court), and the external (popular for border disputes). External arbitration and mediation are used when the conflict cannot be successfully managed within the relevant political system and the solution must be proposed from outside. Mediation has become increasingly popular, with a wealth of institutions operating internally (various round tables, *ad hoc* mediation groups and Commissioners) and externally (the High Commissioner on National Minorities within the OSCE, the Council of the

Baltic Sea States Human Rights Commissioner, the UN Human Rights Committee, etc.). Problems may arise in the wider arena of high-level diplomacy, making the observance of neutrality in decision making enormously difficult.

The last two strategies, *cantonisation and/or federalization* (Switzerland) and *consociationalism or power sharing* (Lebanon), are fully compatible with linguistic human rights. Under cantonisation the relevant multiethnic state is subjected to a micropartition in which political power is devolved to (conceivably very small) political units, each of which enjoys mini-sovereignty. Federalism is similar, with the units usually much larger than cantons. Federalism is based on a federal society, requiring the boundaries between the components of the federation to match the boundaries between the relevant ethnic, religious or linguistic communities.

Principles of *power sharing* and *consociation* operate at the level of an entire state, or within a region of a state. Lijphart (1977, quoted in McGarry & O'Leary 1993, 35) has provided four features for consociational democracies:

- a grand coalition government representing the main segments of the divided society;
- proportional representation, employment and expenditure rules apply throughout the public sector;
- community autonomy norms operate under which ethnic communities have self-government over those matters of most profound concern to them;
- constitutional vetoes for minorities.

As can be seen, the democratically acceptable methods of management either separate the domains of ethnolinguistic interest or demand consensus, which may easily lead to the Hobbesian thought that any solution is better than none. As a result, the solutions achieved might be economically ineffective, further deepening the schism between various linguistic interests. However, such policies provide conditions for language maintenance, with the space for developments controlled by the speakers themselves.

Linguistic human rights

States, which represent the nation-building interest, have obligations vis-à-vis their citizens and residents concerning languages. These obligations are firmly rooted in linguistic human rights, providing standards for the use and acquisition of both minority and national languages. These obligations also cover the issue of the common language. These rights may be found in domestic as well as international law.

In most cases, international law does not deal with languages directly but regards them as

1. markers of identity and dignity;
2. of persons belonging to a specific group;
3. expressed in various language functional domains.

This enables us to use three approaches in clarifying the concept of language rights. The most traditional one is based on the target groups, the second on human rights principles, and the third on the functional domains of language within society. There are three main threatened groups, groups which commonly represent linguistic characteristics different from their environments: linguistic minorities, aliens, and indigenous peoples. Usually they are politically and economically disadvantaged and subjected to acculturation pressures and social discrimination. Although international law recognizes collective rights, all the linguistic rights are attached to individuals. Thus persons belonging to these groups may enjoy these rights in community with other members of their group. The second approach (used largely by, for instance, de Varennes 1996), is based on universal human rights principles of non-discrimination, freedom of expression and minority protection.

According to Skutnabb-Kangas and Phillipson (1994, 71), linguistic human rights in education may be regarded as essentially covering two rights: the right to learn an official language in the country of residence, in its standard form and the right to learn and use one's mother tongue: "International human rights instruments regard linguistic human rights in relation to the mother tongue(s) as consisting of the right to identify with it/them, and to education and public services through the medium of it/them, whereas mother tongues are defined as 'the language(s) one has learned first and identifies with'".

The second distinction concerns whether these rights should be collective, that is, to be enjoyed by the minorities as groups, or individual, to be enjoyed by the individual member of the group (Lerner 1991). The main practical concern of those who stress individual rights at the cost of collective rights has to do with the implications for individuals upon whom duties will be imposed in the name of group rights that might be detrimental to their well-being.

Individual language rights include the right not to suffer undue interference and discrimination. According to Coulombe (1993), this means the right to speak any language at home and on the streets and to use it in private correspondence, to keep native names and surnames, to use it within one's cultural and religious institutions, including newspapers, radio stations and community centers, etc. However, the respect for individual rights does not serve to heal collective social disparities, as individual rights derive from the individual's personal capacity and appear to be insufficient to sustain vulnerable languages.

Collective language rights protect language group membership and its identity, based on an individual's membership in a given community. Coulombe (1993,146–148) distinguishes two kinds of collective language rights: the right to sustain one's language and the right to live in one's language. In the first case the State's duties might include public funding for minority language schools, governmental services in the minority language, or even affirmative action programs for the hiring of members of the linguistic minority in the public services. The second case would require that one's language be used and understood in a variety of everyday situations, both private and public. The distinction between these two seems to be at the level of the participation of the majority and the obligations of the State concerning minority maintenance. Most of the language rights have to be connected to territorially-based linguistic communities that are above a certain critical number, as they are not transportable. These communities themselves have to fulfill certain socioeconomic, demographic and linguistic conditions. The distinctive feature of a group right is that it does not take into account the respective sizes of the right-holder and duty-holder, for example of the majority and minority.

However, there is no right to the continued survival of a linguistic group, as there is no basis for preferring its vital interests to those of a comparable group. Instead, Réaume (1994, 30) suggests the right to linguistic security, based on two key processes. One is the socialization of children into the language through the child's extended family and kinship group and the public educational system (comparable to Fishman's (1991) intergenerational language transmission). The second is the range of contexts for use of the language, which must be sufficiently rich to sustain the complexity that contributes to future development (the issue of language domains). The right to linguistic security can be understood as the right to pursue the normal processes of language transmission and maintenance without interference. This would preclude any attempt to prohibit use of the language in the normal range of contexts or to prohibit the education of children of the group in the language. A collective right to linguistic security would impose duties on other groups not to use numerical superiority or political dominance to prohibit the use of a minority language. Where two or more languages share social structures, there is a threat that social institutions such as the public school system or governmental structures will be organized to suit majority practices exclusively (although such organization may by advertised as the common language policy with a purely instrumental goal). In order to avoid such an outcome, a fair compromise, based on the principles of minority protection, should be found.

Contemporary international law provides the space for introducing fair and acceptable solutions for the maintenance and management of minority languages only in the case of the goodwill of the state. However, most of the principles in international law are insufficient to require that. They either belong to soft law, are too implicit, or deal mostly with individual rights, and establish the ultimate limit to minority protection to the detriment of the majority language.

Conclusion

In the modern world the relationship between language and power is much more sophisticated than the traditional language-nation-state equation presumes. The choice of the common language, tied to substantial benefits, is crucial for the further distribution of power, dividing languages to be linked either to nation building or to minority protection. Nation building itself is often under pressure from the language spread of LWCs, especially when the language-spread model takes the place of the minority-protection model with power relations left intact.

The main focus remains, however, in the power relationship between nation building and minority protection, which is the main domain of linguistic human rights. Here, besides clarifying the rights attached to the common language of the State and minority languages, the collective aspect should be introduced explicitly, providing linguistic security for minorities. From here derives the need for a multiple language planning model that may cover language spread, nation building and minority protection within the same framework, with explicit links and constraints, based on linguistic human rights.

References

Buzan, Barry. "Societal security, state security and internationalisation." In Wæver et al., eds. (1993), 67–77.

Clark, Donald and Robert Williamson, eds. *Self-determination. International Perspectives.* Houndmills, Basingstoke, Hampshire and London: Macmillan, 1996.

Coulombe, Pierre A. "Language Rights, Individual and Communal." *Language Problems and Language Planning,* 17(2)(1993): 140–152.

Dua, Hans R., ed. *Language Planning and Political Theory. International Journal of the Sociology of Language* no. 118, 1996.

Fishman, Joshua A., ed. *Readings in the Sociology of Language.* The Hague, Paris: Mouton, 1968.

Fishman, Joshua A. *Reversing Language Shift. Theoretical and Empirical Foundations of Assistance to Threatened Languages.* Multilingual Matters 76. Clevedon, Philadelphia, Adelaide: Multilingual Matters, 1991.

Galtung, Johan. *The True Worlds. A Transnational Perspective.* New York: Free Press, 1980.

Kallen, Evelyn. "Ethnicity and Self-determination: A Paradigm." In Donald Clark and Robert Williamson, eds. (1996), 113–123.

Laitin, David D. "Language planning in the former Soviet Union: the case of Estonia." In Dua, ed. (1996), 43–62.

Léger, Sylvie, ed. *Linguistic Rights in Canada: Collusions or Collisions?* Proceedings of the First Conference. Ottawa: University of Ottawa, Canadian Centre for Linguistic Rights, 1994.

Lerner, Natan. *Group Rights and Discrimination in International Law.* Dordrecht: Martinus Nijhoff Publishers, 1991.

Lijphart, A. *Democracy in Plural Societies: A Comparative Exploration.* New Haven: Yale University Press, 1977.

Lo Bianco, J. *National Policy on Languages.* Canberra: Australian Government Publishing Service, 1987.

Lustick, Ian. "Stability in deeply divided societies: consociationalism versus control." *World Politics* 31 (1979): 325–344.

Maurais, Jacques. "Regional majority languages, language planning and linguistic rights." *International Journal of the Sociology of Language* 127 (1997): 135–160.

Mazrui, Alamin M. "Language policy and the foundations of democracy: an African perspective." In Dua, ed. (1996), 107–124.

McGarry, John and Brendan O'Leary. "Introduction: the macro-political regulation of ethnic conflict." In McGarry and O'Leary, eds. (1993), 1–40.

McGarry, John and Brendan O'Leary, eds. *The Politics of Ethnic Conflict Regulation. Case Studies of Protracted Ethnic Conflicts.* London, New York: Routledge, 1993.

Ozolins, Uldis. *The Politics of Language in Australia.* Melbourne: Cambridge University Press, 1993.

Phillipson, Robert, Mart Rannut, and Tove Skutnabb-Kangas. "Introduction." In Tove Skutnabb-Kangas and Robert Phillipson, eds. (1994), 1–22.

Réaume, Denise. "The right to linguistic security: reconciling individual and group claims." In Léger, ed. (1994), 23–42.

Skutnabb-Kangas, Tove. "Language and Self-determination." In Clark and Williamson, eds. (1996), 124–140.

Skutnabb-Kangas, Tove and Robert Phillipson. "Linguistic human rights, past and present." In Skutnabb-Kangas and Phillipson, eds. (1994), 71–110.

Skutnabb-Kangas, Tove and Robert Phillipson, eds. *Linguistic Human Rights: Overcoming linguistic discrimination*. Berlin, New York: Mouton de Gruyter, 1994.

Stewart, William A. "A Sociolinguistic Typology for Describing National Multilingualism." In Joshua A. Fishman, ed. (1968), 531–545.

Tomaševski, Katarina. "International prospects for the future of the welfare state." In *Reconceptualizing the welfare state*, 100–117. Copenhagen: The Danish Centre for Human Rights, 1996.

De Varennes, Fernand. *Language, Minorities and Human Rights*. The Hague, Boston, London: Martinus Nijhoff Publishers, 1996.

Wæver, Ole, Barry Buzan, Morten Kelstrup, and Pierre Lemaitre, eds. *Identity, Migration and the New Security Agenda in Europe*. London: Pinter Publishers, 1993.

LEGAL ISSUES

The Existing Rights of Minorities in International Law

FERNAND DE VARENNES

1. The Existing Rights of Minorities

> Does not the sun shine equally for the whole world? Do we not all
> equally breathe the air? Do you not feel shame at authorizing only
> three languages and condemning other people to blindness and
> deafness? Tell me, do you think that God is helpless and cannot
> bestow equality, or that he is envious and will not give it?
> (Constantine the Philosopher (Cyril), 9th Century A.D.[1])

There is not in the present state of international law[2] an unqualified "right to use a minority language", but there are a number of
existing rights and freedoms that affect the issue of language preferences and use by members of a minority or by the State.

The expression "existing rights of minorities" is used here in order to make a distinction between certain standards that are part
of international law, and those principles that are morally or politically desirable, but not legally required.

Moral or political principles, even if they are sometimes described as "human rights", are not necessarily part of international
law. They are things that governments "should" do, if they are
"nice", not something they "must" do. Being nice is not a very con-
vincing argument and is less persuasive than rights and freedoms
that have the weight of the law behind them.

Furthermore, there appears to be a belief, especially here in
Europe, that only citizens who are members of national minorities
are entitled to have their language used by the state if it is a non-
official language. This is often based on the mistaken view that
anything to do with language is a collective right, so therefore only
certain "collective" groups, in particular national minorities, can
claim it. What the following paper will attempt to demonstrate is
that many different aspects of the use of language are already pro-

tected under international law, that these aspects involve individual rather than collective rights, and that they are not dependent on whether individuals are citizens or members of a national minority.

2. The Private Use of a Minority Language

It is essential to make one early fundamental point very clear: state conduct which prevents or controls the use of a language in private activities—be it the language of individuals belonging to a minority or belonging to a majority—can be in breach of a number of rights in international law. Some of these rights may be well established, while others are increasingly recognized in bilateral and multilateral treaties and other documents. All of the existing rights in international law are individual rights and freedoms, although their manifestation may involve more than one individual.

Among existing international human rights in the private sphere are the right to private and family life, the right to freedom of expression, and non-discrimination or the right of persons belonging to a linguistic minority to use their language with other members of their group. How these various rights actually operate in different areas of daily life are described briefly in the following sections.

2.1 To Speak or Write a Language
2.1.1 Use in Private or Public

To forbid family members to use a language among themselves would be in breach of the right to private and family life, as well as the right to freedom of expression. If a government, by legislation or other means, tried to do this in the case of individuals belonging to a linguistic minority, this would in addition be a violation of Article 27 of the International Covenant on Civil and Political Rights, and would in all probability be discriminatory.[3]

There are provisions in both the European Charter for Regional or Minority Languages and the European Convention on the Rights of National Minorities which refer to this first example as a right of "national minorities", but what these two latter treaties do is simply repeat what is already protected in international law—and available to all individuals—and emphasize that individuals who belong to a national minority also enjoy this protection. It is once again critical to remember that even individuals who are not citizens, and who therefore cannot be part of a "national minority", are still entitled to the same human rights in international law, even if this is not precisely referred to in the European instruments previously mentioned.

Another relevant example, especially in the European context, is where a government authority bans the private use of a minority language in public areas (such as banning individuals from having a private conversation in their own language in public streets, or banning the use of a particular language in a public park, etc.). Such attempts are breaches of the right to freedom of expression; they would in all likelihood be a form of discrimination based on language, and would certainly be contrary to Article 27 of the International Covenant on Civil and Political Rights if they restrict the use of a minority language by individuals who are members of such a minority. While in Europe there is a tendency to associate these examples with the rights of members of a national minority, these rights are not restricted to that group. In international law, whether one is a citizen or not does not matter: legally, such restrictive measures by a public authority are generally forbidden.

2.1.2 The Right to Correspond and Communicate

A state cannot forbid individuals to use a minority language in private correspondence or communications (including private business or commercial correspondence by telephone, electronic means, etc.). Such an attempt would clearly be a breach of a variety of rights in international law, including freedom of expression, and the right to private life. It would probably also be in breach of non-discrimination, and the right of individuals to use their own language with other members of their group in the case of a linguistic minority. Certain limitations are, of course, permitted, depending on the nature of the right or freedom involved. For example, some restrictions are permitted to the right to freedom of expression where these are considered necessary for purposes of public health or morality. However, in a general sense none of the permissible limitations under international law would allow for a blanket prohibition on the private use of a particular language for correspondence or communication, and this is particularly true in the case of a minority language.[4]

2.1.3 Cultural and Musical Expression

A prohibition making it illegal to play any song, or to stage theater presentations, operas, etc., either in private or in public, in a particular language would similarly clearly be in violation of rights that already exist in international law, such as freedom of expression, and non-discrimination based on language. It would also be contrary to Article 27 of the International Covenant on Civil and Political Rights if the prohibition prevented individuals belonging to a linguistic minority from enjoying their language or culture with other members of their group. This right is also set out explicitly in a number of instruments.[5]

2.2 Names and Toponymy in a Minority of Non-Official Language
2.2.1 The Name or Surname of Individuals

The right of individuals to use their own names is clearly recognized in international law as part of the right to private and family life,[6] and it is similarly part of the rights of ethnic and linguistic minorities included under Article 27 of the International Covenant on Civil and Political Rights. It is also contained in an increasing number of international and regional treaties and other documents dealing either with national minorities, linguistic minorities or ethnic minorities.[7] A state cannot prevent an individual from having a name or surname which is not in an official language or which does not feature in a prescribed list. Names and surnames constitute a means of identifying persons within their families and the community, and as such are an inseparable part of private and family life. When Bulgaria banned Turkish names a few years ago, or when Slovakia tried to impose certain names or surnames on individuals of Hungarian background, their actions were in breach of international law, although this was not necessarily clearly understood by many until after 1991 when both the United Nations Human Rights Committee and the European Court of Human Rights handed down decisions in this area. This is not a new collective right only available to certain groups, but an individual, fundamental human right that is already part of international law.

However, the right to private and family life does not mean that a state is obliged to register an individual's preferred name or surname officially. As long as individuals are not prevented by the state from using their preferred names or surnames privately, there may not be a violation of the above rights.[8] Nevertheless, state conduct of this type could be deemed as discrimination, as will be pointed out in section 3.

2.2.2 Designations of Localities and Topography

The private use of topographical names in any language cannot be prohibited by a state. This would constitute a violation of freedom of expression, and possibly of Article 27 of the International Covenant on Civil and Political Rights if it prevents individuals who belong to a linguistic minority from using topographical names in their own language when communicating with other members of their group. A number of treaties and other international or regional documents directly mention such a right.[9]

While a government cannot ban the private use of topographical terms or place-names in a non-official language, and particularly a minority language, this does not mean the state itself must officially recognize or use these names or designations. The issue of official toponymy is considered in the next section, since the refusal of a state to recognize or use designations in certain languages may give rise to discriminatory treatment.

2.3 Displays in a Minority Language (or Script)
2.3.1 Public Displays on Private Posters, Commercial Signs, etc.

Under international law, freedom of expression includes the right to linguistic expression. Members of linguistic minorities (as well as all other individuals) have the right to use their language of choice in private activities involving "expression". This includes the use of outdoor commercial signs and posters[10] and applies to the language used in the private display of signs, posters, or other notices of a commercial, cultural or even political nature. International law recognizes that public authorities may require that an official language be used in addition to a non-official language, but probably only up to a point.[11]

In addition to this interpretation in international law, a number of documents also make direct reference to this right.[12]

2.3.2 Private Use of Minority Script on Posters, Commercial Signs, etc.

Since language is a constituent part of freedom of expression, the private use of a particular script, including the script of minorities

(Cyrillic, Greek, Latin, etc.) is protected under international law. A particular script is a component of a language, although relatively few documents actually refer to this.[13] This right is available with respect to all activities in the private sphere, whether or not they involve individuals who are members of a national minority.

2.4 The Media and Telecommunications

2.4.1 The Media and Publication

Media and publication activities fall squarely within the realm of freedom of expression guaranteed under international law. Such activities are also likely to be protected under Article 27 of the International Covenant on Civil and Political Rights and similar provisions in the case of minorities generally. Members of a minority cannot be prevented from publishing privately in their own language, unless it is for reasons permitted under the International Covenant on Civil and Political Rights.

It is important to point out that under the present development of international law a state is not obligated to provide any financial assistance or resources to make publishing in a minority language possible. However, if states do provide financial or material assistance for private publication activities, members of a minority should also be entitled to such assistance in conformity with the right to equality and non-discrimination under international law.

Further specific recognition of this right is found in a fairly large number of treaties and other documents.[14]

2.4.2 Private Broadcasting

There are strong guarantees in international law against prohibitions on the use of a minority language (and other languages) in private media broadcasting such as television and radio. A state which attempts to prevent the use of a particular language in private broadcasting would clearly be in breach of the right to freedom of expression. Such a restriction would, in all likelihood, also constitute a form of discrimination based on language, and may very well also be contrary to Article 27 of the International Covenant on Civil and Political Rights and similar provisions in international treaties and documents in the case of linguistic minorities.[15] However, since these are private activities, a state cannot be forced to provide resources in order to make private broadcasting possible in all the languages used on its territory. Nevertheless, if the government does provide financial support for private broadcasting activities it must do so in a non-discriminatory way, and provide a reasonable proportion of such funding to private broadcasting in minority and non-official languages.

2.4.3 State Licensing and Allocation of Frequencies

The distribution of radio and television frequencies by the state to private parties, and decisions linked to broadcasting licensing are also issues that concern minorities in Europe and elsewhere. If a state refuses to license or to grant frequencies to private media such as radio and television stations which use the language of a minority, or if it makes such licenses or frequencies very difficult to obtain, this could constitute a form of discrimination by public authorities which is prohibited in international law as explained in section 3.

Broadcasting frequencies are not part of the private realm, which means that public authorities are not legally obliged to grant a private broadcasting frequency every time it is demanded by a minority under international standards such as Article 27.

However, the European Court of Human Rights in *Informationverein Lentia and Others v. Austria*[16] pointed out that when exercising their regulatory powers by allocating radio broadcasting frequencies public authorities had to observe their obligations under international legal instruments, which include Article 27 or similar provisions. Thus, a state must take into consideration a minority's right to communicate with its members in their own language, via the airwaves.

In a state where the public authorities favor the majority or official language exclusively, the linguistic and cultural needs of speakers of a minority language are qualitatively and quantitatively disregarded. Such a policy could be a form of discrimination, and is probably a violation of Article 27 of the International Covenant on Civil and Political Rights if linguistic minorities find themselves unreasonably excluded or disadvantaged in terms of operating private stations using their own language.

When the number of speakers of a minority language is fairly large in a geographic area, to refuse a private radio or television license for the broadcasting of services in the minority's language would appear unreasonable and therefore discriminatory since it denies them a benefit or advantage that is available to others: that is, the benefit of radio or television programs in their own language. Because this right is a right to non-discrimination, it is not of decisive importance whether the speakers of a minority language are citizens or not. If there are 600,000 Hungarian speakers in southern Slovakia, or thirteen million speakers of Kurdish in eastern Turkey, whether or not they are citizens should not substantially affect the need to provide for some use of their language. When they are sufficiently numerous and territorially concentrated it would be unreasonable, and therefore discriminatory, for the government to refuse completely to give them the benefit of programs in their own language.

The point is essential and should therefore be repeated: non-discrimination does not imply that there may be no privileged use or recognition of the language of members of a national minority, or, for that matter, of the official language. What is implied by the right of non-discrimination based on language is that while it is quite legitimate to privilege the official language or a national minority language, there are situations where the end does not justify the means. It would be unreasonable not to use other languages under certain conditions and where appropriate, if the number of speakers of such a language is high enough, and if the disadvantages these speakers would face or the particular benefits they would be denied should the language not be used are sufficiently serious.

2.5 Private Educational Activities and Minority Languages
2.5.1 The Right to Create and Operate Private Educational Facilities

Individuals who belong to linguistic, religious or ethnic minorities historically have a long recognized right under international law to create and operate their own educational facilities.[17] This includes the right to use a minority language as medium of instruction.

This right is not absolute: states may still require that all minority students learn the official language up to a reasonable level of fluency.[18] States may also impose "non-linguistic" standards as to the quality of instruction. While states are obliged to recognize officially the validity of education received in these institutions (diploma, university admission, etc.) as long as educational quality standards are met, there is no general obligation to provide financial or other support for such institutions. If states do provide financial or material assistance to private schools, similar support must be made available to minority educational facilities in a non-discriminatory manner.[19]

2.6 Minority Languages and Religious Activities
2.6.1 Worship, Religious Practices or Observance

A prohibition by the state on the use of a minority language during religious worship or other religious practices would be in breach of the right to freedom of expression; it would constitute a form of discrimination, and be inconsistent with international obligations under Article 27 of the International Covenant on Civil and Political Rights and similar provisions.[20]

2.6.2 Marriage and Other Civil Rites

When a particular religious ceremony also involves an official act—as is the case in marriage rites—a state cannot prevent the use of the language of a minority during the private part of the ceremony. To do so would constitute a breach of the right to freedom of expression, and would possibly be a breach of the right to private and family life. In the case of a linguistic minority generally, it would, in all likelihood, also involve a denial of the right of individuals to use their own language with other members of their group.

Although the issue has never been considered at the international level, the state may require that the "official" part of the "private" marriage rites—if it involves a minister, priest, official or rabbi exercising state authority—be in an official language in addition to, but not excluding, the minority language.

2.7 The Use of a Minority Language in Private Economic Activities
2.7.1 The Language of Work and Operations in Economic Activities

As in other private activities, a state cannot prevent an individual or corporate entity from using their preferred language in the economic field. This means that private persons and institutions cannot be stopped from using a minority language in private business relationships.

It is clear that to have legislation or restrictions that exclude the use of a minority language or any other language between an employer and his or her employees, between a small-business owner and a client, or on the advertisements or posters put up in connection with private commercial activities would be a violation of the right to freedom of expression as it is currently understood in international law.[21]

A state may nevertheless require that another language in addition to a minority language be used in private commercial activities in some cases. If a state has adopted measures requiring the use of an official language while not excluding the use of the minority language, then both languages may be used and there would generally be no breach of the right to freedom of expression in such business activities.[22]

There are, however, certain situations in which the requirement to use an official language in conjunction with the preferred language of a minority in private economic activities may be prohibited under international law. For example, the requirement that all the employees of a private business be able to speak the official language perfectly would, in all likelihood, be an unreasonable demand and therefore discriminatory.[23]

2.8 Minority Languages and Private Organizations

2.8.1 Use within Private Groups or Organizations

Any attempt to prevent the use of a minority language in the activities of private groups or organizations such as cultural societies, minority associations, etc., would constitute a breach of the right to freedom of expression under international law.

A state may, nevertheless, require that a private group or organization keep its financial records and other types of documentation in an official language, but it may not prevent the group or organization from also keeping these same documents in their own language. This attempt to prevent the use of a minority language would not only be a breach of the right to freedom of expression, it would probably also be a form of discrimination and, in the case of a linguistic minority, probably a violation of Article 27 of the International Covenant on Civil and Political Rights, as would also be any attempt by the state to prohibit the use of a minority language during the meetings or other activities of private groups or organizations

2.8.2 Use by Political Associations or Parties

Political parties or associations are not part of the administrative structure of the state and may not therefore be prevented from using a minority language, even during elections. Their activities are therefore part of the private domain, even if heavily regulated by the state. A prohibition on the use of a minority language would be contrary to the right to freedom of expression, Article 27 of the International Covenant on Civil and Political Rights, as well as being in all probability discriminatory.

Any use by the public authorities of a minority language (such as the registration of a political party or association, the broadcasting of political messages on state-controlled media, etc.) falls outside of the private domain. These issues mainly involve whether or not a particular restriction or requirement is discriminatory, rather than problems of freedom of expression or Article 27.

3. The Use of a Minority Language by the Public Authorities

There is a growing legal acceptance in treaties that states have a positive obligation to provide public services, benefits and privileges in the language of a specific minority in appropriate circumstances—especially where the numbers and concentration of the speakers of a minority language and the state's resources make this a viable option.

Some caution should, however, be taken. There is a fundamental rift between legal experts who believe that the use of a minority language by public authorities is already well established in international law since it derives mainly from the application of non-discrimination with respect to language, and other experts who, on the contrary, emphasize that such a "right" is an emerging standard which has just begun to appear in legal instruments. Furthermore, there are those who claim that only members of national minorities are entitled to such a right.[24]

The debate is an important one for minorities since it signals the difference between whether a government *must*, in appropriate circumstances, respond to the needs of a minority, or if instead it only *should*. If the former view is correct, it implies that minorities may legally claim the fundamental human right under international law to obtain from public authorities some degree of use of their language as may be appropriate in the circumstances. However, if the latter position is correct, minorities have "weaker" guarantees since only a small number of states have signed legally binding treaties (such as the Framework Convention on the Rights of National Minorities and the European Charter for Regional or Minority Languages). In the case of the European Charter for Regional or Minority Languages, not only are rights restricted to national minorities, they are also restricted to those minorities and areas "selected" by the state, which can also decide to exclude from the application of the charter any minority deemed not worthy of these rights. The Framework Convention on the Rights of National Minorities also limits its application to national minorities, although not with the same "political exclusion" option as the charter.

In terms of what is recognized by international law, there are a few areas where there is wide consensus. Public authorities clearly have, for example, a legal obligation to use or accommodate a minority language in order to communicate information to an individual facing criminal charges in a language he or she understands. In this situation it is clear that public authorities *must* use a minority language.

It is also crucial to remember that non-discrimination, as it is referred to here, is deemed to be applicable to all areas of state involvement and conduct. Under many international treaties and human rights documents, including Article 26 of the International Covenant on Civil and Political Rights, the prohibition of discrimination with respect to language, etc. is a provision applicable to any conduct or legislation by public authorities, and not one specifically limited to other human rights or freedoms as is the case with the European Convention for the Protection of Human Rights and Fundamental Freedoms. The consequences of this distinction can be far reaching for minorities: under the European Convention non-discrimination with respect to language only applies when dealing with a limited number of rights, and not at all in the case of naturalization under the new European Convention on Nationality, while under the International Covenant on Civil and Political Rights non-discrimination based on language applies to every type of state service, preference, benefit, or restriction, including the rules and procedures used to determine who can become a citizen and, indirectly, a member of a national minority.

3.1 Use by Administrative and Public Authorities in General

Where public authorities at the national, regional or local levels deal with a sufficiently large number of individuals who use a particular language, the authorities must provide an appropriate level of service in this language.

For example, in the case of local districts in which minorities are concentrated, local authorities should generally provide for an increasing number of services in the minority language as the number of speakers of that language increases. Beginning at the lower end of what we will call a sliding-scale model, and moving progressively to the higher end, this would imply, for example:

1. making available widely used official documents and forms for use by the population in the non-official or minority language or in bilingual versions;
2. the acceptance by the authorities of oral or written applications in the non-official or minority language and the provision of responses in that language;
3. having a sufficient number of officers who are in contact with the public and able to respond to the use of the non-official or minority language;
4. being able to use the non-official or minority language as an internal and daily language in the work of the public authorities.

Not to provide reasonable responses, that is, responses on a sliding-scale, wherever the number and concentration of speakers of a particular language merit, could be a form of discrimination with respect to language. Individuals who are generally less fluent in the official state language than native users of the language favored by public authorities would experience disadvantages, or would be denied benefits or privileges enjoyed by others simply on the basis of their language. In some situations, especially where it is relatively simple for public authorities to accommodate, to some degree, the language of a large minority, not to use the minority language in a way which would be "appropriate" in the circumstances could be deemed to be unreasonable or arbitrary in light of the subsequent disadvantages faced by members of the minority, and could therefore be seen as discriminatory.

There is an increasing degree of legal and political support for this interpretation. Recent treaties and international instruments often embody this sliding-scale concept as a proper response to the use of the language of minorities, and especially national minorities, by public authorities. The Central European Initiative Instrument for the Protection of Minority Rights (Article 13: "whenever in an area the number of persons ... reaches ... a significant level"), the Framework Convention for the Protection of National Minorities (Article 10: "In areas inhabited by persons belonging to national minorities traditionally or in substantial numbers, if those persons so request and where such a request corresponds to a real need, the Parties shall endeavor to ensure, as far as possible..."), and the European Charter for Minority or Regional Languages (Article 10: "within the administrative districts ... in which the number of residents...justifies the measures specified below and according to the situation of each language"), to name but a few, all recognize that there is a gradation that must be respected as to the degree to which public authorities must use a minority language. If there are certain services to which all individuals are entitled, whether or not they are citizens, then under international law there is a legal obligation to ensure that there is no discrimination based on language.

Finally, it should be pointed out that the expression "administrative or public authorities" refers to all areas of state involvement, including the judiciary, public education, naturalization and, where applicable, public broadcasting and media control. In every area of direct or delegated state activity human rights issues may arise if the state shows a linguistic preference or imposes linguistic restrictions. The next sections deal with those areas of language use by public authorities which are of particular relevance for many minorities in Europe and elsewhere.

3.2 Public Education and Minority or Non-Official Languages
3.2.1 Use as Medium of Instruction

Where a sufficient number of students of a linguistic minority (and in some parts of the world the linguistic majority) are concentrated territorially, it would be unreasonable—and in all likelihood a breach of the right to non-discrimination—for a state not to provide an appropriate degree of use of the minority language as medium of instruction in public schools. If non-citizens are entitled to be educated in public schools, then non-discrimination with respect to language must also be applied to them.

The degree of use of a minority language required by non-discrimination will vary according to what is "reasonable", "appropriate", or "practical" in each situation: the extent of the demand for such instruction, the level of use of the minority language as medium of instruction, the state's ability to respond to these demands, etc. This follows the same sliding-scale model as described earlier and is an approach confirmed in an increasing number of "minority" provisions found in treaties and international instruments.

A state which only allows the exclusive use of an official language in public education may be acting in a discriminatory way if the disadvantages suffered by certain individuals—such as members of a linguistic minority—as compared to the advantages enjoyed by others, is deemed unreasonable given the particular context.[25]

To give a few examples from European practices, Serbian-only education in the Kosovo (Kosova in Albanian) public schools and university system would be a form of discrimination with respect to language under international law in the case of the Albanian-speaking minority, regardless of whether the situation involves a national minority. Since they make up about 90 percent of the total population of Kosovo, it would be unreasonable not to provide instruction in Albanian in these educational institutions. When Estonia eliminates all public school use of Russian as a medium of instruction in about five years time, this will also likely be a case of discrimination with respect to language, once again independent of whether the Russian-speaking inhabitants of Estonia are a national minority, because making up as they do more than 35 percent of the population of the country as a whole, it is unreasonable to prevent the use of the Russian language as a medium of instruction in public schools.

Although the Russian minority in Estonia will still have access to instruction in their own language in private schools supported financially by the government, most international documents dealing with the issue refer to the need for such instruction in public schools where numbers are sufficient.[26] In terms of non-discrimination and international law, Russian-speaking pupils are, in fact, treated differently from those who choose to be educated in Estonian, since they are not allowed to pursue their education in public schools in their mother tongue. Although, admittedly, there must be proof that the pupils are actually disadvantaged to a sufficient degree for the Estonian measures to constitute a form of discrimination, these disadvantages may be demonstrated by the fact that funding for Russian private schools is not at the same level as in public schools, or by other difficulties which may arise for those minority pupils who graduate from private schools rather than public schools.[27]

Just as importantly, a large number of international legal and political documents further acknowledge that public education in a minority language must not exclude the teaching of the majority language. Members of a linguistic minority must be able to learn the official language to a reasonable degree of fluency. The absence of such instruction would represent the creation of "linguistic ghettos", or would exclude minorities from employment or educational opportunities—which would in turn constitute a discriminatory policy under existing international human rights.

3.2.2 Teaching a Minority Language in Public Schools

Where members of a minority are concentrated, but their numbers are not sufficient to make it necessary or possible to use their language as the medium of instruction in public schools, they must, at the very least, be taught their own language if this is practical. This is also widely recognized in many treaties and documents.[28]

3.3 The Judicial System and Proceedings
3.3.1 Judicial Authorities

The language used during court proceedings and by court officials is also an issue of state-endorsed "disadvantages" affecting individuals who are not as fluent as native speakers of the official language. In some situations, because of the severity of this disadvantage, it may be discriminatory not to provide for some appropriate degree of use of the minority language by judges and other court officials. Once again, what this implies is the application of a sliding-scale model which takes into account these disadvantages and the state's resources and ability to respond in a reasonable way.

A number of treaties and non-legal documents recognize the need to use a minority language to an appropriate level in the judicial system. For example, one of the more detailed treaty provisions that applies a sliding-scale model to this area is Article 9 of the European Charter for Minority or Regional Languages. The treaty describes the need to increase the use of a minority language in criminal, civil and administrative tribunal proceedings where "the number of residents justifies the measures". It then goes on to describe in detail how this can be achieved in criminal, civil and administrative proceedings.

3.3. The Right to an Interpreter in Criminal Proceedings

The right to an interpreter is universally recognized in international law and is found in most treaties dealing with human rights. Any person accused, including persons belonging to linguistic minorities, whether they are citizens or not, has the right to an interpreter in criminal cases for the translation of the proceedings, including court documents, if he or she does not understand the language used in the criminal proceedings. A number of international decisions confirm this right and give some indication of its scope and limitations.[29]

This right does not depend on "practical" considerations, such as the number of speakers of a minority language or their territorial concentration in a state. It is an absolute right which may not be set aside once it has been shown that the accused person does not understand the language of the proceedings.

3.3.3 The Right to be Informed Promptly in a Language one Understands

This is another universally recognized right in international law contained in a large number of international treaties. The European Court of Human Rights has also had the opportunity to address the extent of the right to be informed promptly of the nature and cause of a criminal accusation.[30] This is a "linguistic" right available to anyone, citizen and non-citizen alike, regardless of any membership of a minority group. Public authorities must, in this situation, use the language of the person involved, which is generally a minority language. This right is limited to situations where an individual does not understand the language used by state officials in criminal charges.

3.3.4 The Use of Minority Languages during Civil Ceremonies

In the case of civil ceremonies (such as marriage) conducted by public officials exercising state authority, a minority may only claim the right to use its own language in the event that they are territorially concentrated and sufficiently numerous to make it unreasonable for the state not to respond to their preference. This is an example of the application of the right to non-discrimination in language matters. It is also recognized under the sliding-scale model in treaties and other documents which provide for the use of a minority language by administrative authorities in public services where minorities are concentrated in sufficient numbers.[31]

3.4 The Official Use of Names and Toponymy
3.4.1 State Refusal to Register or Recognize Names/Surnames in a Minority Language

As outlined earlier, a state which prohibits the private use of a person's name or surname in a minority language is in breach of the right to private and family life as recognized in international law. However, the right to private and family life does not oblige public authorities to use or officially recognize an individual's name or surname in a minority language.

Such a refusal may, however, be a discriminatory practice if it is deemed to be unreasonable. Since some individuals are denied certain benefits or privileges enjoyed by others (the benefit or privilege of having their name recognized and used by public authorities in their own language), there is a distinction with respect to language that could be argued to be unreasonable and therefore discriminatory. In fact, there are few arguments to support a policy where public authorities refuse to recognize or use an individual's name or surname because it is in a minority language.[32]

3.4.2 Official Toponymy

Another existing right in international law requires that public authorities use place-names in a minority language, if necessary in conjunction with the official language, where "the number of users ... justifies" such a measure. Once again, this can be seen as the state having to adopt a non-discriminatory practice in terms of language preferences.

This is, once again, a recognition that it is "reasonable" for states to accommodate the language of minorities where they are territorially concentrated in sufficient numbers.[33]

3.5 The Public Media and Minority Languages
3.5.1 Public Media and Publications

Like any other type of state service, benefit or activity, the involvement of the state in the public media must conform to the requirements of non-discrimination. Public authorities must adopt a sliding-scale model: if the state controls, operates or finances any media, they must do so in a non-discriminatory fashion and generally reflect–in the time and resources allocated–the relative demographic importance of minorities.

This view of non-discrimination, as well as the provisions of some human rights treaties and political commitments contained in a variety of other documents, suggest that an appropriate and reasonable policy by public authorities involves the sliding-scale model, based on the numerical importance of the speakers of a minority language, their location and geographic concentration, etc.

If the state is actively involved in newspaper publication, it should likewise devote a fair proportion of resources and/or space for the use of minority languages in the event that its population comprises sufficiently large linguistic minorities.

3.6 Political Representation, Minority Languages and the Electoral Process

> Community of language and culture ... does not necessarily give rise to political unity, any more than linguistic and cultural dissimilarity prevents political unity.[34]

3.6.1 Exclusion from Elected Positions and Language Requirements

The electoral process supervised and conducted under the auspices of the state is part of the "public" sphere. Attempts by minorities and others to obtain the right to use their language in this area by claiming that a state is obliged to respect their right to freedom of expression have therefore unavoidably failed when they have been raised at the international level or under the European Convention for the Protection of Human Rights and Fundamental Freedoms.[35]

There are, however, other fundamental human rights that have an important impact on the electoral process for minorities. For example, a law or other state measure which excludes individuals from being candidates or from holding an elected public position because they do not speak the official language may be in breach of international law. It may constitute an unreasonable, and therefore discriminatory, restriction. In this way, members of minorities who would be excluded from running for or occupying an elected office could argue that the state is acting in breach of a fundamental human right in international law.

In light of the importance of a free and democratic process open to all citizens, the exclusion of individuals, who may be members of a minority, because of the linguistic preferences of public authorities is such a serious consequence that it is more than likely contrary to non-discrimination with respect to language in international law.

3.6.2 Denial of the Right of Minorities to Vote

The denial of the right to vote simply because of insufficient fluency in the official or other prescribed language would almost
certainly constitute a violation of non-discrimination with respect
to language in international law, since it excludes individuals who
are only or mainly fluent in a minority language–or other languages–from the right to vote or benefits to be gained by voting
because of a language distinction.[36]

3.6.3 Party Registration and Administrative Use of Minority Languages during Elections

As pointed out in a number of European decisions, neither freedom of expression (nor the limited non-discrimination provision
of the European Convention) guarantees a right to use a minority
language in official state activities connected to the electoral process. In the case of the registration of a political party, the European
Court of Human Rights has indicated there is no unqualified obligation for public authorities to accept such a document.[37]

However, under a general non-discrimination provision contained in Article 26 of the International Covenant on Civil and Political Rights and other documents, this type of function is an example of an administrative activity by public authorities. When
dealing with a numerically important or territorially concentrated
minority, it could be described as unreasonable for public authorities not to use the appropriate minority language to some degree.
This means that under the sliding-scale model of what is
"reasonable" or "appropriate", public authorities would have to use
the minority language for the registration of documents and in
other aspects of the electoral process as may be required in consideration of what is non-discriminatory.

3.6.4 The Use of Minority Languages within Elected Bodies

An elected parliament, assembly, chamber or municipal government
may have a number of restrictions concerning the use of languages
for official deliberations. Even within these political institutions,
there are certain minority rights which are recognized in
international law and which have a significant effect on what the
state may or may not impose in terms of language preferences.

Under general non-discrimination guarantees such as Article 26 of the International Covenant on Civil and Political Rights and other similar provisions, to ban an elected politician from using a minority language during meetings or sessions of Parliament or the National Assembly, or at other levels of government, such as municipal councils, could be discriminatory.

For example, to prohibit or prevent the use of Hungarian during sessions of a municipal council (either by an elected politician or a member of the public) in Vojvodina would be unreasonable because a significant proportion of the population of this municipality are members of a linguistic minority. According to the sliding-scale model discussed previously, it would be a form of discrimination not to respond to the exclusion of, or disadvantages imposed on, individuals who are members of the Hungarian minority, whether that minority is classified as a national minority or not. The use of the Hungarian language in places like Vojvodina, of the Russian language in cities like Narva, and of the Albanian language in parts of Macedonia, must be accommodated because it is reasonable for municipalities to use these languages given the concentration of individuals using the languages. This does not mean that the state must use all of the languages of every minority, or in every situation, as the European Court of Human Rights has previously shown.[38] It is only obliged to use a language to the extent to which it is appropriate given the number of speakers and the particular type of state function concerned.

Especially in view of the fundamental role and prominence of political activities in a democratic setting, it would seem that in international law—and this tends to be confirmed in other international documents—political institutions must be very flexible in taking measures to permit the use of a minority language in order to ensure the effective participation of minorities in public affairs.[39]

3.7 Naturalization, Language and Minorities

America is a political union—not a cultural, linguistic, religious, or racial union ... Of course, we as individuals would urge all to learn English for that is the language used by most Americans as well as the language of the marketplace. But, we should no more demand English-language skills for citizenship than we should demand uniformity of religion. That a person wants to become a citizen and will make a good citizen is more than enough.

(Honourable Cruz Reynoso[40])

As with any other state activity, once a government decides to "act" or to provide an "advantage" or "privilege," it must do so in a non-discriminatory way. In other words, once a government decides to grant citizenship to individuals through a naturalization process or any other procedure, it must abide by human rights principles that are widely recognized in international law. Though citizenship is clearly a prerogative of the state in the sense that the state is not obligated to grant it to anyone, once it has initiated a naturalization process it must respect the human right to equality and non-discrimination in its policies. Furthermore, by denying citizenship to large numbers of individuals, some states have been able to deny to large proportions of their inhabitants a variety of rights and privileges.

It is possible for a state to prevent individual members of a minority from being naturalized, or to make the naturalization process more difficult for them, by using an official or prescribed language requirement, despite claims to the contrary.[41] Members of a minority who are less fluent, or not fluent at all, in the official language may not be able to surmount the disadvantages imposed by the naturalization regulations in order to become citizens.

As confirmed in at least one important international decision,[42] it is possible to have linguistic naturalization requirements that are "unreasonable", and therefore discriminatory in international law if these requirements are unconnected to "the specific conditions of the society in which the people live".

One thing should be made clear: a naturalization policy which shows a marked preference for the official language is not contrary to non-discrimination under Article 26 of the International Covenant on Civil and Political Rights. However, if a substantial percentage of the state's inhabitants belong to a linguistic minority, those areas of the naturalization regulations which only take account of one language for the purposes of obtaining citizenship could appear to "operate in a vacuum", and thus be seen as unreasonable, if they do not take into account the social, historical and demographic realities of the state.

Naturalization policies that only permit those who are fluent in the official language to acquire citizenship could well be discriminatory if, for example, 30 or 40 percent of the state's population all speak another language. While that part of the naturalization legislation that "favors" the official language would be valid, for the purposes of naturalization a language spoken by a substantial part of the population of the country would also have to be given recognition in some way.

An example of a non-discriminatory naturalization policy in the above case would be where citizenship could be obtained by having a sufficient knowledge of either the official language or of the minority language used by a substantial proportion of the population. An "official language only" policy in such a situation would be too restrictive and unreasonable, as the Inter-American Court on Human Rights suggested could occur in the *Costa Rica Naturalization Case*.[43]

In this regard, the new European Convention on Nationality is not helpful. For the first time since the adoption of the Universal Declaration of Human Rights, a major international treaty has completely ignored language use and other areas of potential discrimination. Despite the Inter-American Court clearly stating that it is possible to have naturalization regulations that are discriminatory on the basis of language, it appears that within the Council of Europe political considerations were powerful enough to "castrate" one of the most fundamental human rights recognized in international law.

On a number of occasions the United Nations Human Rights Committee has commented—when considering state reports—that it considers any removal of recognized grounds for non-discrimination as highly suspect. It would thus appear that Article 5(1) of the European Convention on Nationality, by excluding language use and other grounds for non-discrimination, would be "highly suspect" and may actually be inconsistent with the Universal Declaration on Human Rights and Article 26 of the International Covenant on Civil and Political Rights.

To those who have traditionally viewed the Council of Europe as an inspiration for, and strong supporter of, universal human rights, the European Convention on Nationality constitutes an alarming step backward. At the risk of being repetitive, almost every major treaty since the Second World War contains a non-discrimination provision which repeats faithfully the grounds for non-discrimination enumerated in the Universal Declaration on Human Rights. Non-discrimination on the grounds of language in particular is always recognized in international treaties, and is often included in the constitutions of countries that prohibit discrimination. The refusal to include it in the European Convention on Nationality is therefore quite alarming, not to say inexcusable, since it may encourage states to adopt restrictions which, while not contrary to European law, would be contrary to international human rights as contained in the Universal Declaration on Human Rights and the International Covenant on Civil and Political Rights.

As an example which is not beyond the realms of possibility, the government of Yugoslavia could adopt naturalization legislation indicating that those born in the country may not automatically become citizens, even if their parents are both citizens, until and unless they have acquired a perfect command of the official language, written and spoken, or at least a very high standard in that language. Many individuals born after the adoption of this type of legislation and belonging to long established minorities like the Hungarians in Slovakia, the Roma in Bulgaria, or the Albanians in Yugoslavia, might not be able to satisfy such a requirement unless their parents had made the decision to abandon their language and culture completely in order to make sure that their children could become citizens.[44]

Such a scenario is not contrary to the European Convention on Nationality, because non-discrimination based on language is not prohibited in the Convention. Even though this means that many children run the risk of not having citizenship in any country, it is still allowed by the European Convention on Nationality which contains no provision disallowing naturalization laws that may result in situations of statelessness. Article 4 of the European Convention on Nationality only goes so far as to say that the naturalization laws of states must "be based on principles" such as granting every person the right to a nationality and avoiding situations of statelessness. To adopt rules based on a series of principles, legally speaking, does not mean that a state is obliged to grant citizenship to those who would otherwise be without nationality. In just the same way, millions of Chinese residents of Hong Kong discovered, before the territory was handed back to China, that they had never been full citizens of the United Kingdom, nor even of China before 1997. Their position was not in violation of international law, and similar situations could occur in some European countries with new regulations establishing a difference between citizens who have mastered the official language and those who have not, even if they were born in the country and their families have been living there for generations or centuries.

As a final word on this issue, it is important to remember that even if European law contains a flaw and an unfortunate weakness, international law as represented by the International Covenant on Civil and Political Rights offers protection for individuals in Europe who may be the victims of discrimination based on language, even if the human rights system in Europe does not protect them. An individual born in Varna or Kosova who would be denied citizenship only because she or he has not mastered the official language perfectly could still argue that this is a form of discrimination under Article 26 of the International Covenant, even if such an argument could not be used in Europe under the European Convention on Nationality.

4. Conclusion

Unius linguae uniusque moris regnum imbecille et fragile est.

(St. Stephen[45])

Almost one thousand years ago, Saint Stephen, the first king and patron saint of Hungary, wrote in a letter to his son that for a ruler to try to impose a single language on all his subjects was foolish and a sign of weakness.

His words ring true, although the lesson seems to have been lost sight of at various times throughout the centuries.

If history can teach us something, it is that it is foolish to threaten individuals with heavy fines or even imprisonment for privately using a "prohibited" language, as Turkey tried to do with respect to the Kurdish language, and Bulgaria in the case of individuals whose first language was Turkish .

It is also foolish to exclude native-born individuals simply because they do not speak the "right" language, just as it would be foolish to exclude individuals simply because they have different religious beliefs from the majority.

It is foolish for a government not to make some degree of use of the language spoken by hundreds of thousands of individuals in the country, whether they are citizens or not.

It may have taken us almost a millennium, but international law has finally reached the point of recognizing the wisdom of Saint Stephen's advice. The existing rights of minorities in international law provide a framework within which the conduct of the state can be measured in order to avoid unacceptable "foolishness" directed against the inherent human dignity of every individual.

In many areas, the European evolution has also been significant, especially with new treaties like the European Charter on Minority or Regional Languages and the European Convention on the Rights of National Minorities.

Finally, it is important to emphasize that many aspects of these new treaties actually constitute an attempt to elaborate and elucidate well-established international rights and freedoms that guarantee the use of the language of individuals in certain situations, both in private activities and by the state itself under certain conditions, whether or not these individuals are citizens or members of a "national minority".

Notes

1 Quoted in Joshua A. Fishman, ed., *Readings in the Sociology of Language*, 589. The Hague: Mouton and Co. N.V. Publishers, 1968.

2 Most of the documents referred to in this chapter are international treaties which are legal instruments. Some however, such as the Document of the Copenhagen Meeting of the Conference on the Human Dimension, Recommendation 1201 (1993) on an Additional Protocol on the Rights of National Minorities to the European Convention on Human Rights, the United Nations' Declaration on the Rights of Persons Belonging to National or Ethnic, Religious and Linguistic Minorities, and The Hague Recommendations Regarding the Education Rights of National Minorities are not legally binding documents. They are either in the nature of political statements which may have an impact on the interpretation or evolution of legal standards, or are documents prepared by experts in order to clarify existing or emerging rules.

3 See *Ballantyne, Davidson and McIntyre v. Canada*, United Nations Human Rights Committee Communications Nos. 359/1989 and 385/1989, 31 March 1993 (dealing with freedom of expression and language); and *Lovelace v. Canada*, United Nations Human Rights Committee Communication 24/1977, UN Document A/36/40 (dealing with the right to use an indigenous language and enjoy culture with other members of a linguistic and cultural minority).

4 Paragraph 32.5 of the Document of the Copenhagen Meeting of the Conference on the Human Dimension; and Article 10 of the Framework Convention for the Protection of National Minorities.

5 Article 12 of the European Charter for Regional or Minority Languages.

6 *Coeriel and Aurik v. the Netherlands*, United Nations Human Rights Committee Communication No. 453/1991, U.N. Doc. CCPR/C/52/D/ 453/1991 (1994); *Burghartz v. Switzerland*, European Court of Human Rights, judgment of 22 February 1994, 18 E.H.R.R. 101.

7 See, for example, Article 11 of the Central European Initiative for the Protection of Minority Rights; and Article 11 of the Framework Convention for the Protection of National Minorities.

8 See *Guillot v. France*, European Court of Human Rights, 52/1995/558/ 644, judgment of 24 October 1996; and *Stjerna v. Finland*, judgment of 25 November 1994, series A, no. 299-B.

9 Article 14 of the Central European Initiative Instrument for the Protection of Minority Rights; and Article 11 of the Framework Convention for the Protection of National Minorities.

10 *Ballantyne, Davidson and McIntyre v. Canada.*

11 A state would not have complete discretion in terms of the joint use of the official language it can impose. It appears likely from a few national decisions that a state's demand for the use of an official language jointly with a minority language could constitute discrimination in international law if it imposes too heavy a burden. In other words, some requirements for using the official language, without directly excluding the free use of a minority language in private communication activities, could be so unreasonable as to be a form of discrimination. See also Fernand de Varennes, *Language, Minorities and Human Rights*, chapter 3. The Hague: Martinus Nijhoff, 1996.

12 Article 7(2) of Recommendation 1201 (1993) on an Additional Protocol on the Rights of National Minorities to the European Convention on Human Rights.

13 See, on this point, de Varennes, *Language, Minorities and Human Rights*, section 4.6.

14 Article 9 of the Framework Convention for the Protection of National Minorities; and Article 11(2) of the European Charter for Regional or Minority Languages.

15 Article 18 of the Central European Initiative Instrument for the Protection of Minority Rights; Article 9 of the Framework Convention for the Protection of National Minorities; and Article 11(3) of the European Charter for Regional or Minority Languages.

16 Case 36/1992/381/455–459.

17 See, for example, Advisory Opinion on Minority Schools in Albania, Permanent Court of International Justice, Series A/B, No. 64, 3 (1935): 17.

18 Article 17 of the Central European Initiative Instrument for the Protection of Minority Rights; and Article 14 of the Framework Convention for the Protection of National Minorities.

19 Article 16 of the Central European Initiative Instrument for the Protection of Minority Rights; and Article 13 of the Framework Convention for the Protection of National Minorities.

20 Article 12 of the Central European Initiative Instrument for the Protection of Minority Rights.

21 *Human Rights in the Republic of Estonia*, Raimo Pekkanen and Hans Danelius, Special Rapporteurs. In *Human Rights Law Journal*, vol. 13, no 5–6, 236–256 (1991): 241; and *Ballantyne, Davidson and McIntyre v. Canada.*

22 *Ballantyne, Davidson and McIntyre v. Canada.*

23 Article 13 of the European Charter for Regional or Minority Languages.

24 The debate between the two views obviously cannot be explored in detail here. Those interested should read de Varennes, *Language, Minorities and Human Rights*, chapter 4. Briefly, those who see non-discrimination as useful in the area of the use of a minority language by

public authorities in appropriate situations emphasize that a state language preference puts those who are less fluent in that language at a disadvantage, and that under certain conditions such a state preference may be unreasonable–and therefore discriminatory.

25 For example, Article 4 of the Declaration on the Rights of Persons Belonging to National or Ethnic, Religious and Linguistic Minorities; Article 17 of the Central European Initiative Instrument for the Protection of Minority Rights; Article 14 of the Framework Convention for the Protection of National Minorities; and Article 8 of the European Charter for Regional or Minority Languages.

26 See, for example, Articles 12 to 14 of The Hague Recommendations Regarding the Education Rights of National Minorities; Article 14 of the European Charter for Regional or Minority Languages; and Article 8 of the Framework Convention for the Protection of National Minorities.

27 The 1993 Estonian Law on Private Education indicates that Russian schools will receive the same amount of funding as public schools for "instructions costs", but not for "administrative costs". Administrative costs would seem to include the actual purchase, construction and maintenance of schools, rental of offices, payment for support staff, electricity, heating, transportation of students, etc. These costs can be quite substantial—which would seem to suggest that Russian minority students will, in fact, be disadvantaged and will not be treated in the same way as students benefiting from better facilities in public schools.

28 See, among others, Article 5(1) of the UNESCO Convention against Discrimination in Education and Article 14 of the Framework Convention for the Protection of National Minorities.

29 *Isop v. Austria*, Application 808/60, 5, Yearbook of the European Convention on Human Rights 108; *Dominique Guesdon v. France*, Communication No. 219/1986; *Kamasinski v. Austria*, judgment of 19 December 1989, European Court of Human Rights.

30 *Brozicek v. Italy* (1989) European Convention on Human Rights, series A, no. 167.

31 See Article 13 of the Central European Initiative for the Protection of Minority Rights; Article 11 of the European Charter for Regional or Minority Languages; and Article 10 of the Framework Convention for the Protection of National Minorities.

32 Article 11 of the Central European Initiative Instrument for the Protection of Minority Rights; and Article 11 of the Framework Convention for the Protection of National Minorities.

33 Article 14 of the Central European Initiative Instrument for the Protection of Minority Rights; Article 11 of the Framework Convention for the Protection of National Minorities; and Article 10(2)(g) of the European Charter for Regional or Minority Languages.

34 Quoted in Juan F. Perea, "Demography and Distrust: An Essay on American Languages, Cultural Pluralism, and Official English". *Minnesota Law Review* 77 (1992): 269-373, 355.

35 See, for example, *Fryske Nasjonale Partij v. Netherlands* (1986), 45 Decisions and Reports 240 (European Commission of Human Rights), 243.

36 This is referred to in Mathieu-Mohin and Clerfayt, (1987) *European Convention on Human Rights*, Series A, no. 113.

37 *Fryske Nasjonale Partij v. the Netherlands*, 243.

38 Cf. the situation where elected politicians were prevented from taking up their office because they refused to take a parliamentary oath in Dutch, in Mathieu-Mohin and Clerfayt, 25. The European Court on Human Rights essentially concluded that such a linguistic requirement affecting the principles embodied in Article 3 of the First Protocol of the Convention for the Protection of Human Rights and Fundamental Freedoms could not be deemed to be unreasonable, and therefore discriminatory, under Article 14: "The aim is to defuse the language disputes in the country by establishing more stable and decentralized organizational structures ... In any consideration of the electoral system in issue, its general context must not be forgotten. The system does not appear unreasonable if regard is given to the intentions it reflects and to the respondent state's margin of appreciation within the Belgian parliamentary system—a margin that is all the greater as the system is incomplete and provisional".

39 Article 10(2)(e) & (f) of the European Charter for Regional or Minority Languages.

40 Bill Ong Hing, "Beyond the Rhetoric of Assimilation and Cultural Pluralism: Addressing the Tension of Separatism and Conflict in an Immigration-Driven Multiracial Society", *California Law Review* 81 (1993): 863–925, 864.

41 See Council of Europe, "Convention européenne sur la nationalité et rapport explicatif," DIR/JUR (97) 6, at 23–24, where it is stated without any further elaboration that language and a few other grounds of discrimination are not recognized under Article 5(1) of the Convention because they cannot constitute discriminatory requirements in the area of nationality.

42 Advisory Opinion of 19 January 1984 (*Costa Rican Naturalization Case*) Case No. OC–4/84; and Advisory Opinion on Certain Questions, Arising Out of the Application of Article 4 of the Polish Minorities Treaty (*Polish Nationality Case*), Permanent Court of International Justice, Series B, No. 7 (1923): 18. See also de Varennes, *Language, Minorities and Human Rights*, Section 6.4.

43 Advisory Opinion of 19 January 1984 (Case No. OC–4/84.).

44 To those who would argue that such an argument is too far-fetched, it should be mentioned that recently the Prime Minister of Slovakia, when attacked for allegedly considering "ethnic cleansing" through encouraging population transfers between Hungary and Slovakia in August 1997, had apparently also made comments on the possibility of changing the citizenship of Hungarian-speaking citizens of Slovakia. If these individuals were to lose their Slovakian citizenship, even if they could obtain Hungarian citizenship, it would mean they would lose their right to vote, could not obtain certain types of work, and could

even be excluded from owning property, in a country inhabited by their ancestors for centuries.

45 Quoted in the foreword to C.A. Macartney, "National States and National Minorities." New York: Russell and Russell, 1968.

The Slovak State Language Law as a Trade Law Problem

BART DRIESSEN[1]

It is often argued that the increased globalization and liberalization of trade constitutes a threat to linguistic minorities. Without wanting to enter the academic debate, I would like to offer some thoughts from a legal perspective. This paper explores the impact of developments in international trade law and developments in the context of the European Community-Slovak association agreement on the 1995 Slovak State Language Law.[2] Why this Slovak legislation? First because of its topical relevance.[3] Second, because the Slovak language legislation is amongst the most far-reaching of its kind, and a point is often best explained using an extreme example.

Why trade law and European economic integration? It is my contention that Slovakia is currently under a lot of obligations, and in the future will have to agree to even more rules which, although not intended to protect linguistic minorities, will have a direct impact on their situation.

In this paper I will explore how Slovakia's international trade obligations exert an influence on the treatment of linguistic minorities in Slovakia *qua* trade obligations. In order to make the point as clearly as possible, I will attempt to do this from the perspective of the Hungarian minority in Slovakia. This is not because I would deny the importance of the Slovak side of the story or the issues at play in relations with other minorities in Slovakia, but because the Hungarian minority has been rather in the focus of attention.

First some general caveats are in order. Of course, I do not argue that international trade law or economic integration is the panacea for maintaining minority rights in Slovakia. International trade obligations are not designed, and often not fit, to protect minority rights. Economic integration in the European context is fitted to *economic* aims. As a general principle, trade law only comes into play when international, that is, inter-state traffic in goods or services is concerned. When a transaction is purely Slovak, then there is normally little room for international trade law instruments. However, especially where the free movement of goods is concerned, one can think of cases where linguistic requirements are imposed on products or services that will, by definition, have an international impact.

The discussion below must necessarily focus on the most poignant of these issues of conflict. In this sense, the scope of this paper can be but modest. First, a bird's-eye view of Slovakia's position in international trade law will be presented. This will be followed by some observations on selected issues of minority rights in Slovakia. Then I will discuss some of the procedural aspects of the matter.

The Setting: Slovakia's Obligations in International Trade Law

Slovakia does not exist isolated from the rest of the world. It is a member of the World Trade Organization (WTO). It has concluded an association agreement with the EC, and–at least in public and in word–Mr Mečiar's government remains committed to joining the European Union, albeit with markedly less enthusiasm than governments in neighboring associated countries.

First the WTO. WTO law (or, as it was called before 1995, GATT law) is based on two overriding principles: first, WTO Member States such as Slovakia have to abide by the *most-favored-nation* (MFN) principle. This implies, in short, that with respect to all customs duties and charges, rules and formalities in connection with importation and exportation, any "advantage, favor, privilege or immunity" granted by Slovakia "to any product originating in ... any other country shall be accorded immediately and unconditionally" to the like product originating in, or destined for, the territories of all other WTO Member States.[4] In other words, at the border Slovakia may not discriminate between products on the basis of their country of origin or destination.

The second main principle is that of *national treatment*. This implies, among other things, that once products are imported, Slovakia is obliged to treat them similarly to products produced in Slovakia. It follows from GATT panel case law that, in principle, it is not relevant whether the purpose of the measures may have been unrelated to trade policy or to other policy goals.[5] This conclusion would not be different if the policy goal in question related to language rights.

Although these two principles—MFN and national treatment—are fairly simple, many exceptions exist. Most of these are not relevant for the present discussion; where they are, I will discuss them in more detail below. Moreover, since the results of the Uruguay Round entered into force on 1 January 1995, Slovakia, like other WTO Members, is subject to a considerably enlarged and more exacting corpus of trade rules.

Next the association agreement. The association agreements concluded by each of the Central European countries with the European Union are, to a large extent, similar. In addition to establishing a free-trade zone between each associated country and the EC, these agreements bring into force many of the rights and obligations in the field of free movement of goods, persons, services and capital that are applicable within the EC. For most Central European countries, including Hungary and Slovakia, these arrangements with the EC are complemented by the liberalization of trade among themselves within the framework of the Central European Free-Trade Area (CEFTA).[6]

Even with the introduction and implementation of the obligations laid down in the association agreement Slovakia is a long way off from adopting the current body of European Community [EC] law. In order to assist candidates for EC Membership, the European Commission issued a document in 1995 listing the most essential rules governing the internal market that associated countries need to implement before they can accede to the EC. This 482-page White paper on the preparation of the associated countries of Central and Eastern Europe for integration into the internal market of the Union[7] is officially no more than an advice by the European Commission intended to aid the associated countries in preparing for accession. But it can also be seen as a fair statement of the *minimal* future legal obligations of Slovakia in the economic field and, in practice, the European Union uses it as a yardstick to determine whether the associated countries are ready for Membership negotiations. This gives the White Paper political weight equaling the association agreement.

Of course, even this does not fully cover all relevant EC policy initiatives relating to linguistic rights; but these policies will not be discussed here.[8]

Until now, every Central European government has tended to treat its accession to the EC largely as the end sprint in a race in which every country runs for itself. The fact that other Central European countries will also join, and that this will of course have an impact on the applicant country itself, is often overlooked.

Without attempting too much speculation, it would seem that—in some five to ten years—Hungary will be among the first new Members to join the European Union. In view of the European Commission's recommendation not to include Slovakia in the first wave of accessions, it also seems quite certain that Slovakia, if it maintains its current policies, will *not* be among the first. Hence Slovakia, if it wants to prepare seriously for EC Membership, will have to take account of the Membership of Hungary, more so than vice versa.

Substantive Minority Rights in International Trade Law

How do these international trade instruments influence law and practice with respect to the Slovak State Language Law? There are several issues at play. One problem here is that the Law, although rich in penalties, is poor on guidelines as to what to do in international contacts. This creates potentially serious problems in some areas. Another problem is that the body of current and future obligations of Slovakia in the context of the WTO, the association agreement and the accession preparation, is exceedingly large. Therefore, the following remarks can only cover some selected issues and can only attempt to be illustrative, rather than give an exhaustive account, of the issues involved. In what follows, the Law will be analyzed from the point of view of the three above-mentioned sets of international trade obligations and some of the most important conflict zones will be discussed: the audiovisual media, the written media, and language requirements and labeling.

The Audiovisual Media

In practice, many Hungarians in Slovakia can receive television broadcasts from Hungary. While this is certainly not an ideal and full replacement for language broadcasts made by, and catering especially for, the Hungarian minority in Slovakia, the above-mentioned obligations to some extent provide a "safety net" function enabling Hungarians in Slovakia to receive at least some Hungarian-language broadcasts. Moreover, it may be interesting to look at the legal possibilities of running a television station from Hungarian territory that enjoys the protection of the freedom of broadcasting services.

The State Language Law contains several provisions concerning audiovisual media. Article 5(1) of the Law provides that

[r]adio and television broadcasting is in the State language through-out the Slovak Republic. The exceptions are:
a) foreign-language radio broadcasts and foreign-language television broadcasts composed of audiovisual works and other picture-and-sound recordings with subtitles in the State language or which in some other way meet the criteria of basic comprehensibility with re-gard to the State language; ...
c) musical programs containing original texts.
The broadcast in national minority and ethnic group languages is regulated by separate provisions.[9]

Further relevant is Article 5(4):

Broadcasts by regional and local television channels, radio stations and radio facilities take place basically in the state language. Other languages may be used before the broadcast and after the broadcast of a given program in the State language.

It would not seem impossible to interpret this as interference with the retransmission of foreign broadcasts.

What are Slovakia's obligations vis-à-vis the transmission of broadcasts? As far as broadcasters falling under the jurisdiction of Slovakia are concerned, admittedly the corpus of international trade law does not add much. However, there are some rules on broadcasting which may be relevant for linguistic minorities in Slo-vakia since they provide a guarantee for—in particular—the Hungar-ian minority's right to receive *Duna Televízió* from Hungary, wherever local transmission stations are willing to retransmit it.

The association agreement is relevant. Article 97(2) provides in relevant part that "[t]he Parties shall co-ordinate, and where ap-propriate, harmonize, their policies regarding the regulation of cross-border broadcasts ..." In effect, Slovakia will have to adjust its policies to EC legislation in this field. The authors of the White Paper included the EC legislation concerned among the essential cornerstones of the internal market:

[a]udio-visual policy presupposes the existence of national regula-tory systems, in most Member States these are independent bodies un-der the authority of a Ministry. In the United Kingdom, for example, the responsible Ministry is the Department of National Heritage and the Regulatory Authorities are the Independent Television Commis-sion for private broadcasters and the BBC for the public sector. In France, the Ministries for Culture and Communication are responsible and the Conseil Supérieur de l'Audiovisuel is the regulatory Authority. This system of dividing regulation and government ensures the inde-pendence of broadcasting from political interference.[10]

Such independence is the first, but not the only step towards guaranteeing meaningful broadcasting in minority languages in Slovakia.

The crucial piece of legislation regarding the regulation of cross-border broadcasts is EC Directive 89/552/EEC (the Television without Frontiers Directive).[11] Slovakia will have to implement this directive in its domestic legislation, both by virtue of the association agreement and the White Paper.

Other European countries such as Slovakia may adopt, on a recip-rocal basis, the principles of the Television without Frontiers Direc-tive even before they become Members of the European Union.

Moreover, within the framework of the Council of Europe the European Convention on Transfrontier Television has been adopted.[12] Both Slovakia and Hungary ratified this Convention. Many of the obligations in the Directive have an equivalent in the Convention.

The preamble of the Directive stresses that the right of free movement of all services, as applied to the broadcasting and distri-bution of television services,

> is also a specific manifestation in Community law of a more general principle, namely the freedom of expression as enshrined in Article 10(1) of the Convention for the Protection of Human Rights and Fundamental Freedoms ... for this reason the issuing of directives on the broadcasting and distribution of television programmes must en-sure their free movement in the light of the said Article and subject only to the limits set by paragraph 2 of that Article and by Article 56(1) of the Treaty.

A clear linkage is thus made between the free movement of broadcasting (an economic right) and the freedom of expression (a human right). This is the first important point.

The second point, and the cornerstone of the system, is the "sender state principle", meaning that, in principle, states may not prohibit broadcasts emanating from other Member States which fulfill the rules there. This is laid down in Article 2(2) of the Direc-tive: "Member States shall ensure freedom of reception and shall not restrict retransmission on their territory of television broad-casts from other Member States for reasons which fall within the fields co-ordinated by this Directive ..." In the recent *Paul Denuit* Case, the European Court of Justice ruled in this regard that "under the system established by the Directive for allocating obligations between the Member Sates from which broadcasts emanate and those which receive them, it is solely for the Member States from which television broadcasts emanate to monitor the application of the law of the originating Member State applying to such broadcasts and to ensure compliance with the Directive and that the receiving Member State is not authorized to exercise its own control in that regard".[13] The court recognized in the same case that a member state may not oppose a retransmission on its territory of a television program broadcast under the jurisdiction of another Member State if that program does not fulfill the local content criteria of the Directive. In other words, if a program in violation of EC rules is broadcast in state A to state B, it is state A which may act against it, but not state B. This implies *a fortiori* that programs in violation of the laws of state B may not be banned by state B if these programs are broadcast under the jurisdiction of state A.

In other words, EC legislation on television broadcasts is based on two underlying fundamental principles: first, television broadcasting is seen as a function of the freedom of expression. Second, there should be free movement of television broadcasts with respect to broadcasts that fulfill the legal rules in the sender state.

The question now arises how broadcasts should be treated which are broadcast from another state merely to evade the jurisdiction of the state for which they are intended. Within the EC context, there has been a lot of jurisprudence on this; in the European Union, many commercial television stations broadcast from United Kingdom or Luxembourg territory programs especially intended for the Dutch, French or Belgian market in order to evade national standards there. It may be expected that in the future the principles underlying these EC judgments will guide any stations broadcasting into Central European countries as well.

Recitals 14 and 15 of Directive 97/36/EC, which amends the Television without Frontiers Directive, summarize the position succinctly:

> ... the Court of Justice has constantly held that a Member State retains the right to take measures against a television broadcasting organization that is established in another Member State but directs all or most of its activity to the territory of the first Member State if the choice of establishment was made with a view to evading the legislation that would have applied to the organization had it been established on the territory of the first Member State;
>
> ... Article F(2) of the Treaty on European Union stipulates that the Union shall respect fundamental rights as guaranteed by the European Convention for the Protection of Human Rights and Fundamental Freedoms as general principles of Community law; ... any measure aimed at restricting the reception and/or suspending the re-

transmission of television broadcasts taken under Article 2a of [the Television without Frontiers Directive] must be compatible with such principles.

In other words, if a television station in the EC relocates to a neighboring Member State only to avoid language restrictions, the state of reception may only act against this evasion if this would be compatible with the freedom of expression protected by the European Convention for the Protection of Human Rights and Fundamental Freedoms. That will rarely be the case in the context of the Slovak Law.

Until now, the whole discussion may have seemed theoretical. Maybe so; but in another recent case the European Court of Justice clarified exactly when a broadcaster is under the jurisdiction of another state, that is, when broadcasters start to enjoy the free movement of broadcasting. The Court observed that "a television broadcaster comes under the jurisdiction of the Member State in which it is established. If a television broadcaster is established in more than one Member State, the Member State having jurisdiction over it is the one in whose territory the broadcaster has the center of its activities, in particular where decisions concerning program policy are taken and the programmes to be broadcast are finally put together."[14] Although I would be the first to realize the practical difficulties involved, I would like to argue that this body of rules may, in time, open creative possibilities for Slovakia's Magyar minority to broadcast from Hungarian soil to Slovakia with the force of trade law behind them.

Finally, there is yet another set of rules very much of relevance here: as I have already mentioned, both Hungary and Slovakia have subscribed to the European Convention on Transfrontier Television. Article 4 thereof requires that "[t]he Parties shall ensure freedom of expression and information in accordance with Article 10 of the Convention for the Protection of Human Rights and Fundamental Freedoms and they shall guarantee freedom of reception and shall not restrict the retransmission on their territories of program services which comply with the terms of this Convention". The rules contained in the convention are not as specific as those laid down in EC law; they are, on the other hand, already applicable between Hungary and Slovakia. Moreover, the convention contains elaborate provisions for arbitration if a dispute arises between two signatory states and explicitly links the freedom of retransmission with the freedom of expression.

This—admittedly cursory—overview of Slovakia's current and future obligations in the field of audiovisual media leads to some tentative conclusions.

First, the State Language Law gives no guarantees as to the future of TV broadcasting in the Hungarian language in Slovakia. Moreover, past experience has shown increasing state interference with respect to the content and quantity of programming, including the issue of references to geographical names in Slovakia in Hungarian-language broadcasts.

Second, the presumption underlying EC law is that broadcasters and re-transmitters are able to function independently from political interference. It cannot be imagined that Slovakia will ever join the EC if it cannot guarantee the independence of broadcasters from political interference. Such interventions as are allowed are strictly circumscribed and should not curtail freedom of expression.

Thirdly, at some point in the coming five years or so, Hungary is likely to become a Member of the EC. This means that the Television without Frontiers Directive will become topical for any broadcast from Hungarian soil into Slovakia, and may become a potential issue in EC-Slovak relations. Although, ideally, Hungarian-language TV broadcasting *in* Slovakia should be guaranteed, the trade law obligations referred to above may be useful in providing a still significant inroad: broadcasting from Hungary.

Periodicals and Occasional Publications

Article 5(5) of the State Language Law provides that "[p]eriodical and non-periodical publications are published in the State language. Press publications issued in other languages are regulated by a separate provision".15

The English translation of the State Language Law leaves ambiguous the question of whether "published" may also mean "distributed". Certainly, an argument to that effect could be made. There is nothing in international trade law directly stopping Slovakia from regulating the use of language by the press in Slovakia (although, of course, instruments on minority rights are very much relevant). The trade law question is different: can the State Language Law legally restrict the importation and distribution of journals or books in minority languages from neighboring countries? Some current Hungarian-language literature and newspapers marketed in Slovakia are apparently printed in, and imported from,

Hungary. It may be instructive to review the level of protection of these imports under international trade law.

First, it would seem evident that newspapers, periodicals and books are *products*.[16] The most relevant provision is the basic principle of Article XIII:1 of GATT 1994, which provides that "[n]o prohibition or restriction shall be applied by any contracting party on the importation of any product of the territory of any other contracting party ... unless the importation of the like product of all third countries ... is similarly prohibited". In other words, *if* a WTO Member State has the right to restrict imports, it is obliged to do so in a manner that does not discriminate between third countries. In other words, if ever there was a restriction of some kind on the importing of periodicals or literature into Slovakia, in principle such restriction should be applied in a non-discriminatory fashion. Of course, even though the Law is not directed against publications of Hungarian *origin*, it is a fact that the vast majority of such imported publications will originate in Hungary. The GATT panel report *Spain—Tariff treatment of unroasted coffee* provides an interesting precedent for the view that Hungary's rights would be impaired if Hungarian-language publications were restricted and most imports of these originated in Hungary.[17] In the above case, Brazil complained about a distinction in tariffs introduced in Spain between unwashed Arabica and Robusta coffees on the one hand, and "mild" coffee on the other. Although Spain did not discriminate on the basis of the country of origin, Brazil claimed that, in practice, discrimination did exist since Spain's imports of unroasted coffee from Brazil comprised almost entirely unwashed Arabica. Spain argued that it was entitled to make further subdivisions in its customs tariff structure. The Panel noted that, whatever the classification adopted, Article I:1 of GATT requires that the same tariff treatment be applied to "like products." Although the Panel recognized that different types of coffee may have different characteristics, it found that such differences constituted an insufficient reason for allowing different tariff treatment. Moreover, no other GATT member had made a similar distinction in its customs tariffs. In conclusion, even though the Spanish measure was not specifically directed against any particular country, it was still found to be discriminatory.

Second, WTO law severely limits the right of WTO Member States to restrict imports of newspapers, books and periodicals. Article XI of GATT 1994 lays down the main principle that "[n]o prohibitions or restrictions other than duties, taxes or other charges ... shall be instituted or maintained by any contracting party on the importation of any product of the territory of any contracting party ..."

This, of course, does not fully solve the problem. Importing literature or newspapers is one thing; the restrictions in the Language Law are, however, aimed at the *marketing* of Hungarian-language literature and periodicals: "[p]eriodicals and occasional publications *are published* in the state language". This is where the national treatment clause of Article III:4 of GATT 1994 becomes relevant. This provision recognizes that "[t]he products of the territory of any contracting party imported into the territory of any other contracting party shall be accorded treatment no less favorable than that accorded to like products of national origin in respect of all laws, regulations and requirements affecting their internal sale, offering for sale, purchase, transportation, distribution or use ..." The term "affecting" must be interpreted very broadly.[18] It would seem beyond doubt that any law restricting the sale of Hungarian-language newspapers is a law "affecting [their] internal sale, offering for sale, purchase, transportation, distribution or use".

This, of course, raises a question regarding the extent to which Hungarian-language and Slovak-language (or better: Hungarian-origin and Slovak-origin) publications are "like products". Since the Language Law is arguably targeted at the language use of Hungarians and other minorities, and not at the language use of native Slovak speakers, one could argue that Slovakia itself apparently considers Hungarian-origin and Slovak-origin periodicals to be like products. The best–admittedly only partly–relevant precedent was set by the WTO panel in *Canadian periodicals*. The question there was whether periodicals published inside and outside Canada with largely similar content but different advertisements were like products. The panel held they were.[19]

The third GATT principle relevant in this context is Article XX(d) of GATT 1994, which provides for a derogation possibility from the above-mentioned principles by providing that "nothing in this Agreement shall be construed to prevent the adoption or enforcement by any [Member] of measures: ... necessary to secure compliance with laws or regulations which are not inconsistent with the provisions of this Agreement ..." Such exception may not "constitute a means of arbitrary or unjustifiable discrimination between countries where the same conditions prevail, or a disguised restriction on international trade, constitute a means of arbitrary or unjustifiable discrimination between countries where the same conditions prevail, or a disguised restriction on international trade". However, for three reasons Slovakia could not easily rely on Article XX(d) to "save" its Language Law. First, it appears to be standard WTO practice that a country cannot claim the protection of Article XX merely because the underlying objective of the import-restricting legislation was not inconsistent with GATT law.[20] Moreover, a GATT panel has held that there is a proportionality test in Article XX(d).[21] Third, even if Article XX were resorted to, trade restrictions may not lead to the discriminatory treatment of products from different countries.

Let us now look at the same matter from the perspective of the association agreement and the White Paper. As argued above, Slovakia will have to implement the body of existing EC law in the future. With Hungary's accession to the EC expected in about five years, it becomes interesting to look at what the law would be if any dispute arose on the interpretation of the association agreement. Certainly, the interpretation of the corresponding provisions in EC law will play an important role. A recent court case gives some idea of where that law is going.

In 1995, the Commercial Court of Vienna requested a prejudicial ruling from the European Court of Justice on certain questions which came up in the context of a dispute between the Austrian publisher Familiapress and Heinrich Bauer Verlag. The latter, a German publisher, sold publications in Austria offering readers the chance to take part in games with prizes. The way in which this was done was, according to Familiapress, inconsistent with Austrian legislation on unfair competition. Familiapress demanded that Bauer desist from selling its publications in Austria. The question arising was whether the marketing of Bauer's publications could be prohibited if these publications fulfilled the laws of their country of origin (i.e. Germany).

This question relates to Articles 30 and 36 of the EC Treaty. Article 30 establishes as a basic rule that quantitative restrictions and measures with an effect equivalent to quantitative restrictions are prohibited in trade between EC Member States. Article 36 of the EC Treaty, which is almost the same as Article 36 in the EC-Slovak association agreement, provides for an exception to Article 30. It lays down that the freedom of movement of goods does not preclude, *inter alia*, "prohibitions or restrictions on imports ... justified on grounds of public morality, public policy or public security". However, "[s]uch prohibitions or restrictions shall not ... constitute a means of arbitrary discrimination or a disguised restriction on trade ..." Almost similar rules govern trade between the EC, Hungary and Slovakia with respect to goods originating in one of these places.

The first question was whether the matter fell under the scope of Article 30. The court observed that "since it requires publishers established in other Member States to alter the contents of their papers, the prohibition in question jeopardizes access of the product concerned into the market of the Member State of importation and, consequently, hinders free movement of goods."[22]

The next question was whether the Austrians could invoke the exception of Article 36 of the EC Treaty. If they could, then the German journals could be stopped anyway, even if this violated Article 30. The court made some very interesting observations on this issue.

First, it observed that "maintenance of press diversity may constitute an overriding requirement justifying a restriction on free movement of goods". The court explicitly mentions in this context Article 10 of the European Convention on Human Rights and Fundamental Freedoms "which is one of the fundamental rights guaranteed by the Community legal order". It must be kept in mind that, in this case, Bauer was considerably larger than the relatively small Austrian publisher and could flex more muscles.

The Court continued by recalling that "the provisions of national law in question must be proportionate to the objective pursued and that objective must not be capable of being achieved by measures which are less restrictive of intra-Community trade".[23] The question thus arose as to whether the Austrian restriction was proportionate to the maintenance of the pluralism of the press and whether it would be possible to achieve the same objective in a manner less restrictive of Community law and freedom of expression. That matter, in the view of the court, was a factual question to be determined by the Austrian courts.

How does this case relate to the rights of linguistic minorities in Slovakia?

First, the *Familiapress* case was played out in the context of relations between two EC Member States. Consequently, the applicable law was the EC Treaty. The question arises as to whether the judgment can simply be transposed to the association agreement. The EC Treaty is of course not (yet) in force for Slovakia—but Slovakia is bound to the EC-Slovak association agreement which contains similar provisions. Moreover, in the context of CEFTA an almost similar provision[24] is in force between Hungary and Slovakia. Lastly, the EC expects Slovakia to adopt the whole body of Community law in the future.

On the EC side, in some past cases the European Court of Justice has proven hesitant to interpret the corresponding provisions of free-trade agreements similar to Articles 30 to 36 of the EC Treaty, even if the text was identical. For instance, in *Polydor vs Harlequin*[25] the court observed that the case law on Articles 30 to 36, quoted by Harlequin, determined "in the context of the Community the relationship between the protection of industrial and commercial property rights and the rules on the free movement of goods". Therefore, even though the terms of the association agreement concerned were identical to Articles 30 to 36 of the EC Treaty, the court did not consider this sufficient reason for transposing the broad interpretation of the EC Treaty provisions to the association agreement.[26] However, the precedent value of this case seems limited: this case concerned essentially a matter of collision of parallel imports with intellectual property rights. *Familiapress* involved more fundamental issues, namely the freedom of expression. More importantly, the contested restriction on free movement in our case would be a Slovak law rather than a company's intellectual property right. Under these circumstances, it may be expected that an interpretation giving greater emphasis to freedom of movement is warranted.

The *Familiapress* case concerned Austrian legislation aimed at a relatively non-political issue: the curbing of unfair competition. What would the legal position be if Slovak legislation aimed at stopping periodicals and books in a minority language were at issue?

Familiapress gives us some clues as to the proper interpretation of the association agreement.

First, although the exceptions to the freedom of movement of goods must be interpreted restrictively, there is more room for exceptions to free movement of goods in the context of trade with Slovakia than within the EC itself.

Second, the EC Court of Justice has stressed the importance of freedom of expression where the restriction on free trade concerns periodicals. In the case of the State Language Law, this concern for freedom of expression would translate itself into an interpretation favoring free trade.

Third, any restriction on the principle of free movement must be proportionate. It is very difficult to defend any outright prohibition as being "proportionate".

In summary, if the Slovak authorities take the view that Article 5(5) also covers the distribution of publications it would seem that, in the long run, it is unlikely to survive Slovakia's economic integration with Western Europe.

Labeling of Products

Article 8(1) of the State Language Law provides that "[i]n the interest of consumer protection the use of the State language is compulsory in the indication of the contents of domestic or imported goods, especially foods and medicines, in the conditions for guarantees and in other information for the consumer".[27] In the past, the Slovak authorities have, in several cases, interpreted an obligation to use the Slovak language as a prohibition on the use of other languages. Indeed, if Article 8(1) is interpreted in a similar vein, problems will be raised in the field of trade law.

First, EC law does not allow an exclusivity provision in the field of food labeling. A few years ago the European Court of Justice had to adjudicate a very interesting Belgian problem. Dutch is the official language in the Flemish part of Belgium, while the remainder of the country speaks French or German. A company in Flanders had been marketing mineral water in bottles with labels in French or German, but not in Dutch. The company's competitors complained that this was a breach of Belgian legislation (which required that labels should be in at least the language of the region in which the product was for sale). This Belgian legislation was the implementation of EC Directive 79/112, which required that such labels must be "in a language easily understood by purchasers, unless other measures have been taken to ensure that the purchaser is informed".

The court emphasized that the directive only required the prohibition of the sale of products on which the labeling is not easily understood by the purchaser, rather than the imposition of any particular language. Literally speaking, the legislation did not seem to preclude the kind of legislation introduced in Belgium. Nevertheless, interpreting the directive as allowing only the use of the language of the region in which the products are marketed fails to take account of the aim of the Directive, which is the elimination of obstacles to the free movement of goods. Indeed, the Directive allowed for other languages "if other measures have been taken to ensure that the purchaser is informed".[28] In other words, the obligation to use the official language exclusively goes too far and constitutes a measure having an equivalent effect to a quantitative restriction on imports, prohibited by Article 30 of the EC Treaty. In the case of Article 8(1) of the Slovak Language Law, which is specifically intended to attend to language use in southern Slovakia, it would be hard to explain why the sale of products labeled in Hungarian, which can be read by the majority of the population there, would not be "[i]n the interest of consumer protection".

In response to this judgment the European Commission stated that it "has always taken the view that legislation imposing the use of a given language in relations between economic operators cannot be justified as being in the interest of consumers and may constitute an obstacle to trade within the meaning of Article 30 of the EC Treaty on the freedom of movement. Such a requirement, applying when the goods are sold to final consumers, could also prove to be incompatible with Article 30 of the EC Treaty on the grounds that it is disproportionate".[29]

For Slovakia, this means concretely that any future development of this legislation in conformity with the EC-law will imply that compulsory labeling of foodstuffs in Slovak may be problematic.

Lastly, the court has read a similar proportionality test into an EEC Directive imposing linguistic requirements for the labeling of crystal.[30]

Procedural Guarantees

In international economic and trade law considerably more attention has been devoted to procedural guarantees of rights than in international minority rights law. First, as far as WTO law is concerned, any government that feels that its rights under the WTO have been violated may initiate consultations with the country concerned. If these negotiations do not come to anything, the complaining country may request the establishment of a WTO panel. If the panel finds against the violating state, that state can be obliged to comply or—as a final resort—face measures in the form of suspension of concessions.[31]

In practice, since the 1950s no state condemned by an adopted panel report in the GATT system has ever let things go that far. The threat of such measures is a rather strong incentive for states to comply with WTO panel rulings against them.

Slovakia is not (yet) a Member of the EC and, therefore, persons in Slovakia who feel they have been wronged under EC law do not (yet) have recourse to the EC courts. However, the jurisprudence of these courts provides some—albeit not full—guidance on the interpretation of the EC-Slovak association agreement. Moreover, the EC may request consultations with Slovakia in the Association Council established under that agreement. In a few years from now, if Hungary has become an EC Member, the EC will be under greater pressure to force implementation of EC law by Slovakia also vis-à-vis Hungary.

Complementary to this, Slovakia's progress in adopting and implementing the whole body of EC law will be followed within the framework of the pre-accession programs. This may be a further factor likely to encourage Slovakia into observance of linguistic rights vis-à-vis Hungary.

Conclusions

I do not claim to have been exhaustive in introducing the trade law issues related to the Slovak State Language Law. The WTO Agreements constitute a corpus of law of well over 300 pages. The body of EC law to be adopted by Slovakia constitutes tens of thousands of pages, and just the listing in the White Paper of the most crucial legislation already makes a document of 482 pages. I can only hope to have given a flavor of some of the possible implications of economic and trade law on language legislation in Slovakia.

A lot of the above thoughts seem, at first sight, to be relevant only once Hungary has become an EC Member. It is only then that relations between Hungary and Slovakia will be governed by the association agreement. This is partly true. On the other hand, the up-coming accession may already throw its shadow on relations between the two countries in the coming years, both in Slovakia's relations with the EC and in Slovak domestic politics.

Of course, trade law provisions cannot replace an effective system for the protection of minority rights. Current minority law leaves much to be desired. However, for some issues, trade law may have an impact on linguistic rights which is worth taking into account. In some cases, Slovakia's commitments in the field of international trade do have a certain "safety net" function, especially for the Hungarian minority. A denser network of international trade obligations and rights will only enhance this.

Notes

1 The author wishes to thank Sofia Alves for her research assistance and the editors and Iván Gyurcsík for their helpful comments. The responsibility for the text lies, however, solely with the author.

2 I have used the translation prepared by Miklós Kontra in his "On the right to use the language of one's choice in Slovakia", *Canadian Centre for Linguistic Rights Bulletin*, 4:1 (1997): 5–8.

I am not aware of much literature on the border area between minority rights and international economic (trade) law. I would, however, like to mention Bruno de Witte's cogent contribution, "Surviving in Babel? Language rights and European integration", in Y. Dinstein and M. Tabory, eds., *The Protection of Minorities and Human Rights*, 277-300, Dordrecht: Kluwer, 1992; María Amor Martín Estébanez, "The Protection of National or Ethnic, Religious and Linguistic Minorities", in Nanette A. Neuwahl and Allan Rosas, *The European Union and Human Rights*, 133-163, The Hague: Martinus Nijhoff Publishers, 1995; and François Grin and Catherine Hennis-Pierre, "La diversité linguistique et culturelle face aux règles du commerce international: le cas du film et des émissions de télévision", in Sélim Abou and Katia Haddad, *La diversité linguistique et culturelle et les enjeux du développement*, 265-286, Beyrouth (Libanon): Université Saint-Joseph, 1997.

3 For an analysis of the Slovak State Language Law and Slovak language legislation in general from a minority rights point of view see Miklós Kontra, "Szlovákiában szlovákul–Amerikában angolul" (Slovak in Slovakia — English in America), *Valóság* 5 (1997): 60-72; id., "English Only's Cousin: Slovak Only", *Acta Linguistica Hungarica* 43 (1995/96): 345-372; and Bart Driessen, "A new turn in Hungarian-Slovak relations? An overview of the Basic Treaty", *International Journal on Minority and Group Rights* (1997), 1-40.

4 Article I:1 of GATT 1994.

5 The GATT panel in *Special import taxes instituted by Greece, Binding Instruments and Selected Documents* [hereinafter: BISD] 1S/48-49 at § 5).

6 The Member countries of CEFTA are the Czech Republic, Hungary, Poland, Slovakia and Slovenia. Romania is scheduled to join the group.

7 Hereinafter: *White Paper*.

8 For an overview see Martín Estébanez, op. cit.

9 Footnote in original: "SNC Law No 254/1991: Article 3, paragraph 3, according to its newest amendments. SNC Law No. 255/1991: Article 5, according to its newest amendments".

10 *White Paper*, at 210.

11 *Official Journal* (1989) L 298/23; amended by Directive 97/36/EC, *Official Journal* (1997) L 202/60.

12 Convention of 5 May 1989, ETS No 132, http://www.coe.fr/eng/legaltxt/ 132e.htm. The convention entered into force for Slovakia on 1 May 1997, and for Hungary on 1 January 1997.

13 Case C-14/96, *Paul Denuit*, judgment of 29 May 1997, [1997] ECR I-2785, § 32. See also Case C-11/95, *Commission v. Belgium* [1996], ECR I-4115, § 34.

14 Case C-56/96, *VT4 Ltd. v. Vlaamse Gemeenschap*, judgment of 5 June 1997 [1997], ECR I-3143.

15 Footnote in original: "Law No 81/1966 on Periodical Press and Other Telecommunication Instruments, according to its newest amendments".

16 See the WTO panel report in *Canada—certain measures concerning periodicals*, Report of the Panel, WTO doc. WT/DS31/R of 14 March 1997;

Report of the Appellate Body, WTO doc. WT/DS31/AB/R of 30 June 1997 (hereinafter: *Canadian periodicals*).

17 BISD 28S/102.

18 GATT panel report on *Italian discrimination against imported agricultural machinery*, BISD 7S/60 at § 12.

19 §§ 5.22–5.27.

20 § 5.9 of *Canadian Periodicals*; GATT panel report on EEC–Regulations on Imports of Parts and Components, BISD 37S/132, §§ 5.14–5.18.

21 Panel Report on *United States—Section 337 of the Tariff Act of 1930*, BISD 36S/345, § 5.26.

22 Case C–368/95, *Vereinigte Familiapress Zeitungsverlags- und vertriebs GmbH vs Heinrich Bauer Verlag*, judgment of 26 June 1997 [1997], ECR I–3689.

23 Ibid. at § 19.

24 Article 18 of the CEFTA Agreement.

25 Case 270/80, *Polydor vs Harlequin* [1982], ECR 329.

26 For a cogent critique see Stanislaw Soltysiński, "International Exhaustion of Intellectual Property Rights under the TRIPs, the EC Law and the Europe Agreements", *Gewerblicher Rechtsschutz und Urheberrecht Internationaler Teil* 4 (1996): 321–322.

27 Footnote in original: "Law No 634/1992 on Consumer Protection: Article 9, Paragraphs 1, 2 and Article 11. SNC Law No. 152/1995 on Food Products."

28 Case C–369/89, *Piageme asbl v. Peeters bvba* [1991], ECR I–2971, § 15.

29 *Official Journal* (1996) C 56/45.

30 Case C–51/93, *Meyhui NV v. Schott Zwiesel Glaswerke AG* [1994], ECR I–3879.

31 See, for details, Edwin Vermulst and Bart Driessen, "An overview of the WTO dispute settlement system and its relationship with the Uruguay Round Agreements: Nice on paper but too much stress for the system?" *Journal of World Trade* 2 (1995): 131–161.

MARKET ISSUES

Market Forces, Language Spread and Linguistic Diversity

FRANÇOIS GRIN[1]

The Issue

The spread, maintenance and decline of languages is usually seen not as a purely linguistic process, but as the result of the interplay of complex social, political and economic forces. However, despite the fact that much has been written about language dynamics—particularly language decline—our understanding of *how* macro-level forces influence them remains fairly imprecise.

Ten years ago, the sociolinguists René, Appel and Peter Muysken pointed out that we still had no full-fledged theory of language shift (Appel and Muysken 1987). In my opinion, this remains true today, and our understanding of the *cause-and-effect* relationships involved, particularly when it comes to language spread (as opposed to language decline), is incomplete. Much of the work available is descriptive, and most theoretical approaches retain a clearly inductive or hermeneutic orientation; hence, we still do not have a deductive theory with general, testable propositions, although notable progress has been made on some aspects, particularly with the publication of Fishman's *Reversing Language Shift* (Fishman 1991).[2]

In particular, we do not know very much about the influence of economic processes (particularly at the macro level) on linguistic ones. There certainly is, in the economics of language, a growing literature that investigates how economic variables or processes affect language spread, decline and use. In the case of minority languages, the economic effects of state-sponsored maintenance efforts have been studied by Ó Cinnéide and Keane (1988) and Sproull (1996); some more theoretical papers explore changes in patterns of minority-language use over time (Grin 1992 and 1993) or second-language learning and its implications for language spread (Church and King 1993; John and Yi 1995). In these papers, patterns of expansion and decline are viewed as the result of an essentially economic calculus of utility-maximization. However, these contributions only constitute steps towards a fuller, more general understanding of how economic forces shape our *linguistic environment.*

Tackling these questions raises a number of conceptual and empirical difficulties reviewed elsewhere (Grin 1996), and it is no surprise that economists have devoted most of their attention not so much to the effect of economic variables on linguistic ones, but on the *reciprocal* causation—that is, how linguistic variables affect economic ones (Grin, 1999). Even then, these links are usually approached in microeconomic terms. For example, economists of language often investigate how the fact that people belong to some particular language group affects their labor income.[3] This does not, *per se*, amount to a macro-level interpretation of the links between the economic sphere and our linguistic environment. However, if only because it is sound practice to ground macro-level analyses on an understanding of micro-level processes, we can use the latter as a stepping-stone. In this paper, I will therefore attempt to discuss some macro-level implications of the relationship between language and economics. In so doing, I shall be combining the two causal directions mentioned earlier, that is, from linguistic to economic variables and from economic to linguistic variables, but the thrust of the argument is on the latter causal direction.

An integrative treatment of how macro-level economic processes affect our linguistic environment would far exceed the scope of this modest paper. Hence, I shall try to arrive at some meaningful propositions by focusing on a somewhat narrower question, namely: "do market forces exert a positive or a negative influence on linguistic diversity?" Even if this question could be answered in a general way (which, in itself, is not a foregone conclusion), it would constitute but one part of the larger theme; however, it is a very central part, and hence one that I believe is well worth investigating.

The "Unregulated" Context

What then do we know about the effect of so-called free market forces on linguistic diversity? This raises from the start a number of definitional problems which cannot be fully discussed here. However, a few caveats are in order.

First, the "free" market to which I am referring implies freedom to buy and sell goods, services and production factors with only minimal state-imposed restrictions on their nature, quantity or price. This is the case referred to here, in shorthand, as the "unregulated context". The implicit concept of freedom therefore applies to specific areas of human activity (production, consumption and exchange; "production" itself is a broad area that includes "work"). Of course, what shapes people's *desire* or *ability* to work, produce, exchange and consume, as well as the terms on which they do so, can only be considered "free" in a purely formalistic sense: these inclinations, and hence the resulting activities, take place in a context determined by history, culture and power. Therefore, using the concept of "free" markets must not be interpreted as reflecting a naive belief that a broader form of freedom automatically follows from economic liberalism. It simply makes it clear that we are talking about free markets in the standard neoliberal sense.

Elementary Mechanics of Market-Driven Language Spread

The concepts of *supply* and *demand* are essential analytical tools in the study of the unregulated context. For example, we could start by assuming that a certain linguistic environment, at a given time, can be seen as an "equilibrium" resulting from the intersection of a supply curve and a demand curve. The use of supply and demand in the study of language issues raises thorny definitional questions investigated elsewhere (Grin 1997a). A common—but not unproblematic—interpretation is close to that developed by Grenier and Vaillancourt (1983), who do not address supply and demand *for a language in general*, but supply and demand for *language skills on the labor market*. The interpretation then goes as follows: if (for whatever reason) demand for particular language skills increases (e.g., the ability to speak a language of wider communication such as English), this will tend to drive up the price of these skills, and hence the wage rate of people who possess them. As a consequence, more people will have an incentive to learn the language, and English will spread. It should be noted that the expansion of one language does not necessarily require the demise of other languages; hence, the spread of English does not *ipso facto* mean that linguistic diversity is threatened. The two processes may be empirically related, but their theoretical connection is not self-evident and deserves closer scrutiny. In particular, the following three questions need to be addressed if we wish to assess the implications of this market-driven vision of language spread:

- first, can market forces be seen as providing the reason(s) for the *initial* increase in demand?
- second, what exactly happens on the labor market?
- third, what does this tell us about long-term language dynamics *as an outcome of market forces*?

Market Forces as a Primary Impetus

There is little doubt that market forces are closely linked to changes in the *demand* for skills in some language or other; for example, the economic weight of an economy that functions primarily in the English language—that of the United States—will generally encourage European corporations to recruit English-speaking employees able to interact with potential clients and suppliers in the U.S.

However, it is not so much market forces themselves as other processes that provide the initial impetus for this state of affairs. These processes create a *context* within which market forces can *subsequently* cause demand for specific language skills to increase, and then set in motion the mechanism described above. The economists Breton and Mieszkowski (1977) mention clearly *non-market* behaviors such as "displaying substantial military power," "military intervention" and "diplomatic interference" by X-speaking countries as reasons for the dominant position of language X. Focusing on English, Phillipson (1992) has investigated the ways in which language spread can be interpreted as a deliberate policy.

In recent years, the position of English has been attracting the attention of an increasing number of scholars; for example, Crystal (1997) has argued that different causes lie at the origin of its spread. The causes mentioned are *first* political expansion, mainly through colonization, which has given the English language a ubiquitous presence around the globe; British political power was, over time, relayed and replaced by U.S. might; the *second* cause singled out by Crystal is economic clout, initially linked to Britain's pioneering role in the industrial revolution, and then to the rise of the U.S. as the world's leading economic power. There again, the ultimate causes of the spread of English appear to be related to (military) power and (demographic) size, far more than to the *economic* mechanism of the market—or any other purely market-driven rationality. One important implication of the above is that even if one endows markets with characteristics such as "naturalness"—a temptation that many find irresistible, dubious as it may be on analytical grounds—it would in no way allow us to view language spread as a "natural" process, because it is clearly initiated and abetted by non-market processes.

The case of English, however, is unique in that its increasing use has coincided with accelerating technological innovation in Western countries. Crystal (1997) reviews the linguistic aspects of technical progress in the media, international travel and safety, and communications, showing how closely the English language was associated with these developments. His survey confirms how difficult it is to theorize about a unique case, and hence to offer causal explanations of any generality. Crystal is therefore led to conclude that English "is a language which has repeatedly found itself at the right place at the right time" (1997, 110). Apart from being rather circular, such a conclusion provides a good illustration of the point made in this section: although market forces may further language spread, they cannot be seen as the ultimate cause of language spread and are not sufficient to explain the decline of linguistic diversity. However, they may well contribute to these processes once they have been set in motion by primarily non-economic causes; how this works—and how far it can go—is the question to which I now turn.

A Closer Look at Labor Market Dynamics

Let us consider the case in which essentially non-market forces cause some initial increase in the demand for English-language skills on the labor market. This market is conventionally represented with a supply curve and a demand curve in the price-quantity space, where the quantity in question is that of the labor force *with English-language skills* (measured in work hours), and the price is the wage rate offered on that particular segment of the labor market. As usual, the demand curve is decreasing in price (the higher the hourly cost of a worker's labor, the lower the number of hours managers will want to employ), while the supply

curve is increasing in price (the higher the wage rate offered on
the market, the more willing people will be to offer their labor).
Market equilibrium is given by the intersection of supply curve S
and demand curve D, which denotes an equilibrium employment
at q and an equilibrium wage rate at w (fig. 8.1). The increase in
demand for English-language skills causes the demand curve to
shift to the right to D' (*at any given wage rate*, employers are willing to hire more workers with English-language skills, or to increase the number of hours during which they employ their workers). This creates an excess demand for this category of workers,
forcing employers to offer higher wages; more English-speaking
workers will then offer their services; alternatively, English-
speaking workers already in employment will be willing to increase their hours. This determines a new equilibrium at a higher
overall employment level q' and a higher wage rate w'.

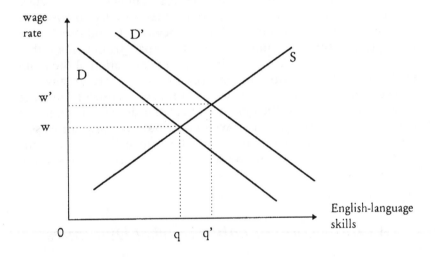

Figure 8.1. Labor-market equilibrium

Let us note in passing that this analytically simple result has been
very under-researched empirically. The reason is that measuring
the evolution of wage rates according to workers' language skills
requires data sets of which there are currently very few. This is
particularly true in the case of *foreign* languages. Although there
are numerous contributions on Canadian (see, e.g., Vaillancourt
1996) or U.S. (see, e.g., Bloom and Grenier 1996) cases, these studies examine the labor market value of English-language skills in

countries where English is an official and/or demolinguistically dominant language. Ongoing research on Switzerland will provide what may well be the first econometric estimates of the rates of return to English as a *foreign* language (recall that English is the first language of less than 0.9 percent of the resident population of Switzerland). Available results there indicate that even after controlling statistically for the usual determinants of income (education, experience, economic sector of activity), a fluent command of English is handsomely rewarded (Grin 1997b).

Let us now venture into the market-induced dynamics of the profitability of English-language skills. As people observe that rewards for this particular skill increase, a larger number of people will decide to learn the language well. They may well be assisted in this choice by the government. A telling example can be found in the Swiss canton of Zurich, where the department of education decided, in November 1997, to increase the allocation of hours for English-language classes, to the detriment of French, Switzerland's second official language.[4] Although the decision was not based on a proper examination of wage differentials accruing to people able to speak English, it mirrors a general perception that English is indispensable to personal material success and to the performance of a technologically advanced economy.

These factors induce a shift of the supply curve to the right: at a given wage level, more people than before have English-language skills to offer on the labor market. This shift is represented in figure 8.2. The interesting result is that the equilibrium quantity of

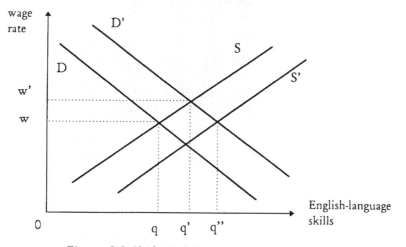

Figure 8.2. Shifts in labor-market equilibrium

English-language skills increases to q", while there is no telling *a priori* where the new wage rate will be. If the rightward shift of the supply curve is a dramatic one, the oversupply of English-speaking workers will cause the wage rate to dip below its initial level; if there is only a modest shift in supply, it is likely to remain above its initial level.

However, the process certainly does not stop here. Quite apart from the fact that whatever forces induced the initial rightward shift in demand may still be operating, the increase in the level of employment of the segment of the workforce endowed with English-language skills generally reinforces the relevance of English as a language of wider communication; for example, it increases the likelihood that among persons from a different linguistic background, English will be the one language they have in common, or the language in which their combined competence level is highest. The precise workings of this class of processes has been approached through the theory of "network externalities" (King and Church 1993; John and Yi 1996); in short, network externalities theory analyzes how agent j's decision to learn, say, a computer standard or some other language, will be made more profitable (and hence more likely) if agent k does the same. A full characterization of the process would require, in addition, a terrain investigation of many technical aspects of inter-group communication, which is far from complete. Independently of the network rationality of language learning, and the more or less complicated technical aspects through which these network effects play themselves out, it may also be the case that the spread of a given language of wider communication affects people's tastes in favor of the language concerned. All these reasons, whether market-driven or not (although market-driven reasons are probably sufficient to generate the dynamics explored here) induce *another* shift of the demand curve to the right. This, as explained above, will in turn induce a further rightward shift of the supply curve, and so on.

What this means is that simple labor market dynamics provide a plausible explanation of language spread *after an initial push from non-market forces*. Language spread appears to have a market-driven momentum of its own, with continuous increases in the number of people equipped with, say, English-language skills (graphically, this is denoted by the increase of q to q', q'', q''', etc.). However, we should observe that this still tells us nothing about the evolution of the wage rate w. Successive shifts in demand drive it up, and successive shifts in supply bring it back down. On balance, it is impossible to say that one effect will systematically dominate, and hard data are lacking for a proper empirical treatment of the issue. Nevertheless, circumstantial evidence can be used to investigate it, as proposed below.

Long-Term Dynamics

The first thing to observe is that, as English-language skills become more widespread, they are likely to become more banal. Two observations suggest that, over time, this is more likely to erode the premium rewarding English-language skills than to increase it. Some indirect evidence can be found in Bloom and Grenier's (1996) in-depth analysis of the evolution of wage differentials between anglophones and Hispanics in the U.S. They conclude (1996, 60) that "a large supply of minority-language speakers depresses wages more among those whose primary language is not the dominant language of the labor market than it drives their wages upward by creating demand for services in the minority language." Admittedly, these findings can be explained away by self-selection behavior into high-proportion Hispanic regions; besides, it only offers a roundabout way of pondering the likely evolution of the returns to English-language skills. Let us, however, make another observation by drawing a parallel with literacy.

There was a time–not too many decades ago in Western societies, and currently in some developing countries[5]–when the ability to read and write was a major asset, either inherited from, or giving access to, a privileged socioeconomic position. As literacy has become generalized, the material and symbolic rates of return on literacy have gone down. It is no longer the case that literacy pays off–rather, illiteracy carries severe material and symbolic penalties. A premium now has to be earned through the mastery of other, *additional* skills. Indirect as it is, this evidence suggests that the generalization of English-language skills, which may well be furthered by the operation of free-market forces, is more likely to reduce than to increase the market value of those skills. This can be represented as a succession of equilibrium points x, x', x'', x''', etc., with a steadily decreasing wage rate, as shown in figure 8.3.

It may well be the case that English-language skills will continue to become generalized; but because they will become mundane, their ability to enrich those who possess them will erode. What will then provide access to higher earnings is likely to be additional skills, just as literacy acquired in childhood now needs to be

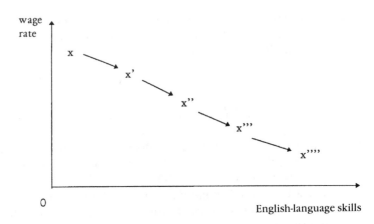

Figure 8.3. Evolution of labor-market equilibrium over time

complemented by vocational or academic training. Linguistic competence in languages *other than* English is high on the list of skills that will become profitable. Consider the following scenario in international trade, probably occurring in the not too distant future. A Saudi ministry official is looking for some industrial equipment for irrigation facilities; this equipment can equally well be supplied by a Singaporean, a Swedish or a French company, each of which delegates a sales representative to Saudi Arabia. Assume the respective products to be similar in price and technical performance (as is increasingly likely to be the case, along with the international integration of markets); further assume that all four actors are fluent in English. Because the products are essentially identical, what will give a company a competitive edge is some *other* attribute, and it is quite likely that a seller's ability to approach the Saudi customer in Arabic will be precisely such an attribute. Evidence on retail sales in Catalonia and Quebec clearly shows that even though buyers are perfectly able to understand a sales pitch and to buy a product in Castilian or in English, they prefer to do so in Catalan or French respectively. Knowledge of the customer's language, of course, offers no systematic guarantee that a contract will be signed. However, over a high number of business dealings, such skills (along with cultural, as opposed to linguistic competence) are likely to make a difference.

The implication is quite clear: the ability to address a customer in his or her language will become a strategic asset for companies, induce them to reward those skills through wage differentials, and hence provide an incentive for people to learn languages other than English. In short, market forces may well contribute to the spread of a language; but their very logic implies limitations on their homogenizing tendencies by generating mechanisms that reward behaviors which maintain diversity. Ultimately, market regulation is largely a system of checks and balances, and it would be missing the point to claim that market forces are only, and by their very nature, detrimental to diversity; the real problem is not market exchange as a form of rationality, but the unequal power structures within which market exchange takes place.

Of course, this encouraging forecast is subject to some restrictions, two of which seem to have particular importance. The first one is that (using the example above) Saudis must not *forget* Arabic the very moment they become fluent English speakers. Since documented cases of language shift (even those resulting in the full displacement of a language) go through a stage of generalized (though usually *subtractive*) bilingualism, it is hard to imagine a scenario in which there would not be a phase of bilingualism during which the market-driven, diversity-maintaining mechanism described above could operate. Obviously, the chances of such a mechanism effectively maintaining diversity are much higher if bilingualism is of the additive kind. Additive bilingualism (even when the non-expanding language is not a minority language in the usual sense) can therefore make a major difference in the long-term preservation of diversity.

The second, and somewhat disheartening point is that market forces may help preserve a *qualified*, but not an unrestricted form of diversity. Arabic is the language of a sufficiently large pool of potential buyers for Singaporean, Swedish or French firms to encourage investment by their nationals in the learning of Arabic; the same cannot be said of lesser-used languages. Sheer market forces, in the unregulated context, apparently contain no built-in mechanism that could help preserve them. This is not to say that market forces cannot be harnessed to this end; however, this is only possible in what I call the *regulated* context, which is described below.

The Regulated Context: The Case of Gaillimh le Gaeilge

Unhampered market forces may provide built-in safeguards against linguistic uniformity; unfortunately, they offer no guarantees for the preservation of minority languages with little economic clout.

The same observation can be stated differently, by saying that in general, minority languages have no *market* value. However, it does not follow that they have no *economic* value. One should not forget that, ultimately, economics is not about financial or material performance, but about *utility*, or satisfaction, and that money is merely, in sound economic theory, a means to an end.

This is clearly exemplified by environmental commodities. Clean air and unspoilt landscapes, as such, have no market value, and they cannot be bought or sold like a car, a bottle of wine or an employee's time. Nevertheless, they have economic value, because the enjoyment of clean air and unspoilt landscapes generates utility. However, because there is no market for such assets, unhampered market forces are likely to induce behaviors that will result in the destruction of those assets (or in an inadequate supply thereof, which is analytically the same thing). This problem is known in the literature as *market failure*. Linguistic environments present striking similarities with the natural environment; this argument is developed elsewhere (e.g. Grin and Hennis-Pierre 1997), showing that what applies to one, quite probably applies to the other. In particular, policy intervention is indispensable to avoid the undersupply of environmental goods and, for similar reasons, of linguistic diversity. Such intervention transforms the unregulated into a regulated context. As it is used here, the term "regulated" denotes a situation in which market forces are constrained by public policy measures. Policy measures do not necessarily take the form of mandatory behavior (e.g., requiring companies, by law, to package and label their products bilingually); they may actually use market mechanisms. For example, the tax schedule can be amended in order to offer fiscal benefits to those firms that have a particularly commendable language-use policy.

The recourse to market mechanisms has opened a whole range of environmental policy measures aimed at the preservation of environmental quality. They can prove more effective than prohibition or mandatory behavior, if only because they are not seen as quite as meddlesome; their rationale is to modify the framework conditions within which market forces operate (as in the fiscal example in the preceding paragraph), and then to rely on those market forces to induce the behavior desired.

Examples of language policies that rely on market forces to preserve linguistic diversity are still very few. Efforts have been made to promote the visibility of minority languages in business and commerce (Price 1997), but it is not always the same thing as a clear reliance on market forces to assist in the task of minority language maintenance (and hence, the preservation of diversity).

One current example that goes further in this direction is that of the *Gaillimh le Gaeilge* ("Galway with Irish") project, initiated in 1988 by the Comhdháil Náisiúnta na Gaeilge (CnaG), a non-government organization that federates various bodies involved in the promotion of Irish. CnaG began by commissioning a study (Cinnéide and Keane 1988) to evaluate the economic impact on the city of Galway and the surrounding Gaeltacht (Irish-speaking area) of the various government measures in favor of Irish. The report showed that the amounts spent yearly on Irish language promotion by the authorities generated IR£13.1m in *added* business for the city of Galway (or IR£17m for Galway and the surrounding Gaeltacht area taken together). CnaG then used this finding to impress on local businesses (for example, through the Chamber of Commerce) that in the regulated context created by government intervention, Galway and its region vastly benefited from the survival of Irish. The language could actually be seen as an income-generating asset, one that is highly valuable in a rather peripheral location such as the western fringes of Ireland. Hence, the case could be made that it was in the interests of business owners themselves to do their part to strengthen the position and visibility of Irish in local economic and commercial life. As a result, CnaG has been able to persuade an increasing number of providers of goods and services (particularly in restaurants, hotels and retail shopping) to put up bilingual Irish-English outdoor signs, propose bilingual menus, use bilingual stationery and forms, or even advertise bilingually. Many local branches of national or international corporations have joined the *Gaillimh le Gaeilge* project, which provides strictly no financial support for the bilingualisation of business operations, but stresses instead the fact that it is very much in the interests of businesses to go bilingual as far as possible. Since the inception of the project, an estimated 135 businesses have introduced bilingual signs, and 83 use Irish for other purposes such as invoice forms or stationery. Many of those joining in do not want to appear to be lagging behind what is increasingly perceived as a modern trend.[6] In this way, business people's market-driven concern to ensure that their image keeps abreast of that of their competitors concurs to affirm and maintain linguistic diversity.

The story of *Gaillimh le Gaeilge*, which has done much to re-legitimize the natural use of Irish in an urban commercial setting, is one in which outside intervention has used market forces with consummate skill in order to turn the latter to the advantage of a minority language. Such success, of course, cannot be taken for

granted and requires continuing attention to protect what is still a
marginal strategic inroad. Nevertheless, it indicates that much can
be gained by exploiting opportunities to harness market forces for
the benefit of diversity, instead of attempting, often vainly, to
combat them. In addition, this result has been reached at little cost
to the authorities, whose financial involvement, mostly in the form
of an annual grant to support the project, can be estimated at
IR£40,000 per year.

Conclusion: On Policy Implications

In this paper, I have tried to show that the effect of market forces
on linguistic diversity is a complex one–more complex, at least,
than is sometimes claimed in the literature; those claims may proceed from a confusion between the phenomenon of *globalization,*
and what is usually called, with little attention to its dynamics, "the
market".

The main results of this investigation are the following:
- Market forces certainly contribute to the spread of languages
  of wider communication—at this time, the language that most
  visibly (that is, most globally) benefits from this is undoubt-
  edly English—although other languages can expand regionally
  to the detriment of more local ones.
- However, it is usually non-market forces that give the primary
  impetus to the process whereby a language progressively ac-
  quires the status of a language of wider communication; there
  is nothing "natural" about language spread.
- Market forces do not necessarily result in the demise of all
  other languages, even in the long run, because market dynamics contain a built-in system of checks and balances.
- When unhampered market forces do contribute to language
  death, as is certainly the case for lesser-used languages, this reflects the fact that these languages have no *market* value; economic value, however, includes non-market values generated
  outside the sphere of market exchange.
- The absence of market value does not mean that these languages have no *economic* value.
- Using commonalities between linguistic diversity and environmental assets like clean air or unspoilt landscapes, it is
  possible to justify economically the recourse to policy instru-

ments that will modify the market context and induce diversity-preserving behavior.

- Such intervention need not imply an uphill battle against market forces, but can use chinks in the market armor to turn these forces to advantage in the struggle for the preservation of linguistic diversity.

In conclusion, I would like to return to the observation made earlier that the initial impetus of language spread has to be traced back to *non-market* causes. It follows that existing inequalities between languages (and their prospects for the future) are ultimately the result of causes such as political, *geo*political and military inequality, along with technical processes whose logical articulation with power play are, as yet, not fully understood–as evidenced by the somewhat circular character of Crystal's explanation of the dominant position of English.

What matters here, from a policy standpoint, is that the argument according to which policy measures suggested to reverse patterns of language shift and preserve diversity can be rejected on the basis of their allegedly "non-economic" nature is doubly flawed. First, because a proper understanding of linguistic diversity (including its substantial similarities with environmental assets) provides a strong case for welfare-increasing policy interventions which are, as such, perfectly justified on economic grounds; this latter point becomes even more cogent once it is recognized that policy intervention can use market forces instead of running against them. Second, because if linguistic inequality is the result of behavior like military, political or cultural imperialism (which implies a departure from pure market exchange), it is difficult to argue that efforts made to restore some modicum of equality should be bound by the confines of the free market–let alone a narrow understanding of the latter. The only logically valid grounds for demanding that diversity-increasing policies pass the test of market compatibility would be the joint assumptions that linguistic diversity is not worth preserving, and that the quest for some degree of equality is not legitimate. Conversely, the main reason why it is important to understand why and how market forces can contribute to the maintenance of linguistic diversity is not because market compatibility represents some incontrovertible requirement, but quite simply because, from a strategic standpoint, market-compatible policy measures can be among the most effective.

This brief foray into the policy implications of the effects of market forces on linguistic diversity can serve to remind us of a basic truth that has been all but forgotten in the current fascination with the (indeed fascinating) workings of free markets: that the market is just an arrangement, generally good, but not perfect, for the regulation of human exchange and, as such, is a means to an end, not an end in itself. Many of the most revered theorists of economic science were fully aware of this (see Bürgenmeier 1994 on Leon Walras). Recognition of non-material goals, such as environmental quality or linguistic diversity, can usefully put some priorities back into place: market forces are there to serve welfare, not the other way around.

Notes

1 The author thanks Jean-Marie Grether and Robert Phillipson for helpful comments, as well as the Swiss National Science Foundation (grant no. 4033–041060) for financial support.
2 See also the two theme issues of the *International Journal of the Sociology of Language*, 1995, precisely on the theme of language spread.
3 This line of research, in economics, definitely belongs to *micro*economics, even when using large data sets where the unit of analysis is a typical, not an actual individual. In other social sciences, by contrast, this level of analysis would often be defined as "macro".
4 This decision has elicited strong negative reactions, and its implementation has been immediately postponed.
5 My use of the term "developing" does not imply anything about the socioeconomic model towards which the countries concerned "should" (or should not) develop. It simply refers to low values of a variety of socioeconomic indicators, whether per capita GDP, literacy rates or life expectancy at birth.
6 On the Gaillimh le Gaeilge project, see CnaG annual reports, e. g. Comhdháil Náisiúnta na Gaeilge (1996). The author wishes to express thanks to CnaG director Peadar Ó Flatharta for supplying first-hand information on the experiment.

References

Appel, René, and Pieter Muysken. *Language Contact and Bilingualism*. London: Edward Arnold, 1987.
Bloom, David and Gilles Grenier. "Language, employment, and earnings in the United States: Spanish-English differentials from 1970 to 1990." *International Journal of the Sociology of Language*, 121 (1996): 45–68.

Breton, Albert, and Peter Mieszkowski. "The economics of bilingualism." In W. Oates, ed., *The Political Economy of Fiscal Federalism*, 261–273. Lexington, Mass: Lexington Books, 1977.

Bürgenmeier, Beat. "The misperception of Walras." *American Economic Review* 84 (1994): 342–352.

Church, Jeffrey and Ian King. "Bilingualism and network externalities." *Canadian Journal of Economics* 26 (1993): 337–345.

Comhdháil Náisiúnta na Gaeilge. *Gaillimh le Gaeilge. Tuarascáil bhliantúil 1996* (Galway with Irish. Yearly Report, 1996). Baile Átha Cliath/Dublin, 1996.

Crystal, David. *English as a Global Language*. Cambridge: Cambridge University Press, 1997.

Fishman, Joshua. *Reversing Language Shift*. Clevedon: Multilingual Matters, 1991.

Grenier, Gilles, and François Vaillancourt. "An economic perspective on learning a second language." *Journal of Multilingual and Multicultural Development*, 4 (1983): 471–483.

Grin, François. "Towards a Threshold Theory of Minority Language Survival." *Kyklos* 45 (1992): 69–97.

——. "The relevance of thresholds in language maintenance and shift: a theoretical examination." *Journal of Multilingual and Multicultural Development* 14 (1993): 375–392.

——. "Economic approaches to language and language planning: an introduction." *International Journal of the Sociology of Language* 121 (1996): 1–16.

——. "Aménagement linguistique: du bon usage des concepts d'offre et de demande" (Language planning: on the proper use of the concepts of supply and demand). In N. Labrie, ed., *Etudes récentes en linguistique de contact* (Recent Studies in Contact Linguistics), 117–134. Bonn: Dümmler, 1997a.

——. *Langue et différentiels de statut socio-économique en Suisse* (Language and socioeconomic status differentials in Switzerland). Berne: Office fédéral de la statistique, 1997b.

——. "Economics." In J. Fishman, ed., *Handbook of Language and Ethnic Identity*, 9–24. Oxford: Oxford University Press, 1999.

Grin, François, and Catherine Hennis-Pierre. "La diversité linguistique et culturelle face aux règles du commerce international: le cas du film et des émissions de télévision" (Linguistic and cultural diversity in the face of international trade rules: the case of films and television broadcasting). In S. Abou and K. Haddad, eds., *La diversité linguistique et culturelle et les enjeux du développement* (Linguistic and cultural diversity and the challenge of development), 256–286. Beyrouth: Université Saint-Joseph, and Montréal: AUPELF-UREF, 1997.

John, Andrew and Kei-Mu Yi. "Language, learning and location." *Discussion Paper* No. 264, The Jefferson Center for Political Economy, University of Virginia, 1996.

Ó Cinnéide, Mícheál, and Michael Keane. *Local Socio-economic Impacts Associated with the Galway Gaeltacht.* Gaillimh/Galway: Coláiste na hollscoile Gaillimhe, 1988.

Phillipson, Robert. *Linguistic Imperialism.* Oxford: Oxford University Press, 1992.

Price, Adam. *The Diversity Dividend. Language, Culture and Economy in an Integrated Europe.* Brussels: European Bureau for Lesser-Used Languages, 1997.

Sproull, Alan. "Regional economic development and minority language use: the case of Gaelic Scotland." *International Journal of the Sociology of Language,* 121 (1996): 93–117.

Vaillancourt, François. "Language and socioeconomic status in Quebec: measurement, findings, determinants, and policy costs." *International Journal of the Sociology of Language,* 121 (1996): 69–92.

Linguistic Diversity, Human Rights and the "Free" Market

TOVE SKUTNABB-KANGAS

Globalisation carries with it a danger of uniformity [...] Peace means diversity [...] it means multiethnic and multilingual societies.
(From UNESCO's *The Human right to peace. Declaration by the Director-General*, 1997, 9)

The State of the World's Languages

Today we have at least around 7,000 (maybe up to 10,000) *oral* languages[1] and thousands of *sign* languages.[2] The *big killer languages*, the top ten oral languages in the world (in terms of number of mother-tongue speakers), all with more than 100 million speakers, are Chinese, English, Hindi/Urdu, Spanish, Arabic, Portuguese, Russian, Bengali, Japanese and German. They comprise only between 0.1 and 0.15% of the world's oral languages but account for close to 50% of the world's oral population.

A very small group of the world's oral languages, numbering less than 300, are spoken by communities of one million speakers and above. In addition to the big killer languages they comprise *middle-sized languages*, which to many of us may seem small, like Hungarian, Slovak, Croatian, Finnish, Swedish, Danish, Czech, Estonian, and Esperanto. Among these, only French and Italian have over 50 million speakers. Demographically, these fewer than 300 languages account for a total of over 5 billion speakers, or close to 95 % of the world's oral population.

On the other hand, somewhat over half of the world's (oral) languages, and most of the sign languages, are used by communities of 10,000 speakers or less, and most of them are spoken in one country only (84 % of all the world's oral languages are endemic to the country). These are the *small and threatened languages*. But, half of these, in turn, meaning around a quarter of the world's oral languages, are spoken by communities of 1,000 speakers or less, according to Dave Harmon (1995). Demographically, their speakers total only about 8 million people, less than 0.2 % of an estimated world population of 5.3 billion. Over 25 % of the world's languages account for only 0.2 % of speakers. These *really small and endangered languages* are the most vulnerable oral languages of the world (and all sign languages are threatened).

Michael Krauss from Alaska is one of the linguists who has worked hard to make the world aware of the threat to languages (e.g. Krauss 1992). He estimates (1995) the number of oral languages that are assured of still being around in 2100 at only around 600, well below 10 % of the present oral languages. Again, this count does not consider sign languages.[3] Already today, Krauss claims, between 20 and 50 % of the world's oral languages are no longer being learned by children, meaning they are "beyond endangerment, they are living dead and will disappear in the next century". According to this prognosis, then, not only are most of those languages with fewer than 10,000 speakers, that is, over half of today's languages, going to disappear, but also most of the ones which have between 10,000 and one million speakers. All this just in the next hundred years.

Languages are today being killed and linguistic diversity is disappearing at a much faster pace than ever before in human history.

Now we could just say: so what? Is it not a natural development? Will it not be easier when all of us speak the same language, or only a few big languages?

No.

Linguistic and cultural diversity are as necessary for the existence of our planet as biodiversity. They are correlated: where one type is high, the other one is too. Mark Pagel points out that in North America "languages, like all biological species, get thicker on the ground as you approach the equator" (Pagel, as reported by Nicholas Ostler in *Iatiku: Newsletter of the Foundation for Endangered Languages* 1, 1995, 6).

Luisa Maffi, President of Terralingua,[4] also says (1996) that there are "remarkable overlaps between global mappings of the world's areas of biological megadiversity and areas of high linguistic diversity", and likewise a "correlation between low-diversity cultural systems and low biodiversity" (Maffi 1996).[5]

However, the relationship between linguistic and cultural diversity on the one hand, and biodiversity on the other, is not only correlational. There seems to be mounting evidence that it might be causal. According to Maffi, ethnobiologists, human-ecologists and others have proposed "theories of 'human-environment coevolution'", including the assumption that "cultural diversity might enhance biodiversity or vice versa" (ibid.).

In this perspective, the first conference investigating this relationship, called "Endangered Languages, Endangered Knowledge, Endangered Environments" (organized by Maffi at the University of California, Berkeley, October 1996) stressed "the need to address the foreseeable consequences of massive disruption of such long-standing interactions" (ibid.).

The processes of language loss also "affect the maintenance of traditional environmental knowledge—from loss of biosystematic lexicon to loss of traditional stories" (ibid.).

The United Nations Environmental Program (UNEP), one of the organizations behind the 1992 Rio Biodiversity Conference, produced a massive book on global biodiversity assessment that summarizes current knowledge about biodiversity (Heywood 1995; see also Groombridge 1992). Now UNEP also acknowledges the connection between biological resources and human resources. It is in the process of producing a companion volume to the biodiversity book, on Cultural and Spiritual Values of Biodiversity (Posey & Dutfield [eds.], in press). The chapter on Language Diversity (Maffi & Skutnabb-Kangas, in press) argues that "the preservation of the world's linguistic diversity must be incorporated as an essential goal in any bioculturally-oriented diversity conservation program" (from Executive Summary).

It is interesting that the loss of biodiversity has had massive attention all over the world—many people are worried about it. But few people talk of loss of linguistic diversity. Still, linguistic diversity is today disappearing much faster than biological diversity, in the sense that the percentage of languages that will perish/be killed in the next century is larger than the percentage of all biological species that will be killed during the same period.

"Preservation of the linguistic and cultural heritage of humankind" (one of UNESCO's declared goals) has been seen by many researchers and politicians as a nostalgic primordialist dream (creating employment for the world's linguists). The perpetuation of linguistic diversity is, however, a necessity for the survival of the planet, in a similar way to biodiversity (Maffi & Skutnabb-Kangas, in press).

But what does this have to do with linguistic human rights?

Linguistic Genocide and the Market-Value of Languages

For the maintenance of linguistic and cultural diversity on our planet and the development of languages, educational language rights are not merely vital but the most important linguistic human rights. If children are not granted the opportunity to learn their parents' idiom[6] fully and properly so that they become (at least) as proficient as their parents, the language is not going to survive. Normally parents transmit their languages to their children. They do it partly by using the language themselves with the children, and partly, and increasingly importantly, by choosing their own language as the medium of education for their children or by otherwise ensuring that their children get full competence in their language in school. When more and more children gain access to formal education, much of the more formal language learning which earlier happened in the community must happen in schools. Where the school does not support the intergenerational transmission of the parents' language to children, it *may* be a conscious, voluntary choice by one or both parents, where they *are* aware of the long-term consequences of the non-transmittance for the children themselves, for the relationship between parents and children and sometimes even for the future of the language. But in most cases I would claim that there may not have been any conscious choice with real alternatives. Then it may be a question of linguistic genocide.

When the United Nations did preparatory work for what later became the International Convention for the Prevention and Punishment of the Crime of Genocide (E 793, 1948), linguistic and cultural genocide were discussed alongside physical genocide and were seen as serious crimes against humanity (see Capotorti 1979). When the Convention was accepted, Article 3, covering linguistic and cultural genocide, was voted down and it was thus not included in the final Convention of 1948.

What remains, however, is a definition of linguistic genocide which most states then in the UN were prepared to accept. Linguistic genocide is defined (in Art. 3, 1) as

> Prohibiting the use of the language of the group in daily intercourse or in schools, or the printing and circulation of publications in the language of the group.

Linguistic genocide, as defined by the UN, is practised throughout the world. The use of an indigenous or minority language can be prohibited overtly and directly, through laws, imprisonment, torture, killings and threats (as in Turkey today vis-à-vis the Kurds, according to human rights organizations; e.g., *Human Rights in Kurdistan* 1989; *Helsinki Watch Update* 1990; see also Skutnabb-Kangas & Bucak 1994 and Hassanpour, this volume).

The use of a small language can also be prohibited covertly, more indirectly via ideological and structural means. Especially in the West, but increasingly everywhere where literacy and formal education play an important role in children's socialization, educational systems are the direct agents of this killing. Every time there are indigenous or minority children in day-care centers and schools with no bilingual teachers authorized to use the languages of the children as the regular teaching and child-care media, this is tantamount to prohibiting the use of minority languages "in daily intercourse or in schools". This is the situation for most immigrant and refugee minority children in all Western European countries and in the United States, Canada and Australia, as well for most indigenous first nations, both earlier and, for many, still today (see, e.g., Fettes, in press; Hamel 1994; Jordan 1988).

But behind education and other types of direct agents we have those structural agents which are decisive for what alternatives exist in the educational system and in other market places where languages are allocated certain values—both economic values and, partially but not completely through this—market values (see Grin, this volume, on the implications of the difference). Languages are validated or invalidated. Their standing on the market for linguistic capital is assessed. This is where languages compete with each other, and this is where the linguicist hierarchisation of languages[7] takes place. Linguicism is defined as "ideologies, structures and practices which are used to legitimate, effectuate and reproduce an unequal division of power and resources (material and immaterial) between groups which are defined on the basis of language" (Skutnabb-Kangas 1988, 13).[8]

When linguistic diversity disappears through linguistic genocide (meaning languages are killed; they do NOT disappear through any kind of natural death, but are murdered), the speakers are assimilated into the realms of other languages. The top ten languages in terms of numbers are the real killer languages, and English is foremost among them (see Phillipson 1992; Graddol 1997). These are the languages whose speakers have allocated to themselves and to their languages more power and (material) resources than their numbers would justify, at the cost of speakers of other languages.

Using the metaphor of the languages themselves as killer languages may be vivid. However, it is the market forces behind the languages, behind the relative validation or invalidation, that are important to analyze. François Grin gives an exposé of this market elsewhere in this volume. I will only add a few sociological notes on alternative responses to changes under and after modernism. What I loosely call "the 'free'-market response" is centralisation, homogenisation, monocultural efficiency—and the consequences for linguistic diversity are disastrous. An alternative response could be through diversity, including implementing linguistic human rights.

"Free" Markets: Trying to Re-create the Illusion of Pre-modern Certainties, in a Post-modern World of Insecurities, with Fundamentalist Modernist Means

Dow Templeton Associates, part of one of the world's most powerful transnational complexes, puts their forecast for the next millennium very simply, under the subtitle "Global village" (*Dow 2000*. Third Quarter [1997], 1): "Individual value systems, cultures and traditions will be maintained, but English will become the universal language and capitalism will become the dominant social system."

It is interesting that transnational Dow expresses the parallel between a universal/dominant language and a universal/dominant economic system so clearly and so simply—not to say simplistically. Nevertheless, it is something for politically naive linguists to take note of.

An active agent in killing languages faster than ever is the development that has accelerated since the disintegration of the Soviet Union, namely the triumphalist proclamation of the "free"-market system as The Global System For Ever. Of course, it is everything but free (see, e.g., Escobar 1995—see also Grin [this volume] for a neoliberal standard definition). This proclamation has in fact constructed the "free-market" system as a *political* system rather than an economic system only.

There does not seem to be enough reason for this triumphalism. In its image-building claims it draws on individualist postmodern (or at least late-modernism-related) ideologies of mobility, change and unlimited choice—but the exact opposite seems to figure prominently in the lack of choice that it offers. In its prognoses, here symbolized by the Dow Templeton quote, it seems to belong to the early phases of modernism. Sociologist Göran Therborn defines the phases in the development from premodernity to modernity[9] and further to postmodernity, on a viewpoint axis where *PRE-MODERNITY* is "looking back, over its shoulder, to the past, to [its] ... experience and ... example of wisdom, beauty, glory". *MODERNITY* "looks at the future, hopes for it, plans for it, constructs, builds it."

Dow's prognosis above is a typical project for modernity, planning for future.

However, according to Therborn and others, that is no longer where we are. *POST-MODERNITY* "has lost or thrown away any sense of time direction. The past as well as the future and the present have become 'virtual realities,' or simultaneously combinable elements" (Therborn 1995, 4–5). Therborn's analysis tallies with that of another guru of postmodernism, Zygmunt Bauman, whose catch phrase "all that is solid melts in the air" captures (or, ironically, consolidates) the essence of postmodernism. Bauman claims (1997) that safety and security of life has disappeared with modernism. Instead, we have uncertainty, existential anxiety, Unsicherheit—and it is here to stay. We are/have to be or become reconciled to it. But it is not a fear of natural catastrophes but fear of results of human action; it is manufactured uncertainty. There is a lack of existential grounding: jobs disappear; traditional skills (or any skills on a long-term basis) no longer have a (lasting) market value; human partnerships, including the most intimate ones, are fragile. All are on the move—even if we never leave the place where we were born or where we stay: the ground is moving from under us, in spite of us. This may be good for some adventurous spirits, but for most of us it means anxiety. All of us have within us both enjoyment of adventure (as the postmodernist ideal has it) but also a fear of not being in control. Uncertainty creates, according to Bauman, fundamentalist, neotribal sentiments: let's make the world a bit simpler, more constrained.

The Dow prognosis above seems to me to be a perfect example of a result of this uncertainty: let's make the world simple, let's have one world language and one world economic system. And we who belong to the neotribe of capitalist English-speaking elites will gain and maintain control and be able to recognize the McDonaldized world. Outside, on the streets, the safe and homogenized and environmentally disastrous McDonalds and Pizza-Huts are the same everywhere. Inside, the hotels belong to the same chain with the same CNN—you could be anywhere in the world.

This is a powerful, but at the same time desperate solution: trying to re-create the illusion of premodern certainties, with modernist means, in a postmodern world–and ruining the planet as a side effect.

The development model with capitalism and English as both the means and the goals has been exported worldwide, neocolonising the "South" countries.[10] It is now being aggressively exported to Eastern and Central Europe (even if Western investments have lagged somewhat behind Western ideology). It has also operated in a similar fashion domestically in the North's own marginalised, "undereveloped" areas. A description of the process in the Arctic areas of the rich Nordic countries (Jussila & Segerståhl 1988, 17) could just as well relate to Africa—and, maybe, to Central and Eastern Europe? "Economic growth and its implications are present in the modernization process ... in the marginalised areas. All productive activities have been gradually geared towards markets after the emergence of money economy in these areas. The use of local resources is today a means for acquiring both financial and social prestige, which in turn sets aside ideas of a sustainable use of resources, although the knowledge of sustainability would exist."

It is also imperative to compare the "educational aid to development" and its results in former colonies in underdeveloped countries (countries that we in the West have consciously underdeveloped and continue to underdevelop—cf. Rodney 1983), with what is happening in Central and Eastern Europe. Are there parallels?

In much of Africa and Asia, the dominant role of English in secondary and higher education, on the route towards upward social mobility, remains unchanged, with substantial "aid" from British and American donors consolidating the position of English. As a result, there is a growing mismatch between actual language use in the society, societal goals and educational means, with the result that education is largely failing to deliver the goods (Alexander 1995a, 1995b; Heugh 1995a, 1995b; Luckett 1995; Rubagumya 1990). The picture is broadly similar in most former colonies (World Bank 1988; Haddad et al. 1990). Symptoms of crisis and financial straits make injections of cash from the World Bank more attractive, and the Bank and the IMF (International Monetary Fund) seem to have African countries in their pockets.[11]

There are grave grounds for doubting the appropriacy of such development assistance. Why should the Western world, where mass education is fraught with unresolved problems, be able to resolve acute problems elsewhere? (See Kozol 1991 on schools in diverse areas of the USA. In Britain, the pattern is equally patchy: according to the annual report on the conditions of schooling in England, drawn up by the Office for Standards in Education, "Half the primary schools and two-fifths of secondary schools are failing to teach children to a satisfactory standard" [reported in the *Guardian Weekly*, 11 February 1996].) How can decentralized education correspond to local needs when the "distance educators" who pull the financial and ideological strings know neither local cultures nor local languages? How is it that mostly monolingual English-speakers are running around the world as experts on how multilingual people in other parts of the world can become still more multilingual (by learning English), when Britain and the United States are notoriously failing to teach their majorities even the first elements of another language? I am reminded of the story of Dan Quayle, who visited Latin America as the US Vice-President and apologized for not knowing Latin—or the American headmaster who said to a minority student that if English was good enough for Jesus it was good enough for him ... These are fundamental ethical questions. Accountability must relate not merely to budgets but to a wide range of cultural and ecological concerns.

Historically, both *development* and *human rights* are central to UN activities and figure in innumerable declarations, beginning with the Charter of the United Nations (Article 55 commits its members to the promotion of higher standards of living, solutions to international economic, social, health and related problems, and international cultural and educational cooperation, and universal respect for human rights and fundamental freedoms. The same Article also outlaws discrimination on the basis of language). There is, however, an inherent contradiction between the commitment to development (as promoted by the UN's agencies, and multilateral and bilateral donors) and to human rights, since much of the evidence is that development programmes, e.g. the structural adjustment policies of the World Bank and the IMF, have "been found to harm rather than promote human rights" (Tomaševski 1993, 45). It is an additional paradox that much mainstream "aid" in the late 1980s was made conditional on human rights observance, particularly political rights, at a time when such "aid" was jeopardizing human rights. Criticism of the neglect of human rights in development aid has often been expressed by NGOs which, for instance, have documented that the interests of indigenous groups have been sacrificed on the altar of "economic progress" (ibid., 51; see also Stavenhagen 1990, 1995).

Summing up, market economy, and the creation of larger and more centralized economic, administrative and political units has, despite a rhetoric of democracy and local participation, been the order of the day in the "first" and "third" worlds. It also seems to be re-emerging in the former "second" world. The socioeconomic, techno-military, and political structural changes inevitably connected with the "modernization" process cause stress on both *nature* and on *people*, their socioeconomic conditions of life, and their languages and cultures (figure 9.1). These processes have resulted in an accelerated *environmental degradation* (= nature under stress), and *growing gaps* between the Haves and the Have-nots (or Never-to-haves as many of our Indian colleagues say), and in *linguistic and cultural genocide* (= people under stress). Education systems, as currently run, contribute to committing this linguistic and cultural genocide.

Alternative Responses to Changes

BACKGROUND REASONS

Socioeconomic, techno-military and political structural changes

RESULTS in

Environmental degradation	Linguistic and cultural genocide	Growing gaps between haves and have-nots

CREATES STRESS UPON

NATURE	PEOPLE	
	Languages and cultures	Socioeconomic conditions of life

THESE RESPOND, ALTERNATIVELY,

THROUGH MARKETS & MONOCULTURAL EFFICIENCY: Economic efficiency first priority; larger and more centralized economic and political units; OR	THROUGH DIVERSITY: Sustainability through diversity first priority; flexible, resilient and democratic economic and political units

WHICH RESULTS, ALTERNATIVELY, in

bio-diversity	linguistic and cultural diversity	living conditions	bio-diversity	linguistic and cultural diversity	living conditions
disappears	disappears; homogenization	deteriorate; polarization	maintenance	maintenance, development	sustainable; democratization

(This figure is partially inspired by the flow chart in Jussila & Segerståhl 1988, 18.)

Figure 9.1. Alternative responses to socioeconomic, techno-military and political structural changes

An important priority for research would be to define policies for preservation and development of environmental, linguistic and cultural, economic and political diversity.[12] This would also include studying the role of human rights in the different responses.

Human Rights and the "Free" Market

What is the response of the human rights system to giving free range to market forces? Human rights, especially economic and social rights, are, according to human rights lawyer Katarina Tomaševski (1996, 104), to act as *correctives to the free market.*

The first international human rights treaty abolished slavery. Prohibiting slavery implied that *people* were not supposed to be treated as market commodities. ILO (The International Labour

Organisation) has added that *labor* should not be treated as commodity. But price-tags are to be removed from other areas, too. Tomaševski (ibid., 104) claims that "The purpose of international human rights law is ... to overrule the law of supply and demand and remove price-tags from people and from necessities for their survival".

These necessities for survival include not only basic food and housing (which would come under economic and social rights), but also basics for the sustaining of a dignified life, including basic civil, political *and cultural* rights. In Johan Galtung's terms, it is not only material, somatic needs that are necessities for survival, but also non-material, mental needs (see Table 9.1).

Table 9.1 Types of basic needs and basic problems

TYPES OF BASIC NEEDS
vs.
Impediments to their
satisfaction

	DIRECT (intended)	STRUCTURAL (built-in)
Material needs (SOMATIC)	SECURITY vs. violence	WELL-BEING vs. misery
Non-material needs (MENTAL)	FREEDOM vs. repression	IDENTITY vs. alienation

(based on Galtung 1988, 147)

Education is part of "well-being" and "identity", and a prerequisite for "security" and "freedom". Education, including basic educational linguistic rights, is one of the necessities from which price-tags should be removed.

This means that it is the duty of each government to create conditions under which people are able to provide these necessities for those unable to do so themselves. Many people cannot do this, some of the reasons being that the right to work is not a fundamental inalienable individual human right. Neither is the right to fair trade at a collective level. If people cannot provide the necessities themselves, it is the duty of governments, according to human rights principles, to provide the necessities for them. If individual governments are unable to do so, it is the duty of the international community.

If this really happened, we would not need to worry about the fate of the world's languages. But it does not. Most states are either unwilling or unable to deliver—or both.[13] This unwillingness will be shown below, in the scrutinizing of the protection of educational language rights in some human rights instruments— which are, after all, signed and ratified by states. The capacity of states to deliver is partially eroded by the restrictions on sovereignty in the age of postmodernist globalisation which has replaced the *universalism* of the modernization period (Bauman 1997). *Universalisation*, seen by some idealists as positive (civilization was spread to more and more countries, differences were going to be leveled out), in fact had to do with westernisation and homogenisation. In Bauman's analysis (1997), the difference between the two is that *universalisation* was seen as something with active agents (we made it happen) whereas *globalisation* is (constructed as) something that happens to us, a natural process that moves by itself. The only possible actions by states are negative: to remove hurdles, obstacles from its way: to drop constraints on the "free" market, to make capital flexible, to make workers replaceable, movable and controllable, *not* take any positive action but only remove constraints on capitalism. Bauman uses the claims by Tietmeyer, the German finance magnate, as an example: according to Tietmeyer the key task for states in the world today is to secure the confidence and trust of investors. The state must remove any obstacles to this confidence. Tietmeyer's claims are accepted at face value; he does not need arguments to support his claims. In his world, the investors are the only volatile element/force. In Bauman's analysis, on the other hand, behind this lies the collapse of institutions of political control over trade and capital.

The earlier tests of the sovereignty of a state had to do with the extent to which the state had political control over the economy, the military, and culture, and the extent to which it was self-sufficient and sovereign and could provide for its citizens (see also Hassanpour, this volume). The postmodernist state has no control over the traditional markers of sovereignty; sovereignty has disappeared–or is shaky beyond repair. *Glocalisation* has replaced globalisation. There is a globalisation of finance and capital; they are extraterritorial. Everybody can buy the same tanks; i.e. military control has disappeared. And American culture is everywhere (see

Phillipson, this volume). Preservation of local law and order (the only area where states are "sovereign") represents localization. States use their power to control those who might want to prevent the removal of obstacles to globalisation.[14] Tietmeyer's investors are in Bauman's view interested in *weak but sovereign states*: states have to be weak in order not to be able to prevent the globalisation which multi- and transnationals need, on the other hand, they have to be capable of securing the safety of international businessmen on the streets everywhere and to control workers, i.e. to have control over the state apparatuses for violence for internal purposes. Most wars today are intrastate wars, not wars between states.

The often quoted fact of the top 358 multimillionaires (who have as much liquid cash as the poorest 45 % of the population of the world put together) is just one example of increasing inequality, one of the consequences of structural changes in globalisation (one of the "stress on people" factors in figure 9.1). But instead of analyzing the structural poverty resulting from, among other factors, the structural unemployment inherent in the "free markets" as a result of globalisation, the poor are constructed as being poor because of inherent deficiencies (including a lack of competence in dominant languages). If the Asian Tigers could do it, everybody can—if they don't, it's their own fault. The images of the poor have also undergone historical change (for an excellent analysis of this, see Gronemeyer 1992). They were temporarily poor through no fault of their own, and they helped the rich camels to get through the eye of the needle. They were there to be spiritually salvaged. They suffered from temporary unemployment or illness, and were only in need of short-term help in order to become useful and self-sufficient again.

Now the poor are seen as structurally poor and unemployed, hence bad consumers—and under the "free" market that is a crime. The criminalisation of poverty leads to the poor being legitimately controlled by the state (in the welfare state by social workers, and increasingly the police) and not "helped." Not ethnic cleansing but economic cleansing—townships, bantustans for the poor of the world. Thus the local state removes the obstacles for the globalising free market. Signing the half-secretly negotiated MAI (Multilateral Agreement on Investment) further accelerates this development.

This is the answer of market forces to the postmodern problems of their own making. A human rights oriented answer could be different. According to our earlier analysis, one of the important tasks for states would be to guarantee the satisfaction of basic human needs for everybody. This could be done if human rights and economic rights came together, controlled by a democratic political process.

But in global *human rights policies* there is a conspicuous silence regarding economic and social (or welfare) rights, coupled with very vocal anti-welfare approaches. In global and European *economic policies*, human rights are hardly mentioned, except when legitimating economic benefits for the industrialized countries by referring to alleged (and often real) human rights violations in underdeveloped countries. Also, in renegotiating *political, military and economic alliances*, Western countries skillfully play the card of alleged human rights violations.[15]

Tomaševski sums it all up (1996, 100): "the ideology of the free market has exempted economy from public control (sometimes even influence) and thus eliminated the basis for human rights, when these are understood as an exercise of political rights to achieve economic, social and cultural rights".

Globalising access to information has enabled counterhegemonic forces to ensure that there is growing sensitivity to human rights. At the same time, there is also a growing inability to secure these rights on the part of progressive forces in civil society. The gap between rhetoric and implementation is growing, with all the growing inequalities.

The message from both sociologists like Zygmunt Bauman and human rights lawyers like Katarina Tomaševski is that unless there is a redistribution of *resources* for implementing human rights, nothing is going to happen. It is no use spreading human rights or knowledge of human rights unless the resources for implementation follow, and that can only happen through a radical redistribution of the world's material resources.

This cannot be done under the "free" market system. One of the richest men in the world, George Soros, who has made a fortune in the financial markets, thinks that "the untrammeled intensification of *laissez-faire* capitalism and the spread of market values into all areas of life is endangering our open and democratic society. The main enemy of the open society ... is no longer the communist but the capitalist threat" (1997, 45). The wrongs are going to continue.

Why Linguistic Human Rights in Education?

Human rights ("correctives to the free market") are supposed to be about rectifying human wrongs. Language rights are needed to remedy language wrongs. Linguistic human rights are an essential dimension of human rights. There are strong reasons why states should in fact support linguistic and cultural diversity and linguistic rights, for *egoistic* reasons (in the interest of their own elites), not only for human rights reasons. Linguistic and cultural identity are at the core of the cultures of most ethnic groups (Smolicz 1979). Threats towards these identities can have a very strong potential to mobilize groups. Still, as Asbjørn Eide (1995, 29–30) of the UN Human Rights Commission points out, cultural rights have lacked importance and received little attention both in human rights theory and in practice, despite the fact that today "ethnic conflict" and "ethnic tension" are, according to Eide, seen as the most important potential causes of unrest, conflict and violence in the world. Just as the absence of economic and social rights in the period between the "world" wars promoted the emergence of totalitarian regimes, absence or denial of linguistic and cultural rights are today effective ways of *promoting* conflict and violence, which, despite multiple causes, can all too easily take ethnically and linguistically defined or articulated forms.

This has been acknowledged by many researchers from several fields. For instance Jurek Smolicz, Australia formulates it as follows: "... attempts to artificially suppress minority languages through policies of assimilation, devaluation, reduction to a state of illiteracy, expulsion or genocide are not only degrading of human dignity and morally unacceptable, but they are also an invitation to separatism and an incitement to fragmentation into mini-states" (Smolicz 1986, 96).

It has also been acknowledged by politicians, for instance in creating in the OSCE (Organisation for Security and Cooperation in Europe) the position of a High Commissioner on National Minorities, "as an instrument of conflict prevention in situations of ethnic tension" (Rothenberger 1997, 3). When launching The Hague Recommendations Regarding the Education Rights of National Minorities (see below), The High Commissioner, Max van der Stoel (1997, 153), stated that "...in the course of my work, it had become more and more obvious to me that education is an extremely important element for the preservation and the deepening of the identity of persons belonging to a national minority. It is of course also clear that education in the language of the minority is of vital importance for such a minority".

Granting linguistic and cultural human rights would be a step towards *avoiding* "ethnic" conflict, avoiding disintegration of (some) states, and avoiding chaos and anarchy where the rights of even the elites will be severely curtailed because of increasingly civil-war-like conditions, especially in inner cities. Many western states use today larger sums to control this anarchy (with the help of the state machinery of violence) than their education allocations. However, the link between language rights and other human rights, including economic and social rights on the one hand, and civil and political rights on the other hand, is seldom acknowledged.

Whether humanity has a moral obligation to prevent linguicide, or whether this would be interference in an inevitable process in which only the fittest survive, has been debated at several levels—some partly inspired by primordial romanticism (as in many revitalization movements), some by instrumentalist "modernism" (as in old and modern colonial situations, including the possible neocolonisation of Central and Eastern Europe by the United States and Western Europe). An attachment to one's language or mother tongue as a central cultural core value seems, like ethnicity, to combine: draw on primordial, ascribed sources but to be shaped and actualized by (achieved) econo-political concerns (Fishman 1989; Smolicz 1979).

In addition, linguistic human rights are a necessary (but not sufficient) prerequisite for the maintenance of linguistic diversity on the planet, as discussed earlier. Educational language rights are at the core of both efforts. Schooling, in addition to migration, was explored as one of the important causal factors in language loss at the Berkeley conference on endangered languages (see above). In a couple of generations schooling has succeeded in killing languages which without formal education had survived for millennia. Formal schooling may soon reach the entire world population.

My estimation is that languages which are not used as main media of instruction will cease to be passed on to children at the latest we reach the fourth generation of groups in which everybody goes to school—and many languages may be killed much earlier. The language which is used as the main medium in minority education is decisive for the future of languages on the planet (and too many of those who decide about minority education worldwide are (monolingual native) speakers of the killer languages).

Next we will discuss the extent to which present linguistic human rights, especially in education, are sufficient to protect and maintain linguistic diversity. This short summary presents a gloomy picture.

Is Language as Important as Other Human Characteristics in Human Rights Law?

In many international, regional and multilateral human rights instruments, language is mentioned in the preamble and general clauses (e.g. both Art. 2, Universal Declaration of Human Rights, and Art. 2.1, International Covenant on Civil and Political Rights [ICCPR, 1966], in force since 1976), as one of the characteristics on the basis of which discrimination is forbidden, together with

> race, colour, sex, religion, political or other opinion, national or social origin, property, birth or other status...

The four original basic characteristics cited in Article 13 of the United Nations *Charter* are *race, sex, language, or religion*, with signatories committing themselves to promote

> ... universal respect for, and observance of, human rights and fundamental freedoms for all without distinction as to race, sex, language, or religion.

This suggests that language has been seen as one of the most important characteristics of humans in terms of human rights issues in the key documents that have pioneered the post-1945 UN effort.

Even so, the most important linguistic human rights are still absent from human rights instruments. Despite fine declarations of the intent to promote diversity, including linguistic diversity, binding international law on human rights still denies linguistic human rights, especially in education. This is not only in contrast to the spirit of the human rights instruments in general and in their preambles, but is also in contrast with how several other human attributes are dealt with in human rights law. A special, negative treatment is given to language: language gets much poorer treatment in human rights instruments than other important human attributes such as gender, "race" or religion.

Opt-outs, Modifications and Alternatives in Educational Clauses

But after the lofty non-duty-inducing phrases in the preambles of the human rights instruments, moving to the real business, namely the binding clauses, and especially to the educational clauses, there is a change of position. All or most of the *non-linguistic* human characteristics (race, sex, religion, etc.) are still there and are accorded positive rights: the clauses or Articles dealing with them create obligations and contain demanding formulations in which states are firm duty holders and are obliged to ("shall") act in order to ensure the specified rights (i.e. positive rather than negative rights). Here modifications, opt-out clauses and sliding-scale alternatives are rare.

In binding educational clauses, however, one of two things can often be noted. Either language disappears completely, as, for instance, in the Universal Declaration of Human Rights (1948) where the paragraph on education (26) does not refer to language at all.

Similarly, the International Covenant on Economic, Social and Cultural Rights (adopted in 1966 and in force since 1976), having mentioned language on a par with race, color, sex, religion, etc. in its general Article (2.2), omits reference to language or linguistic groups in its educational Article (13.1), even though it *does* explicitly refer to "racial, ethnic or religious groups":

> ... education shall enable all persons to participate effectively in a free society, promote understanding, tolerance and friendship among all nations and all racial, ethnic or religious groups...

Alternatively, *if* language-related rights are specified, the Article dealing with these rights, in contrast to the demanding formulations and the few opt-outs and alternatives in Articles dealing with other characteristics, is typically so weak and unsatisfactory that it is virtually meaningless. For example, in the UN Declaration on the Rights of Persons Belonging to National or Ethnic, Religious and Linguistic Minorities, adopted by the General Assembly in December 1992, most of the Articles use the obligating formulation "shall," and have few let-out modifications or alternatives—except where linguistic rights in education are concerned. Compare, for example, the unconditional formulation in Article 1 with the education Article 4.3:

> 1.1. States *shall protect* the existence and the national or ethnic, cultural, religious and linguistic identity of minorities within their respective territories, and *shall encourage* conditions for the *promotion* of that identity.
> 1.2. States *shall* adopt **appropriate** legislative *and other* measures *to achieve those ends.*

> 4.3. States **should** take **appropriate** measures so that, **wherever possible**, persons belonging to minorities have **adequate** opportunities

to learn their mother tongue **or** to have instruction in their mother tongue. (emphases added, "*obligating*" in italics, "**opt-outs**" in bold.)

Clearly the formulation in Art. 4.3 raises many questions. What constitutes "appropriate measures," or "adequate opportunities," and who is to decide what is "possible"? Does "instruction in their mother tongue" mean through the medium of the mother tongue or does it only mean instruction in the mother tongue as a subject?

Similarly, in the European Charter for Regional or Minority Languages (22 June 1992), a state can choose which paragraphs or subparagraphs it wants to apply. Again, the formulations include a range of modifications including "as far as possible", "relevant", "appropriate", "where necessary", "pupils who so wish in a number considered sufficient", "if the number of users of a regional or minority language justifies it", as well as a number of alternatives, as in "to allow, encourage *or* provide teaching in *or* of the regional or minority language at all the appropriate stages of education" (emphases added).

While the Charter demonstrates the unquestionably real problems of writing binding formulations which are sensitive to local conditions, just as in the UN Declaration above, its opt-outs and alternatives permit a reluctant state to meet the requirements in a minimalist way, which it can legitimate by claiming that a provision was not "possible" or "appropriate", or that numbers were not "sufficient" or did not "justify" a provision, or that it "allowed" the minority to organize teaching of their language as a subject at their own cost.

A new Council of Europe Framework Convention for the Protection of National Minorities was adopted by the Committee of Ministers of the Council of Europe on 10 November 1994. We again find that the Article covering medium of education is much more heavily qualified than any other. Thus the situation is not improving despite new instruments in which language rights are mentioned, or even treated in detail.

Draft Universal Declaration of Linguistic Rights

Introduction

This section analyses some aspects of the draft Universal Declaration of Linguistic Rights, handed over to UNESCO in June 1996, in particular educational language rights. The Declaration is the first attempt at formulating a universal document dealing exclusively with language rights, and it relates to all the groups mentioned above—although not to sign language users. It is a vast document which has already gone through 12 drafts.[16] Its 52 Articles are wide-ranging and specify many linguistic rights.

The Declaration grants rights to three different entities: *individuals* (i.e. "everyone"), *language groups*, and *language communities*. Where the beneficiary is "everyone" unconditionally, the rights are *individual* ("inalienable personal rights," Art. 3.1). Where the beneficiary is the language group or community, the rights are *collective*. And where the beneficiary is *a member of* a linguistic group or community, the rights are, in most cases, individual, but conditional. Even in this Declaration, it is clear already in Article 3.1 that educational language rights, in contrast to cultural rights, are not seen as inalienable:

> This Declaration considers the following to be inalienable personal rights which may be exercised in any situation:
> - the right to the use of one's language both in private and in public; ...
> - the right to maintain and develop one's own culture; ...

These individual rights (including the rest of Art. 3.1) are the only ones which apply to all without any conditions.

Collective rights in the Declaration apply to a (historical) language community (which includes both traditional national minorities[17] and also all numerically small peoples, such as indigenous peoples, in addition to dominant linguistic majorities) or to a language group, which is

> any group of persons sharing the same language which is established in the territorial space of another language community but which does not possess historical antecedents equivalent to those of that community. Examples of such groups are immigrants, refugees, deported persons and members of diasporas (Art. 1.5).

Rights of Language Communities and Language Groups

Communities have more rights in the Declaration than the other categories. With respect to communities, Article 8.2 says that

> All language communities are entitled to have at their disposal whatever means are necessary to ensure the transmission and continuity of their language.

This could be interpreted as meaning that all language communities are entitled to receive from the state the funds needed to organize mother-tongue-medium education from kindergarten to university. However, when we read Article 8.2 alongside other Articles in the same section, we see that it belongs to the category of pious preamble which everybody can applaud but which carries no legal obligations. No duty holders are specified for granting the "means" mentioned in Article 8.2 above, or the "equal rights" or "necessary steps" mentioned in Articles 10.1 and 10.3 below:

> All language communities have equal rights (Art. 10.1).

> All necessary steps must be taken in order to implement this principle of equality and to render it real and effective (Art. 10.3).

And when we come to the Articles dealing with education, the same piety prevails, while no duty holder is specified:

> All language communities are entitled to have at their disposal all the human and material resources necessary to ensure that their language is present to the extent they desire at all levels of education within their territory: properly trained teachers, appropriate teaching methods, text books, finance, buildings and equipment, traditional and innovative technology (Art. 25).

> All language communities are entitled to an education which will enable their members to acquire a full command of their own language, including the different abilities relating to all the usual spheres of use, as well as the most extensive possible command of any other language they may wish to know (Art. 26).

> The language and culture of all language communities must be the subject of study and research at university level (Art. 30).

In many ways these "rights" sound like a dream–and that is probably what they will remain. They are at present completely unrealistic for any except, maybe, a few hundred of the world's language communities, most of them dominant linguistic majorities.

Groups have fewer rights than communities. Article 3.2 spells out collective rights for groups:

> This Declaration that the collective rights of language groups *may* include ... the right for their own language and culture to be taught (emphasis added).

In the case of groups, collective rights to one's own language are thus not seen as inalienable. In addition, Article 3.2 says nothing about where the language should be taught (whether only in private schools, or after school, or in state-financed schools) and for how long. Again, no duty holder is specified.

Does "Everyone" Have Language Rights?

Only education in the language of the territory is a *positive* right for "everyone." There is no mention of bilingual or multilingual territories in the Declaration. Every territory seems to have only one "language specific to the territory," i.e., territories are seen as monolingual. This means that for those who speak a language other than the language of the territory, education in their own language is not a positive right. In addition, the Declaration grants members of language communities the right to "the most extensive possible command" of any *foreign* language in the world, whereas the rights granted to "everyone" include only the (negative—"does *not exclude"*) right to "oral and written knowledge" of one's *own* language. This is clear if one compares the formulations at the end of Article 26 on language communities with Article 29 which spells out the (negative) right of "everyone":

> All language communities are entitled to an education which will enable their members to acquire a full command of their own language, including the different abilities relating to all the usual spheres of use, as well as **the most extensive possible command of any other language** they may wish to know (Art. 26 on rights of language communities).

> 1. Everyone is entitled to receive an education **in the language specific to the territory where s/he resides.**
> 2. This right does not exclude the right to acquire **oral and written knowledge of any language** which may be of use to him/her as an instrument of communication with other **language communities** (Art. 29 on rights of "everyone", emphases added).

Furthermore, Art. 29.2 is formulated so as to suggest that "everyone's" own language can be learned only if it is a useful instrument when communicating with other language communities. This means that it could, in principle, be excluded if it is not known by any entity defined as a language community, or if it is not used as a *lingua franca* between people where some represent language communities. If it is "only" known and/or used by language groups or by individuals representing "everybody", it can be excluded from any provision in Article 26. This is extremely important when considering the fact (section 2) that most threatened languages are used in one country only.

It is likely that language policies following the principles in the education section, with its lack of rights, will force all those not defined as members of language communities to assimilate. This interpretation of indirect assimilation through education is strengthened when noting the reservation in Articles which otherwise might grant "everyone" more language rights. According to Art. 23.4, "...everyone has the right to learn any language." "Any language" could also be interpreted as the mother tongue of those who otherwise are not granted positive mother-tongue learning rights–except that rights prevail only "within the context of the foregoing principles" (Art. 23.4) and these support only the languages and self-expression of language communities, i.e. not the language of "groups" or "everyone":

> 1. Education must help to foster the capacity for linguistic and cultural self-expression *of the language community of the territory where it is provided.*
> 2. Education must help to maintain and develop *the language spoken by the language community of the territory where it is provided.*
> 3. Education must always be at the service of linguistic and cultural diversity and of harmonious relations *between different language communities* throughout the world.
> 4. Within the context of the foregoing principles, everyone has the right to learn any language (Article 23, emphases added).

The Declaration thus clearly gives language communities very extensive rights but leaves "everyone" with very few rights. This makes the *Declaration* vulnerable in several respects. As we know, there are many states which claim that they do not have minority language communities, and which do not want to grant these communities any language rights. Self-determination is not an unconditional right in international law, neither internally, in terms of autonomy of some kind, nor externally (see contributions to Clark & Williamson, ed. 1996). This means that a declaration which grants most of the rights to linguistic communities, without specifying firm duty holders, makes these communities completely dependent on the acceptance of their existence by states, an acceptance that many states are not willing to grant. "Language groups" are in a still weaker position–these may be seen by many states as individuals only, not representatives of any "group". And those individuals who are not members of any language communities or groups, even according to the fairly vague definitions of these entities in the Declaration, are in the weakest position. It is for these reasons that the existence of firm individual rights is enormously important and would be a logical continuation of the tradition of human rights being individual. Such rights are, however, the weakest part of the Declaration.

The new draft Universal Declaration thus does not give any positive educational language rights to every individual, regardless of the category to which s/he belongs—and this is exactly what individual human rights are supposed to do. An individual human right is, by definition, an unconditional, fundamental right which every individual in the world enjoys simply because that individual is a human being. It is a right which no state is allowed to take away. The Declaration suggests a monitoring body to be set up by the United Nations, and suggests sanctions against states that interfere with their citizens' rights. At present, the text is only a draft recommendation that has no immediate prospect of being approved.

In addition, even the educational language rights for language communities are formulated in such a way that the whole Declaration runs the risk of being seen as full of pious, unrealistic wishes which cannot be taken seriously. For most African, Asian and Latin American countries, the rights in the Declaration are at present practically, economically and even politically impossible to realize, as was clearly expressed at the first UNESCO meeting at which the Declaration was discussed. It therefore seems extremely unlikely that it will be accepted in its present form.[18] This will probably also be the fate of the UN draft Universal Declaration on Rights of Indigenous Peoples, according to its chair, Erica Irene Daes (1995). Despite careful negotiations over a decade, several countries, most importantly the United States, are probably going to demand substantial changes which undermine the progress achieved in the Declaration (Morris 1995). This draft Declaration formulates language rights strongly, especially in education. If these rights were to be granted in their present form, some 60 to 80 percent of the world's oral languages would have decent legal support. Implementation is, of course, a completely different matter.

The draft Universal Declaration of Linguistic Rights, clearly less than ideal in its present form, represents the first attempt at formulating language rights at a universal level to reach a stage that permits serious international discussion to start. From the point of view of maintaining the planet's linguistic diversity, the immediate fate of the UN Draft Universal Declaration on Rights of Indigenous Peoples is probably more important, however, because it has at least some chance of being accepted, signed and ratified–even if in a form which reduces the rights granted in the present draft.

Recent Positive Developments

New Interpretation of Article 27

There might be some hope for some groups, however, in a few promising recent developments. The UN ICCPR Article 27 still grants the best legally binding protection to languages:

> In those states in which ethnic, religious or linguistic minorities exist, persons belonging to such minorities shall not be denied the right, in community with other members of their group, to enjoy their own culture, to profess and practise their own religion, or to use their own language.

In the customary reading of Art. 27, rights were only granted to individuals, not collectivities. And, "persons belonging to ... minorities" only had these rights in states which accepted their existence. This has not helped immigrant minorities since they have not been seen as minorities in the legal sense by the states in which they live. More recently (6 April 1994), the UN Human Rights Committee adopted a General Comment on Article 27 which interprets it in a substantially broader and more positive way than earlier. The Committee sees the Article as:

- protecting all individuals on the State's territory or under its jurisdiction (i.e. also immigrants and refugees), irrespective of whether they belong to the minorities specified in the Article or not;
- stating that the existence of a minority does not depend on a decision by the State but requires to be established by objective criteria;
- recognizing the existence of a "right"; and
- imposing positive obligations on the States.

The Hague Recommendations Regarding the Education Rights of National Minorities

The second positive development is the new educational guidelines issued by The Foundation on Inter-Ethnic Relations for the OSCE (= Organisation for Security and Cooperation in Europe) High Commissioner on National Minorities, Max van der Stoel, The Hague Recommendations Regarding the Education Rights of National Minorities & Explanatory Note (October 1996). These guidelines were worked out by a small group of experts on human rights and education (including the author of this article). In the section "The spirit of international instruments," bilingualism is seen as a right and responsibility for persons belonging to national minorities (Art. 1), and states are reminded not to interpret their obligations in a restrictive manner (Art. 3). In the section on "Minority education at primary and secondary levels", mother-tongue medium education is recommended at all levels, including bilingual teachers of the dominant language as a second language (Articles 11–13). Teacher training is made a duty of the state (Art. 14). Finally, the Explanatory Note states that

> [S]ubmersion-type approaches whereby the curriculum is taught exclusively through the medium of the state language and minority children are entirely integrated into classes with children of the majority are not in line with international standards (p. 5).

This means that the children to whom the Recommendations apply might be granted some of the central educational linguistic human rights. The question now is the extent to which the 55 OSCE countries will apply the Recommendations, and how they will interpret their scope (see the Special Issue volume 4:2, 1996/1997 of *International Journal on Minority and Group Rights,* which is about the Hague Recommendations). The Recommendations could, in principle, apply to all minorities, even the "everyone" with very few rights in the Draft Universal Declaration on Linguistic Rights discussed above (and since indigenous peoples are supposed to have at least all the rights that minorities have, they too might peruse the Recommendations while waiting for their own Declaration).

The recent People's Communication Charter, an NGO-initiative, might also help (see Hamelink 1994, 1995).

Conclusion

At present, though, while we can hope that these two positive developments might have some effect, overall there is not much cause for optimism. My conclusion is that we still have to work for education through the medium of the mother tongue to be recognized as a human right. And if this right is not granted, and implemented, it seems likely that the present pessimistic prognoses of over 90% of the world's oral languages not being around anymore in the year 2100, err *on the side of optimism.*

Language shift *can* thus be "voluntary" at an individual level: a result of more benefits accruing to the individual who agrees to shift than to someone who maintains her mother tongue. But in most cases of language shift it seems that either sticks, punishment, or carrots, economic or other benefits, have been at work—or, increasingly, ideological persuasion, hegemonic mind-mastering, that is, linguicist agents. Likewise, the choice of which languages are granted support, and of what kind, in the education system as mother tongues and foreign or second languages often follows linguicist "free"-market principles, with more benefits accruing to those who support the killer languages as both media of education and as first foreign languages in education.

To sum up, then: if people are forced to shift their languages in order to gain economic benefits of the kind which are in fact bare necessities for basic survival, this is a violation of not only their economic human rights but also their linguistic human rights. Violations of linguistic human rights, especially in education, may lead, and have led, to both ethnically articulated conflict and to reduction of linguistic and cultural diversity on our planet. But granting human rights, even linguistic human rights, even in education, on paper, something that is hardly done today, does not help much without a radical redistribution of resources. With a "free" market this is not likely to happen, because, as Soros (1998, 27) puts it: "Markets reduce everything, including human beings (labor) and nature (land), to commodities. We can have a market economy but we cannot have a market society".

Notes

1 Grimes' *Ethnologue*, 13th edition (http://www.sil.org/ethnologue) lists 6,703 languages; David Dalby's new *Linguistic Atlas* claims around 10,000. Most of the figures in this Article are based on Harmon (1995).

2 Every time "language" is written here, it means "oral language", unless otherwise indicated. We know very little about sign languages, demographically and otherwise. See note 3.

3 For important analyses of the invalidation of these, see Branson & Miller 1989, 1993, 1995, 1996, 1997, in press; for Hungary, see Muzsnai, this volume.

4 Terralingua is a nonprofit international organisation devoted to preserving the world's linguistic diversity and to investigating links between biological and cultural diversity (President: Luisa Maffi; Web-site: http://cougar.ucdavis.edu/nas/terralin/home.html).

5 For empirical evidence and an excellent discussion of the complexities of assessing these correlations, see Harmon (1995).

6 Using the term "idiom" (rather than "language") signals that it really means "what the parents speak (or sign)", regardless of whether this is called a language, a dialect, a sociolect, a vernacular, or whatever–it does NOT need to be the standard or official language of the area/country, or what people have replied in census questions about mother tongue, or written.

7 The linguicist hierarchisation through glorification of dominant languages, stigmatization of dominated languages and rationalisation of the relationship between them (Skutnabb-Kangas & Phillipson, in press) can be compared with the hierarchisation which Bauman (1997) describes as *"chronopolitics"* in the universalisation process: everything that was different from the West was put down chronologically, placed on a scale where it was seen as similar to something that might have existed in the West in an earlier historical phase. An example would be the frequent reference in Denmark to a distance of 150 years to be covered on the plane from a Turkish village, via Istanbul, to Copenhagen, i.e. Bauman's chronopolitics is similar to evolution theories in development studies.

8 Linguicism (Skutnabb-Kangas 1988, 13) is a major factor in determining whether speakers of particular languages are allowed to enjoy their linguistic human rights. Lack of these rights, for instance the absence of these languages from school timetables, makes indigenous and minority languages invisible. Alternatively, minority mother tongues are constructed and presented as non-resources, as handicaps which are constructed as "preventing" indigenous or minority children from acquiring the majority language (= the only valued linguistic resource), so that minority children should get rid of them in their own interests. At the same time, many minorities, especially minority children, are in fact prevented from fully acquiring majority resources, and especially ma-

jority languages, by disabling educational structures in which instruction is organised through the medium of the majority languages in ways which contradict most scientific evidence on how education for bilingualism should be organised (see, e.g., Cummins 1996; Pattanayak 1981; Ramirez et al. 1991; Skutnabb-Kangas 1984, 1990, 1999).

9 With some classics, the change was from military to industrial society (Saint-Simon); from a religious to a "positive", scientific stage of social evolution (Comte); from Gemeinschaft to Gesellschaft (Tönnies); from mechanical to organic solidarity (Durkheim); and from traditional to rational (Weber).

10 The model is in complete contradiction with the South countries' own definition of what development is, a definition which would also correspond to the human rights and basic needs oriented approach in this paper: *DEVELOPMENT*: "A process of self-reliant growth achieved through the participation of the people acting in their own interests as they see them, and under their own control. The primary objective is to satisfy the basic needs of all the people through a democratic structure of government that supports individual freedoms of speech and organization, and respects all human rights. (This description is based on the definition provided in *The Challenge to the South, the Report of the South Commission)*" (Harris 1997, 213).

11 This was how a South African MP formulated it in an interview on 14 November 1997. We (Robert Phillipson & TSK) have heard Hungarian and Baltic colleagues claim the same about their own countries. "Every year Africa transfers to its creditors–principally northern governments, the World Bank and the IMF–around $10 billion, more than the region spends on health and education combined... For every dollar on health, the Ugandan government spends five on debt repayment... Zambia is spending 10 times more on repaying the IMF than on primary education" (Watkins 1996, 14). Watkins also notes that Germany, Japan, Britain and the US have notoriously rejected proposed plans to alleviate the situation. The overlap with a list of countries which have notoriously tried to prevent the acceptance of linguistic human rights is not surprising.

12 There are caveats, though. There are no longer any "bad" or "good" solutions, only relatively better or worse solutions. Both the bipolar possibilities (either *universality* (universal ideas, ideologies, solutions) or *tolerance of diversity and pluralism*) have certain benefits and certain dangers, according to Baumann (1997). Believing in "universal truths" (like "communism" or "capitalism" or the "free market") can, in the worst case, lead (and has led) to genocide. "Tolerance" can also lead to tolerating genocide without doing anything (e.g. Bosnia, Nigeria). "Tolerance" can also be expressed in demands for autonomy of choice in an individualistic neoliberal way, in consumer societies, where any kind of restrictions or limits are seen as negative. This might also include the prevention of any kind of positive intervention to achieve the "regulated context" which Grin (this volume) sees as necessary for harnessing market forces for the preservation of at least some linguistic diversity.

13 One reason not discussed here is, of course, that even basic human rights do not apply to all humans, and very clearly not to most of those who are speakers of the most threatened languages.

14 Bauman (1997) claims that if the globalisation of information levels out cultural differences and cultures in general, a policy of fragmentation implied in localisation may, on the other hand, favor differentiation. You can have whatever cultural values but still get Western tanks, computers, etc. There is a lack of cohesion, illogically, in the policy.

15 The concept of "human rights" is often used in international relations arbitrarily and selectively by "donor" governments so as to attempt to trigger "democratic" elections or to sanction states that commit gross human rights abuses; in effect it is used as a political tool rather than a rigorous concept rooted in international law (Tomaševski 1997).

16 The declaration was the result of an initiative undertaken by The International Pen Club (Committee for Translation and Linguistic Rights), and CIEMEN (Mercator Programme, Linguistic Rights and Law).

17 "Minority" is a notoriously difficult concept to define—see Andrýsek 1989, and Skutnabb-Kangas & Phillipson 1994, note 2 and references, for an overview of the criteria used in different definitions. See also Capotorti 1979; Thornberry 1991; de Varennes 1996.

18 There is a small Follow-up Committee, trying to raise support for the Declaration, and a Scientific Council (of which TSK is a member) which is supposed to advise UNESCO on a revision.

References

Alexander, Neville. "Multilingualism for empowerment." In Kathleen Heugh, Amanda Siegrühn, and Peter Plüddemann, eds., *Multilingual Education for South Africa*, 37–41. Johannesburg: Heinemann, 1995.

——. "Models of multilingual schooling for a democratic South Africa." In Kathleen Heugh, Amanda Siegrühn, and Peter Plüddemann, eds., *Multilingual Education for South Africa*, 79–82. Johannesburg: Heinemann, 1995.

Andrýsek, Oldrich. *Report on the definition of minorities*. Netherlands Institute of Human Rights, Studie- en Informatiecentrum Mensenrechten (SIM), SIM Special No., 8 (1989).

Bauman, Zygmunt. "Universalism and Relativism–Reaching an Impossible Compromise." Keynote lecture presented at the conference *Development and Rights*, Roskilde University, 8–10 October, 1997.

Branson, Jan and Don Miller. "Beyond Integration policy–the deconstruction of disability." In L. Barton, ed., *Integration: Myth or reality*, 144–167. Brighton: Falmer Press, 1989.

——. "Sign Language, the Deaf and the Epistemic Violence of Mainstreaming." *Language and Education* 7(1) (1993): 21–41.

——. "Sign Language and the Discursive Construction of Power over the Deaf through Education." In Davis Corson, ed., *Discourse and Power in Educational Settings,* 167–189. Creskill, N.J.: Hempton Press, 1995.

——. "Writing Deaf subaltern history: is it a myth, is it history, is it genealogy? is it all, or is it none?" In T. Vollhaber & R. Fischer, eds., *Collage. Works on international Deaf history,* 185–194. Hamburg: Signum Press, 1996.

——. "Nationalism and the linguistic rights of Deaf communities: Linguistic Imperialism and the recognition and Development of Sign Language." Revised version of paper presented at the symposium "Current Issues and Future Prospects in the Study of Language Policy and Planning" at AILA 96, the 11th World Congress of Applied Linguistics, August 1996, Jyväskylä, Finland, 1997.

Branson, Jan and Don Miller. "National Sign Languages and Language Policies." In Ruth Wodak & David Corson, eds., *The Encyclopedia of Language and Education.* Volume 1, Language Policies and Political Issues in Education, 89–98. Dordrecht: Kluwer Academic, 1997.

Capotorti, Francesco. *Study of the Rights of Persons Belonging to Ethnic, Religious and Linguistic Minorities.* New York: United Nations, 1979.

Clark, Don & Robert Williamson, eds. *Self-Determination: International Perspectives.* London: The Macmillian Press, 1996.

Cummins, Jim. *Negotiating Identities: Education for Empowerment in a Diverse Society.* Ontario, California: California Association for Bilingual Education, 1996.

Daes, Erica-Irene. "Redressing the Balance: The Struggle to be Heard." Paper to the Global Cultural Diversity Conference, Sydney, 26–28 April, 1995.

Eide, Asbjørn. "Economic, social and cultural rights as human rights." In Asbjørn Eide, Catarina Krause, and Allan Rosas, eds. *Economic, Social and Cultural Rights. A Textbook,* 21–40. Dordrecht, Boston & London: Martinus Nijhoff Publishers, 1995.

Escobar, Arturo. *Encountering Development. The Making and Unmaking of the Third World.* Princeton Studies in Culture/Power/History. Princeton, N.J.: Princeton University Press, 1995.

Fettes, Mark. "Life of the Edge: Canada's Aboriginal Languages Under Official Bilingualism." In Tom Ricento, and Barbara Burnaby, eds. *Language and Politics in the United States and Canada: Myths and realities,* 117–149. Mahwah, N.J.: Lawrence Erlbaum, 1998.

Fishman, Joshua A. *Language and Ethnicity in Minority Sociolinguistic Perspective.* Clevedon and Philadelphia: Multilingual Matters, 1989.

Galtung, Johan. *Methodology and Development. Essays in Methodology,* Volume III. Copenhagen: Christian Ejlers, 1988.

Graddol, David. *The Future of English?* A guide to forecasting the popularity of the English language in the 21st century. London: British Council, 1997.

Grin, François. "Market forces, language spread and linguistic diversity." In Miklós Kontra, Robert Phillipson, Tove Skutnabb-Kangas, Tibor Várady, eds. *Language: A Right and a Resource,* 169–186. Budapest: Central European University Press, 1999.

Gronemeyer, Marianne. "Helping." In Wolfgang Sachs, ed. *Development Dictionary. A Guide to Knowledge as Power*, 53–69. London, N.J.: Zed Books, 1992.

Groombridge, B., ed. *Global Biodiversity: Status of the Earth's Living Resources*. World Conservation Monitoring Centre. London: Chapman & Hall, 1992.

Haddad, W. D., M. Carnoy, R. Rinaldi & O. Regel. *Education and development: evidence for new priorities*. Washington, D.C.: World Bank (Discussion paper 95), 1990.

Hamel, Rainer Enrique. "Indigenous education in Latin America: policies and legal frameworks." In Tove Skutnabb-Kangas & Robert Phillipson, eds., *Linguistic Human Rights. Overcoming linguistic discrimination*, 271–287. Berlin and New York: Mouton de Gruyter, 1994.

Hamelink, Cees J. *Trends in world communication: on disempowerment and self-empowerment*. Penang: Southbound, and Third World Network, 1994.

——. *The Politics of World Communication. A Human Rights Perspective*. London, Thousand Oaks & New Delhi: Sage, 1995.

Harmon, David. "The status of the world's languages as reported in the *Ethnologue*." *Southwest Journal of Linguistics* 14 (1995): 1–33.

Harris, Phil. "Glossary." In Peter Golding and Phil Harris, eds., *Beyond Cultural Imperialism. Globalisation, communication & the new international order*, 208–256. London, Thousand Oaks and New Delhi: Sage, 1997.

Hassanpour, Amir. "Language rights in the emerging world linguistic order." In Miklós Kontra, Robert Phillipson, Tove Skutnabb-Kangas, and Tibor Várady, eds. *Language: A Right and a Resource*, 223–241. Budapest: Central European University Press, 1999.

Helsinki Watch. *Destroying ethnic identity. The Kurds of Turkey. An update, September 1990*. New York and Washington, D.C., 1990.

Heugh, Kathleen. "From unequal education to the real thing." In Kathleen Heugh, Amanda Siegrühn, and Peter Plüddemann, eds., *Multilingual Education for South Africa*, 42–51. Johannesburg: Heinemann, 1995a.

——. "The multilingual school: modified dual medium." In Kathleen Heugh, Amanda Siegrühn, and Peter Plüddemann, eds., *Multilingual Education for South Africa*, 79–82. Johannesburg: Heinemann, 1995b.

Heywood, V.H., ed. *Global Biodiversity Assessment*. Cambridge & New York: Cambridge University & UNEP (United Nations Environmental Program), 1995.

Human Rights in Kurdistan. *Documentation of the international conference on human rights in Kurdistan*, Hochschule Bremen, 14–16 April. Bremen: The Initiative for Human Rights in Kurdistan, 1989.

Jordan, Deirdre. "Rights and claims of indigenous people. Education and the reclaiming of identity: the case of the Canadian natives, the Sami and Australian Aborigines." In Tove Skutnabb-Kangas and Jim Cummins, eds., *Minority Education: from shame to struggle*, 189–222. Clevedon: Multilingual Matters, 1988.

Jussila, Heikki and Boris Segerståhl. *Cultural and societal change in the North–the role of innovation in development*. Oulu: Research Institute of Northern Finland, Working Papers 56, October 1988.

Kozol, Jonathan. *Savage inequalities. Children in America's schools*. New York: Harper, 1991.

Krauss, Michael. "The world's languages in crisis." *Language* 68 (1992): 4–10.

——. Paper at a conference of the American Association for the Advancement of Science, reported in *The Philadelphia Inquirer*. 19 February, 1995, A15.

Luckett, Kathy. "National additive bilingualism: towards a language plan for South African education." In Kathleen Heugh, Amanda Siegrühn, and Peter Plüddemann, eds., *Multilingual Education for South Africa*, 73–78. Johannesburg: Heinemann, 1995.

Maffi, Luisa. Position Paper for the Interdisciplinary Working Conference "Endangered Languages, Endangered Knowledge, Endangered Environments." Terralingua Discussion Paper 1. Web page, see note 4, 1996.

Maffi, Luisa and Tove Skutnabb-Kangas & Jonah Adrianarivo. "Language diversity." In Darrell Posey, and Graham Dutfield, eds., *Cultural and Spiritual Values of Biodiversity*. Leiden & New York: Intermediate Technologies, Leiden Univeristy & United Nations Environmental Programme (in press).

Morris, Glenn T. "12th Session of UN Working Group in Indigenous Peoples. The Declaration Passes and the US Assumes a New Role." *Fourth World Bulletin. Issues in Indigenous Law and Politics*. University of Colorado at Denver. 4 (1995): 1–2.

Muzsnai, István. "The recognition of sign language: a threat or the way to a solution?" In Miklós Kontra, Robert Phillipson, Tove Skutnabb-Kangas, Tibor Várady, eds., *Language: A Right and a Resource*, Budapest: Central European University Press, 1999.

Pagel, Mark. (as reported by Nicholas Ostler in *Iatiku: Newsletter of the Foundation for Endangered Languages* 1 [1995]: 6).

Pattanayak, D. P. "Tribal education and tribal languages: a new strategy." In D. P. Pattanayak, *Language, education and culture*, 166–177. Mysore: Central Institute of Indian Languages, 1991.

Phillipson, Robert. *Linguistic imperialism*. Oxford: Oxford University Press, 1992.

Phillipson, Robert. "International languages and international human rights." In Miklós Kontra, Robert Phillipson, Tove Skutnabb-Kangas, Tibor Várady, eds., *Language: A Right and a Resource*, 25–46. Budapest: Central European University Press, 1999.

Ramirez, J. David, Sandra D. Yuen, and Dena R. Ramey. *Executive Summary: Final report: Longitudinal study of structured English immersion strategy, early-exit and late-exit transitional bilingual education programs for language-minority children, Submitted to the U.S. Department of Education*. San Mateo, CA: Aguirre International, 1991.

Rodney, Walter. *How Europe Underdeveloped Africa.* London: Bogle-L'Ouverture, 1983.

Rubagumya, Casmir M., ed. *Language in education in Africa: a Tanzanian perspective.* Clevedon: Multilingual Matters, 1990.

Skutnabb-Kangas, Tove. *Bilingual or Not: the Education of Minorities.* Clevedon: Multilingual Matters, 1984.

——. "Multilingualism and the Education of Minority Children." In Tove Skutnabb-Kangas and Jim Cummins, eds. *Minority Education: from shame to struggle,* 9–44. Clevedon: Multilingual Matters, 1988.

——. *Language, Literacy and Minorities.* London: The Minority Rights Group, 1990.

——. *Linguistic Genocide in Education or Worldwide Diversity and Human Rights?* Mahwah, N.J.: Lawrence Erlbaum Associates, 1999.

Skutnabb-Kangas, Tove and Sertaç Bucak. "Killing a mother tongue–how the Kurds are deprived of linguistic human rights." In Tove Skutnabb-Kangas and Robert Phillipson, eds., in collaboration with Mart Rannut. *Linguistic Human Rights. Overcoming linguistic discrimination,* 347–370. Contributions to the Sociology of Language 67. Berlin & New York: Mouton de Gruyter, 1994.

Skutnabb-Kangas, Tove and Robert Phillipson. "Linguistic human rights, past and present." In Tove Skutnabb-Kangas and Robert Phillipson, eds., in collaboration with Mart Rannut. *Linguistic Human Rights. Overcoming linguistic discrimination,* 71–110. Contributions to the Sociology of Language 67. Berlin and New York: Mouton de Gruyter, 1994.

——. "Linguistic Human Rights and Development." In Cees Hamelink, ed., *Ethics and development. On Making Moral Choices in Development Cooperation,* 56–69. Kampen: Kok, 1997.

——. (in press). "Linguistic human rights." *Gazette. The International Journal for Communication Studies,* Special volume on Human Rights, ed. Cees Hamelink, 60:1 (1998): 27–46.

Smolicz, J. J. *Culture and Education in a Plural Society.* Canberra: Curriculum Development Centre, 1979.

Smolicz, Jerzy J. "National Language Policy in the Philippines." In Bernard Spolsky, ed. *Language and education in multilingual settings,* 96–116. Clevedon/Philadelphia: Multilingual Matters, 1986.

Soros, George. "The Capitalist Threat." *The Atlantic Monthly,* February 1997, volume 279, 2 (1997): 45–58.

——. "Toward a Global Open Society." *The Atlantic Monthly,* January 1998, volume 281,1 (1998): 20–32.

South Commission. *The Challenge to the South.* Oxford: Oxford University Press, 1990.

Stavenhagen, Rodolfo. *The Ethnic Question. Conflicts, Development, and Human Rights.* Tokyo: United Nations University Press, 1990.

Stavenhagen, Rodolfo. "Cultural rights and universal human rights." In Asbjørn Eide, Catarina Krause, and Allan Rosas, eds., *Economic, Social and Cultural Rights. A Textbook,* 63–77. Dordrecht, Boston and London: Martinus Nijhoff Publishers, 1995.

van der Stoel, Max. "Introduction to the Seminar." *International Journal on Minority and Group Rights. Special Issue on the Education Rights of National Minorities* 4,2 (1996/1997): 153-155.

Therborn, Göran. *European Modernity and Beyond. The Trajectory of European Societies 1945-2000.* London: Sage, 1995.

Thornberry, Patrick. *International Law and the Rights of Minorities.* Oxford: Clarendon Press, 1991.

Tomaševski, Katarina. *Development Aid and Human Rights Revisited.* London: Pinter, 1993.

——. "International prospects for the future of the welfare state." In *Reconceptualizing the welfare state,* 100-117. Copenhagen: The Danish Centre for Human Rights, 1996.

——. "Development Aid and Human Rights." Keynote lecture presented at the conference *Development and Rights,* Roskilde University, 8-10 October 1997.

de Varennes, Fernand. *Language, Minorities and Human Rights.* The Hague, Boston, London: Martinus Nijhoff, 1996.

World Bank. *Education in sub-Saharan Africa. Policies for adjustment, revitalisation and expansion.* Washington, D.C.: World Bank (summarized in *Comparative Education Review,* February 1989), 1988.

Watkins, Kevin. "IMF holds a gold key for the Third World." *Guardian Weekly,* 16 June 1996.

Language Rights in the Emerging World Linguistic Order: The State, the Market and Communication Technologies

AMIR HASSANPOUR

The transition from feudalism to capitalism in Western Europe was associated with the increasing intervention of the state in the linguistic life of individuals and communities.[1] If the pre-modern state was distinguished by its general inability to centralize power, the modern state, often labeled the "nation-state", achieved a remarkable centralization of political, economic, cultural and linguistic power. Even in states that are cited as models of "civic" rather than "ethnic" nations, for example, France, Britain and the U.S., there is a tradition of legislating the universal use of the national language and the banning of other languages (de Varennes 1996, 10–19). It is not surprising, therefore, that the first struggles for equal rights in the realm of language coincide with the increasing centralization of political and linguistic power in early-nineteenth-century Europe (ibid., 16–18).

In modern states, individuals are treated as citizens entitled to a diversity of *rights*. According to the liberal democratic tradition, this regime of rights imposes considerable limits on the power of the state over citizens (Waldron 1993, 575). Ironically, however, it is the institution of the state that grants these rights. While the state recognizes, constitutionalizes or guarantees such rights, individuals only "exercise their rights" to the degree that the state permits (Schneider 1993, 508).

Many poststructuralists and postmodernists reject modernity's state-centered politics by pointing to the advent of a radical rupture in governance, the regime of rights, and citizenship. According to one account, there is a "growing dispersion of the capacities of governance to agencies 'above' and 'below' the nation state... States are losing their monopoly over who governs in their territories; nation-states are becoming just one, albeit vital, part of a division of labor in governance and the nature of that division is no longer under their exclusive control" (Hirst 1996, 98, 99). According to another, Foucauldian, theorist of this "new era" or "post-modern world order", the "facts of sovereignty and territoriality as described by international law, then are becoming transnational legalistic fictions. As the proliferating sub/supranational nuclei of decentralized power now author(ize) contra-governmentalistic law-unmaking and law-breaking within uncertain territories, each sovereign finds itself on its own territory constantly challenged from within and without" by divisive forces such as "ethnic tribal-ism", "linguistic separatism", "religious fundamentalism, pan-national racialism, or global environmentalism..." (Luke 1997, 8).

In this actually existing "cyberspace", sovereign territorial powers "cannot determine for themselves what laws will be, for whom, and why" (ibid., 12). Modernity's "centered sovereignty" is replaced by "decentred power centers, illegitimate law-making bodies, unruly rule-setting agencies". Throughout the world, these "decentralized power nuclei set the rules within their particular domains of space, regions of operation, or communities of meaning where the rulings of govern-mentalizing states are ineffective, illegitimate, or powerless" (ibid., 14).

Other poststructuralists envision a "global civil society" in which the actions of non-state actors allow the theorist to challenge the representation of the state as "a pure presence and a sovereign identity reflecting a coherent source of meaning" (Marden 1997, 51). Here, the main concern is not the loss, real or imagined, of state sovereignty. The problem is, rather, to deny the state "a single coherent sovereign presence". This may, then, bring into play "other modes of sovereign being besides the privileged figure of the state". Once the irreducibility of the state is abandoned, it will be possible to see alternative sources of sovereignty; closure may give way to new openings (ibid.).

This chapter examines the implications of postmodernist claims about the erosion of state sovereignty in light of the struggle of the Kurds for language rights in Turkey. Turkey pursues a harsh policy of killing the Kurdish language, spoken by no less than twelve mil-lion people within this country. Writing, printing, broadcasting, and teaching in Kurdish have been harshly punished as crimes against the "indivisibility of the Turkish nation" and its "territorial integrity". In spite of the totalitarian "closure" of the Turkish state, a group of Kurds in Western Europe in the latter part of the 1990s undermined its sovereign rule by exercising the right to native-tongue broadcasting and teaching via satellite television. While this is an overlapping exercise of sovereignty, the chapter argues that the state continues to play a significant role in the regulation of linguistic and political power.

Med-TV: A Non-State Nation's Access to Satellite TV

In May 1994, MED Broadcasting Ltd., founded by a group of Kurds in Europe, launched the first Kurdish satellite television channel, Med-TV (see Hassanpour 1997 for a more detailed history). This was "in response to calls over recent years, particularly from the Europe-wide Kurdish diaspora, for a television station of its own" (Med-TV, 1995). The license for the channel was issued in London by the Independent Television Commission, which requires the licensee to comply with British broadcasting codes including "due impartiality in the treatment of matters of political controversy or public policy."[2] Broadcasting began with a daily menu of three hours, which was gradually expanded to eighteen hours a day by late 1997. Med-TV's office is in London but most of the production work is undertaken in their studios in Brussels and Stockholm.

The channel gets its name from the Medes who, according to Med-TV, established one of west Asia's ancient civilizations and were the ancestors of the Kurds. Today, "Kurdish identity is still defined by its own distinct language, culture and traditions" (Med-TV, 1995). Yet the Kurds, "numbering 35 million worldwide... are the largest nation in the world today without a recognized homeland... For the first time in history, the Kurdish people can now see their own lives, their own reality, reflected on television screens across the world. Med-TV hopes to assist in the regeneration of the Kurdish language and the identity of this dispossessed nation whilst informing the Kurdish public of the world, national and international events". One of the aims of the Kurdish Foundation Trust, which provides financial assistance, is to "assist in the development of the cultural identity of the Kurdish people and the Kurdish language throughout the world" (ibid.).

Programming is quite diverse. There are three newscasts a day, in two dialects of Kurdish and in Turkish. Current affairs and debates on politics and other topics are very popular. Leaders of Kurdish political parties from all parts of Kurdistan frequently participate in debates. Viewers from Kurdistan and Europe participate in live talk shows and telephone debates . Documentaries include in-house productions and a diverse selection from various producers usually aired with Kurdish voice-over. Entertainment and cultural programming includes film, drama, music, theater, science, etc. Children's programming is extensive including Kurdish language teaching, play, and cartoons. Religious programming is provided for the majority Muslim population as well as minorities. There is also weekly programming in the third major Kurdish dialect, Dimili (also called Zaza), and in other languages such as Assyrian, Arabic, and English.

The Closure of the Turkish State

The Republic of Turkey was founded in 1923 on an official ideology, Kemalism (the ideas of Kemal Atatürk, founder of the Republic of Turkey), which prescribes Turkish ethnonationalism, etatism and secularism as the main pillars of the political system (Muller 1996). The state, constitutionalized as a sacred institution, has virtually stifled civil society (Kadioğlu 1996). The army, the most important state organ, has conducted, in less than fifty years, three coups d'état (1960-61, 1971-73 and 1980-83) in order to keep Kemalism intact. The leaders of the last coup arranged for the scripting of a constitution (1982) which praised them for protecting "the integrity of the eternal Turkish Nation and motherland and the existence of the sacred Turkish State" (text in Flanz 1994, 3; the words quoted were dropped in the 1995 amendments to the document). The constitution declares the closing of political space in absolute terms; the boundaries of closure are Turkishness:

> This Constitution, determining the eternal existence of the Turkish Homeland and Nation and the indivisible integrity of the Grand Turkish State is entrusted for safekeeping by the TURKISH NATION to the patriotism of its sons and daughters who are devoted to democracy, is to be understood, interpreted and implemented by its IDEAS, BELIEFS and COMMITMENT in deference to and with absolute loyalty to its letter and spirit... no thought or consideration contrary to the Turkish national interests, the principle of indivisible integrity of the Turkish existence with its state and territory, Turkish historical and moral values, and the nationalism, principles and reforms and modernization of Atatürk can be protected...(Republic of Turkey, 1995, 1; emphasis in the original).

The paramount concern of the constitution is ensuring the "indivisible integrity" of the state. For instance, one of the "fundamental aims and duties of the state" is to safeguard "the indivisibility of the country" (Article 5). Citizens are given a prominent place in many constitutions, and in the Turkish case, "[N]o Turk shall be deprived of citizenship, unless he commits an act incompatible with loyalty to motherland" (Article 66). The free operation of printing presses and freedom of the press are guaranteed only if they do not threaten the "indivisible integrity of the State with its territory and nation..." (Articles 28 and 30; these and subsequent references to the Constitution are from the text in Flanz 1994).

The extensive policy of Turkification of the Kurds since the mid–1920s resulted in widespread resistance including several armed uprisings. Indeed, resistance to assimilation since the mid–1980s has been more extensive in Turkey than Iraq, Iran or Syria. Militarily, the guerrilla war waged by the Kurdistan Workers Party (better known by its Kurdish acronym PKK) since 1984 is the longest uninterrupted armed resistance on record in Kurdistan. Resistance on the political and cultural front, both by PKK supporters and others, has been equally unrelenting. By the mid–1990s, some members of the Turkish intelligentsia and the business elite voiced their opposition to the military suppression of the Kurds and called for their recognition as a non-Turkish people. However, for both the army generals and the majority of the civil hierarchy it is an either/or situation—either the Kurds or no Turkish state. The war led to the destruction and depopulation of about 2,685 villages between 1984 and 1996, the displacement of about one million Kurds, and other acts of violence.[3] These measures amount to "ethnic cleansing."[4]

The "international community" is very tolerant of Turkey for the obvious reason that Ankara is an indispensable ally of the West in a strategically vital part of the world. While non-state actors such as human rights activists and organizations, intellectuals and others support Kurdish rights, the agenda of Western powers is in no vague terms the protection of the sovereignty and "territorial integrity" of the Turkish state by, among other things, providing extensive military and financial support to Ankara.[5] However, the European Union encourages Turkey to integrate the Kurds by granting them cultural and linguistic rights.

The Erosion of Turkish Sovereignty

Med-TV has threatened the Turkish state's "single coherent sovereign presence" in politically and culturally significant ways. Article 42 of the constitution stipulates that "no language other than Turkish shall be taught as mother tongue to Turkish citizens at any insti-

tutions of training or education". This Article has been implemented with utmost force, making many disobedient teachers,
textbook writers and publishers, and students pay a high price
(Chyet 1995). Ankara has even used diplomatic power to prevent
Kurdish education outside its borders, in Denmark and elsewhere
(Skutnabb-Kangas 1981, 279–80). While the Kurds have individu-
ally resisted the ban on education by secretly teaching themselves
and their children to read and write in their language, Med-TV provides such instruction to millions of viewers on a daily basis. For
example, the program *Roj Ba Mamosta* (Hello, Teacher!) has a
classroom setting where a teacher instructs children in their native
tongue, using a blackboard, books and other teaching materials.
Children's programming promotes one of the slogans of the Kurdistan Parliament in Exile, which calls on the Kurds to learn, write
and read in their language. Equally serious is Med-TV's violation of
another provision of Article 42 which requires that "[T]raining and
education shall be conducted along the lines of the principles and
reforms of Atatürk". Thus, the channel tries, quite successfully, to
dismantle the Kemalist project of building a nation-state based on
Turkish ethnonationalism.

Although in 1991 Turkey repealed the law that banned the use
of non-Turkish languages like Kurdish, the constitution and various
laws allow the government to suppress the language. Broadcasting
in Kurdish is still illegal. In order to divert audiences from viewing
Med-TV, some government officials have considered lifting the ban
on Kurdish broadcasting, but this is still far from materializing. In
1992, Prime Minister Demirel dismissed as "unconstitutional" the
idea of Kurdish programming by Turkey's state television. In 1996,
a television station in Diyarbekir was allowed to air Kurdish music
selected from a list of songs approved by security officials. This
program was later discontinued. Under such conditions, the very
fact that Med-TV broadcasts in Kurdish and is being extensively
viewed amounts to violation of state sovereignty.

Given these constitutional prerogatives, it seems that every second of Med-TV's broadcasting undermines Turkish sovereign rule.
The logo "Med-TV", which is always present in the upper left cor-
ner of the screen, is an assertion of Kurdishness (the Kurds are
Medes not Turks). It also asserts, from a nationalist perspective,
Kurdish rights to statehood. The logo's colors of red, yellow and
green are the colors of the Kurdish flag; moreover, the flag itself
appears frequently in the programming, ranging from news and
information to entertainment and culture. The daily menu begins
with a grand orchestra performing the Kurdish national anthem,

Ey Reqîb (O Enemy!). The presence of the Kurdish national flag and anthem means that Med-TV treats the Kurds not as an audience but as citizens of a Kurdish state. This is, therefore, more than a war of meanings and identities. It is a conflict between two nationalisms—one that has achieved state power and one that struggles for statehood.

"Symbolic violence", that is, making people ashamed of their language, culture and origins, was as extensive as physical violence against the Kurds. Using the name "Kurd" was made illegal and, when reference was inevitable, the people were referred to as "Mountain Turks" (*Dağli Türkler*), who were identified as retrogressive tribal groups that resist the civilizing mission of the Turkish state. Kurdish was declared a Turkish dialect corrupted by non-Turkish languages. Many Kurdish personal and geographical names were banned and replaced by Turkish names (Akin 1995). As recently as the 1980s, Turkish embassies were trying to extend the ban on Kurdish names to refugees and immigrants in Western countries (Helsinki Watch 1988, 10; Pierse 1997).

Territoriality and Satellite Television

Since the 1980s, death squads have been active in Turkey. Extrajudicial killings are practiced, apparently because the judicial elimination of all opposition would be too visible at a time when Ankara is actively seeking full membership in the European Union. However, like other states, Turkey also violates its own laws by legal means. For instance, a state of emergency has been in force in the Kurdish provinces since 1987. The emergency regime with its statutory orders and decrees, especially the widely condemned Anti-Terror Law of 1991, allows the government to convict almost anyone of terrorism (Helsinki Watch 1991).

The suppression of Med-TV, unlike that of print media, could not be confined within the borders of the country. The channel operated in multiple spaces that only partly coincided with the territorial boundaries of the state. The offices, their staff, and production facilities were outside the borders of Turkey and dispersed in at least three EU member states. The transmitter, unlike the offices of the Kurdish newspaper *Özgür Gündem* (simultaneously blown up in two different cities), was extraterrestrial and beyond the physical reach of Turkey. The audiences were also divided between the Middle East and Europe, the Kurdish "southeast" and the Turkish provinces. Television initiatives, unlike print media, need to be licensed, and Med-TV's license was issued in Britain, a country that could not readily comply with Turkish demands for the suppression of the channel. In interviews with the media, helplessness was clearly voiced in the discourse of Turkish authorities.

The suppression of Med-TV requires the combined use of legal action and violence. The physical absence of owners, program producers and broadcasters made it difficult for the state to take legal action against the channel, although legal power could be used against anyone who dared to act as reporter, cameraperson, interviewee, advertiser, or telephone caller.

Compared to other mass media, television is the most expensive and technologically complex medium in terms of production, transmission, and reception. This makes it difficult for non-state actors or non-business groups to have access to the medium. Faced with financial difficulties, Med-TV seeks advertising income; however, in spite of a sizable audience of about fifteen million, political restrictions have so far turned away potential advertisers.

The absence of Kurdish state power or political freedom also limits the ability of the channel to report from Kurdistan. Television reporting requires a crew of at least one cameraperson and a reporter, which is difficult if not impossible to hide in police states. Also needed in transnational broadcasting are studio facilities and satellite links. Moreover, it is risky for individuals, whether officials or members of the public, to participate in interviewing, perform music, or appear on the screen. However, resistance is also extensive. In a society with an insatiable hunger for native-tongue television, clandestine reporters and audience members use telephones, fax machines, and camcorders, and smuggle videos out of the country.

New forms of violence were used against Med-TV in the Kurdish provinces: satellite dishes were smashed, and viewers, dish vendors, dish installers, and coffee-houses with satellite dishes were intimidated (for details, see Hassanpour 1997). A more effective form of repression is cutting off electricity from villages and small towns during prime-time hours when Med-TV is on the air (Ryan 1997). Since the channel was forced to change its satellite provider in 1996, viewers had to adjust their dishes to an angle different from Turkey's satellite channels. This allowed the police to detect viewers, resulting in more violence against them. As a result of technical problems as well as political pressure, the channel lost some of its viewers. On 1 July 1997, Med-TV began airing on Eutelsat in addition to Intelsat. However, jamming prevented its reception from the Eutelsat transponder.

The Extraterritoriality of State Power

Diplomacy extends state power beyond its territorial base. Combining diplomacy with espionage, Turkey moved to silence the channel in Europe. Turkish embassies were ordered to collect information on the financial and organizational structure of the channel and how it had been able to broadcast through Eutelsat.[6] In direct contacts between heads of state, Turkey asked Britain and other European Union countries to take action against the channel. Under the terms of the Council of Europe Convention on Trans-Frontier Television, the ITC provided the Turkish government with information about the licensing of Med-TV.

Ankara demanded the revoking of the license by arguing, among other things, that the "broadcasts threaten Turkey's territorial integrity and make propaganda for the terrorist organization PKK."[7] However, lacking evidence to connect the licensee to PKK or any political organization, the Independent Television Commission was not in a position to comply with Turkey's demands.

The embassy has also mobilized Turkish immigrants in England to harass the ITC by writing letters and compiling petitions which repeat Ankara's disinformation against the channel, accusing it of "terrorism" and "hate propaganda", and calling for the revocation of its license. A Med-TV director received threatening letters[8] while another was physically attacked by four men in a train station in Germany.

Considering the pressure from Turkey, the ITC's ability to maintain an arm's length relationship with the executive branch of the British government is significant. The Commission's resistance to becoming a springboard for extending Turkey's media policy to Europe has implications beyond Med-TV. Whatever the outcome, British and EU policy on Med-TV will establish a precedent for communication rights and freedoms in the evolving global regulation of media. The question is one of allowing dissident voices or non-state peoples a space in the global village.

If the most convenient legal action, that is, the revoking of the license, is not forthcoming, the democratic state still has recourse to other venues. On 18 September 1996, Britain, Belgium and Germany conducted one of the worst offensives against a media institution. Police simultaneously raided Med-TV offices in London and its studio, Roj N.V., in Brussels, while in Germany Kurdish homes were searched. The office's files, diskettes and computers were seized in a three-hour search by Special Branch officers

(Black 1996). The raid in London was carried out under the Prevention of Terrorism Act. The police stated that the aim was financial investigation.

In Brussels, a 200-strong special forces unit attacked the studio and detained ninety-seven people. Everyone was handcuffed, forced to lie on the floor, and forbidden to speak to one another. Five employees of the channel were arrested on charges of money laundering and criminal conspiracy. The special forces took files, mailing lists, videos and computers, damaged the premises, and sealed the studio. The office of the "Kurdistan Parliament in Exile" in Brussels was also searched. On 9 October police searched houses belonging to Kurds in six Belgian cities. The aim was apparently to seek confirmation from the Kurdish community that Med-TV raised money through extortion. On 27 October the Turkish daily, *Hürriyet,* wrote that the raids in Brussels followed an agreement between Belgian police and the chief of Turkey's internal security. The arrested staff were released and re-arrested several times between 18 September and 30 October when the last four were released. Med-TV's decision to expand its delivery system in Europe, via cable, invited further Turkish interference in the internal affairs of other countries.

The market is an important actor in the world of satellite television. Satellite technology was first developed and monopolized by the state but the market today is a partner in launching, owning and running communication satellites. According to one observer, a "satellite aristocracy" now rules in the sky (Joxe 1994). However, while Turkey was successful in working with telecommunications businesses, the satellite market proved not to be a totally closed space.

Med-TV began broadcasting in May 1995 on a contract with France. Bowing to pressure from Turkey, France Telecom refused to renew Med-TV's Eutelsat transponder lease when it expired a year later. This was followed by the refusal of Portuguese Telecom to honor its contract. Portuguese, Spanish and German companies, too, followed suit. Then, when the Polish PTT unilaterally breached a contract, vetoed by the Polish government, the channel was forced off the air on 2 July. Although Turkey celebrated its victory, Med-TV resumed test transmissions on 13 August after signing a contract with an American company, Intelsat. Ankara protested the deal and called for U.S. government intervention. When the Eutelsat service, this time leased through Slovakia, resumed in July 1997, it was jammed (between 1 and 23 July) and Ankara pressured this country to withdraw the service.

Turkey also mobilized the private sector against the channel. Ankara was apparently involved in the resignation of three lawyers who had been working for Med-TV and in the closing of the channel's bank account.[9] According to one source, "several West European banks, legal firms and other companies have refused to work with Med-TV, apparently for fear of alienating the Turkish authorities."[10] Turkey pioneered new forms of sabotage in international broadcasting. During a live studio debate on Med-TV, telephone calls from two guest speakers phoning from their home in Diyarbakir in Turkey were intercepted and replaced with music and electronic jamming. On 14 December 1995, broadcasting was jammed, apparently for the first time in the history of satellite television, when Abdullah Öcalan, leader of the Kurdistan Workers Party, was scheduled to announce a unilateral cease-fire.

Deterritorializing Sovereignty

It is clear from the above that a separation, however limited, between sovereign rule and its territory, has already occurred in Turkey. Med-TV, as a broadcaster, and Turkey, as a state, share the same land and population, that is, the northern parts of greater Kurdistan or, to use state discourse, Turkey's "southeast". There is one territorial base and two contenders for loyalty. The channel's power derives from a Kurdish audience politicized by the nationalist movement led, in Turkey, primarily by PKK.

In spite of the imbalance of power between Turkey and Med-TV on the international level, the channel is not totally helpless. One of its weaknesses, that is, the enormous cost of satellite broadcasting, is, in part, compensated by running the station along the lines of community television. The dedication of the staff and the voluntary work of many viewers and supporters is a source of strength. It is remarkable that broadcasting resumed immediately after the main studio in Brussels was ransacked and closed.

Med-TV is supported by non-state actors. For instance, Britain's Lord Avebury, who chaired the Parliamentary Human Rights Group in London, expressed his concerns about Turkey's intentions. In an Early Day motion one day after the channel was forced off the air in July 1996, the British MP John Austin-Walker protested the European governments' bowing to Turkish pressure (Drucker 1996, 9). Two members of the European Parliament tabled questions to the Council of Europe about the cooperation of

EU members with Turkey in the raids on Med-TV in London and Brussels in September 1996. The leader of the Socialist Group in the European Parliament condemned Turkey for actions against Med-TV and against the "Kurdish people as a whole". The executive director of "Article XIX International Centre Against Censorship" protested the police raid in Brussels. The International Federation of Journalists and the Association of Professional Journalists of Belgium submitted a strong protest to the court in Brussels. Med-TV is also supported by minority broadcasting institutions and individuals. For instance, the television network of the Basque non-state nation has provided Med-TV with material to be aired by the channel. Turkey's fight against Med-TV has raised consciousness about the need for solidarity among minority broadcasting institutions.

While the silencing of Med-TV requires coordinated efforts by several states and market forces, the survival of Med-TV would also require cooperation among the forces of civil society on the global level. The imbalance of power is evident here, too. The inter-state system of cooperation is well established and lavishly funded by taxes, including those collected from the viewers of Med-TV. By contrast, while actors in civil society are numerous and potentially powerful, they are scattered and fragmented; they have no embassy networks, no legislative organs, and no intelligence and military coalitions. Any non-state institution such as Med-TV would need considerable financial and organizational resources to rally the kind of support that is vital but not automatically available.

Med-TV has disturbed Turkey's constitutional blueprint for a pure, sovereign Turkish presence in the "southeast". It has established relations with Kurdish viewers not as members of an audience but rather as citizens of a Kurdish state, and, by doing so, it is exercising deterritorialized sovereignty. Every day, viewers experience the citizenship of a borderless state with its national flag, national anthem, national television and national news agency. Indeed, every day Med-TV raises the Kurdish flag in about two million homes. It is obvious that Turkey treats each satellite dish as a Kurdish flag hoisted on the rooftops of every building in the "southeast". Government authorities have, in fact, considered banning dishes in Kurdish provinces. In the town of Batman, officials changed the colors of traffic lights from the red-yellow-green of the Kurdish flag to red-yellow-blue (Loewy 1996). The experience of Kurdish citizenship is further enhanced every time the Europe-based Kurdistan Parliament in Exile sets foot in Kurdish homes through the channel's regular coverage.

Banning satellite dishes is difficult to enforce in larger urban areas.[11] Another alternative, that of cutting off electricity to many communities, would also be difficult to continue for a long time. A more effective option, that is, democratization of the political system, has not yet been considered. This would entail, among many changes, discarding Turkish ethnonationalism as the foundation of state and society. It is interesting that the option of legalizing Kurdish broadcasting, as put forward by some Turkish authorities, makes no pretense of democratization. The discourse of government officials is straightforward; if Kurdish broadcasting is allowed, it would aim at replacing Med-TV's Kurdish nationalism with Kemalism. A pro-Kurdish paper, *Demokrasi*, called this "Contra-TV", referring to the U.S. backed Contras of Nicaragua. Such a television initiative, whether private or public, would find it difficult to compete with Med-TV as long as the Kurds are suppressed.[12]

Conclusions

The experience of Med-TV demonstrates the ability of a non-state, privately owned satellite channel to exercise, as well as grant, language rights in a country where the state strictly denies such rights to Kurdish citizens. Broadcasting from multiple national (Britain, Belgium) and international spaces (the geostationary orbit), the channel has granted the Kurdish citizens of Turkey as well as other Middle Eastern countries the right to communicate audiovisually in their language. The small but powerful television screen is transformed into multiple classrooms where language, politics, national identity, history, and other forms of popular knowledge are taught on a daily basis.

Television creatively combines visual images, sound and music with the spoken and written varieties of language. The popularity of the medium allows Med-TV to act as a legislator of language or, rather, a language academy. This is all the more significant in the case of Kurdish, which is a threatened language, divided by the international borders of Turkey, Iran, Iraq and Syria, split into four major dialect groups, and written in three different alphabets. If traditional academies generally target the written language of the educated, Med-TV regulates the language-use of millions of people both literate and orate.

The "legislative" powers of Med-TV go beyond the realm of language and culture. By communicating and implementing the decisions of the Kurdistan Parliament in Exile (at least in connection with the promotion of the Kurdish language), Med-TV seems to exercise both legislative and executive powers. The failure of the Turkish state to silence the channel has given it, at least in the eyes of viewers, more than the semblance of executive power. Many viewers see Med-TV as the realization of one of their dreams of sovereignty.

Med-TV thus seems to confirm postmodern claims about the withering away of states, nations and boundaries. A small group of private individuals are dismantling a vast machinery of linguicide, run by one of the top military powers of the world, and supported by the "international community" of Western powers. However, theorizing this dramatic decentering of a highly centralized state power as the beginning of a "new era" may be too optimistic. Indeed, even some poststructuralists would reject such "virtual geography" or "cosmopolitan optimism" for failing to explain, among other things, the continuing trend of nationalist revival, ethnic cleansing, and formation of new nation-states. They admit the enduring presence of the state but reject a state-centrist theoretical framework (see, e.g., Marden 1997, 39; Brown 1995). The persistence of old and new structures of power is often lost in the fast pace of a changing world that is difficult to catch up with intellectually.

The experience of Kurdish makes better sense when put in the context of the emerging world linguistic order. The spoken languages of the world, more than six thousand in number, interact in a hierarchical system, characterized by a highly unequal division of power. There are small and big languages, written and unwritten, national and local, international and national, state and non-state, official and non-official, and living and dying. The world language system is indeed the site of extensive competition, domination and repression. The state and the market are the two most powerful regulators of this linguistic order.

It is estimated that in prehistoric times, there were some 10,000 to 15,000 languages in the world. Almost half of these languages have disappeared, leaving behind only about 6,000 today. Considering the accelerating pace of language death, some linguists estimate that about 3,000 languages are likely to become extinct within the next century. These dying languages include 90 percent of Australia's 250 languages, 45 of Russia's 65 languages, 50 percent of the languages of the former Soviet Union, and more than one-third of South America's languages (Krauss 1992; see, also, Skutnabb-Kangas, this volume).

New communication technologies are not autonomous factors serving the world's languages neutrally or equitably. Kurdish access to satellite television is, in fact, the exception rather than the rule. It was made possible by a combination of factors, which are themselves products of the changing world order – for example, the formation of a sizable diaspora of workers and political refugees, the brutal national oppression perpetrated by despotic Middle Eastern states, the persistence of the Kurdish nationalist movement, and the conflict between Turkey and the European Union.

The surface of our planet is divided among some 200 states, which in turn share the world's 6,000 languages. The great majority of these states are multilingual. Even when languages are legally equal, they usually remain unequal in the market. For instance, while French is legally equal to English in Canada and is the only official language in the predominantly francophone Québec province, it is dwarfed by the cultural and economic power of English. If Kurdish is threatened by the dictatorship of the state, French, one of the world's most prestigious languages, is threatened by the dictatorship of the market. Underrating the power of the market and the state does not enhance the struggle for maintaining our rich heritage of languages. The extremist position in poststructuralism totalizes "openings" by ignoring "closures". A more constructive approach, at least for language rights activists, is to see the dialectics of opening and closure. The evolving world linguistic order is both the prison-house and sanctuary of languages. With eighteen hours of daily programming today (March 1998), Med-TV operates as the "national" television of a non-state nation. The short, turbulent life of the channel dramatizes the coexistence and conflict of these opposites.[13]

Postscript (July 1999)

After this paper was written (March 1998), Turkey continued its efforts to take Med-TV off the air while it helped an enemy of PKK, the Kurdish Democratic Party of Iraqi Kurdistan, to launch a rival station, KTV, in late 1998. KTV's regular programming began in January 1999 with extensive anti-PKK propaganda (for a report on the channel see, Amberin Zaman, "Swords into rabbit ears: Kurdish rivals launch TV broadcast battle across tense border", The Washington Post, 4 February 1999, p. A24).

In November 1998, PKK leader Abdullah Öcalan, living clandestinely in Syria, was expelled from this country when the Turkish Army warned Damascus to stop helping the organization. Soon Öcalan ended up in Italy where he sought asylum. Med-TV was the only channel to devote its entire programming to the event, and played a major role in rallying Kurdish support for his cause. However, he had to leave Italy and seek asylum elsewhere. In mid-February 1999, Öcalan made headline news when Turkey abducted him in an operation involving the US, Israel, Greece and Kenya. Med-TV increased its programming from 18 to 24 hours, and tried to provide Kurdish perspectives on the events, and air the statements and positions of PKK and its leaders. (Andrew Buncombe, "Diaspora hear the word on Kurd TV", The Independent, 19 February 1999, p. 12). On 6 March, Turkish Prime Minister Bülent Ecevit urged his European and NATO counterparts to close down Med-TV and a Kurdish newspaper published in Europe.

The ITC announced, on 22 March, that it had suspended the channel's licence for a period of 21 days. Med-TV was given three weeks to convince the ITC to allow the channel to remain on the air. Turkey welcomed the decision and called on ITC to revoke the license. The Kurds and others supporting freedom of the press protested by a wave of demonstrations. After three weeks, the ITC was not convinced and, on 23 April, it served a notice revoking the licence to take effect in 28 days. In ITC's words,

> Med TV's licence was suspended on 22 March by the ITC under Section 45A of the 1990 Broadcasting Act, following four broadcasts which included inflammatory statements encouraging acts of violence in Turkey and elsewhere. These were judged by the ITC as "likely to encourage or incite to crime or lead to disorder". This is against UK law, as set out in the 1990 and 1996 Broadcasting Acts.

(for a list of Med-TV's breaches of Programme Code, see ITC website www.itc.org.uk)

On 29 May, Kurdish programs were aired for six hours daily on Britain's Cultural TV (CTV). All the broadcasts were pre-recorded so that their contents could be checked for compliance with ITC codes. The programs were produced by a Belgian firm, BRD, at Med-TV's studios. In June, Turkey began pressing Britain to crack down on CTV, claiming that it was making propaganda on behalf of PKK (Ian Black, "Turks want 'pro-Kurd' TV censored by Britain", Guardian, 21 June 1999).

Turkey and its NATO supporters were able to silence Med-TV on the eve of the channel's fourth birthday. By July 1999, Turkey continued to deny the Kurds broadcasting and other communication and linguistic rights. At the same time, CTV continued Kurdish broadcasting within the same satellite footprint as Med-TV's.

Notes

1 This chapter, the revised version of a paper presented at the Budapest conference on linguistic human rights, is based on my continuing research on Med-TV, including "Satellite Footprints as National Borders: MED-TV and the Extraterritoriality of State Sovereignty" (*Journal of Muslim Minority Affairs*, 18, no. 1 [1998]: 53–72). I am indebted to Tove Skutnabb-Kangas and Bart Driessen for their excellent comments; I am alone responsible for the contents.

2 Jon Davey, director of Cable & Satellite, Independent Television Commission, London, response to my inquiry, 13 October 1995.

3 According to "State of Affairs in Turkey", Update no. 67, 4 July 1997, prepared by the Washington Kurdish Institute (Internet source).

4 "Turkey and the Kurds: Ethnic Cleansing", *The Economist*, 333, No. 7894 (17 December 1994): 52–53.

5 According to U.S. government sources, Turkey imported $950 million worth of arms mainly from the U.S. in 1994. With a total of 811,000 troops, it ranks seventh among the world's armed forces ("Turkey is world's sixth largest arms importer", *Turkish Daily News*, 5 July 1996).

6 Reported in *BBC Summary of World Broadcasts*, Part 2 Central Europe and the Balkans; BALKANS; TURKEY; EE/2270/b, 5 April 1995.

7 The Associated Press, "Kurds Pioneer Broadcasting to Ethnic Groups Without a Homeland", 15 August 1995.

8 The Associated Press, "Kurds Pioneer Broadcasting."

9 My interview with Mr. Haluk Sayan, director of Med-TV, London, 12 July 1995.

10 Edward Mortimer, "An Identity Crisis..." *The Financial Times*, 3 January 1996, quoted in Med-TV (March 1995). *The International Impact of Med-TV*, London: Med-TV, 29.

11 According to a Med-TV press release, Necati Bilican, the governor of the state of emergency area, threatened in February 1997 the banning of satellite dishes in the Kurdish region. Operations were conducted against dishes in at least 48 villages ("More threats against Med-TV", London, 17 February 1997).

12 For a brief report, see "Turkey Said to be Considering Allowing Kurdish Broadcasts", *Turkish Daily News*, 2 June 1996.

13 In January 1998, the Independent Television Commission fined the channel £90,000 (US $144,000) for breaching the commission's rules of

impartiality. In early March, Med-TV received a warning from the commission for broadcasting an interview which constituted "encouragement and incitement to crime". The interviewee was a military commander of the Kurdistan Workers Party.

References

Akin, Salih. *Désignation du peuple, du territoire et de la langue kurde dans le discours scientifique et politique turc.* Thèse, Doctorat en Sciences du Langage, École doctorale de Lettres, Université de Rouen, France, 1995.

Black, Ian. "Police Raid Kurdish TV in London". *The Guardian* (London), 20 September 1996.

Brown, Robin. "Globalization and the End of the National Project". In John MacMillan and Andrew Linklater, eds., *Boundaries in Question: New Directions in International Relations,* 55–68. London: Pinter Publishers, 1995.

Chyet, Michael. "Sabri, the Teacher", *Kurdistan Report*, no.21 (May-June, 1995): 51, 57.

Drucker, Catherine. "MED TV: Satellite Television for Kurdish Speakers". *Contact Bulletin* (The European Bureau for Lesser Used Languages) 13, no. 3 (Autumn 1996): 9.

Flanz, Gisbert. "Turkey". In A. Blaustein and G. Flanz, eds., *Constitutions of the Countries of the World.* Dobbs Ferry, N.Y.: Oceana Publications, Inc., 13 August 1994.

Hassanpour, Amir. "Med-TV, Großbritannien und der Türkische Staat: Die Suche einer Staatenlosen Nation nach Souveränität im Äther". In Carsten Borck, Eva Savelsberg and Siamend Hajo, eds., *Ethnizität, Nationalismus, Religion und Politik in Kurdistan,* 239–78. Münster: LIT Verlag, 1997.

Helsinki Watch. *Destroying Ethnic Identity: The Kurds of Turkey.* New York: Helsinki Watch, March 1988.

Helsinki Watch. *Turkey: New Restrictive Anti-Terror Law, 6.* New York: Helsinki Watch, 10 June 1991.

Hirst, Paul. "Democracy and Civil Society". In Paul Hirst and Sunil Khilnani, eds., *Reinventing Democracy,* 97–116. Oxford: Blackwell Publishers, 1996.

Idiz, Semih D. "Ankara's sleuthing providing the facts Europeans maintain they lack on PKK's cover organizations". *Turkish Daily News*, 26 June 1996.

Joxe, Alain. "Stratégie de l'aristocratie satellitaire", *Les conquêtes de l'espace.* Paris: Le Monde diplomatique: [Série] Savoire 3 (1994): 64–67.

Kadioğlu, Ayşe. "The Paradox of Turkish Nationalism and the Construction of Official Identity". *Middle Eastern Studies* 32, No. 2 (April 1996): 177–193.

Krauss, Michael. "The World's Languages in Crisis". *Language* 68, No. 1 (1992): 4-10.

Loewy, Reuben. "Kurdish Problem Just Won't Go Away for Turkish Leaders". *The Globe and Mail* (daily paper, Toronto), 2 January 1996.

Luke, Timothy. "Reconsidering Nationality and Sovereignty in the New World Order". *Political Crossroads* 5, Nos. 1 & 2 (1997): 3-17.

Marden, Peter. "Geographies of Dissent: Globalization, Identity and the Nation". *Political Geography* 16, No. 1 (1997): 37-64.

Med-TV. *Kurdish Satellite Television*. London: Med-TV, Fall 1995.

Muller, Mark. "Nationalism and the Rule of Law in Turkey: The Elimination of Kurdish Representation during the 1990s". In Robert Olson, ed., *The Kurdish Nationalist Movement in the 1990s: Its Impact on Turkey and the Middle East,* 173-199. Lexington, Kentucky: The University Press of Kentucky, 1996.

Pierse, Katherine. *Cultural and Language Rights for the Kurds*. London: Medico International and Kurdish Human Rights Project, 1997.

Republic of Turkey. "An Act Amending the Preamble and Some Articles of the Constitution of the Republic of Turkey No. 2709 of 7.11.1982". In Ömer Faruk Gençkaya, ed., *Republic of Turkey Supplement*. In Gisbert H. Flanz, ed. *Constitutions of the Countries of the World. Turkey,* 1-8. Dobbs Ferry, New York: Oceana Publications, Inc., 1995.

Ryan, Nick. "The Land of Sun". Unpublished paper, May 1997.

Schneider, Elizabeth. "The Dialectic of Rights and Politics: Perspectives from the Women's Movement". In D. Kelly Weisberg, ed., *Feminist Legal Theory,* 507-26. Philadelphia: Temple University Press, 1993.

Skutnabb-Kangas, Tove. *Bilingualism or Not: The Education of Minorities*. Translated by L. Malberg and D. Crane. London: Multilingual Matters Ltd., 1981.

——. "Linguistic diversity, human rights and the 'free' market". In Miklós Kontra, Robert Phillipson, Tove Skutnabb-Kangas, Tibor Várady, eds. *Language: A Right and a Resource,* 187-222. Budapest: Central European University Press, 1999.

de Varennes, Fernand. *Language, Minorities and Human Rights*. The Hague: Martinus Nijhoff Publishers, 1996.

Waldron, Jeremy. "Rights". In Robert Googin and Philip Pettit, eds., *A Companion to Contemporary Political Philosophy,* 575-85. Cambridge, MA: Basil Blackwell Ltd., 1993.

LANGUAGE PLANNING ISSUES

Separating Language from Ethnicity: The Paradoxes of Strict Language Policies and Increasing Social Harmony in the Baltic States

ULDIS OZOLINS

Since the renewed independence of the Baltic states in 1991, language policy issues have become a critical point in local politics and have attracted considerable international interest. Reinstating national languages as the official languages of the renewed states was seen as essential in overturning the previous Soviet population and language policies that had brought widespread russification and threatened existing national cultures. However, language policy has never been an internal matter alone: from the beginning of national assertion in the late 1980s, language policy became an external affairs issue, with Moscow, Western Europe, and many other commentators berating, warning or in other ways seeking to exert influence. The Baltic states have adopted language policies which are often criticized from outside; yet, as we will show, these policies are gaining considerable support from the populations within their states, even those who are represented as being the most excluded by language or related citizenship policies.

We examine the evidence that can now be gathered on the course of language policies in the Baltic states, and raise questions about the paradoxical nature of language policies and democratic stability in this region.

Overcoming the Heritage of Soviet Language Policy

For the Baltic states, language issues are related to both the long period of Soviet language policies since World War II, and, even more critically, to the demographic changes wrought on the Baltic states by Soviet industrialization and population policies. These have led to a sharp decline in the proportion of local nationals in the population of these republics, particularly in the case of Estonia and Latvia. The demographic situation is presented in table 11.1, which contrasts the pre-World War II era (when the Baltic states were independent countries) and the postwar period.

Table 11.1

Proportion of local nationals as percentage of total population

	Last prewar census	1989	1995
Estonia	88.1	61.5	64.2
Latvia	77	52	54.8
Lithuania	83.9	79.6	81.3

(Kaiser 1994; Economist Intelligence Unit 1996–7)

While each of the three states had significant minorities before World War II, which were each made up of citizens and which had considerable cultural autonomy, the Soviet-period settlers brought a tide of russification. These settlers rarely spoke the local languages–in the 1989 census, for example, only some 20 percent of Russians in Latvia spoke Latvian, only 12 percent in Estonia spoke Estonian, while some 35 percent of Russians in Lithuania spoke Lithuanian.

Soviet language policy was officially one of bilingualism, with local republic languages as well as Russian being used in schools, administration, culture and politics. Yet this policy of bilingualism in fact led to asymmetric bilingualism: Russian-speaking settlers received and expected to receive all services in Russian in any republic; they also expected to be able to work in Russian in any sphere, thus expecting locals to use Russian in their dealings with these monolingual Russian-speaking officials or workers. Locals needed to be bilingual in their own language and in Russian, but Russians could remain solidly monolingual (Lewis 1972; Kreindler 1985; Kirkwood 1989; Marshall 1996). Russian schools were established for the children of settlers, although there were no schools for settlers of other Soviet nationalities—thus, other nationalities who were outside their own republics tended to be russified. Russian was promoted as the international language and language of interethnic communication, and achieved greater sociolinguistic functions as it slowly took over at many administrative, occupational and educational levels.

Language considerations were fundamental to the processes of national self-determination in the Baltic republics from the late 1980s onwards (Lieven 1993). Language was inextricably linked to the very salvation of a national identity under such an intense demographic and cultural threat. While still part of the Soviet Union, all three republics passed language laws in 1988–9, re-establishing their local languages as the official languages of the republics and introducing a series of measures that have determined language policies ever since:

- The language policies were fundamentally aimed at the eradication of most aspects of official Soviet two-language polices, in favor of the local national languages. The national languages are now used at all levels of official administration so that, for example, local nationals can be guaranteed to receive services in their national language. There has been complete decyrillization in signage and public notices, with Russian virtually disappearing from public display.
- Language requirements have been introduced for all who work in public contact positions, whether in government or in private enterprise; language proficiency tests for those in these positions have been held from 1992.
- Cultural autonomy has been granted to the various minority groups, in line with pre-war policies that guaranteed cultural autonomy as defined by the Versailles treaty (Loeber 1993). There has been particular emphasis on helping groups who were not recognized during the Soviet period; for example, schools have been re-established for many minority groups such as Poles, Jews and Ukrainians. Existing institutions for Russians (e.g. the extensive school system) are being maintained where significant numbers of Russian children still live. Minority policy is to treat Russians as one more minority group, though it is a minority with special characteristics, as analyzed below.
- Finally, and most controversially in the case of Estonia and Latvia, language requirements are central to issues of naturalization and citizenship. All three Baltic states see their status as being the continuation of their prewar independence, interrupted by a prolonged Soviet occupation. However, in considering who should be the citizens of these renewed states, Estonia and Latvia took a radically different view from that taken by Lithuania. Lithuania considered its minorities to be so small that it took the so-called zero-option, granting citizen-

ship of the new Lithuanian state to all residents apart from certain military and security units. Estonia and Latvia, on the other hand, considered that it would be impossible to grant citizenship to all settlers, some of whom were antagonistic to the idea of independent states and few of whom knew the national languages. Both states defined as citizens all those (of whatever nationality) who were citizens of these states in 1940, and their descendants. For those who had arrived after 1940, a process of naturalization was agreed to after considerable debate, and elementary speaking and writing ability in the national language was made part of the criteria for naturalization. Indeed the citizenship laws as eventually adopted by Estonia and Latvia are essentially language-based laws, with other less controversial features like a period of residence, some knowledge of local history and the constitution, and an oath of loyalty. Dual citizenship is not allowed for settlers from the Soviet period.

The Baltic states all explicitly rejected a two-language state model, that is, having two official languages, the national language and Russian. Such a model was seen as guaranteeing the continuing hegemony of Russian and asymmetric bilingualism, and the steady erosion of national identity, not to mention a continuing official Russian presence with links across the border. This has often been difficult for Western commentators or institutions to accept, and has angered Moscow, which has posited itself as the protector of all "Russian speakers".

It is important to stress that the language laws have been explicitly directed at *overturning an existing language situation*. Population and language policies had led to a situation where, in Estonia and Latvia, Russian was in some cases a more widely spoken language than the national language, and with no incentives for monolingual Russian speakers to increase their linguistic repertoire. Politically, the language laws meant the overturning of the previous privileges enjoyed by Russian-speaking settlers in being able to insist on the use of their language. This privilege was taken for granted during the Soviet period. Sociolinguistically, the laws have meant reasserting the dominance of the national languages in all areas of life, particularly in administration and public interaction where Russian had assumed *de facto* prominence.

The language laws do not regulate what language must be used by individuals in interactions; however, they do stipulate that all persons in positions involving contact with the public must be able to communicate in the national language. An important aspect of these language laws is that they reach into the private economic sphere—all those working in shops or businesses with direct client contact must be able to communicate in the national language.

These language laws have been attacked from several quarters. Most savagely perhaps, they were attacked in the late 1980s and early 1990s by the various pro-Soviet groupings that opposed independence for these states and indeed opposed any diminution of the status of Russian (Alksnis 1991). The most vociferous of these groups, the various "Interfront" organizations, were not, however, able to gain any significant support from the sizable Russian populations.

Significantly, far more sustained criticism and venom towards these language requirements comes not from local residents but from Moscow, where Russian foreign policy has consistently, but with very varying degrees of success, attempted to make these issues objects of international condemnation.

In response to largely Russian concerns, an almost never-ending series of international observers and delegations have come to the Baltic states at various times–Rannut wearily recounts that since the gaining of independence in 1991 some fifteen such missions have visited Estonia alone, "none of which have found any gross or systematic violations of human rights" (Rannut 1994, 208). All of these observers of the Baltic states have come to similar conclusions: that there are no systematic abuses of human rights, that minor frictions and lack of clarity and communication exist on a very few issues, and that issues should be resolved with common sense and patience. Even some Russian authors acknowledge that the issue is no longer about the violation of international standards, although they still point out the need for the Baltic states to take account of the particular position of the Soviet-period settlers (Shamshur 1994).

The language laws have also met quite strong opposition from another quarter—European institutions. The Council of Europe and the Organization for Security and Cooperation in Europe have been asked from time to time to comment on legislation and other issues in the Baltic states—a practice adopted by the Baltic states in their wish to integrate into European structures. These institutions accepted the Baltic states' citizenship legislation after considerable examination and negotiation, but recently seem to have adopted some harsher views on language policy. We return to their role below.

There have been quite varied responses to the Baltic language situation in scholarly studies. Several Baltic scholars themselves

have led the way in the analysis of the Baltic language situation
(Rannut 1991, 1994; Druviete 1995, 1996; Ozolins 1994, 1996) and
there have been a number of others who have drawn parallels with
other situations–interestingly enough in several instances with
Quebec (Grin 1991; Maurais 1992; de Varennes 1995/6). Other
Western scholars have carried out detailed work with Baltic colleagues (Kirch and Laitin 1994; Laitin 1996). Laitin's 1996 work
argued that the language situation in Estonia seemed to have some
of the preconditions for extended ethnic conflicts and the failure
of language rationalization, but that these have, in fact, been successfully avoided because of specific factors associated with the
break-up of the Soviet Union, and that nation-building will in fact
be able to proceed in the Baltic on the classic model of a nation-
state with its national language.

Again, perhaps surprisingly, the most negative attitudes to the
Baltic states come from those concerned with European integration. Smith, Aasland and Mole (1994) argue, on the basis of a sample of Russian residents in four cities in the Baltic, that there is
overwhelming condemnation of language laws and citizenship
laws. The samples, particularly in Tallinn and Riga, are so overwhelmingly unequivocal on this that they seem to confirm every
Interfront or Moscow concern about locals feeling disenfranchised
and discriminated against. Yet the evidence presented in this study
is so much at odds with every other empirical study carried out at
this time (see the discussion of Rose and Maley 1994 below) and
every study since, that the entire basis of their approach needs to
be questioned. Certainly any social scientist working in the Baltic
would know exactly where to find samples of Russian residents
who held such views, but the question of representativeness must
be asked.

Even more worrying, from a scientific point of view, are David
Arter's completely unsupported and seemingly random assertions
on the situation in the Baltic states and the obstacles to the integration of the populations there. Arter, Professor of European Integration at Leeds, argues that

> In the Baltic states, the principal obstacle to national integration has
> stemmed from the imperialistic attitude of the political class repre-
> senting the indigenous majority towards the ethnic minorities of the
> former Imperial power (Russians, Byelorussians and Ukrainians)...
> Hardline nationalists held that citizenship should be conferred only
> on those who lived in the Baltic republics before 1940, along with
> their descendants .... (Arter 1993, 247)

It is difficult to square such comments with any understanding of actual Baltic politics. The author clearly is not aware that this citizenship model was held not by "hard-line nationalists" but by virtually every major political party in Estonia and Latvia. To accuse the elites and governments that actually have come to power in these countries of extreme nationalism seems to be a complete misreading of Baltic politics and betrays, more worryingly, a serious lack of attention to detail—the parliaments are in fact heavily representative of managerial, organizational and varied personal interests, with identifiably nationalist representatives being in a distinct minority. Arter's argument also presupposes just who is indeed responsible for the lack of integration—particularly integration into new states that a proportion of the settlers, who were unable to speak the language of those states, neither wanted, nor supported. It is a completely unwarranted inversion to cite the previous colonial masters as helpless victims, and the fledgling Baltic states as now wielding imperialistic [*sic*] and autocratic power. Arter's contribution may explain some of the inflexible templates that champions of European integration wish to impose upon Eastern European countries, but is completely misleading on the particulars of politics and language in the Baltic.

At an even greater distance than Arter, popular historian Francis Fukuyama in the United States has also contributed to this issue, asserting, on the basis of even less attention to detail, that Baltic language and citizenship policies were discriminatory and should be opposed by the US government (*New York Times* 19 December 1992).

When the Baltic states adopted their language and citizenship policies there were, as in the authors cited above, dire warnings of how exclusionist policies could lead to ethnic conflict, lack of integration, disenfranchisement of large numbers of residents, and, potentially, ethnic violence and civil war. Yet the question must be asked: what is the empirical evidence, now, after more than five years of Baltic independence and when language policies have had some chance of being implemented? What do we find in terms of resident attitudes and behavior towards these policies? Are concerns of growing ethnic conflicts justified?

The Paradoxes of Language and Political Stability in the Baltics

In every instance, the empirical evidence reveals almost the opposite of these dire predictions. Over the past few years, while difficulties, both economic and political, have abounded, we have in

fact seen a period of growing social harmony, the lessening of ethnic tensions, a greater acceptance of the learning and use of national languages, and even some improvement of the economic
situation. We need to explain this seeming paradox: the existence
of quite strict language laws which have drawn such criticism, and,
at the same time, growing ethnic harmony.

Laitin's (1996) work is instructive here. As noted above, he argued that at the time it gained independence, the situation in Estonia was fraught with difficulties in terms of re-establishing a traditional nation-state and achieving language rationalization. There
were significant numbers of Russian speakers in the country
whose access to good channels of communication to the outside
world meant they were able to publicize their situation, and international attitudes were skeptical of attempts to reimpose a unitary
nation-state upon ethnically diverse populations. Specifically on
the language and citizenship laws, Laitin correctly predicted that
there would be no overt ethnic conflict for two reasons. Firstly,
Estonian enjoys high status in Estonia and is indelibly embedded as
the language of politics, culture and administration, unlike the
situation in many other ex-colonial regimes where there may be
attempts to institute a weakly-supported language as a national
language. Secondly, he argues that the specific circumstances of
the break-up of the Soviet Union have left the non-Estonian minority in a situation in which they will find it economically more ex-
pedient to follow Estonia's economic success (certainly vis-à-vis
economically struggling Russia) than to follow any Russian-
oriented cultural or political groups. Economic advancement will
bring about increased language rationalization. Laitin in fact argues
that English may eventually become the language of inter-ethnic
communication in Estonia, given the reluctance of Russian speakers to learn Estonian, but that Estonian hegemony will be accepted.

Other empirical evidence of the actual linguistic and political
situation in the Baltics supports Laitin's conclusion with respect to
diminishing ethnic tensions, but we can go beyond Laitin's trust in
economic advancement and the status of Estonian. In what follows,
we explore the actual situation across four dimensions—the sociological, political, sociolinguistic and psychological, finally suggest-
ing some tentative hypotheses on how these factors can also help
us to understand some of the paradoxes of democratization in this
region.

Sociologically, it is crucial to understand that the "Russian
speakers", the object of Moscow's expressed concern, are not at all
one homogeneous group but are, in fact, quite diverse and even

internally divided in terms of their attitudes to the new nations and their place within them. Several authors have alluded to this, not least Russian authors studying Russian settlers in the "near abroad". Even Smith et al., for example, quote Semyonov who argues that Baltic Russians may well constitute "a motley, unorganized mass, which in a political sense does not represent movements and parties but a crowd" (Smith et al. 1994, 203). Yet this "crowd", in a sociological sense, reveals important internal differences. This was illustrated in the long process of the differentiation of the Baltic states from the Soviet Union, with Russians and other non-local nationals spread along the whole spectrum from total support for independence to hostile opposition to such a move.

More recently, sociolinguistic surveys have revealed quite strong gender differences in the extent to which people want to learn the national language and want their children to learn it. Young Russian males, particularly from the most well-off families, are least likely to want to learn local languages (Druviete 1995, 30; Volkovs 1996); as the attitude of this group is well known and generally despised by other Russians, we see class as well as gender differences coming into play. Russian women overwhelmingly favor learning the national languages. Volkovs argues that these kinds of sociological differences among the Russian group mean it is very difficult to talk of anything other than the steady disintegration of this group as an entity.

The interethnic mixing that is seen very clearly in Latvia also works against ethnic conflict: not only is there a high rate of ethnic intermarriage in Latvia, but in eastern Latvia, where Russian communities have historically resided longest, a majority of Russians are citizens according to the 1940 benchmark.

Politically, it is the argument of this paper that, as a central paradox, the measures that were seen to exclude a large part of the population—citizenship and language laws—have in fact provided the basis for continuing political stability. The central case here is that of restrictive citizenship in the case of Estonia and Latvia. If the zero-option had been taken in these countries, with all residents accepted as citizens, it could well have led to a permanent political and constitutional crisis, with a large Russian bloc mobilizing on the basis of ethnicity and demanding the retention of a two-nation and two-language state, leading to the kind of prolonged stand-offs seen in the late 1980s in the Supreme Soviet. Ethnic mobilization would then have become the dominant mode of politics in the Baltic. In fact, while present citizenship laws are restrictive, Russian residents do not on the whole see themselves as threat-

ened by these governments, which have not been overtly nationalist and have rarely acted strongly on any ethnic issues. As the non-
citizen residents gradually acquire citizenship, they will join an
already established political fabric not marked by intense ethnic
mobilization (Broks et al. 1997).

Such a stance on the part of non-citizens is not a recent phenomenon but is characteristic of the responses of these groups
since the beginning of democratization in the late 1980s. In this
area, there were some instructive differences between Latvia and
Lithuania on the one hand, and Estonia on the other. In the case of
Latvia, for example, while the period from 1989 to, say, 1994 saw a
catastrophic decline in living standards, high inflation, critical en-
ergy shortages, the closing down of large government enterprises
followed by growing unemployment, a decline in the social order
and—if many of the authors mentioned above are to be believed—a
rise in extreme nationalism, not a single strike by Russian workers
occurred during this period. The hardline Interfront found little
popular support, despite its ready access to the media and often
institutional support both at home and internationally. Lithuania
displayed a similar picture.

In Estonia, on the other hand, there was some political opposition, particularly from the heavily Russian-populated eastern border region of Narva. Estonian law allowed non-citizens to participate in municipal elections, and the Russian-dominated councils
had a protracted struggle with the central government over a
number of issues, a situation used repeatedly by Moscow to point
to discrimination. This stand-off lessened in the mid 1990s, with
growing acceptance of the current Estonian political direction and
policies on the part of local Russian politicians, who often de-
parted from the hard-line demands of Moscow, much as Laitin
(1996) had predicted.

Sociolinguistically, all surveys have revealed a marked increase
in the learning of the national languages and, above all, a decided
change in attitude towards the acceptance of the language regimes
now in place. Rose and Maley's 1994 work was the most significant
to document the marked decline in ethnic tensions in the Baltic
states from 1994, ironically the time when the citizenship laws
were finally in place and the language laws had had time to take
effect. Rose and Maley's survey of Russians in the three Baltic states
revealed a set of attitudes markedly different to that reported by
Smith et al. The proposition "People like us should not be made to
learn a Baltic language", which could be seen as a relatively
straightforward test of attitudes to the new language regime, had

more than half of all Russian respondents *disagreeing* (see table 11.2).

Table 11.2
"People like us should not be made to learn a Baltic language" (%)

	Russians in Estonia	Russians in Latvia	Russians in Lithuania	Total
Strongly agree	11	13	9	11
Agree	26	21	24	23
Disagree	36	25	30	30
Strongly disagree	22	22	25	23
Don't know	5	19	12	12

(Rose & Maley 1994, 56)

Similar positive results from more qualitative surveys are cited in Druviete (1995, 1996) for Latvia, and in Kirch and Laitin (1994) for Estonia. Here, a crucial distinction in attitudes to language can be seen between those expecting to achieve citizenship and those not expecting to. For example, some 30 percent of those not wishing to obtain citizenship had no desire to master Latvian, whereas for those desiring to become citizens the figure was only 5 percent (Druviete 1995, 68). Of those with little desire to learn Latvian and obtain citizenship, a significant number of the younger respondents were looking forward to emigration, while older respondents pointed to their age and the fact of having no talent for languages.

An important factor here is how language relations are actually played out in daily behavior and interaction. While language laws lay down requirements for public contact positions and stipulate the language of official administration, most Baltic citizens continue to speak Russian to Russian-speaking monolinguals and generally do not confront non-speakers of the Baltic national languages, thus not threatening them. Russian language schools, media and other institutions continue to exist, and the language used in personal interactions is not covered by law. Thus, despite seemingly exclusionary language laws, linguistic tolerance can be seen in everyday life; the legitimate right of these new states to have their own national languages is broadly recognized and, consequently, there is more willingness to learn the national languages.

The linguistic and legalistic, rather than ethnic, basis of language and citizenship requirements is slowly being appreciated by most:

after all, people are only asked to be able to speak a language if they want certain positions or status (citizenship, public office) or in certain occupations; they are not being asked to change their identity. In the face of this, most arguments in support of official two-language policies have been reduced to rather incoherent defenses of monolingualism.

Psychologically, it must be recognized that we are seeing a peculiar aspect of post-socialist accommodation, where individual response rather than collective action can be noted. While Laitin stresses the macroeconomic consequences of the success of the Baltics as a factor in ensuring legitimation and the lack of overt ethnic conflict, other factors may be just as important. It is hypothesized here that the generally apolitical and low-key response of non-citizens and non-speakers of the national languages has many causes, two of which are paramount: one is the generally non-confrontational manner of the Baltic governments and citizens towards non-citizens. Equally important, however, is the factor of Soviet political socialization, which systematically dissuaded people from involving themselves in politics or from believing that they had any relation to the major issues of the day. A major issue now is what kinds of political and social identification can fill the void filled for so long by Soviet socialization.

Table 11.3

Multicultural self-identification (% April 1992, February 1993)

"Do you feel yourself to be a representative of the following cultures...?"

Culture of identification

| | Estonians | Russians | |
	1993	1992	1993
Estonian	99	43	65
Russian	15	85	96
European	82	–	48
World	49	31	38
Soviet	11	42	59
Some other	10	4	18

(Kirch & Laitin 1994, 16)

Perhaps the most interesting material on identification comes from Estonia, in Kirch and Laitin's 1994 collection which, considering previous hostility between Russian and Estonian populations, showed a remarkable degree of acceptance of the Estonian state on the part of Russians and positive attitudes towards continuing to live there. The surveys in this collection showed that between 1992 and 1993 a *declining* proportion of Russian respondents reported rather high, or very high, ethnic tensions, and this was the period in which the most vociferous debate (and external condemnation) of the citizenship laws was taking place. The surveys also showed the complexity of identity shift: in one significant table (see table 11.3), both Estonian and Russian respondents were asked "Do you feel yourself to be a representative of the following cultures..."

This table clearly reveals "the more manifold cultural identification of non-Estonians". We see here the compatibility between a growing identification with Estonia and, at the same time, a growing self-identification as Russians and a growing sense of identity as Soviets–understandable, perhaps, of people who see themselves in the specific "post-Soviet" situation of having been citizens of a larger entity who enjoyed some freedom of movement within that entity, and who are now forced to adjust to new geopolitical circumstances. This need for individuals to reorient their identification and sense of belonging militates against immediate political action.

In these specific post-Soviet circumstances, the power of socialization tends to lead individuals towards non-political forms of accommodation, particularly where economic well-being can be calculated. However, economic considerations are not the only ones. Another example of personal accommodation is given in relation to citizenship where, once again we see a paradox: after intense debate over this issue (including international urging for easy or automatic citizenship) and after surveys revealing a widespread desire to attain citizenship, there is, in fact, an extremely slow take-up of citizenship through naturalization. In Latvia, naturalization will take place over several years, being made available first to those born in Latvia and below the age of twenty-five. Early figures for Latvia show that for the period from the beginning of 1995 to the end of 1997, some 120,000 persons were eligible to apply for citizenship, but by 30 June1997, only 7,152 had applied, and only 5,944 had been granted citizenship. This astonishingly low rate of application has yet to receive scholarly analysis, but it seems that particular personal factors may be important. This age group is liable for military service, which may explain some reluctance on the part of young males to apply for citizenship (although it does not explain the reluctance of young females). Another factor is that the acceptance of Baltic citizenship will entail the loss of the individual's old Soviet passport, after which visits to Russia or other CIS countries will entail applying for visas; for those holding old Soviet passports, no visa is required. Such personal considerations may be far removed from the principled arguments about citizenship, zero-options and inclusiveness that have dominated political debate on this issue, but they may well be more compelling for individuals, and are instantly recognizable to anyone familiar with post-Soviet life. Non-citizens may choose to remain so not because of lack of loyalty or lack of language, but because personal considerations may make life as a non-citizen perfectly comfortable and, in fact, more comfortable for certain pursuits. The particular benefits arising from citizenship (public sector employment, the right to vote) may well be outweighed by the costs.

Non-citizens are making strategic and personal decisions on citizenship, just as they are with language use. Also important is the fact that the difference between life as a citizen and life as a non-citizen is likely to differ less and less. Already, surveys show that while non-citizens and citizens may well disagree about the past (e.g. the value of the Soviet period), there is much more agreement over present grievances or attitudes towards the future, including attitudes towards the government and on major economic or social issues (Karklins 1994; Zepa 1997).

***

Much of the criticism of the Baltic states in their approach to language and citizenship makes reference to universal rights or international standards of behavior, yet as we have seen these are often far removed from the ways in which individuals accommodate themselves to new regimes and how they pursue their own interests. In matters of citizenship, of course, there are no international standards, since sovereign states insist absolutely on their own control over this matter, and international bodies can do no more than recite general procedural issues of predictability, open processes, clear criteria, etc. Moreover, Estonia and Latvia see it as ironic that they are willing to give citizenship to those who are able to speak and understand the national language, while some *Western* European countries will not grant citizenship to certain minorities no matter how well they speak the national language, reserving citizenship on a *jus sanguinis* basis.

Rather more has been done in terms of international debate on linguistic rights (Skutnabb-Kangas et al. 1994; de Varennes 1995/96), with several major charters or drafts now being formulated, such as the "Universal Declaration of Linguistic Rights" drafted at a conference in Barcelona in 1996, the "European Charter for Regional or Minority Languages" of 1992, or the "Hague Recommendations Regarding the Education Rights of Minorities" of 1996. However, Skutnabb-Kangas, in much of her work, forcefully argues how little and how patchily actual language rights are formulated or guaranteed in individual states, whatever the supposed international agreements. On the other hand, from the perspective of the Baltic states, arguments that they are somehow not obeying international standards in their treatment of Russian speakers (the usual argument) are difficult to fathom. First, universal statements are often couched in such generalities that it is possible to argue that there is indeed complete compliance (Phillipson and Skutnabb-Kangas 1995). As one telling example, one need only consider the following part of the "Preliminaries" to the draft Barcelona declaration, which, among other considerations, explicitly listed the following as needing to be taken into account in determining language policy:

> ... that invasion, colonization, occupation and other instances of political, economic or social subordination often involve the direct imposition of a foreign language or, at the very least, distort perceptions of the value of languages and give rise to hierarchical linguistic attitudes which undermine the language loyalty of speakers; and ... that the languages of some peoples which have attained sovereignty are immersed in a process of language substitution as a result of a policy which favours the language of a former colonial or imperial power.... (Barcelona Declaration, p.5 of text)

The Baltic states would, of course, see this consideration as directly applying to them, and their language policies as being devised specifically as a consequence of this situation. Some European leaders have supported this view (Bildt 1994). Thus, any arguments over conformity to international standards can certainly be met on their own terms.

Secondly, however, it has become clear in relation to the Baltic states that the issues are not conformity to some international or European standard but are quite different, relating to issues of security and foreign policy much more than to any actual concern with language issues *per se*. Significant here is the far greater involvement recently of the Organization for Security and Cooperation in Europe (OSCE) in issues of minorities and language—ostensibly to prevent minority issues from causing security concerns. The OSCE has notably sharpened its attitudes towards Estonian and Latvian language laws in recent years, even though these laws are essentially the same as those of a decade earlier. Despite the endless delegations that have reported no infringements of human rights in the Baltics, and fully functioning Russian-language school systems, media and other institutions, the OSCE still sees ethnic conflict there as potentially destabilizing, and in increasingly heated correspondence has reiterated concerns that language requirements of various kinds be softened or eliminated. The Baltic states are keen to achieve their own integration into European structures, but they are unlikely to yield to such views when they are, in fact, able to develop economies and democracies of far greater stability than many countries around them. Nor will it be necessary for them to make such appeasement. Estonia, for example, is now being treated seriously as a candidate for the EU—clearly, macropolitical and macroeconomic factors will be the deciding ones.[1]

Ultimately, the Baltic states see no incompatibility between their own language policies and orderly and democratic government or the well-being of their minorities. There is now some recognition of this in international scholarship. In an "Excursus on the language rights problems in the new Estonia," the Hungarian author György Szépe (1994) takes account of recent work on linguistic human rights and comments specifically on the Estonian situation:

> This is a very complex issue; we have to admit that human rights (and linguistic human rights) are very important and central issues, but they are not adequate tools to solve the problems of an entire historical age. The invasion of the new coloniser—exemplified by the Russian immigrants to Estonia after the occupation of that small country in 1940—can endanger the existence of the linguistic community of the country. Estonia's reaction in requiring a positive attitude to the language of the country by the (former) colonisers is not a novel aggression but a restitution of the previous peaceful stage. (1994, 47)

He ends by offering one reminder: "Without interfering in the dispute, may I remark that human rights are meant to protect the underdog rather than the (past, present or potential) overdog" (ibid.), and there are no doubts as to who has been (and very much still is) the underdog in this context.

Note

1 This article was completed in early 1998; that year was to subsequently see an intensification of the campaign by OSCE to alter both Latvia's citizenship law (leading to a closely contested referendum on this in October 1998), and a new language law. OSCE particularly criticized proposed language law operations in the private economic sphere. In connection with the latter, the OSCE also released its "Oslo Recommendations" on language rights of national minorities, which argued that international norms demanded the provision of services in other languages on demand for minorities, and prohibited language regulation in the private economic sphere. OSCE continued to warn that nonadherence to these guidelines would jeopardize entry into Europe. In 1999 the Latvian Parliament passed a new language law repeating the earlier provisions for the law to apply to the private economic sphere, but this law was returned to Parliament by the President for further consideration. At the time of publication this issue remains unresolved. The details of events in 1998 are treated in U. Ozolins "Between Russian and European hegemony: current language policy in the Baltic States" in *Current Issues in Language and Society,* forthcoming, 1999.

References

Alksnis, V. "Suffering from Self-Determination." *Foreign Policy* no. 84 (1991): 61–71.

Arter, David. *The Politics of European Integration in the Twentieth Century.* Aldershot: Dartmouth, 1993.

Bildt, C. "The Baltic Litmus Test." *Foreign Affairs* 73, no.5 (1994): 72–85.

Broks, J., U. Ozolins, G. Ozolzile, A. Tabuns and T. Tisenkopfs. "The Stability of Democracy in Latvia: Pre-requisites and Prospects." *Humanities and Social Sciences Latvia.* Double edition: no.4 (13) (1996); no.1 (14) (1997): 103–134.

Druviete, I., ed. *The Language Situation in Latvia.* Part I [in English.] 1995; Part II [in Latvian], 1996; Riga: Latvian Language Institute,

Economist Intelligence Unit. *Country reports: Estonia, Latvia, Lithuania,* 1996–7.

Grin, F. "The Estonian language law: presentation with comments." *Language Problems and Language Planning* 15, no. 2 (1991): 191–201.

Kaiser, R. J. *The Geography of Nationalism in Russia and the USSR.* Princeton: Princeton University Press, 1994.

Karklins, R. *Ethnopolitics and Transition to Democracy. The Collapse of the USSR and Latvia.* Washington: Woodrow Wilson Center Press, and London: Johns Hopkins University Press, 1994.

Kirch, M. and D. Laitin. *Changing Identities in Estonia. Sociological Facts and Commentaries.* Tallinn: Estonian Science Foundation, 1994.

Kirkwood, M., ed. *Language Planning in the Soviet Union.* London: Macmillan, 1989.

Kreindler, I. T., ed. *Sociolinguistic Perspectives on Soviet National Languages.* Berlin: Mouton de Gruyter, 1985.

Laitin, D. "Language planning in the former Soviet Union: the case of Estonia." *International Journal of the Sociology of Language,* no.118 (1996): 43–61.

Lewis, E. G. *Multilingualism in the Soviet Union.* The Hague: Mouton, 1972.

Lieven, A. *The Baltic Revolution.* New Haven: Yale University Press, 1993.

Loeber, D. A. "Language rights in independent Estonia, Latvia and Lithuania, 1918-1940." In S. Vilfan, ed., *Ethnic Groups and Language Rights.* Aldershot: Dartmouth, 1993.

Marshall, D. F. "A politics of language: language as a symbol in the dissolution of the Soviet Union and its aftermath." *International Journal of the Sociology of Language,* no.118, 7–41.

Maurais, J. "Redéfinition du statut des langues en Union Sovietique." *Language Problems and Language Planning* 16, no.1 (1992): 1–20.

Ozolins, U. "Upwardly mobile languages: the politics of language in the Baltic states." *Journal of Multilingual and Multicultural Development* 15, nos. 2 & 3 (1994): 161–9.

——. "Language policy and political reality." *International Journal of the Sociology of Language,* no. 118 (1996): 181–200.

Phillipson, R. and T. Skutnabb-Kangas. "Linguistic Rights and Wrongs." *Applied Linguistics* 16, no. 4 (1995): 483–504.

Rannut, M. "Linguistic policy in the Soviet Union." *Multilingua* 10, no. 3 (1991): 241–50.

——. "Beyond linguistic policy: the Soviet Union versus Estonia." In T. Skutnabb-Kangas and R. Phillipson, eds., *Linguistic Human Rights: overcoming linguistic discrimination.* Berlin: Mouton de Gruyter, 1994.

Rose, R. and W. Maley. *Nationalities in the Baltic States: a survey study.* Glasgow: Centre for the Study of Public Policy, 1994.

Shamshur, O. "Current ethnic and migration issues in the former USSR." *Current Issues in Language and Society* 1, no. 1 (1994): 7–27.

Smith, G., A. Aasland, and R. Mole. "Statehood, Ethnic Relations and Citizenship." In G. Smith, ed., *The Baltic States. The National Self-Determination of Estonia, Latvia and Lithuania.* London: Macmillan, 1994.

Szépe, G. "Central and Eastern European language policies in transition (with special reference to Hungary)." *Current Issues in Language and Society* 1, no. 1 (1994): 41–64.

de Varennes, F. "The protection of linguistic minorities in Europe and human rights: possible solutions to ethnic conflicts?" *Columbia Journal of European Law* 2, no. 1. Fall/Winter (1995/6): 107–143.

Volkovs, V. "The National Self-Esteem of the Latvia Russian Youth." [In Latvian.] *Latvian Journal of Sociology and Political Science,* no. 7 (1996): 26–7.

Zepa, B. "State, Regime Identity and Citizenship." *Humanities and Social Sciences Latvia.* Double edition: no. 4 (13) (1996); and no. 1 (14) (1997): 81–102.

Language Policy in a Changing Society: Problematic Issues in the Implementation of International Linguistic Human Rights Standards

INA DRUVIETE

A new State Language Law (Latvijas Republikas Valsts valodas likums) was submitted to the Latvian Parliament in November 1995. It was adopted on July 8, 1999. Discussions about this draft project have been taking place for more than three years, involving not only wide circles of Latvian society, but also foreign specialists and international organizations. The State Language Law raises some problematic issues that are significant not only for a specific language law in one particular country. Case studies viewed against the background of existing internationally binding norms for linguistic rights may give rise to new ideas concerning the further development of universal concepts with respect to these rights. Before the case studies are discussed, a general background description of the context in which language policy is carried out in Latvia will be presented.

Latvia: Ethnoprofiles and the Sociolinguistic Situation

The Republic of Latvia was established in 1918, and after being annexed by the Soviet Union during World War II, once again regained its independence on 21 August 1991. The latest data in the Civil Register (1997) show that the population of Latvia totals 2,475,500, of whom 56.5 percent are Latvians, and 43.5 percent are representatives of other nationalities, including Russians (30.4 percent), Belarussians (4.3 percent), Ukrainians (2.8 percent), Poles (2.5 percent), Lithuanians (1.4 percent), Jews (0.6 percent), Gypsies (0.3 percent), Germans (0.2 percent), Estonians (0.1 percent), Livs (0.01 percent), and other nationalities (0.9 percent)

(Vēbers 1997). During the fifty years of Soviet power the percentage of Latvians in the total population of Latvia fell drastically (in 1935 Latvians made up 77 percent of the total population) whilst Russian, Ukrainian, Belarussian and other ethnic groups from the former Soviet Union increased substantially, both in absolute numbers and as a percentage of the total population. Knowledge of the Latvian language amongst the immigrants was very low. According to the 1989 census, Latvian language skills were possessed by 21.1 percent of the Russians, 15.5 percent of the Belarussians, 8.9 percent of the Ukrainians, 22.8 percent of the Poles, 40.3 percent of the Lithuanians, 27 percent of the Jews, and 52.3 percent of the Gypsies. Ninety-five percent of the non-Russians, among them 64.4 percent of the Latvians, know Russian (Druviete 1997a). Almost exclusively the Russian language functioned in the administrative apparatus on the state level, in big enterprises and in numerous local offices. The Russian language was the main medium of communication between the inhabitants of Latvia. At schools more lessons were allotted to Russian than to Latvian; moreover, Latvian was not mandatory at Russian schools. Between 1988 and 1991, the struggle to regain independence also manifested itself as a fight for the rights of the Latvian language in Latvia.

In 1988, the Latvian language regained its status as the state language. On 5 May 1989, the Language Law was adopted. It stated that the official (state) language of Latvia was Latvian and provided for the right to learn the Latvian language to be granted to all inhabitants of Latvia. However, the law was not consistent and still paid homage to the regime, providing "special rights" for the Russian language. This inconsistency did not help to change the language situation in Latvia.

As the Republic of Latvia restored its independence, the Language Law was amended in 1992 and the special role and rights accorded to the Russian language were deleted. However, it was emphasized that the state would ensure that proper respect was paid to all languages used in the Republic of Latvia. The implementation of the amended Language Law, mainly by administrative methods, was a turning point in attitudes towards the Latvian language and, in recent years, the level of ability to speak Latvian has risen among the non-Latvian population in Latvia. According to a sociolinguistic survey, 45 percent of the inhabitants of Latvia whose native language is other than Latvian, possessed Latvian language skills in 1995 (Druviete 1995). This is partly due to various provisions of the Language Law, especially Article 4, which provides that public servants both at the state and local-government levels, as well as persons who have everyday contact with the general public, must be able to understand and use the Latvian language.

Without the interest of the population in the Latvian language and their conscious wish to learn it, the priority status of the Latvian language will not be stable and irreversible, and the quality of the Latvian linguistic environment will not be high. Since 1996, with the assistance of the United Nations Development Programme, the National Programme for Latvian Language Training was established. This program uses a ten-year model for Latvian language training for those residents of Latvia who have little or no Latvian language skills. The $3.2 million required for the first two years of the UNDP project have been contributed by Denmark, the Netherlands, Norway, Finland, Sweden, and the European Union. The British Know-How Fund provides an in-kind contribution in the form of educational resource materials for the Latvian Language Program Unit. Some 180,000 schoolchildren, and as many adults, will learn the Latvian language under this program.

Law on State Language

In the same way as any other independent state, Latvia is inevitably developing into a civic nation. In Latvia's case, the integration process is complicated by its ethnic diversity and the poor Latvian language skills among certain groups of inhabitants. The Latvian Saeima (Parliament) has recently adopted new laws which include special provisions for the linguistic integration of Latvian society–the Education Law and the Law on State Language. Both laws have sparked discussions in the press about the linguistic problems facing Latvia.

There are direct and indirect links between language policy and sociopolitical, historical and economic reality. Language policy has to take into account the real circumstances which exist objectively and which cannot be changed voluntarily in a short period of time. Particular attention must be given to this dual character of language policy when discussing language legislation in countries where serious political and economic change has recently taken place. In Latvia, language policy is about how best to promote the acquisition and use of Latvian through organized governmental and societal efforts, in order to change the language situation in

Latvia. The main goal of language policy in Latvia is to create a linguistically normalized society, with the titular language functioning as the only official language but with loyal bilingual minorities, existing in a legal framework of cultural autonomy.

The philosophy behind the Language Law in Latvia is prescriptive, not only descriptive. The clear task of changing the sociolinguistic reality is advanced. To implement this goal, a complex system of measures is presently being carried out. Among these measures, the most important are Latvian-language training, language proficiency certification, language requirements for naturalization, and language inspection activities.

The language laws of the Baltic states have sometimes been criticized for deciding the role of competing languages and for enabling too much official intervention in language use in society. A market-based approach to competing languages in Latvia would be the best way towards language shift among Latvian speakers within the next two to three generations.

Nevertheless, there are problems involved in present language policy if we analyze it from the point of view of the preservation of the Latvian language. As R. Karklins points out, "few outside commentators have realized the weak position of the Latvian language in Latvia" (Karklins 1994, 142).

The existing international legislation on minority language rights (e.g. the European Charter for Regional or Minority Languages, the Framework Convention on National Minorities) are strongly based on the following concepts: (1) the official (or state) language is invariably the language of the majority; (2) language rights are associated with minority rights only; (3) speakers of the official languages of a state enjoy the full scope of linguistic rights. None of these presuppositions is correct in the case of Latvia.

In most cases it is taken for granted in the language rights literature that minorities are, or at least tend to be, bilingual in their mother tongue and the official language. Most human rights experts stress the obligation of the minority to learn the official language (Skutnabb-Kangas 1998; see also The Hague Recommendations Regarding the Education Rights of National Minorities & Explanatory Note). This right and duty to learn the state language is important not only because it ensures that linguistic rights do not result in the segregation of linguistic minorities, but also because it makes clear that the maintenance of minority languages should be neither at the expense of the full participation of minorities in the life of the nation, nor at the expense of the rights of majorities.

In Latvia, only about 45 percent of the representatives of minorities possess Latvian language skills at present. The bilingualism of the rest of the minorities should be a necessary prerequisite for integration into society, and there have to be some kind of positive stimuli which promote that outcome. At present there is a weak instrumental, and even weaker integrational, motivation for Russian speakers to be bilingual. Latvia's linguistic legislation, according to commonly accepted standards of linguistic rights, ensures that the resident minority's language (i.e. Russian) is given preference in almost all spheres of everyday life as well as there being wide access to information and entertainment in Russian in the mass media. Therefore it seems necessary to involve one more concept in discussing the linguistic rights of minorities–the concept of linguistic self-sufficiency and its consequences in the life of the nation and for the sociolinguistic position, or even survival, of the official state language. If we insist on the application of a maximal scope of minority language rights to Russian (e.g. its use in all official situations, in higher education, and for visual information), the existing linguistic self-sufficiency of Russian speakers would be reinforced and the rights provided for one language group would entail direct violations of elementary linguistic human rights, as well as the threat of linguistic assimilation for the other, namely, for Latvians (Druviete 1997b). Also, a precise use of terminology in the Latvian case is extremely important. As a consequence of the political changes in the region, Latvians formally turned from being a minority in the former centralized state to being the majority in the newly established state, whereas the Russians, who had earlier formed a majority, formally became a minority. However, a corresponding change in the real status of the respective languages did not, and could not follow automatically. As T. Skutnabb-Kangas (1994, 178) writes, "Russian is thus a majorized minority language (a minority language in terms of numbers, but with the power of a majority language), whereas the Baltic languages are minorized majority languages (majority languages, in need of the protection usually necessary for the threatened minority languages)". International law does not provide mechanisms for the protection of "majorities" or "majority languages". The problem is how to avoid political hypocrisy when considering the inequality between the main languages in competition in Latvia. The extralinguistic factors to be taken into account are: (1) the poor economic situation in Latvia; (2) the limited market for Latvian language goods and services; (3) the geopolitical situation of Latvia, that is, its situation as a neighboring country to the main Russian-speaking territory; and (4) the numerical, political and economic power of the speakers of the main competing language (that is, Russian), both in Latvia and abroad.

These considerations were taken into account in the preparation of the new version of the Language Law. In this Article, only two provisions from the Law on the State Language will be analyzed, namely the provision regarding language use in private enterprises and the provision regarding the spelling of foreign proper names in Latvia.

Language Use in Private Enterprises/Companies

Article 7 of the law states: "In the Latvian Parliament, in all enterprises (companies), institutions, civil institutions and organizations (except national cultural heritage associations and religious organizations) the language used in meetings and in other working sessions is the official state language. If foreigners take part in these meetings, any other language may be used, but upon the request of a single participant the organizer must provide a translation into Latvian".

Organizations created for language-related purposes (e.g. departments of foreign languages, language societies), as well as organizations which do not fall under the jurisdiction of Latvia, are also included in the list of exceptions. Nevertheless, this Article regulates language use in meetings held at the workplace not only in state-owned, but also in private enterprises and companies.

Some experts claim that this Article may be seen as interference in private affairs and may thereby limit the free space which international human rights law seeks to establish and protect.

Firstly, we must clarify the concept "private affairs," and establish the difference between "personal, informal affairs" and "private entrepreneurship". Of course, there cannot be any regulation of language use in private life. But does "private life" include situations in which dozens, hundreds or thousands of people are employed? This is one form of ownership of the means of production. Due to the rapid privatization process, only about 10 percent of all enterprises in Latvia were state property or public property in 1998. The electricity companies, the fuel industry, the communications industry, and other vital branches of Latvia's economy are, today, private companies.

Secondly, private entrepreneurship is subject to state regulations in all countries. Latvia has a "Law on Entrepreneurial Activity," a "Law on the Registration of Enterprises", a "Law on Limited Liability Companies", etc. The activities of private companies are thus supervised by the state, and there is a constant regime of regulation, monitoring and enforcement. Why, then, should the regulation of one particular activity, namely the use of language in meetings in private companies, be a violation of human rights?

Article 27 of the International Covenant on Civil and Political Rights states: "In those states in which ethnic, religious or linguistic minorities exist, persons belonging to such minorities shall not be denied the right, in community with the other members of their group, to enjoy their own culture, to profess and practice their own religion, or to use their own language". Article 7 of the Latvian draft law is not about the use of language by those who are "in community with other members of their group", but the use of language in organizations and enterprises where persons belonging to different linguistic groups are employed. Neither can the workplace meetings be classified as private communication. Thus, the regulation of language use in private enterprises cannot be considered interference in private affairs.

But let us take the opposite view, that a private enterprise, irrespective of the number of employees, belongs to the private sphere. The only legitimation for interference by the state in relation to individual rights and freedoms would be on the basis of clear public interest (Article 8 of the European Convention on Human Rights and Fundamental Freedoms). Can the authors of the law be sure that state involvement in the regulations mentioned above is required in the interests of national security, public safety, or the economic well-being of the country?

Latvian society is inexorably developing into a civic nation on the basis of respect for the independence of the state and a common language, metaphorically and *de facto*. This process is hindered by a poor knowledge of Latvian among certain groups of inhabitants, who cannot therefore participate fully in the life of the nation.

Since 1988, when the Latvian language regained its status as the official state language, a well-developed system for Latvian second-language instruction, both for pupils in schools and for adults, has been developed. Latvian language skills among representatives of minorities have increased significantly (in 1989 about 20 percent of non-Latvians possessed Latvian language skills; in 1999, the proportion was about 70 percent). More than 350,000 employees have passed the state-language proficiency test required for registration. Nevertheless, there is considerable evidence that the process of Latvian-language acquisition partially came to a halt in the last two years (Druviete 1997c). The reasons for this may have to do with lack of motivation to use Latvian.

The use of Latvian is problematic in private firms and enterprises owned by Russian speakers. Private business is one of the main niches for persons who have neither Latvian citizenship nor Latvian language skills. The levels of income and economic welfare in private businesses are much higher than in state-owned businesses. As these firms mostly use Russian or English in their contacts with each other or to conduct international business, the Latvian language is not necessary from an economic point of view. Interpreters and translators are widely used to fulfill the demands of the Language Law, while the actual language used for office work and during meetings in the workplace is Russian.

The Language Law (1989; with amendments and additions in 1992) included norms on language choice by lower-ranking persons which must be seen as democratic (Article 4), and free language choice in enterprises (Article 6). However, these norms have contributed to the maintenance of two linguistic collectivities that were already in existence during the Soviet period: Russian entrepreneurs, and bilingual Latvian speakers who control the administrative sphere and who, according to the present Language Law, are obliged to speak Russian with lower-ranking persons if such persons so require. Even if some individuals will do so, we cannot expect a whole community to learn and use the language of another community if there are no economic or legal stimuli to do so.

The Russian language and the other main competitor, English, possess two crucial features: they are very widely spoken and function as languages of international communication. The Latvian language has no such "carrots" to offer. Under the conditions of the market economy the only compensatory mechanisms for Latvian can be of a legal nature. The State Language Law therefore includes the norm about the language of work in certain kinds of enterprise. It calls for state interference in the language situation in private enterprises in order to protect the rights of Latvian speakers, and also the right of other well-integrated minorities to use Latvian in entrepreneurial activity.

We can, of course, foresee difficulties in implementing this norm. It will be difficult to control the use of language if the proportion of Latvian speakers in the enterprise is below 50–60 percent. Problems can also be expected in the case of joint ventures.

One possibility might be to use quantitative criteria on the number of employees (as in Quebec–see, e.g., Maurais 1987).

Personal Names

Article 11 of the Framework Convention for the Protection of National Minorities states: "The parties undertake to recognize that every person belonging to a national minority has the right to use his or her surname (patronym) and first names in the minority language and the right to official recognition of them, according to modalities provided for in their legal system". Article 7, paragraph 2 of Recommendation 1201 (1993) of the Parliamentary Assembly of the Council of Europe also states that "Every person belonging to a national minority shall have the right to use his/her surname and first names in his/her mother tongue and to official recognition of his/her surname and first names".

Claims have been made that these norms have not been observed in Latvian linguistic legislation. Fernand de Varennes, for instance, states that "Latvia provides, perhaps, the most recent and unfortunate example of an Article 27 violation, having recently adopted a language law which follows the same type of measures popular in oppressive regimes like Franco's" (de Varennes 1995/96, 127). Article 18 of the 1992 language law does state: "Foreign given names and surnames shall be written and used in Latvian in conformity with the rules for transforming given names and surnames of other languages into Latvian" (State Language in Latvia, 1994, unofficial translation).

The English version of this Article could give grounds for misunderstanding. The original text does not contain the words "in Latvian," and "rules for transforming" simply means "rules of spelling." But what is the essence of this norm? Let us describe it first, and then discuss whether or not it is a violation of linguistic human rights.

From a linguistic point of view, Latvian is a typical example of inflectional languages. The noun has singular and plural forms, two genders, and seven cases, and affixes are used to mark several grammatical categories simultaneously. Proper names behave like any other nouns in Latvian (which is not the case in German, for instance, where gender is not marked in surnames). In Latvian, it is impossible to use nouns, including proper names, without endings. Latvian names and surnames have different endings according to the gender of their bearer. With very few exceptions, the use of different masculine and feminine endings is universally accepted within the Latvian community and has been mandatory since the 1930s. Surnames within the same family differ: some have masculine endings (*-s, -is, -us*) and some feminine endings (*-a, -e*), irrespective of the origin of the surname. For example, the husband's name may be *Ints Kalns, Juris Locis, Andrejs Ivanovs* or *Gatis Veinbergs*; the wife's name would then be *Inta Kalna, Anna Loce, Ilze Ivanova, Maija Veinberga*.

In written Latvian, according to a tradition that goes back more than 450 years, all foreign proper names (first names, surnames, place names) are spelt in accordance with their pronunciation (i.e. not their spelling) in the respective original language, using Latvian graphemes which are as close as possible to foreign phonemes (*Thames–Temza, Pittsburgh–Pitsburga*). An ending which marks the gender, the number and the grammatical role is added in Latvian. Otherwise the foreign proper name cannot be assimilated into the syntactic structures of Latvian.

These two principles lay behind the centuries-long tradition and the norm in the language law with respect to the spelling of foreign proper names. A fifteen-book series on "Regulations on the Spelling of Foreign Proper Names in Latvian" has already been published to ensure the adequacy and identification of this spelling (covering English, German, Russian, Lithuanian, Estonian, Arab, Bulgarian, Italian, Polish, etc. proper names). Let me give a few examples to show the conversion process in practice:

> *Tove Skutnabb-Kangas–Tuve Skutnaba-Kangasa*
> *Robert Phillipson–Roberts Filipsons*
> *Max van der Stoel–Makss van der Stūls*
> *Colin Baker–Kolins Beikers*

It is very important to stress that the name and surname of the person are not changed. English *Michael* (spelt "*Maikls*" in Latvian) and German *Jochen* (spelt *Johens* in Latvian) have never been changed to the respective Latvian forms. The English *George* would be written in Latvian as *Džordžs*, the French *Georges* as *Žoržs*, but not as the Latvian name of the same origin, *Juris*. In pronunciation they are as close as possible to the original language, only an ending is added. In the case of proper names in Latvian and another language that share a common origin, efforts are made to preserve all the details of the pronunciation in the donor language. For example, the English names *Andrew, Mary* and

David are spelt in Latvian as *Endrjū, Mērija, Deivids,* although the respective Latvian names are *Andrejs, Marija, Dāvids.*

I agree that this principle may appear strange and that Latvians are probably the only nation using the Latin script who employ the principle of phonetic transcription when dealing with foreign proper names, both in official documents and in informal publications. The other Baltic language, Lithuanian, returned to original spelling in official documents a couple of years ago. It is also true that this kind of spelling is quite inconvenient in the contemporary world, if we take into account the increasing amounts of information exchange and people's increasing mobility.

But does it constitute a violation of linguistic human rights?

Yes, if we consider that it is a universal, indisputable right for every individual to see and use their names and surnames in a certain visual, graphic form in all languages, irrespective of the grammatical structure and spelling traditions of these languages.

No, if we take into account the three main arguments against calling the Latvian practice a violation of linguistic human rights.

First, it concerns the use of the respective proper name only when used in the Latvian language; there is no interference in the use of the proper name in the individual's native language or in other languages. "However, the right to private and family life does not mean a state is obliged to officially register an individual's preferred name or surname. As long as individuals are not prevented by the state from using their preferred names or surnames privately, there may not be a violation under the above rights" (de Varennes 1997, 4).

Secondly, the name itself has not been changed; due to this transcription system the pronunciation of the name is usually even more precise than in those languages which employ the original form. This is because Latvians know from the spelling how to pronounce the name.

Thirdly, the use of the original spelling is, in any case, only possible within the same script system (mainly Latin and Cyrillic). Even then problems arise with respect to the use of special diacritics. If graphemes have to be transliterated from one graphic system to another, changes in the visual image are unavoidable. When the Russian name *Георгий Васин* is rendered in French as *Gueorgoi Vassine* (the official spelling used in the French part of Russian passports) and *Надежда Буш* as *Nadejda Bouch*, the same principle is at work as in Latvian—that of changing the graphic form in order to reach a maximally adequate pronunciation.

If it is unanimously agreed that the Latvian practice is incompatible with internationally accepted norms for linguistic rights, governmental efforts to change it will follow. But would these efforts be successful? It is almost impossible to regulate by law certain linguistic processes pertaining to the language system. Even if a decree were to be adopted regarding the use of the original form of foreign proper names in passports and other official documents, the problem would not be solved for at least a decade. A double standard would then exist, since the traditional spelling would, in any case, be used in belles-lettres, press publications, private communications, and other spheres which cannot be influenced by normative acts. As an example of how deep-lying the spelling tradition is, let me mention that there is very little response to repeated invitations by some Latvian linguists (including the author) to use original spellings at least in brackets. Latvia is a case where "in a certain respect the authority of the linguistic institutions is stronger than that of the legal institutions with regard to their respective norm systems" (Bartsch 1987, 86). Psychological stereotypes are, of course, also involved. School education and the recent practice of Russification encourage average Latvians to accept the thesis that "language is law above the law" naturally.

The Latvian use of foreign proper names is an exciting matter for discussions with respect to the linguistic and sociolinguistic (political) aspects of language legislation. It shows that intralinguistic factors may sometimes also influence legal aspects of language policy.

Conclusion

The impact of global and regional linguistic processes, as well as of international minority and language legislation, on the language situation in Latvia seems to be unpredictable at present. There should be no doubt about the necessity for language legislation which promotes the use of Latvian. Considering the recent political and ethnodemographic processes in the region, Latvia and the other Baltic states are among those countries where consistent implementation of reasonable language policy principles is essential for the maintenance of the language. The Latvian experience requires that more problem areas be introduced into discussions about LHRs—for example, the rights of official-language speakers when changes in language hierarchy are promoted, the impact of the linguistic self-sufficiency of a minority on the integration of society as a whole, and, last but not least, the use of LHR concepts when applied in quite different political situations.

It is very likely that the most controversial Articles of the new State Language Law will be changed in the nearest future. This would not mean that all the problems have been solved. It would merely be a temporary solution for political reasons, while the sociolinguistic problems would remain and would reappear again and again. I therefore suspect that a bureaucratic, literal implementation of some international documents in the present language situation in Latvia would lead to results that would be contrary to the basic idea of linguistic rights—if the basic idea is to protect a language from extinction and to protect Latvian-language speakers from involuntary linguistic assimilation. It is also true that the main concern of politicians and international experts is not the widening or restriction of the sociolinguistic functions of Latvian and Russian in Latvia. From a political point of view, their main task is to prevent possible conflicts between language collectivities, since such conflicts would hinder the political and economic development of the region. If we do not take into account the historical, psychological and demographic components of the language situation, the Latvian Law on State Language could, at first glance, look like a conflict-provoking agent. In reality, it embodies conflict-preventing potential. This is one of the paradoxes in transitional societies (Broks, Ozolins, et al. 1997). Both an overt and a covert policy of societal bilingualism in Latvia at the state level would interrupt the slow but satisfactory process of political integration in Latvian society, strengthening the segregationist tendencies between the two main linguistic communities with results that would be difficult to predict.

References

Bartsch, Renate. *Norms of Language. Theoretical and Practical Aspects.* London and New York: Longman, 1987.

Broks, Janis, Uldis Ozolins, et al. "The Stability of Democracy in Latvia: Prerequisites and Prospects." *Humanities and Social Sciences. Latvia* 4, no.1 (1997): 103–34.

Druviete, Ina, ed. *The Language Situation in Latvia. Sociolinguistic Survey. Part 1. Language Use and Attitudes among Minorities in Latvia.* Riga: Latvian Language Institute, 1995.

Druviete, Ina. "Latvia." In H. Goebl et al., ed., *Contact Linguistics. An International Handbook of Contemporary Research,* volume 2 (1997a): 1906–1912.

——. "Change of Language Hierarchy in Latvia: Language Skills and Attitudes to Language Policy." *Recent Studies in Contact Linguistics.* Plurilingua XVIII, 84–91. Bonn: Dümmler, 1997b.

——. "Linguistic Human Rights in the Baltic States." *International Journal of the Sociology of Language* 127 (1997c): 161–185.

Karklins, Rasma. *Ethnopolitics and Transition to democracy. The Collapse of the USSR and Latvia.* Washington: The Woodrow Wilson Center Press, 1994.

Maurais, Jacques. "L'expérience québécoise d'aménagement linguistique." *Politique et aménagement linguistiques. Textes publiés sous la direction de Jacques Maurais,* 359–416. Québec: Conseil de la langue française, 1987.

Skutnabb-Kangas, Tove. *Linguistic Human Rights in Education. Language Policy in the Baltic States.* Conference Papers, 173–191. Riga: Gara pupa, 1994.

——. "Linguistic Diversity, Human Rights and the 'Free' Market." (This volume.)

de Varennes, Fernand. "The Protection of Linguistic Minorities in Europe and Human Rights: Possible Solutions to Ethnic Conflicts?" *The Columbia Journal of European Law* 2, no.1 Fall/Winter (1995/6): 107–43.

——. *The Existing Rights of Minorities in International Law.* Preliminary Draft Prepared for the Conference "Linguistic Human Rights," Budapest, 17 October 1997.

Vēbers, Elmārs. *Latvijas valsts un etniskas minoritates* (Latvia and its ethnic minorities). Riga: Institute of Philosophy, 1997.

EDUCATION AND ETHNICITY ISSUES

The Recognition of Sign Language: A Threat or the Way to a Solution?

ISTVÁN MUZSNAI

Introduction

A language is a powerful tool. A natural language is a product of the human brain and has the potential to represent the human thinking process. Apart from thought processes, a language may also reflect a specific way of life or culture, and it is for this reason that specific cultures can also be identified by a certain language.

Peaceful coexistence is a matter of trust. While this mutual trust is unbroken there is no reason to feel any threat from another party; there is no reason to withhold rights or privileges, and there is no reason to fight for independence. However, if mutual trust can no longer be maintained, a period of conflict and struggle is imminent. One way of demonstrating superiority is by depriving the less powerful of their human rights.

If a minority group is deprived of linguistic human rights, members of that group rightly feel that their cultural and linguistic survival is threatened. Members of the group fail to achieve educational, economic and political equality. This social injustice inevitably gives rise to numerous minor, or not so minor, cultural conflicts between members of the majority and members of the minority, and a struggle for equality and independence begins.

People belonging to a majority might feel threatened by those who use a different language. This suspicion is very often not without reason, since, if a minority group is powerful enough, they might prefer to claim an autonomous, independent existence instead of being ruled by others. In this way the unity or integrity of a society might be threatened by the separation of minority groups. A linguistic minority is usually also an ethnic minority, and if ethnic issues are not handled wisely, constant ethnic conflicts will be present.

One linguistic minority which is not an ethnic minority and which has never put forward any claims to self-determination that could represent a threat to a nation-state is the Deaf community.

Since there cannot be any threat from the Deaf towards the integrity or unity of a state, one might imagine that the Deaf were the first linguistic group to be granted full linguistic human rights. In this article we will investigate the extent to which this is true.

The Development of Education for Deaf People

In 1880, the hearing educators of the Deaf people of the world came to the conclusion at their Milan congress that the most effective way of educating Deaf children was through oral language, by avoiding any manual component of expression. This professional decision sealed the fate of sign language. The Deaf minority was told that it was in their own interest not to use their primitive way of gesturing. Thus, for a long period of time, signing was regarded as something to be ashamed of. Nevertheless, Deaf people still used it among themselves, but only in secret.

It took about seventy years before a leading American linguist, Bill Stokoe, and his colleagues made their first attempts to restore the social status of sign language (Stokoe 1960, 1–94). Since then, much progress has been made worldwide regarding the rehabilitation and public acceptance of sign language and of Deaf people.

During the past two centuries, a methodological question has dominated the philosophy behind the education of Deaf people: is the manual (based on sign language) or the oral (based on spoken language) teaching method more promising for the "blank mind" of a Deaf person? These two options marked the opposite extremes of a methodological continuum on which a combined method could be found at a midpoint. Individual teachers generally chose an in-between position, depending on their students and the circumstances, on their styles or preferences, and on their tastes or beliefs. The pendulum has kept swinging ever since between the two extremes (Lane 1984, 457–460).

However, regardless of the methodology chosen by educators, the education of Deaf people still remained deficient, and was not able to meet its goals. Deaf children remained grossly undereducated compared to their hearing peers. Failures in the education of the Deaf were partly due to a lack of linguistic access to curricular content, and partly to the fact that below-grade-level performance was accepted and expected from Deaf students (Johnson, Liddell, and Erting 1989, 3–14). Pedagogic success cannot be guaranteed by methodology only. A linguistic clarity/distinctness and pedagogic competency is also required for effective teaching.

Recently, a different theoretical polarization has emerged in the education of the Deaf. The earlier, traditional view of Deafness is now considered a pathological paradigm, in contrast to which an anthropological paradigm represents a completely new perspective (Erting 1981, 221–238; Corwin & Wilcox 1985). The anthropological paradigm shifts the focus from method to pupils, from deficiency to cultural identity. In this way, both sign language and Deaf people's culture came into the forefront with respect to their education. This shift of paradigm holds the promise of improvements in the education of Deaf children. However, little can be expected from the traditional, pathological attitude towards teaching.

Unfortunately, since the 1960s Hungary has been unable to join the rest of the international community in many of these positive developments. Firstly, the political climate in Hungary in the 1960s was not favorable to human rights issues. Also, the centralized educational policy made it impossible to break away from the outdated, but officially sustained belief in the unsuitability of sign language for teaching purposes.

Even in 1998, eight years after the beginning of a general liberalization process in Hungary, advocates for the recognition of sign language had not succeeded in changing the firm stance of the professional educators of the Deaf, most of whom are hearing people themselves. I am not aware of any other free country in the world where Deaf people can so easily be dominated and treated as minors by a small group of hearing educators. This makes the situation in Hungary of particular significance with respect to the official recognition of sign language.

After some brief demographic details we will discuss a few aspects of the current educational practice with respect to Deaf people in Hungary in the light of relevant research findings. Concrete examples will be taken from a school at which the author has taught (Muzsnai, ms). International linguistic human rights standards will then be examined and the effects of their possible implementation on current Hungarian education for Deaf people will be discussed.

Educational Practice in Light of Research Findings–a Hungarian Case Study

Deaf Children in Hungarian Schools

In the 1993/94 academic year, a total of 1,046,479 children went to school in the six- to fourteen-year-old age group. Of these, 1,234 attended schools for the Deaf or schools for the hard-of-hearing. It is a fair assumption that some hearing-impaired children attended normal schools, but their numbers are unknown.

In the following, I will be referring to my documented experience in the Budapest School for the Deaf and will refer to the school as "the case-study school". I was engaged with students in teaching situations on the preschool level, as well as on lower-primary, upper-primary, and secondary levels.

In the 1997/98 academic year the school had 133 pupils, 112 in the school proper, and 21 in the kindergarten. There were 19 classes for the 112 school children and three for those in the kindergarten. Forty-three of the children lived in the school's dormitory. The school had 38 qualified teachers teaching subjects like mathematics, history, etc. These teachers were, without exception, culturally hearing, female educators. There were 37 other teachers who were also qualified to teach the Deaf, but whose classes took place after the school lessons proper. In this group of teachers, four male teachers were included, two of whom were Deaf themselves.

The Pathological Versus the Anthropological Paradigm

Hungarian teachers of Deaf children are currently, consciously or unconsciously, teaching according to the pathological paradigm. However much teachers intend to improve the existing situation, their overall efforts are dominated by what they see as negative features of the picture of Deaf people. They focus on loss of hearing and are obsessed by the numerical indices defining that loss. Instructors emphasize the sounds that the person is, or is not, able to pronounce or lip-read. This obsession with negative aspects inevitably leaves its mark on the whole educational process. The emphasis, as is typical of all deficiency-based theories in the education of minority children (see Skutnabb-Kangas 1990, 23, table 5), is placed on what is lacking, and after some time the affected Deaf child herself may also be under the spell of what is lacking. The victim is blamed, and starts believing herself to be deficient.

The most important teaching activity under the pathological paradigm becomes the training of hearing, to be followed by the training of speech, and then training the rhythm of hearing. Articulation drills and training in attentiveness to sounds are the issues of greatest importance.

Unfortunately, the training of intellect, the developing of mental capacities, and the developing of the students' personalities are inevitably relegated into the background. Teachers have become accustomed to generally low performances by their Deaf students, and therefore do not expect high standards from them. The pathological paradigm cannot help but regard the act of signing as a pathological phenomenon, as opposed to the act of speaking which is seen as the "normal" means of interactive communication.

Current research, however, is almost exclusively in favor of the anthropological paradigm in the education of the Deaf (Saulnier and Moores 1992, 21; Erting 1981, 232; Ewoldt 1990, 87; Kelly 1990, 205; Kluwin 1992, 2–3; Martin 1990; Moores and Meadow-Orlans, eds. 1991, 15; Spencer 1991, 220). Teachers who have adopted the recommended new, anthropological paradigm, accept the fact of Deafness as a given, but at the same time start seeking for positive features of personality which stimulate further learning, and traits that are worth developing.

In this process educators with an anthropological approach never devalue sign language, even if a few of them might sometimes believe it to be something pernicious. Instead of dwelling on negative aspects, proper education begins with activities that have a positive perspective. Based on solely linguistic considerations, sign language can function as an invaluable, unique tool in supplying linguistic input for a Deaf child at an early age, when nothing else is able to perform this important task. Even if a Deaf child might, at some point, acquire some spoken language (that is, understanding via lip-reading and, to some extent, speaking herself), by the time spoken language has been acquired to the extent that it might serve as a similar tool for input, it is already too late. There are limits to developmental processes that cannot be ignored. After the expiration of the critical period for language acquisition, acquisition of a language of any kind will require a heroic effort and will result only in limited success. Therefore, the acquisition of sign language should be encouraged as early as possible. Moreover, it is pointless to start teaching spoken language to Deaf children before this has been accomplished (Fisher 1994, 1–11). Postponing the sign-language acquisition process also delays primary socialization and other early development processes.

Undeniably, Deaf people and sign language are closely related. An objective linguistic appraisal of sign language can further help to destroy unreasonable prejudices against both. The wise question for an educator to ask would then be: how can sign language be harnessed in the education of Deaf people? How can it be used as a mediator or as a working tool? The positive emotional ties between Deaf people and sign language will be an invaluable asset when using sign language in teaching Deaf children. If the development of Deaf people's thinking processes is determined to a significant degree by their access to sign language, educators surely have a responsibility to guard and stimulate its growth and development.

The fact that the education of the Deaf is now directed and carried out by hearing teachers cannot be used as a legitimization for depriving Deaf children of the opportunity to be educated in their own language. Deaf children must have the right to education through their own language, and not through a language that will never become their own. A prerequisite for this change is moving from the pathological, to the anthropological paradigm (Corwin and Wilcox 1985).

Sign Language as a Prerequisite for Learning an Oral Language

One element of the overall educational goal is to teach at least some of the receptive and productive spoken language skills of the hearing society to Deaf students. In fact, this is a rather ambitious, demanding task. Unfortunately, in the education of the Deaf in Hungary, the proper prerequisites are not provided for reaching this goal. The learning of oral language skills can be realistically expected from Deaf children only after they possess some idea of what a language is and how it functions. This basic knowledge is most easily obtained through sign language.

Without a solid L1 language base it is almost impossible to begin L2 learning. Yet Hungarian schools for the hearing-impaired often engage in such practice. For instance, in 1997, at the Budapest School for the Deaf where I teach, none of the pupils in a class of six-year-olds had acquired an L1 language base by the beginning of their school career.

This was made evident to me by the fact that their way of thinking did not follow the kind of logical pattern which I could use at that time with my three-year-old daughter. They were struggling to acquire two incompatible languages, while at the same time we were trying to teach them curricular material.

The language of the hearing majority can, in my view, be successfully taught to Deaf children only after the sign language of the Deaf community has been acquired. This fact is proven by the overall high performance of the Deaf children of Deaf parents, who begin their school career after having acquired the sign language of their parents "perfectly", that is, at an age-appropriate level. However, this fact is ignored by most teachers.

The macro movements of signing are a very useful medium through which any linguistic input can be mediated to Deaf children, and especially to those under the age of five. Sign language is visually perceivable at a very early age. In contrast, such young children cannot realistically be expected to focus on minute lip-movements.

In the case-study school, Deaf children of Deaf parents were able to use the sign language which they had acquired from their parents from the beginning of their school career. They also willingly shared it with the Deaf children of hearing parents, as an effective visual tool in communication. Its primary importance, however, lies in the building of a solid language base in the human brain. Among Deaf children it is equally effective as a way of sharing information, expressing their feelings, or manifesting their will. However, teachers in Hungary turn to sign language only as a final tool, a last resort—if they turn to it at all.

Teachers' Attitudes Towards Deafness: Signing Versus Speaking

However well Deaf children acquire spoken-language skills, they never become quasi-hearing people. They will always remain Deaf people, however successful, clever, and self-confident they become, and however proficiently they speak. The sign-rejecting professional attitude of teachers reveals their general attitude towards Deaf people, since the identification of a language with its user is unavoidable. If teachers insist that full human potential can be achieved only by hearing and through speech, this attitude will certainly have an adverse effect on the development of Deaf children's identities.

On the other hand, such an attitude is also an example of linguicism, a view akin to ethnicism and racism (Skutnabb-Kangas 1990, 11; see also this volume). It is important to investigate the roots of this attitude in order to encourage teachers to reflect a more healthy human perspective. If there is something wrong with being Deaf, then Deaf children can never really feel good about themselves. It is detrimental to depreciate openly and with official power something that other people appreciate and cherish!

In a lower-elementary class in the case-study school, half of the group of six children had Deaf parents. As a result, they were able to communicate fluently in sign language; nevertheless their linguistic competence in that area was not respected; it was not even taken into consideration. However, their behavior was much more mature, their overall capabilities more developed, and their level of intellectual ability considerably higher than among the children of hearing parents. Despite this, the spoken/vocal modality was set before them as an example to follow, as the only means by which human beings can be adequately trained and educated.

This kind of "professional" attitude excluded any possible benefits that this specific group might have gained from having sign language and the culture of the Deaf community available to them. The sign-language competence of these children was not tapped into–nor were any of the teachers able to communicate fluently in this language.

Unfortunately, the attitude of the teachers was contagious. Very soon, the children who had previously been proud of their useful heritage lost pride in their not-highly-valued language proficiency and adopted their teachers' attitude. It is much easier to pull down and destroy something than to build up something of genuine value. This mental shift was not difficult to achieve, since the children were unconsciously aware that their parents were not formally well-educated nor very successful in academic terms.

First-hand experience and research findings on teacher background suggest that students at elementary schools for the Deaf are almost exclusively exposed to hearing, female cultural role models (Woodward, Allen, and Schildroth 1988, 189–190). This means that students in our schools for the Deaf have very limited contacts with adequate adult Deaf models. Therefore, teachers of Deaf students have to do their best to demonstrate a deep respect for the valuable asset that Deaf parents, as realistic Deaf role models, represent, as well as a real respect for the sign language they cherish.

Which Language is the Mother Tongue of a Deaf Child?

In the preschool class (for six- and seven-year-olds) in the case-study school, none of the children had Deaf parents. In a situation where both parents of a Deaf child are Deaf themselves (a situation which exists among only 10 percent of all Deaf children), sign language obviously becomes the mother tongue or the first language of that child long before he or she goes to school.

In every other case, where hearing mothers and fathers bring up Deaf children, however much the hearing parents might want their spoken language to become the mother tongue of their Deaf child, this, unfortunately, will not happen. It is impossible for the Deaf child naturally to acquire the language of his or her hearing parents.

Since only the visual modality is available to them, Deaf children who join a group of other Deaf children in a preschool setting for Deaf children only, acquire sign language from the other children who have already acquired it from their Deaf parents. This visual language takes over all the functions that a mother tongue should otherwise accomplish with respect to personality development. Therefore this visual language must be considered as the first language–or mother tongue–of all Deaf children (Skutnabb-Kangas 1994, 139–143.)

In these early years, only the macro movements of signing can serve as a source enabling Deaf children to obtain a cohesive linguistic input, a basis for linguistic competence, and the prerequisites for mental development. It is beside the point to argue about who has the right to decide on behalf of the Deaf children of hearing parents which method of instruction should be provided to achieve the best results. That decision was made the moment that the natural acquisition of a spoken language was blocked by the auditory channel. The only sensible advice that professionals can offer to parents in the case of prelingual Deafness is this:

1. Give full support to the earliest possible acquisition of sign language by Deaf children. (This will become the child's first language [L1]. Those children whose parents are willing to learn sign language as their second language will be at an even greater advantage [Ahlgren 1994, 60].)

2. Later on, provide bilingual education for Deaf children. This is the only way in which Deaf students can successfully overcome some of the disadvantages inevitably arising from lack of hearing (Svartholm 1993, 234–245).

It is of paramount importance to avoid the false route of an oral-only approach which in fact does not work in most cases, but causes a tremendous amount of deprivation and frustration for almost every Deaf person during their school career. Bilingual education, on the other hand, is respectful of human dignity and provides the best opportunities for personality development–which even includes acquiring oral skills in second- language learning (Skutnabb-Kangas 1994, 143–144).

The Effects of Meaningless Versus Meaningful Activities

By the time Deaf pupils in the case-study school had reached the upper grades of the primary level they had become resigned to not finding any meaning behind their learning activities. The unreasonable and incomprehensible emphasis on oral imitation meant that students neglected to seek meaning in what they did in school. They did not understand what they were doing, grammatical drills did not make any sense to them, and spoken or written sentences lost their semantic content as well. School became a stage in life which made little sense to Deaf children and where they could achieve little success.

In contrast to this educational practice, a child's spontaneous learning can be a meaningful activity, and one which can provide motivation for the task of learning.

If a task makes no sense to a child, or is not fully understood, it is very difficult to motivate that child to perform the task. An adult might somehow be able to force a child to do something that he or she does not feel motivated to do, but the child will suffer as a result, and the task will not be accomplished properly. This kind of activity is lacking in self-gratification and causes frustration for both the student and the teacher. This type of "studying" produces a great deal of stress and frustration, emotional immaturity, and instability (Hafer 1995).

The Destructive Effects of Constant Frustration

The approach currently used in the education of Deaf children would only be legitimate if proper emotional fulfillment could somehow counterbalance the amount of emotional distress associated with the oral-only method. However, there is little attempt at present to control the behavioral effects of continual frustration. Effective learning cannot take place in such an emotionally insecure environment, yet a relaxed atmosphere was rarely to be found within the walls of the school for the Deaf, especially in higher-grade classes. Apart from not being able to accomplish minimal educational goals in schools for the Deaf, the constant stress and emotional disturbance have a definite pathogenic effect on both students and teachers.

The Deaf as a Linguistic/Cultural Minority

The pathological paradigm dominates the education of the Deaf in Hungary–as these glimpses of educational practices demonstrate. Deaf people are regarded as people with a physical handicap who need professional (sometimes even surgical) assistance. Professional teachers consider themselves entitled to carry out pedagogical experiments on Deaf children without seeking the prior consent of their parents. Teachers seem to be doing this with much self-confidence, and with a false sense of superiority. Of course, hearing parents also give their consent because the hearing teachers convince them of the unacceptability of signing. But what else can be expected from hearing teachers who have themselves been trained according to pathological premises? No wonder there is a vicious circle.

An anthropological approach, however, which takes the positive assets of the Deaf person and of sign language into consideration, would be a much more appropriate paradigm here. By recognizing sign language as a unique asset of Deaf people, the Deaf would be regarded as a linguistic/cultural minority (Anderson 1994, 12). Anyone who lives close to, or among Deaf people can observe that in every respect (customs, distinctive language, particular culture) they do, indeed, fulfill the criteria for recognition as a minority group. There is a world of difference between looking at someone as a medical, audiological problem, and regarding a Deaf person as a member of a cultural minority. And this is also the key to healthy self-respect among Deaf people themselves!

The gap between the academic performance of Deaf students and that of their hearing peers is obvious to any observer, and this gap will increase if the intended improvements do not meet Deaf people's expectations. It is essential that Deaf people themselves are actively involved in their own education (Padden and Humphries 1988, Ch. 6).

The Hungarian Case Study Summed Up

The overall impression with respect to the current education of the Deaf in Hungary is that it is fundamentally problematic: every aspect of it is filled with conflicts of a cultural nature. All these ills, however, could be treated with a single panacea: granting Deaf children the right to be educated primarily in their sign language.

If sign language were recognized, conflicts would begin to disappear. Recognition of sign language would lead to the provision of bilingual education for the Deaf. And if bilingual education were fully implemented, there would be no reason for the current cultural conflicts.

Should we risk granting Deaf children the right to be educated through sign language? Certainly we should! The only way out of all these conflicts is to give full recognition to sign language and the culture of the Deaf.

Implementing international legal standards by recognizing the rights of the Deaf minority is a first step in the right direction.

International Legal Standards

In the following we shall examine some of the relevant human rights standards and the effect of their possible implementation on the current education of the Deaf in Hungary, on the basis of The Hague Recommendations Regarding the Education Rights of National Minorities, written for the OSCE High Commissioner on National Minorities (Foundation on Inter-Ethnic Relations 1996, 1–19). These Recommendations are an interpretation of current human rights standards (see van der Stoel 1997; Thornberry and Gibbons 1997; see also Skutnabb-Kangas 1998 and this volume, on their origins and scope).

According to The Hague Recommendations Regarding the Education Rights of National Minorities, human beings have the right to maintain their national identity (1996, 5). This must be true even if human beings belong not to a national, but to a linguistic minority, such as the Deaf community (even if the Deaf are not specifically mentioned in The Hague Recommendations). This is the basic, fundamental, inalienable right of Deaf people, one which they are currently denied from childhood onwards in Hungary. They are not provided with an objective social mirror, they are not encouraged to develop themselves, and they are only able to acquire a distorted image of their identity as Deaf people. It is one of the essential tasks of the education of the Deaf to provide a healthy picture of the identity and culture of Deaf people (Markowicz and Woodward 1978, 29–38).

The identity mentioned above can, just like other minority identities, "only be fully realized if they acquire a proper knowledge of their mother tongue during the educational process" (Hague Recommendations, 5). At the same time, Deaf people "have a responsibility to integrate into the wider national society through the acquisition of a proper knowledge of the state language" (ibid., 5). So far, only the second, obligatory, part has been taken seriously since Deaf students' entire school careers have been devoted to the future hope of integration through the best possible acquisition of spoken Hungarian, while their identities and world-knowledge as Deaf people has been relegated into the background for the sake of ultimate integration. Besides, the goal has been unrealistic, at least in terms of the means used in the oral approach. Those involved in the education of Deaf students must take seriously the fact that the mother tongue of both Deaf children and Deaf adults is sign language. Those educating Deaf children must provide proper support and maintenance for sign language (ibid., 5).

The Need for Bilingual Teachers

In addition to all the other teaching being given by bilingual teachers (see below), The Hague Recommendations also suggest that the "official State language should also be taught as a subject on a regular basis preferably by bilingual teachers who have a good understanding of the children's cultural and linguistic background" (ibid., 7). No minority education can be realized without bilingual teachers, and such bilingual teachers must first be trained (ibid., 7). This training is the most urgent challenge, but the challenge cannot be met until sign language itself is recognized.

Deaf students must have the right to bilingual education which most appropriately meets their special needs. It is the duty of the education authorities to carry out strategic planning and train bilingual teachers in advance. A thorough analysis of current trends in the education of the Deaf reveals that Hungary lags behind, with its hearing-educator-centered, one-sided oral approach to the education of Deaf students. The launching of bilingual teacher training will very likely be further delayed until a radical shift of paradigm has taken place in Hungary among professional educators of the Deaf (Johnson, Liddell, and Erting 1989, 15-23).

The Mother Tongue as the Main Medium of Education

The Hague Recommendations acknowledge "the pivotal importance of the first years of education in a child's development" (ibid., 6). Can it be possible that only teachers of the Deaf are unaware of the importance of sign language for Deaf children? The document speaks not only of the recognition of the child's language, but also of the teaching of it, and the active use of it as the main medium of education in preschool, kindergarten, primary and secondary schools (ibid., 6-7).

The Hague Recommendations suggest that it is only towards the end of the primary level that "a few practical or non-theoretical subjects should be taught through the medium of the State language" (1996, 7). Even in secondary school, "a substantial part of the curriculum should be taught through the medium of the minority language. The minority language should be taught as a subject on a regular basis" (ibid., 7).

Regular and continuous use of sign language in the educational setting will also support the self-development of sign language, and in this way a conscientious cultivation of language development will be maintained.

Provision for the Neglected Tertiary-Level Education

Linguistic rights at the tertiary level can also be supported by implementing proper training for educational interpreters and note-takers for Deaf students. It is obvious that granting rights at this level is also tied to the recognition of sign language as the accepted mother tongue of Deaf people. This recognition will hopefully open up full-time employment for those who currently provide essential services to medical and legal professionals without being adequately rewarded for their invaluable services. Today, these services are mostly provided by freelance interpreters, often the hearing children of Deaf parents. The services provided by professional interpreters for the Deaf should be rewarded at the same level as those provided by interpreters of any foreign language. Sign language has also to be accepted as fulfilling the foreign language requirement in higher education institutions.

Conclusions

People are generally afraid of changes. Change poses a threat to them. The suggested shift of paradigm will no doubt involve additional expenses and additional training, and the provision of additional services. However, if we take into account the prospective benefits, such as reduced cultural conflicts, decreasing social tensions, improved education, and an elevated social status for Deaf people, we shall see that it is worth risking a shift of paradigm in the education of Deaf students. These changes are not only desirable, they are almost inescapable. Instead of being a threat, the recognition of sign language prepares the way for bilingual education for Deaf people, which will reduce cultural conflicts between Deaf students and hearing teachers, Deaf people and hearing people.

Acknowledgments

I owe a debt of gratitude to two of the editors of this book, Tove Skutnabb-Kangas and Miklós Kontra, for their patience, encouragement and help during the writing of this paper.

References

Ahlgren, I. "Sign Language as the First Language." In I. Ahlgren and K. Hyltenstam, eds., *Bilingualism in Deaf Education,* 55–60. Hamburg: Signum, 1994.

Anderson, Y. "Deaf People as a Linguistic Minority." In I. Ahlgren and K. Hyltenstam, eds., *Bilingualism in Deaf Education,* 9–13. Hamburg: Signum, 1994.

Bockmiller, P. "Hearing-impaired children: Learning to read a second language." *American Annals of the Deaf.* 126, 7 (1981): 810–813.

Bergman, E. and B. Bragg. *Tales from a Clubroom.* Washington, D.C.: Gallaudet University Press, 1981.

Charrow, V. and J. Fletcher. "English as the second language of deaf students." *Developmental Psychology* 10, 4 (1974): 463–470.

van Cleve, J. V., ed. *Deaf history unveiled: interpretations from the new scholarship.* Washington, D.C.: Gallaudet University Press, 1993.

Cokely, D. "Sign language: teaching, interpreting and educational policy." In Baker and Battison, eds., *Sign Language and the Deaf Community,* 137–158. Silver Spring, MD: National Association of the Deaf, 1980.

Corwin, K. and S. Wilcox. "The search for the empty cup continues." In *Sign Language Studies 1972–1993,* 48, 249–268. Burtonville, MD: Linstok Press, 1985.

Erting, C.J. "An Anthropological Approach to the study of the Communicative Competence of Deaf Children." *Sign Language Studies* 32 (1981): 221–238.

——. "Cultural Conflict in a School for Deaf Children." In P.C. Higgins, and J.E. Nash, eds., *Understanding Deafness Socially,* 123–150. Springfield, Ill.: Charles C. Thomas Publisher, 1986.

——. "Acquiring linguistic and social identity: Interaction of deaf children with a hearing teacher and a deaf adult." In M. Strong, ed., *Language learning and deafness,* 192–219. New York: Cambridge University Press, 1988.

——. "Deafness and literacy: why can't Sam read?" *Sign Language Studies* 75 (1992): 97-112.

Ewoldt, C. "The early literacy development of deaf children." In D.F. Moores and K.P. Meadow-Orlans, eds., *Educational and developmental aspects of deafness,* 85-114. Washington, D.C.: Gallaudet University Press, 1990.

Fisher, S. "Critical periods: Critical issues." In B. Schick and M.P. Moeller, eds., *Proceedings of the tenth annual conference on issues in language and deafness,* 1-11. Omaha: Boys Town National Research Hospital, 1994.

Hafer, J.C. "Curricular Issues In Early Education." Paper read at the 18th International Congress on Education of the Deaf. Tel-Aviv, Israel, 16-20 July 1995.

The Hague Recommendations Regarding the Education Rights of National Minorities & Explanatory Note. The Hague: Foundation on Inter-Ethnic Relations, 1996.

Higgins, P. C. and J. E. Nash, eds. *Understanding deafness socially.* Springfield, Ill.: Charles C. Thomas, 1987.

Humphries, T. "An introduction to the culture of deaf people in the United States: content notes and reference materials for teachers." *Sign Language Studies* 72 (1991): 209-240.

Johnson, R. "Sign language of the deaf: psychological, linguistic, and sociological perspectives." *American Anthropologist* 82, 3 (1980): 624-625.

Johnson, R. and C. Erting. "Linguistic socialization in the context of emergent and deaf ethnicity." *Working Papers in Anthropology,* 1-23. New York: Wenner-Gren Foundation, 1984.

Johnson, R.E., S. Liddell, and C. Erting. *Unlocking the curriculum: Principles for achieving access in deaf education.* Washington, D.C.: Gallaudet Research Institute, 1989.

Kannapell, B. "Bilingual education: A new direction in the education of the deaf." *The Deaf American* 26 (1974): 9-15.

Kelly, L.P. "Cognitive theory guiding research in literacy and deafness." In D.F. Moores and K.P. Meadow-Orlans, eds., *Educational and developmental aspects of deafness,* 202-231. Washington, D.C.: Gallaudet University Press, 1990.

Kluwin, T.N. "Introduction." In T.N. Kluwin, D.F. Moores, and M.G. Gaustad, eds., *Toward effective public school programs for deaf students: Context, process and outcomes,* 1-4. New York: Teachers College Press, 1992.

Lane, H. *When the Mind Hears. A History of the Deaf.* New York: Random House, Inc., 1984.

Livingston, S. "An alternative view of education for deaf children." Parts I and II. *American Annals of the Deaf* 131, 1 (1986): 21-25, and 131,3 (1986): 229-231.

Lucas, C. et al. "Bilingualism and Deafness: An Annotated Bibliography." *Sign Language Studies* 55 (1987): 97-139.

Mahshie, S. N. *Educating deaf children bilingually.* Washington, D.C.: Gallaudet University Press, 1995.

Markowicz, H. and J. Woodward. "Language and the maintenance of ethnic boundaries in the deaf community." *Communication and Cognition* 11 (1978): 29–38.

Martin, D.S. "Review of Education and Deafness by P. Paul and S. Quigley." In *Sign Language Studies 1972–1993*, 66: 85–91. Burtonsville, MD: Linstok Press, 1990.

Martin, D.S., ed. *Cognition, education, and deafness.* Washington, D.C.: Gallaudet University Press, 1985.

—., ed. *Advances in cognition, education, and deafness: Directions for research and instruction.* Washington, D.C.: Gallaudet University Press, 1991.

Mayberry, R. and E. Eichen. "The long-lasting advantage of learning sign language in childhood: Another look at the critical period for language acquisition." In *Journal of memory and language* 30 (1991): 486–512.

Meadow-Orlans, K.P. "Understanding Deafness: Socialization of Children." In P.C. Higgins and J.E. Nash, *Understanding Deafness Socially*, 29–57. Springfield, Ill.: Charles C. Thomas Publisher, 1987.

Moores, D.F. and K.P. Meadow-Orlans, eds. *Educational and developmental aspects of deafness.* Washington, D.C.: Gallaudet University Press, 1990.

Mottez, B. "Deaf identity." *Sign Language Studies* 68 (1990): 195–216.

Muzsnai, I. "Whose interest is to be served by the education of the hearing impaired?" (In Hungarian). *Gyógypedagógiai Szemle.* Vol. XXV, no. 2 (1997): 139–142.

—. "Hungarian Education for the Deaf: Accessible or Not?" Manuscript, 1998.

Nash, J.E. "Learning to be Deaf." *Journal of Contemporary Ethnography* 17, 2 (1988): 229–233.

Nover, S.M. "Politics and language: American Sign Language and English in Deaf Education." In C. Lucas, ed., *Sociolinguistics in deaf communities,* 109–163. Washington, D.C.: Gallaudet University Press, 1995.

Padden, C. and T. Humphries. *Deaf in America: Voices from a Culture.* Cambridge, Mass.: Harvard University Press, 1988.

Paul, P. and S. Quigley. *Education and Deafness.* New York: Longman, 1990.

Reagan, T. "The deaf as a linguistic minority: educational considerations." *Harvard Educational Review* 55, 3 (1985): 265–277.

Rutherford, S.D. "The culture of American deaf people." *Sign Language Studies* 59 (1988): 129–147.

Saulnier, K. L. and D.F. Moores, eds. *A ten-year perspective, 1982–1992.* Washington, D.C.: Gallaudet Research Institute, 1992.

Siple, P., N. Hatfield, and F. Caccamise. "The Role of Visual Perceptual Abilities in the Acquisition and Comprehension of Sign Language." *American Annals of the Deaf* 123, 7 (1978): 852–856.

Skutnabb-Kangas, T. *Language, literacy and minorities.* London: Minority Rights Group, 1990.

———. "Linguistic Human Rights: A Prerequisite for Bilingualism." In I. Ahlgren and K. Hyltenstam, eds., *Bilingualism in Deaf Education,* 139–159. Hamburg: Signum, 1994.

———. "Human rights and language wrongs–a future for diversity." In P. Benson, P. Grundy, and T. Skutnabb-Kangas, eds., "Language rights." Special issue of *Language Sciences* 20, 1 (1998): 5–27.

Skutnabb-Kangas, T. and R. Phillipson. "Linguistic human rights, past and present." In T. Skutnabb-Kangasand R. Phillipson, eds., *Linguistic Human Rights,* 71–110. Berlin, New York: Mouton de Gruyter, 1994.

Spencer, P. E. and K. P. Meadow-Orlans. "Analysis: Issues in the growth and development of hearing-impaired learners." In D.S. Martin, ed., *Cognition, education, and deafness,* 34–40. Washington, D.C.: Gallaudet University Press, 1985.

Spencer, P. E., D. Deyo, and N. Grindstaff. "Symbolic play behaviors of normally-developing deaf toddlers." In D.S. Martin, ed., *Advances in cognition, education, and deafness: Directions for research and instruction,* 216–222. Washington, D.C.: Gallaudet University Press, 1991.

Statistical Tables on Primary Education in 1993/94, by the Hungarian Ministry of Public Education. (In Hungarian.) In *Gyógypedagógiai Szemle.* Vol. XXV, no. 3 (1997): 233–235.

Stewart, D. "Bilingual education: Teachers' opinion of signs." *Sign Language Studies* 39 (1983): 145–167.

van der Stoel, M. "Introduction to the Seminar." *International Journal on Minority and Group Rights.* Special Issue on the Education Rights of National Minorities 4, 2, 1996/1997 (1997): 153–155.

Stokoe, W. C. *Sign Language Structure. An Outline of the Visual Communication Systems of the American Deaf.* Burtonsville, MD: Linstok Press, 1960.

Supalla, T. "Deaf folklore film collection project." *Sign Language Studies* 70 (1991): 73–82.

Svartholm, K. "Bilingual Education for the Deaf in Sweden." *Sign Language Studies* 81 (1993): 291–332.

Thornberry, P. and D. Gibbons. "Education and Minority Rights: A Short Survey of International Standards." *International Journal on Minority and Group Rights.* Special Issue on the Education Rights of National Minorities 4, 2, 1996/1997 (1997): 115–152.

Wilcox, S. *American deaf culture: an anthology.* Silver Spring, MD: Linstok Press, 1989.

Woodward, J. "Some sociolinguistic problems in the implementation of bilingual education for deaf students." In F. Caccamise and D. Hicks, eds., *Proceedings of the second national symposium on sign language research and teaching,* 183–209. Silver Spring, MD: National Association of the Deaf, 1978.

Woodward, J., T. Allen, and A. Schildroth. "Linguistic and cultural role models for hearing-impaired children in elementary school programs." In M. Strong, ed., *Language Learning and Deafness* (1988), 184–191.

Woodward, J. and T. Allen. "Models of Deafness Compared: A sociolinguistic study of deaf & hard-of-hearing teachers." *Sign Language Studies* 79 (1993): 113–132.

Linguistic Human Rights Problems among Romani and Boyash Speakers in Hungary with Special Attention to Education

ANDREA SZALAI

This paper will point out and analyze some problems of language use and human rights among the largest minority in Hungary—the Gypsies (see below for the term)—with special attention to education.[1] The approaches and solutions offered by two paradigms, one sociologically and one culturally oriented, are presented and evaluated, and some alternatives are suggested.

Data on Gypsies in Hungary

Specialist literature dealing with Gypsy communities from the point of view of various disciplines often indicates that majority societies tend to regard such heterogeneous populations as the Gypsies in terms of ethnicity, social status and linguistics. Problems in defining ethnicity are well reflected in the statistical data on the size and proportions of the Gypsy population, data which also illustrates how Gypsies are at the mercy of the host society and its exo-definitions. Statistics frequently differ in several countries, including Hungary, depending on whose definitions are used. In this study, I refer only to those investigations which include information on the languages spoken by Gypsies.

In spite of problems of classification and definition (see Ladányi–Szelényi 1997), according to the results of the 1990 census (see table 14.1) or the data on native language gathered in the 1971 (*Report* 1971) representative survey on Gypsies, it can be stated that Gypsies are the largest linguistic minority in Hungary. Data on the linguistic diversity of Gypsies in Hungary can only be found in the 1971 sociology survey. On the basis of the figures referred to above, 71 percent of the population considered as

Gypsies on the basis of other criteria are linguistically assimilated
and have Hungarian as their mother tongue. Around 21 percent
speak some variant of Romani. Approximately 8 percent speak
dialects of Romanian (*Report* 1971, 14) and mainly identify
themselves, according to their mother tongue, as Boyash this being
the ethnonym and linguonym at the same time.

Table 14.1

The size of the Gypsy population (according to nationality and
language) based on census figures. (See *Statistical Yearbook of
Hungary* 1992, 22-23.)

Year	Declaring Gypsy as mother tongue	Declaring Gypsy as nationality
1941	18,640	27,033
1949	21,387	37,598
1960	25,633	56,121
1970	34,957	–
1980	27,915	–
1990	48,072	142,684

Groups of both native Romani and Boyash speakers are further
divided into ethnic and language subgroups. An analysis of the
correlations between self-identification and the speech situation is
beyond the scope of this paper. Based on categorization according
to mother tongue, I differentiate in this article between native
Hungarian, native Romani and native Boyash Gypsies. In this study
I use the term "Gypsy" rather than the term "Rom", which is
frequently used in political contexts. My reason for this is that I
consider self-identification relevant, and want to include the whole
"Gypsy" group. Only the native Romani speakers in Hungary use
the ethnonym "Rom" as their self-identification in order to identify
their own ethnic group and language, whereas neither the native
Hungarian-speaking Gypsies nor the Boyash group identify
themselves by this name.

The 1971 investigation estimated the total number of Gypsies to
be 320,000 (around 3 percent of the entire population of
Hungary). The 1993-94 survey set the approximate number at
500,000, which is around 5 percent of the entire population
(Havas–Kemény 1995, 4.) However, bilingual Gypsies in Hungary
are likely to be underrepresented in these data, for methodological
reasons. The data are based on questionnaire responses and are

likely to be affected by social hierarchy with respect to linguistic prestige: some Gypsies may have avoided mentioning their knowledge of the Romani or Boyash language. It is probable that the number of speakers who are, at least to a certain extent, bilingual, is in reality higher (Réger 1995, 87).

Still, the large majority of Gypsy children in Hungary are, in fact, probably not bilingual. This also means that the educational problems that most Gypsy children face are not the result of their being bilingual. They are mostly the consequences of the sociocultural disadvantages they experience as a result of the social stratum to which they belong, as well as the inadequate educational methods used in schools and the prejudices of the majority group. Such prejudices often treat social problems as if they were caused by the ethnic origin of the victims.

In order to solve these problems, educational content and methods must be changed and the views of the participants in the educational process need to be revised (see Radó 1997). However, this is not enough, since there are macrosocietal background factors that go beyond the competency of the educational system. In the following pages I will confine my inquiry to the educational linguistic problems of Romani-Hungarian and Boyash-Hungarian bilingual children. But first I would refer to the legal frames of minority education and of language use in Hungary.

Gypsy Minority Education and Educational Linguistic Rights

The Legal Framework

One great achievement of the Hungarian Act No. LXXVII of 1993 on the Rights of National and Ethnic Minorities[2] (henceforth the "Minority Act") is that it recognizes Gypsies as one of the thirteen minorities in Hungary, and provides equal rights in terms of language use as well.

The Minority Act requires, for instance, that schools organize a minority class or group whenever parents of at least eight children belonging to the same ethnic or national minority so request (Minority Act, Article 43 [4]). In such a case, the parents can choose the teaching language; it can be the minority mother tongue only, the minority mother tongue and Hungarian, or

Hungarian only (ibid., 43 [2]). State supplementary benefits to the institution in question are guaranteed to cover additional costs incurred by the minority pre-school and school. The magnitude of these costs will be decided by the existing Finance Act (Minority Act, Article 44, 55 [2, lit.a]; and the Public Education Act, Supplement One, Part Two, items 2a and 4). Since 1991, these financial possibilities have been extended to education programs for Gypsy children. However, a ruling for the minimum requirements of such minority education programs to be financed in this manner only came into existence at the end of 1997 (see *Directive* 1997). Institutions providing minority education are required to take the ruling into consideration when drawing up teaching and syllabus programs.

The Minority Act and the Public Education Act (1993, no. LXXIX) provide for linguistic rights of groups and individuals belonging to national or ethnic minorities. According to Kontra (1997a, 1717) these rights appear to be characterizable by a position somewhere between overt permission and promotion on the grid proposed by Tove Skutnabb-Kangas and Robert Phillipson (1989; 1994, 80).

But the endorsement of educational linguistic human rights for Gypsies is brought about in a manner differing from that usual for other minority groups. In the following section I shall discuss some of the possible reasons for this.

If one interprets the education of Gypsy children within the framework of minority education, several paradigms would be worth considering. I shall discuss only two important paradigms that often come into conflict in the area of the legal regulations governing Gypsy children's education, as well as in everyday practice.

Two Paradigms

One main approach to classifying the educational problems faced by Gypsy children is a sociologically oriented approach. From this perspective, Gypsies can be defined as a group with a marginal status, with economic, societal, regional and cultural disadvantages, suffering from an underclass position and from the effects of prejudice on the part of the majority population. Inequality is emphasized in this paradigm. Societal and political practices based on the sociologically oriented paradigm regard equality of opportunities and the compensation of disadvantages as their main aim in relation to Gypsies, that is, they offer instrumentally oriented solutions based on granting more economic and social rights. In accordance with this, those components of Gypsy culture which are emphasized can usually be described in terms of deprivation, which is a characteristic of the poor.

The other tendency is represented by a culture-oriented approach. The representatives of this paradigm consider the Gypsy minority groups as primarily ethnic communities, with an autonomous and organic culture. They focus on the maintenance and operations of this culture, and examine language as a means in this process. The solutions offered are based on cultural affective rights, including—maybe—linguistic rights.

Naturally, the two paradigms show a number of overlapping areas, and problems also arise which are beyond social, economic, and cultural rights. Irresolvable contradictions only seem to arise when one or the other of the two views is being considered of absolute (and exclusive) relevance.

Deficit theories, typical of the sociological standpoint, dominate investigations about legal rules and educational practice in the context of the Gypsy minority, although one also encounters, here and there, a culture-oriented ideology, representing more enrichment-oriented theories.[3]

The statement of the Minority Act (Article 45[2]) which deals with the education of the Gypsy minority is based on the dominance of the sociological aspect. The text states: "In order to reduce the educational disadvantages of the Gypsy minority, special educational conditions may be created".

The impact of deficit theories can also be abundantly felt in the terminology and stance of other documents dealing with minority education. Both in the 1997 Ministerial Directive on the Education of National and Ethnic Minorities, and in the National Core Curriculum (NAT 1995, 19), references to educational questions relating to the Gypsy minority discuss remedial education.

According to the Directive, remedial education for Gypsies "does not require the teaching of the Gypsy language, but if parents request it, the variety of Gypsy spoken by them is also taught in school" (*Directive* 1997, 3628).

"Ethnic knowledge" is stipulated as a subject area, although it can be taught either as a separate subject or integrated into other subjects. Within the framework of the education of minorities provision is made for the teaching of the various languages spoken by Gypsies.

Here the Directive and the National Core Curriculum (henceforth NAT) contradict each other. The NAT (see Kontra

1997b, 140–141) assumes that the majority of Gypsy learners speak Hungarian as their first language. It makes provision for the study of the minority language only within the framework of the traditional teaching of minority languages. (This allows learners to study a minority language as a foreign language, for four hours per week.) With this, a new self-contradiction is born, for on page 18 we read that "the language may be taught as a second language and may be used as a medium of instruction, as one of the thirteen minority first languages in Hungary" (NAT 1995, 18). The NAT not only discriminates in language matters, but also expresses minimalist expectations regarding the first steps in the education of those belonging to the Gypsy minority, stating that the educational target is for "the learner to meet the requirements of his age group" (NAT 1995, 19).

In cases where the school does not provide "Gypsy language teaching", the school is obliged to choose from at least three of the educational areas listed below, and to teach them for four hours each week. The alternatives are called a) subject development; b) development of minority self-awareness; c) socialization and communicative development; d) regular participation in organized Gypsy activities; e) individual progress. In addition, the Directive prescribes three classroom hours per week to be used for "activities developing special abilities" (see *Directive* 1997).

While allowing for exceptions, the conditions described above involve a preconception that Gypsy children will not meet the minimum school requirements, and that they are socially, communicatively and educationally challenged and therefore unable to achieve success in the school environment. This attitude is given absolution by the requirements of the educational establishments, which thereby construct certain groups of learners—in this case those belonging to the Gypsy minority—as being in need of remedial education. Developmental proposals are almost exclusively directed at the children, rather than at educational methodologies, attitudes and content.

Problems in the organization, content and quality of remedial programs for Gypsy children at the preschool and early school levels are well illustrated in a study (Setényi 1996) examining the proposals for Gypsy minority education programs collected by the Hungarian Ministry of Culture and Education from 1994 to February 1996. The nursery schools and schools which handed in proposals demanded a supplementary normative subsidy for the remedial program. I shall select from the results only those which relate to the minority language and culture.

A large proportion (87 percent) of the preschool remedial programs planned and outlined by the nursery schools contain general socialization goals, significantly connected to an awareness of personal hygiene. Of the preschool programs examined, only 11 percent contained any form of ethnic awareness, in most cases comprising no more than the reading aloud, or possibly teaching, of a few Gypsy folktales. Of the proposals submitted by schools, 52 percent contained nothing outside the traditional supplementary teaching of the two basic subjects, mathematics and Hungarian language and literature, giving as aims a competence corresponding to minimum requirements. Only 23 percent of the applications included elements of ethnic awareness in addition to supplementary, remedial teaching. Only one school mentioned the preservation of "the Gypsy language" (Setényi 1996, 143–144).

It appears to be the case that the normative subsidy targeted to cover the financial needs of institutions of minority education is used for different purposes in Gypsy minority programs than in other "national minority" programs.[4]

While educational programs for non-Gypsy minorities emphasize the children's linguistic and cultural identities, Gypsy educational programs focus on compensation for sociocultural deprivation.

I admit that such remedial programs, which often need to comprise social welfare support elements, are necessary and important. The opportunity to apply for supplementary normative subsidies for these programs can encourage schools and teachers and thus may contribute to the success of the programs.

However, I do not entirely subscribe to the idea that such programs, which hardly contain any considerations of minority language or ethnic awareness, should be called Gypsy programs.

Gypsy programs, in their present form, can be regarded as social programs rather than ethnic or minority programs. The "minority" label in itself does not improve the situation. The concepts of "Gypsy" and "poor" often overlap in majority values, and thus become synonymous in their interpretation and in educational practice.

Challenges and Possible Solutions?

Changes in educational regulations may induce changes in the educational practices analyzed above. The regulations neither prohibit nor prescribe the teaching of either of the native languages used by the Gypsy communities, but they clearly require the integration of elements of the minority culture into the curricula (*Directive* 1997).

However, this alone cannot result in a qualitative improvement in education. Nursery schools and schools are left without help to develop educational programs that contain Romani or Boyash language and/or ethnological elements. Appropriate sample curricula, textbooks, language books or educational supplementary materials are not available in sufficient numbers. Due to the inadequacy of teacher training, the majority of teachers lack even basic cultural, linguistic, and sociological knowledge concerning the different groups of the Gypsy minority. In this respect the prescribed requirements in educational regulations are far ahead of the real existing options in everyday practice.

A further problem is that there are only a small number of qualified teachers who use Romani or Boyash as their mother tongue or as a second language, and hardly any of the trained teachers and nursery-school teachers speak one of these languages as a foreign language, even at an elementary level. To achieve a quality change in minority education it is essential to incorporate up-to-date knowledge about Gypsies into teacher training and further training, besides supporting and encouraging the development of syllabuses and materials. This objective can also be found among the recommendations for the Gypsy educational development program designed by the Ministry of Culture and Education (Gypsy Educational Development Program 1995, 8–9). It is also worth considering employing native Romani or Boyash educational assistants at least in those primary schools attended by large numbers of bilingual Gypsy children.

The teaching of the Romani and Boyash languages, and the problems in connection with education in these languages in general, are complicated by the contradictions within the present legal regulations, namely, the requirement of the Public Education Act which prescribes that only those teachers can be employed as teachers of a national and ethnic minority language and literature, and for teaching through the medium of that language, who are adequately trained and have been awarded a teaching degree in the language in question (see Public Education Act, Article 17 [1], lit b. and 17 [3], lit a., b).

The requirements above cannot, at present, be met as there is no possibility to receive a degree in teaching the Romani and Boyash languages in Hungarian higher education. At a few teacher training colleges and university faculties of humanities, students can learn these languages as foreign languages, but only in very short courses. At present, these languages can only be learned in their native speech communities, with the help of a limited variety of materials which were not primarily designed for linguistic or language teaching purposes.

Present-day regulations contain a number of sources of conflict. On the one hand they provide legal grounds for reluctant schools to refuse the introduction of the teaching of the Romani or Boyash languages as subjects. On the other hand, schools that undertake the task of teaching these languages against all difficulties will inevitably contravene the Act, since no teacher will be able to boast a degree in teaching these languages.

Due to the problems mentioned above, a revision of the regulations seems unavoidable. Naturally, certain compromises need to be made so that legal frameworks converge with the possibilities existing in reality. This does not necessarily mean leveling, if the state contributes to the creation of the minimal professional, structural and financial conditions required by the Act. The training of native minority teachers is also laid down in the Minority Act (Article 46[2]) as a task and responsibility of the state.

In summary, we can state that in most cases preschool and school establishments are unable to contribute to the maintenance and development of linguistic competence of Romani- and Boyash-speaking children, and nothing urges them to do so. The development of language skills is restricted to the Hungarian language. This reinforces the dominance of the majority language, which, because of an already diglossic, asymmetric bilingual situation, might contribute to linguistic assimilation.

Finally, when developing educational programs, it is essential to take into consideration the fact that Gypsies are regarded as a homogeneous group only by the majority group and the legal system. There are, however, efforts towards cultural unification (Szuhay 1995) and the creation of a high culture in the Romani language. These are landmarks in a potentially long and controversial process, the outcome of which is unpredictable.

Because of the diversity, it is difficult to envisage and describe the range of knowledge that might provide the elements for ethnically oriented education. The main plea here is, therefore, that only after thoroughly surveying local conditions and demands should experts start developing educational programs with language teaching and ethnic content, and that such programs should be based on the language and traditions of the local Gypsy community. In addition, based on structural parallelisms, one could refer to differences from, and similarities with, other Gypsy and non-Gypsy groups.

In view of this it seems illusory to expect any rapid change in the educational state of Gypsies. It can also be presumed that revision of legal regulations alone will not be able to solve the problems indicated.

In what follows I would like to analyze some of the recent processes of Hungarian language planning and language policy in relation to Gypsies, to see the extent to which present trends and tendencies might contribute to the validation of the educational linguistic rights of Romani and Boyash speakers.

Tendencies in Romani and Boyash Language Planning and Language Policy Before and After 1989

To understand the present situation, it is important to be familiar with the main features of state policy and language policy with respect to Gypsies before 1989.

In the socialist era, Gypsies were not regarded as an ethnic minority group. The frequently discussed "Gypsy question" was perceived as a social problem which, it was hoped, could be solved by means of welfare and administrative methods. The assimilation of Gypsies was believed to be the solution. The main characteristic of this trend was that any cultural efforts by Gypsies (in terms of literacy, the press, theater, minority institutions, education), together with the development of the Romani and Boyash languages, were seen as harmful, as factors that hindered the "integration" of Gypsies into the majority society (see *Resolution* 1961).

A theoretical basis for this policy was provided by research carried out by József Vekerdi. Although to some extent useful in providing grammars for Romani dialects, glossaries, and editions of texts, Vekerdi's views on Romani language and culture were extremely prejudiced and professionally unacceptable (see, for example, Vekerdi 1979, 1988). His attitude had a negative influence on the validation of Gypsy minority linguistic and cultural rights.

A full presentation of Zita Réger's professional criticism of Vekerdi's views is beyond the scope of this paper (see Réger 1988, 1995). However, some reflection on points raised by Vekerdi is necessary, as current linguistic emancipation efforts are still greatly influenced by his views.

One of Vekerdi's central claims (a claim which was also to become a public belief) suggests that languages of Gypsies only offer a narrow range of communication possibilities. This is often associated with the statement that the Romani language has a limited vocabulary. This opinion simply ignores the sociolinguistic explanation essential for an understanding of the present linguistic situation. This sociolinguistic explanation focuses on the diglossia which permanently characterizes Romani-Hungarian and Boyash-Hungarian bilingualism and the functional division between the minority and majority languages. As Zita Réger has observed (Réger 1995, 81), Romani and Boyash are primarily used in communication within the group, generally in informal situations. Apart from this, cultural anthropological and ethnological research (see, for example, Kovalcsik 1993, 1998; Stewart 1989, 1994) has also shown that Romani possesses a "high form", a distinctive verbal genre used on important communal occasions. The term "vorba" describes this formal speech, as distinguished from "duma", the social vernacular.

In my opinion, the struggles for civil and cultural rights that have taken place since 1989 can be interpreted as an opposing discourse, in reaction to the assimilation-oriented approach which has even questioned the raison d'être of the culture and language of ethnic Gypsies. Efforts towards linguistic emancipation can be interpreted in this context too.

When considering the task of modernizing corpus planning, status planning and acquisition planning, one should take into consideration the predominantly oral nature and diglossic state of the Romani- and Boyash-medium cultures.

The creation of literacy in the Romani and Boyash languages is a very important stage in the planning process. It is only recently (in the late 1980s and, in the case of Boyash, in the 1990s) that language books, grammars and dictionaries were first published for this purpose.

Present language-planning efforts in Hungary are focused on treating Boyash not only as a dialect of Romanian, but as a separate language—with all the rights due to it as such.

There are both linguistic and ethnic reasons that might contribute to the development of the Romanian dialects spoken by the Boyash in Hungary as an autonomous and separate language. According to the somewhat limited data we have at our disposal, it seems that the Boyash oral dialect of Romanian detached itself at least a century and a half ago. Isolated since that time from the mother language, its development has been influenced by the southern Slavonic and Hungarian languages. This may well explain why neither Romanian innovations nor literacy have left any mark on Boyash. To this day, there is no connection with Romanian literacy and high culture.

Most Boyash people define their own ethnicity and language as "Boyash" in their mother tongue in intra-group communication. This endo-definition is used when they talk both about Romani-speaking groups whom they unanimously call "lăkătar," and about non-Gypsies. In intergroup communication, and when using the majority language, they refer to themselves and their own language as "Gypsy", in opposition to Romani-speaking groups and in opposition to non-Gypsies as well. Moreover, non-Gypsy society also identifies the Boyash as Gypsies. In other words, non-Gypsies do not identify the Boyash as speakers of Romanian, but differentiate them from themselves as Gypsies. Since their ethnic and linguistic internal identification is "Boyash", and their external (self-)definition is "Gypsy" (see Szalai 1997), it can be concluded that in spite of their Romanian origins in terms of mother tongue they have no contact either with the standard Romanian language or with the Romanian ethnic identity.

This fact is also taken into consideration by contributors to the first bilingual teaching materials for Boyash children (see Kovalcsik 1994; Kovalcsik–Orsós 1994; Orsós 1994, 1997; Varga 1997). The language in which these books are written shows the characteristics of the Boyash vernacular. The written form of the Boyash language in these materials is based on Hungarian orthography. Sounds which do not exist in the Hungarian language are denoted either by combinations of Hungarian letters or by borrowing letters from standard Romanian orthography. This also allows Boyash adults who are familiar with the Hungarian alphabet to approach a written version of their own language for the first time in their life.

The negative (language) policy analyzed earlier has naturally influenced, partially even created, some of the problems in Romani and Boyash language planning. This might explain why ideological, subjective aspects sometimes dominate in solving problems that would normally require primarily professional, linguistic and educational considerations. The following two examples are intended as an illustration of this state of affairs.

The author of one recently published Boyash dictionary (Varga 1997) increased the number of lexical entries by treating additional meanings of words as new entries, instead of including them in one entry. By doing so, she broke a standard rule of dictionary making. In the background, we can discern an attempt to demonstrate the equality of the Boyash language with other languages with literary traditions. The author regards the size of the dictionary and the number of lexical items it contains as a measure of the equality of languages. In normal circumstances, she would have made efforts to justify this. Paradoxically, her actions followed the logic of the professionally absurd view that she intended to disaffirm.

A similar motivation can be traced in the changes made to a Romani language book (Máté 1994). The new book has basically the same structure and content as an earlier version, but it is now published with a new title and under the name of a different author. This new book omits the presentation of grammatical rules governing the integration of borrowed lexemes into the morphological and phonological system of Romani. This hyper-purist approach[5] has probably been adopted in order to prove the autonomy of the language and its incontestable inner resources. However, the rules that have been omitted are evidence of the vitality, stability and integrity of the Romani grammatical system.

In my interpretation, these trends indicate that prejudices against Gypsies that have been present in linguicism[6] directed against both Romani and Boyash, greatly influence both the Gypsy and non-Gypsy societies. It may be for this reason that experts in charge of Romani or Boyash language planning perceive it as their "duty" to disaffirm negative views. Their argumentation, however, in contradiction with their original purpose, implicitly maintains and reproduces the approach that characterized the rightly criticized statement regarding the extremely narrow communicative potential of the Romani and Boyash languages. This can be observed, for example, in the exaggeration and over-communication of the significance of vocabulary size. This procedure implies the assumption that features resulting from a permanent diglossic bilingualism are interpreted as deficits which reduce the value and prestige of the language.

However, in order to break out of the diglossic state, it is, of course, also necessary to expand the range of use and functions of the Romani and Boyash languages and to develop the necessary sets of linguistic tools for serving different communicative functions. The bilingual textbooks and dictionaries mentioned above may greatly contribute to the development of literacy in Romani and Boyash, as well as to language acquisition within formal settings. However, the conditions for publication and distribution of these and other similar books and dictionaries definitely need improving.

Finally, I would like to mention a recent development which has had a positive impact on the status of the Romani and Boyash languages, namely, the state language exam.[7] Since 1992 it has been possible to take an exam in Romani, and, since 1996, in Boyash. The language examination certificates are equal in value and appearance to those of other languages. This may result in a rise in the prestige of the Romani and Boyash languages. In the long run, it may even reinforce the identity and self-esteem of the speech communities. The language exam could be one of the ways to achieve the long-awaited linguistic and societal emancipation, and a step towards equity and linguistic rights for the Gypsies.

At present, however, it still seems to fulfill functions that are mostly related to protocol. There are several types of challenge to be faced in trying to ensure that the exam is a step in the right direction, and some of them will be briefly outlined here.

The way in which the language examination certificate itself is formulated still reflects attitudes towards the languages which certainly do not serve the aim of emancipation. Regardless of whether one takes an exam in Romani or in Boyash, the certificate will be awarded for an exam passed in the "Gypsy language". This represents the undifferentiated, homogenizing view held by the majority society with respect to Gypsies and their languages. As I pointed out earlier, the majority of non-Gypsies in Hungary have a unified view of Gypsies, and as a result, know nothing about variations in language and culture among Gypsy ethnic groups. This can be the only explanation for why the same certificate is mistakenly issued for two very different languages purely because the speakers of both languages are considered Gypsies. This mistake needs to be rectified urgently in order to avoid possible further complications, for instance, in the event that the same speaker intends to take an exam in both languages.

In my opinion, the problem is rooted in the fact that the language exam follows the structure and task types of language exams that have been implemented for languages with old written traditions. On the one hand, the application of the same method may be considered as a symbolic gesture of equality, and thus emancipation. On the other hand, because of their diglossic status, the Romani and Boyash languages in fact require a different approach. A few examples follow.

A "normal" language exam, such as an exam in French, Italian, Russian, or Bulgarian, does not require that the candidates do corpus planning in the exam situation. The present exam measures understanding and productive skills in spoken and written language. The latter may cause difficulties for Boyash and Romani speakers, since their languages are normally restricted to oral use and there is no standard orthography. Since most of those wishing to take the exam in these languages are formally educated young people who have already acquired the language via family socialization, they can anticipate this difficulty and may develop certain strategies to overcome it.

Yet another problem is that–mainly because of diglossic use–the nature of the corpuses of Romani and Boyash is not such that candidates can necessarily create texts in different registers and genres in an exam-relevant way (e.g. professional texts). By the means available to the Romani language it would be very difficult to render texts originally written in Hungarian on such subjects as financial transactions or the manufacturing of modern household appliances. Likewise, it is almost impossible to translate texts about Santa Claus holidays in Finland, or how the Reichstag was wrapped in aluminum foil. The examples are taken from my own 1996 Romani exam experiences.

These tasks create a paradoxical situation, even for a native speaker. For a correct translation, one has to implement a linguistic modernization or reform at all levels of the language, without having linguistic samples on which to base it. Thus, candidates have no option but to do a corpus planning job on the spot, which is not really a task for them, or for that situation. Concerning the outcome of the translation task, it can really only be decided whether a particular sentence is correct or ungrammatical according to the grammatical rules of that language–correctness of vocabulary cannot really be decided.

Consequently, it would be worth concentrating on the linguistic patterns of relevant speech situations, that is, registers used by Romani and Boyash speakers. If we follow the simple logical statement which claims that in a language we can only know and have access to such things as exist in the language in question (Réger 1988, 163), it is therefore fair to test only these elements. Doing this would not, of course, reduce the value of the language or the language exam.

Conclusions

The main task for the near future in language policy and planning is the harmonization of status planning and corpus planning tasks.

The disproportionate relationship between status (an exam language, i.e. high status) and corpus (inadequate resources have so far been devoted to corpus planning for all registers), which culminates in the exam situation, might be rectified as a result. The harmonization might also function as an incentive for the allocation of further resources, not only to necessary corpus and acquisition planning, but also to solving the social and economic problems which were largely responsible for the creation of the diglossic situation in the first place.

What is needed is a combination of the concerns of both the sociologically and the culturally oriented paradigms.

This change of approach could promote a more successful implementation of the human and civil rights of those belonging to the Gypsy minorities, including social, economic, cultural and linguistic rights to an equal degree.

Notes

1 I would like to express my gratitude to all those who helped me in my work with their remarks and questions. I give my special thanks to Tove Skutnabb-Kangas for her tireless professional and spiritual help and support and to Miklós Kontra and György Szépe for their useful advice. I also thank the experts of the Collegium Martineum Foundation and the Boyash an Roma youngsters working there for the great debates.

2 On the political and linguistic situation of minorities in Hungary and on the linguistic aspects of the Minority Act, see Kontra 1997a.

3 On the consequences of the two kinds of theory and their influence in minority education policies, see Skutnabb-Kangas 1990.

4 We do not consider here the financial problems of education that, in practice, often result in having to spend this supplementary support on the maintenance of the school (see Forray 1994).

5 In connection with the similar manifestation of linguistic purism and its possible relationship to minority language maintenance, see Huss 1998.

6 Linguicism is defined as "ideologies, structures and practices which are used to legitimate, effectuate and reproduce an unequal division of power and resources (material and immaterial) between groups which are defined on the basis of language" (Skutnabb-Kangas 1988, 13; see also Skutnabb-Kangas, this volume).

7 Hungarians who obtain a state language certificate in a foreign language are eligible for a salary bonus if they work in the state sector. At the time of writing, the National State Language Exam Board offers exams in fifty-two languages.

References

Directive. A művelődési és közoktatási miniszter 32/1997 (XI. 5.) rendelete a Nemzeti, etnikai kisebbség óvodai nevelésének irányelve és a Nemzeti, etnikai kisebbség iskolai oktatásának irányelve kiadásáról (Decree of the Minister of Culture and Education on the Directive regarding national and ethnic minority nursery-schools and the publication of the Directive on national and ethnic minority school education). *Művelődési Közlöny*, Vol. XLI, no. 35 (16 December 1997), 3625–3632.

Forray, R. Katalin. "A nemzeti-etnikai oktatás kiegészítő állami támogatása. Szakértői jelentés" (State supplementary subsidy of the education of national and ethnic minorities). Budapest: Oktatáskutató Intézet, 1994.

Gypsy Educational Development Program. Budapest: Művelődési és Közoktatási Minisztérium, 1995.

Havas, Gábor and István Kemény. "A magyarországi romákról" (On the Roms of Hungary). *Szociológiai Szemle* no. 3 (1995): 3–20.

Huss, Leena. "Who is to say what my language is worth?" *Linguistic purism vs. minority language maintenance.* Manuscript. Centre for Multiethnic Research, Uppsala University, 1998.

Kontra, Miklós. "Hungary." In Hans Goebl et al., eds., *Kontaktlinguistik.* Vol. 2, 1708–1723. Berlin and New York: Mouton de Gruyter, 1997a.

——. "Tannyelvi diszkrimináció és cigány munkanélküliség" (Language of instruction discrimination and Gypsy unemployment). *Fundamentum.* Vol. 1, no. 2 (1997b): 139–140.

Kovalcsik, Katalin. "Men's and Women's Storytelling in a Hungarian Vlach Gypsy Community." *Journal of the Gypsy Lore Society.* Ser. 5, vol. 3, no. 1 (1993): 1–20.

——. *Florilyé dă primăvără. Tavaszi virágok. I–II. Beás cigány iskolai énekeskönyv* (Flowers of the spring. Songbook of the Boyash Gypsies). Pécs: Gandhi Középiskola-Fii Cu Noi, 1994.

——. "Linguistic ideology in a Transylvanian Vlach Gypsy community." *Acta Linguistica Hungarica.* Vol. 45. no. 2 (Romani linguistics and culture). In press.

Kovalcsik, Katalin and Anna Orsós. *Fátá ku păru dă ar. Az aranyhajú lány. Beás cigány iskolai népmesegyűjtemény* (The girl with the golden hair. A collection of Boyash folktales). Pécs: Gandhi Középiskola, 1994.

Ladányi, János and Iván Szelényi. "Ki a cigány?" (Who are the Gypsies?). *Kritika.* No. 12 (1997): 3–6.

Magyar statisztikai évkönyv 1992. Statistical Yearbook of Hungary. Budapest: Központi Statisztikai Hivatal, 1993.

Máté, Mihály. *Lovareski shib. Lovári nyelvkönyv* (Lovari language book). Kaposvár: Csokonai Vitéz Mihály Tanítóképző Főiskola, 1994.

Minority Act. 1993. évi LXXVII. törvény a nemzeti és etnikai kisebbségek jogairól (Act on the Rights of National and Ethnic Minorities, no. LXXVII of 1993). *Magyar Közlöny.* No. 100 (22 July 1993): 5273–5286.

NAT. *Nemzeti Alaptanterv* (National Core Curriculum). Budapest: Művelődési és Közoktatási Minisztérium, 1995.

Orsós, Anna. *Beás nyelvkönyv. Pă lyimbă băjásilor* (Boyash language book). Kaposvár: Csokonai Vitéz Mihály Tanítóképző Főiskola, 1994.

——. *Beás–magyar kéziszótár. Vorbé dă băjás* (Boyash-Hungarian dictionary). Kaposvár: Csokonai Vitéz Mihály Tanítóképző Főiskola, 1997.

Public Education Act. Az 1993. évi LXXIX. törvény a közoktatásról (Az 1995. évi CXXI. törvénnyel és az 1996. évi LXII. törvénnyel egységes szerkezetbe foglalt szöveg) (Act on Public Education, no. LXXIX of 1993). *Művelődési Közlöny.* Vol. XL, no. 25 (31 August 1996): 1498–1571.

Radó, Péter. "Jelentés a magyarországi cigány tanulók oktatásáról" (Report on the education of Gypsy pupils in Hungary). Manuscript. Budapest, 1997.

Réger, Zita. "A cigány nyelv: Kutatások és vitapontok" (The Romani language: Research and points of contention). *Műhelymunkák a nyelvészet és társtudományai köréből.* No. 4 (1988): 155–178.

——. "The language of Gypsies in Hungary: An overview of research." *International Journal of the Sociology of Language.* No. 111 (1995): 79–91.

Report. Beszámoló a magyarországi cigányok helyzetével foglalkozó, 1971-ben végzett kutatásról. 1976. A kutatást Kemény István vezette (Research report on the situation of the Gypsies in Hungary. Research director: István Kemény). Budapest: MTA Szociológiai Intézet, 1971.

Resolution. "A cigánylakosság helyzetének megjavításával kapcsolatos egyes feladatokról. Az MSZMP KB Politikai Bizottságának határozata" (Tasks related to the improvement of the Gypsy population. Resolution of the Political Committee of the Central Committee of the Hungarian Socialist Workers' Party, 20 July 1961). In Barna Mezey, ed., *A magyarországi cigánykérdés dokumentumokban. 1422–1985.* Budapest: Kossuth, 1986.

Setényi, János. "Felzárkóztató programok az alapfokú oktatásban" (Gypsy remedial programs in elementary education). *Regio.* Vol. 7, no. 2 (1996): 141–149.

Skutnabb-Kangas, Tove. "Multilingualism and the Education of Minority Children." In Tove Skutnabb-Kangas and Jim Cummins, eds., *Minority education: from shame to struggle,* 9–44. Clevedon: Multilingual Matters, 1988.

——. *Language, Literacy and Minorities.* London: Minority Rights Group, 1990.

Skutnabb-Kangas, Tove and Robert Phillipson. *Wanted! Linguistic human rights.* ROLIG-papir 44. Roskilde: Roskilde University Centre, 1989.

Stewart, Michael S. "True speech: Song and moral order of a Hungarian Vlach Gypsy community." *MAN* 24, no. 1 (1989): 79–101.

——. *Daltestvérek. Az oláhcigány identitás és közösség továbbélése a szocialista Magyarországon* (Brothers in song. The persistence of Vlach Gypsy identity and community in socialist Hungary). Budapest: T-Twins–MTA Szociológiai Intézet–Max Weber Alapítvány, 1994.

Szalai, Andrea. "A 'mi' és az 'ők' határai" (The characteristics of the 'us' vs. 'them' opposition in the language use of Boyash Gypsies). *Regio.* Vol. 8, no. 1 (1997): 104–126.

Szuhay, Péter. "Constructing a Gypsy national culture." *BOOKS.* Vol. 5, no. 3 (1995): 111–120.

Varga, Ilona. *Beás–magyar, magyar–beás szótár* (Boyash-Hungarian, Hungarian-Boyash dictionary). Piliscsaba: Konsept-H, 1997.

Vekerdi, József. "A cigány nyelv és kultúra" (The Gypsy language and the Gypsy culture). In Elemér Várnagy and József Vekerdi, eds., *A cigány gyerekek nevelésének és oktatásának problémái,* 17–48. Budapest: Tankönyvkiadó, 1979.

—. "The Gypsies and the Gypsy problem in Hungary." *Hungarian Studies Review.* Vol. 15, no. 2 (1988): 13–26.

Contempt for Linguistic Human Rights in the Service of the Catholic Church: The Case of the Csángós[1]

KLÁRA SÁNDOR

In 1991, the Catholic priest of a Moldavian village in Rumania publicly humiliated twenty people in his congregation, saying that they had sold their souls for a mess of pottage when they traveled to Budapest for the visit of the Pope (Csoma and Bogdánfalvy 1993, 165). These people, together with hundreds of pilgrims from other Moldavian villages, gave the Pope a petition written in Polish, that is, John Paul II's mother tongue. The text was simple: *Help us, our Holy Father, send us Hungarian priests!* (Magyar 1994, 81).

This story might sound a little strange at first. Why would it be a betrayal for a Catholic to go to a mass celebrated by the Pope? And why would the inhabitants of Moldavian villages ask for Hungarian priests? However, to students of the culture, history and present life of the little-known ethnic group, the *Csángós,* both phenomena are well known. Historical sources show that since the sixteenth century Catholic priests in Moldavia have not served religion exclusively, and that the Csángós have repeatedly asked Rome for priests who could speak their mother tongue. This paper attempts to shed some light on this situation, and to call attention to an ethnic group which is almost totally unknown and which is excluded from access to the human rights system. Analogous cases to those listed in the introduction to *Linguistic Human Rights* (Skutnabb-Kangas and Phillipson, eds. 1994, 18–22) could also be quoted from the life of the Csángós. It is obvious that the Rumanian state has some responsibility in the continuous denial of the Csángós' linguistic rights. But here I will deal with the role of another state that seems to have more of a responsibility in the assimilation of the Csángós: the Vatican.

Who are the Csángós?

The Csángós live in Rumanian Moldavia in the foothills of the Eastern-Carpathians, in about ninety villages scattered in the valleys of small rivers. Today there are two large towns in this area: Roman (Hungarian: *Románvásár*) and Bacău (Hungarian *Bákó*).

According to widely accepted estimates[2] the number of Csángós is about 240,000. By now, most of them have undergone language shift and speak only Rumanian, but about 62,000 Csángós are bilingual and have maintained their Hungarian-origin vernacular (Tánczos 1997, 379).

The Csángó dialects have always been roofless dialects, unaffected by standard Hungarian which was developed in the nineteenth century. For speakers of Hungarian, the intelligibility of Csángó dialects varies from village to village; most are largely, or totally, incomprehensible to them. Csángós do not understand, or understand only with great difficulty, Hungarian varieties, which were influenced to a remarkable extent by the Hungarian language reform movement of the nineteenth century. Besides these facts, there are several other reasons for considering the Csángó dialects as dialects of an Ausbau-language[3] which is very close to, but different from, Hungarian. The Csángós themselves call their mother tongue *Csángó*, and are keenly aware of its difference from *pure Hungarian*.[4]

The forebears of the Csángós migrated to Moldavia from Hungary in two large waves. The first wave arrived there in the fourteenth and fifteenth centuries as the defense system of the Hungarian Kingdom moved eastward. Most of these settlers populated the regions surrounding the town of Roman. As the population grew constantly, new villages were settled in a southerly direction, along the river Siret (Hungarian: *Szeret*), near the town of Bacău. The second wave of Hungarian migration arrived in Moldavia in the sixteenth to eighteenth centuries. These people were *Székelys*, members of a strong community living in eastern Transylvania. The Székelys enjoyed the privileges of collective nobility; they had their own autonomous military and jurisdictional areas, and were exempt from paying taxes either to the royal court or to the voivode (the ruler) of Transylvania. The notion of collective nobility, however, did not mean equal rights and equal prosperity within the community, and, in addition, from the eighteenth century on the Habsburg rulers tried to integrate the Székelys into their empire by depriving them of their privileges. This migration was motivated by both economic and political factors. The Székely groups settled in areas to the west and south of Bacău. The newcomers often settled in the villages of the first settlers, so the two migration waves mixed with each other. The ethnonym *Csángó* has two equally plausible etymologies, both of which are Hungarian. Most probably, first the Hungarians in Transylvania used the name to refer to one group of Moldavian Hungarians, and later the name came to denote all Hungarian speakers in Moldavia.

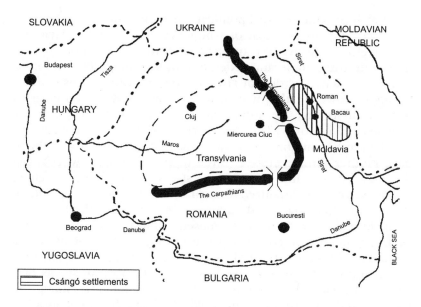

Map 15.1. Csángó-Hungarian settlements in Moldavia, Rumania

The Csángó villages have always had only very few connections with Hungary. From the end of the fifteenth century, the only real contact the Csángós had with Hungary was through the church: as an affiliate of the Franciscan province in Transylvania, a monastery was founded in Bacău. The isolation of the Csángós was completed in the early seventeenth century when Rome took over all Catholic activities in Moldavia. The Csángó settlements are also rather isolated from each other. The Csángó lifestyle and the geographical location of the villages preclude everyday contact between the Csángó communities.

The strong sense of isolation both from Hungary and from each other conserved a medieval-like culture. Most of the Csángós are peasants who own and cultivate their own land using rather undeveloped methods, lacking almost any mechanization. Until very recently their economy was almost exclusively a subsistence economy. To this day they have no handicraft industry, and a secular Csángó intelligentsia could never emerge. All of these factors have resulted in the conservation of an archaic rural culture. Folk art and folklore are not ancient relics but an integral part of the everyday life of the Csángós.

The Csángós, as a group, do not have real political representation. Although an association of Csángó-Hungarians was founded

in 1989, it provides no real political representation, partly because
it has few members (most of whom were born in Moldavia but
now live in Transylvania), and partly because of its close connections with the Democratic Federation of the Hungarians in Rumania, whose activities do not always serve the real interests of the
Csángós. However, the main problem for the Csángó-Hungarian
Association is that the Rumanian state does not recognize the
Csángós as a minority. They are therefore denied all the rights enjoyed by other minorities in Rumania, for example, the right to
have mother tongue classes (three or four lessons a week). The
Rumanian state denies the minority status of the Csángós, arguing
that they are "Hungarianized Rumanians" who must re-assimilate to
their original language and culture. This idea is not the invention
of the Rumanian state. It has been used by the Vatican for centuries
as an argument for converting the Orthodox Rumanians to Catholicism. The similarity, or virtual identity, between the Rumanian
state's argument and that put forward by the Vatican seems puz-
zling, but a close examination of the role of religion among the
Csángós and the history of the Moldavian Catholics gives us a key
to solving the puzzle.

The Role of Religion in Csángó Life

In addition to their economic and cultural conditions, the religious
life of the Csángós also shows features characteristic of the Middle
Ages. Religion, indeed, is not simply a component of Csángó culture but a way of life which determines morality and has a very
strong and natural influence on all aspects of existence. For example, the most important holidays for the Csángó communities are
the annual feasts on the days of the patron saints of local churches,
and pilgrimages to other churches. To this day, communities freeze
out those who do not follow the strict religious prescriptions
(Kotics 1997). Disrespect for religious morals is severely punished
by priests who publicly humiliate people, and sometimes excommunicate them (Kallós 1993, 101). This then means that the role
religion plays in the life of the Csángós is even more powerful than
that of the state. Csángós generally accept the priest's views without criticism, and, of course, they accept everything the priest says.
It is normally the priests who have almost exclusive social control
in the Csángó communities (Kotics 1997, 49–50).

In addition to the generally accepted pre-eminence of religion, another fact reinforces the prestige of the Catholic Church among the Csángós, namely, the fact that they did not participate in the formation of the Hungarian nation which took place in the first half of the nineteenth century, that is, about a century after the last Csángó migration to Moldavia. Moreover, they did not take part in the formation of *any* nation. As a consequence, their ethnic identity is not connected to any national identity, but is of a form which harmonizes, again, with their medieval-like world view. The main components of this identity are Christianity (in their case Roman Catholicism) and loyalty to the territory in which they live.[5] Religion is the only major feature that distinguishes the Csángós from their Orthodox Rumanian neighbors who live in a very similar way; and in those areas where the Csángós have shifted their language to Rumanian, Csángós and Rumanians speak the same language. Thus the main opposition which defines Csángó ethnic identity is religion: when a Csángó is asked about his or her nationality, the most likely answer is "I'm Catholic".[6]

The Role of the Catholic Church in the Assimilation of the Csángós

Today only about 25 percent of Csángós can speak a Csángó dialect; 75 percent have become Rumanian monolinguals. The processes of minority language shift in modern Europe are normally governed by economic and cultural factors, with or without various assimilating techniques used by the state.[7] However, in the case of the Csángós, the major driving forces behind language shift are other than economic. This is shown by, among other things, the fact that the first domain in which Csángós have undergone language shift is religion, in contradistinction to the usual pattern whereby the language of religion is the last to change (Sándor 1996b). The explanation lies in history.

The following reconstruction of Csángó religious life is based on more than two hundred documents such as letters, descriptions, and church inventories.[8]

Until the end of the sixteenth century there were two Hungarian episcopates in Moldavia. Their function was gradually taken over by a new episcopate in Bacău, while a Franciscan monastery was founded there as an affiliate of the Franciscan province in

Transylvania. At the time, the Catholic priests in Moldavia were Hungarians. In the sixteenth and seventeenth centuries, Moldavia was the scene of wars among Ottoman, Transylvanian and Wallachian troops. Due to the permanent wars, poverty, and plague, many of the Moldavian Catholic communities stayed without a priest. As a consequence of the spread of the Reformation in Hungary and Transylvania, there was a need for Catholic priests within the Carpathian Basin. The Transylvanian Franciscans were therefore no longer able to send sufficient numbers of monks to Moldavia. In 1622, a missionary organization named *De Propaganda Fide* took over the spiritual care of the Moldavian Catholics. It sent mostly Italian, sometimes Bosnian and Croatian priests to Moldavia, although from time to time the people asked for Hungarian priests. In the seventeenth century, Jesuits arrived in Moldavia. Many of the documents complain of the scandalous life of both the Italian monks and the Jesuits: they stole ecclesiastical objects, they lived together with women, and they had no contact with their flock since they did not speak their language. Meanwhile, the episcopate of Bacău went from Hungarian to Polish jurisdiction. However, the Polish bishops of Bacău did not reside in Moldavia, leaving the local priests without supervision. Thus, in this unhappy period, four different organizations of the Catholic Church were present in the area: the priests under Polish control, the Jesuits, the Italian missionaries (who belonged to one branch of the Franciscan order, the *Fratres Minorum Conventualium*), and the Bosnian missionaries and Hungarian monks (who belonged to the other branch of the Franciscan order, the *Fratres Strictioris Observantiae*). To make matters worse, the four parties often fought each other and paid little attention to serving their people. Under such circumstances the institution of folk religion developed to such an extent that it became the main domain of religious life. Deacons, who were members of the communities, fulfilled almost all the functions of the priests in the mother tongue of the community, including baptisms and funerals. However, the language of the liturgy continued to be Latin, and the people could not communicate with their foreign priests.

The eighteenth century did not bring any remarkable changes. Although the Jesuits disappeared from Moldavia, people had no church services in their mother tongue except for a few villages where Hungarian Franciscans served. In the last decades of the century, Austria took control over the northern part of the area. Meanwhile, the Vatican issued an order that church services should be celebrated in the mother tongue of the flock, but the reports of the

Austrian consuls sent disinformation to Rome, claiming that the Moldavian Catholics did not need Hungarian priests. When Csángó complaints reached the Vatican through unofficial channels, the Pope's answer stated that their priests spoke the language of the *country*. This was often true, in fact, since the Italian priests could easily learn the genetically closely related Rumanian tongue.

In the first decades of the nineteenth century the situation changed from bad to worse. During this time the Rumanian nation state was born, national feelings became stronger, and the Csángós became the target of the state's overt assimilation policy. The Rumanian Orthodox Church found it humiliating that on the territory of the Rumanian state Rome pursued missionary activity as if it were not a Christian area, and therefore Rome called back the monks. In 1884, the episcopate of Bacău was dissolved and an archbishopric was founded in Bucharest and a bishopric in Iaşi, the capital of Moldavia. Owing to the foundation of Catholic seminaries in these two cities, the need for priests decreased. However, both the young Rumanian Catholic Church and the young Rumanian Catholic priests proved to be much more demanding than their predecessors over questions of language. Towards the end of the nineteenth century schooling became widespread in Moldavia. The language of instruction was exclusively Rumanian, but as religion was taught at church and not at school, bilingual catechisms could be used. In 1895, a law prohibited this practice; religion taught in Rumanian became a compulsory subject at school and the bilingual catechisms were replaced by monolingual Rumanian ones. Although in the church the use of Csángó was forbidden by the priests, the local religious leaders (the deacons) used it until the 1930s. At that time the prohibition of the Csángó tongue was made official by a bishop's order affecting not only the liturgies but also the services of the deacons. In order to change the language of the folk religious practices, a school for deacon training was founded as early as 1923; the old Hungarian prayers and songs were translated and printed in Rumanian; prayer-books written in Hungarian were collected and burnt (Tánczos 1995, 57 and 1996, 220–221), and deacons who did not work in Rumanian were dismissed. In the 1930s young couples who did not know the catechism in Rumanian were not allowed to have a wedding ceremony in the church; a priest could excommunicate people who spoke Csángó during collective labor in their homes;[9] later on, the *Securitate*, the Rumanian state security organization, could accuse old deacons of spying if they found printed Hungarian or handwritten Csángó prayers in their houses (Tánczos 1995, 57 and 1996, 220–221).

Table 15.1 lists those Catholic organizations which have been present in Moldavia from the sixteenth century on, and the languages they have used to address their Hungarian-speaking folk. Table 15.2 summarizes the status of Hungarian in the religious life of the Csángós.

Table 15.1

Catholic organizations in Moldavia

Name	Inspector	Period	Languages used (besides Latin)
Bacău episcopate	Hungary	To end of 16th century,	Hungarian
	Poland	17th–18th centuries	Italian, Polish, Rumanian
	Austria	18th–19th centuries	Italian, Rumanian
Fratres Strictioris Observantiae	Hungary	Up to 1622	Hungarian
Fratres Minorum Conventualium	The Vatican (De Propaganda Fide)	1622–1884	Italian, Rumanian
Order of Jesuits	Order of Jesuits	17th century	Italian, Polish, Rumanian
Iaşi episcopate and seminar	Rumania	1884 onwards	Rumanian
Bucharest archbishopric and seminar	Rumania	1884 onwards	Rumanian

Table 15.2

The use of Hungarian in Catholic religious life in Moldavia

Up to 1622	supported
17–18th centuries	tolerated
1895	prohibited in churches
1938	prohibited in folk religion (for the deacons)

The enthusiasm of the Catholic priests in Moldavia for murdering the Csángós' vernacular is as strong today as it has ever been. In 1990, at a young priest's first mass, two older priests put down their priestly symbols and left the church when, after reading from the Gospel in Rumanian, the young priest started to read the text out in Hungarian (Tánczos 1995, 64). The young priest was born in the same village and studied in Transylvania rather than in Iaşi. His mother tongue is a variety of Csángó which is linguistically closer to modern Hungarian than other Csángó dialects, an idiom spoken by 97 percent of the inhabitants of the village.

In 1991, in another village, the priest ordered a group of young people to kneel by the walls of the church during the Sunday morning mass because they had gone on a trip to a Transylvanian village which wanted to build a sister-village partnership (Tánczos 1996, 114).

Recently, considerable numbers of Csángós have been trying to find jobs in Hungary, and, since 1990, a Csángó class has been organized every year in Transylvania for thirteen-year-old children. Many of them stay on to attend secondary schools as well. The Moldavian priests often warn their congregations that they should call back their children from the Transylvanian schools and their relatives from Hungary. If they fail to do so, the Catholic Church may excommunicate them (Csoma and Bogdánfalvy 1993, 165; Tánczos 1996, 115).

Although the inventory of similar cases is shamefully rich, one more recent case should suffice. In 1995, an ethnographer who was collecting archaic prayers in Moldavia was arrested and detained by the police for a day because a local priest found him "suspicious" (Tánczos 1996, 159–173).

The above-mentioned cases might suggest that these conflicts have nothing to do with the Roman Catholic Church. Rather, they may have arisen simply as products of history or as a result of the private actions of some nationalist priests. However, a closer scrutiny of the facts reveals more hidden relationships.

The Vatican's responsibility in developing the present situation lies in the fact that although it has always had information about the shameful circumstances of its flock in Moldavia, namely that people could not even go to confession because their priests did not speak their mother tongue, it nevertheless always found its own interests in world politics to be much more important. Firstly, when in the first half of the seventeenth century the Vatican's main goal was re-union with the Orthodox Church, it sent Italian missionaries rather than ordinary Hungarian priests to Moldavia. It was for this reason that it supported the activity of the Jesuits in the area. The Jesuits had good connections to the Moldavian Voivode's court, and if they had succeeded in catholicizing the Moldavian nobility, a great step would have been taken towards Romanizing the whole of Moldavia. The Vatican's preference first for Poland, then for Austria, determined its decision not to grant the requests of the Moldavian Catholic communities for Hungarian priests. From the nineteenth century onwards, Hungarian clergymen, including members of the episcopacy, have been asking the Pope to examine the needs of the Moldavian Catholics so that the liturgy be made available in Csángó in those villages where the people want it. For some reason the Vatican seems unable to grant this demand, probably because the Vatican accepts first of all the reports of the local bishops and the legate sent to Rumania, all of which inform Rome about satisfied congregations.[10]

Unquestionably, the local organizations of the Catholic Church in Moldavia have their own responsibility in the murdering of the mother tongue of the Csángós. However, it is hard to believe that their actions are independent of Rome's control. For instance, the local clergy arranged for the replacement of Hungarian patrons of churches by non-Hungarian saints (Lükő 1936, 17; Tánczos 1996, 138–139); had altar-pieces showing Hungarian saints repainted or replaced, for example, the picture of the first Hungarian king, Saint Stephen, was replaced by a picture of Saint Stephen the Protomartyr (Magyar 1994, 79); and mistranslated Hungarian hymns into Rumanian by leaving out the "troubling" parts of the original hymns (Lükő 1936, 17).

The implementation of such changes is outside the competence of the local Catholic clergy. Such acts obviously trigger changes in the identity of the flock. However, the most effective way of changing the identity of the people is through the education of priests. In the extremely poor Csángó communities men who hope to have a better life can achieve their goal most easily by becoming priests. In addition to the economic gains, priests also command the highest prestige in their communities. Unsurprisingly, Csángó children go to the Catholic seminaries of Bucharest and Iaşi with great pleasure (Magyar 1994, 75), even if, as a consequence, they can hardly communicate with their own community, including their family, for several years. During their education they learn how to be proper citizens of their state, and how to become absolutely loyal to those who made it possible for them to achieve a much better life. The literature on the Csángós calls this the "janissary"-method of education, because the system operates on the analogy of the well-known military training system of the Ottoman Empire (Mikecs 1941, 434; Magyar 1994, 75).[11] Because priests have absolute social control in the Csángó communities, the state has little to do to assimilate the Csángós. As deeply religious people, the Csángós accept whatever their priest says, even if—as oftentimes is the case—he calls their mother tongue the tongue of the devil.

Before the latest census in Rumania in 1992, a bishop's encyclical letter ordered the priests to instruct their flock as to what nationality they should declare (Csoma and Bogdánfalvy 1993, 165). Csángós were instructed not to choose *Csángó*, which was one of the options, but *Rumanian* because they were *Roman* Catholics (Csoma and Bogdánfalvy 1993, 165; Tánczos 1996, 115 and 1997, 389). Such an instruction can be remarkably successful because in colloquial Rumanian the words *român* "Rumanian" and *romano* "Roman" sound deceptively similar. However, this verbal trick, used in 1992, goes back to the union politics of the Vatican. One argument in support of re-union with the Orthodox Church (meaning, in fact, its catholicization) was that all Rumanians were Catholics who had taken their faith with them from the Roman Empire, but only those Rumanians could keep the ancient faith who were Hungarianized by the Catholic Hungarian kings in Moldavia, namely: the Csángós. As they return to their ancient language (that is, as they shift to Rumanian) so should the Orthodox Rumanians return to the Catholic Church (Lükő 1936, 16; Mikecs 1941, 434).

The argument that the Csángós are Hungarianized Rumanians was revitalized in a book published in 1985 (Mărtinaş 1985).[12] This idea has become extremely popular with Rumanian politicians, since, if the Csángós are ethnic Rumanians who have been linguistically assimilated to Hungarians, they belong to the majority nation and hence minority rights should not be accorded to them. Table 15.3 shows the similarities in the arguments used by the Vatican and in the Rumanian assimilation policies (parentheses indicate that an argument is an implicit one).

Table 15.3

The argumentation of the Vatican and of the Rumanian State

Statement	The Vatican	Rumania
(1) Csángós do not need Hungarian priests	(+)	+
(2) Csángós are Hungarianized Romanians	+	+
(3) Csángós saved the ancient faith	+	
(4) the Rumanians must also return to their ancient faith (i.e. Roman Catholicism)	+	
(5) the Csángós must return to their ancient language (i.e. Rumanian)	(+)	+
(6) Csángós are *Roman Catholics (romano-catolic)*, that is, *Rumanian Catholics (român catolic)*	+	+

The modern Rumanian nation state's assimilationist policy towards the Csángós coincides with the Vatican's goals which have been followed for centuries in Moldavia. It is important to remember that priests command the highest prestige and absolute authority in the extremely religious Csángó communities. When they promote involuntary language shift, they run little risk of violating any international norms because their language-shift promotion takes place orally, and there are no written church laws or orders which demonstrably violate linguistic human rights.

This strategy of the priests is extremely powerful since the unconditional prestige of the priests lends absolute prestige to the Rumanian language, in such a way that Rumanian is perceived as the best language in all domains of language use. In such a situation people do not have to be forced to shift languages, they undergo language shift voluntarily. Their attitudes to their priests pave the way for their language shift. Such a policy targets the core element of a group's identity, in the case of the Csángós their religion, and through it, almost as a side effect, can achieve language shift. Arguably, there is no intention that the Csángós become Orthodox; what is being changed is merely the "character" of their Roman Catholicism or the vehicle of their religious life from Hungarian to Rumanian.

The number of Csángós who still speak Csángó either as their mother tongue or as their second language is about 60,000. Unless the current rapid process of language shift can be stopped by efficient revitalization, the Csángós are destined to disappear in the Rumanian melting pot. Today, many Csángós insist on practicing their religion in their mother tongue but they are denied this linguistic human right. Their history and current fate exemplify the linguistic assimilation of a minority group without any overt violation of their *language* rights.

Notes

1 I want to thank Miklós Kontra and Peter Trudgill for their help in formulating the English version of this text.
2 The data-gathering methods used in the last Rumanian census (1992) make the results rather undependable. Although the options for nationality included "Hungarian" and "Csángó" as well, in many cases the census-takers marked the Csángós' nationality as Rumanian without so much as asking them the question. In other cases they used loaded

questions like "You are Rumanian, aren't you?" (Csoma and Bogdánfalvy 1993). Since all the Csángós are Catholic, and they are the only Catholic inhabitants in Moldavia, estimates are based on the number of Catholic people in Moldavia.

3 An Ausbau-language is "a variety which derives its status as a language, rather than a dialect, not so much from its linguistic characteristics [...] but from its social, cultural and political characteristics" (Trudgill 1992, 11). Examples of Ausbau-languages include Swedish and Norwegian, or Volga Tatar and Bashkir, which are mutually understandable for each other's speakers but are nevertheless regarded as distinct languages.

4 In traditional Hungarian linguistics Csángó is regarded as a dialect of Hungarian. The main argument put forward by Hungarian dialectologists and historical linguists is that "it has always been considered as a dialect of Hungarian." From a historical point of view, Csángó is unquestionably of Hungarian origin. However, from a sociolinguistic point view, it seems to be a roofless Ausbau-language (Sándor 1996a).

5 Because the Csángó villages have never formed a cohesive geographical unit during their history, Csángós lack not only a common endo-ethnonym, but a "we-consciousness" and a sense of common origin as well. Their identity is very fragile between the strong Rumanian and Hungarian national identities.

6 The roots of this identification reach back to the sixteenth and seventeenth centuries when, except for some small German communities, all the Catholics in Moldavia were Hungarians. At that time the Rumanian words for "Hungarian" and "Catholic" became synonyms, as did the respective Hungarian words as well. Catholic priests were called "Hungarian priests" both by the Csángós and their Rumanian neighbors, even if the priests were Italian, German or Polish. This is the reason why Catholics are sometimes called *ungur* "Hungarian" in Rumanian, even in villages where no one speaks Hungarian anymore. Later the Csángós accepted Hungarian *csángó* and Rumanian *ceangău* as their names, and these words displaced the Hungarian designation *magyar* "Moldavian Hungarian" and the Rumanian word *ungur* "Moldavian Hungarian". In the meantime, most of the Csángós underwent language shift to Rumanian, and *csángó* and *ceangău* today mean "Moldavian Catholic," irrespective of the mother tongue of the people.

7 See, for example, the language shift of the Hungarians in Burgenland, Austria (Gal 1979).

8 The documents are published in Benda (1989), and Domokos (1987). In the next three paragraphs I refer to my sources only when they are different from Benda or Domokos.

9 For instance, corn-husking, spinning, and weaving are still done cooperatively, usually in the house of a member of the community.

10 This policy of the Vatican is still valid today as I learned from an interview which I conducted with Endre Gyulay, the bishop of Southeast Hungary, in September 1997.

11 The janissary (from Turkish *yeni çeri,* "new army") troops used to be the elite of the Ottoman army. Christian children were gathered, often taken by force in the occupied territories, and were converted to Islam and given the finest military education. They were totally isolated from civil society, but enjoyed privileges. Many of them achieved high positions in the Ottoman state, and as they had neither family nor any other civil background, they became absolutely loyal to the sultan.

12 The content of Mărtinaş' book is briefly summarized in English by Baker (1997, 664).

References

Baker, Robin. "On the origin of the Moldavian Csángós." *The Slavonic and East European Review* 75 (1997): 658–680.

Benda, Kálmán. *Moldvai csángó-magyar okmánytár 1–2* (Moldavian Csángó-Hungarian Archives 1-2). Budapest: Magyarságkutató Intézet, 1989.

Csoma, Gergely and János Bogdánfalvy. "Népszámlálás a moldvai csángó falvakban" (Census data gathering in the Moldavian Csángó villages). In Péter Halász, ed., *"Megfog vala apóm szokcor kezemtül..."*, 165-167. Budapest: Lakatos Demeter Egyesület, 1993.

Domokos, Pál Péter. *A moldvai magyarság* (Hungarians in Moldavia). Budapest: Magvető, 1987.

Gal, Susan. *Language Shift. Social Determinants of Linguistic Change in Bilingual Austria.* New York, London: Academic Press, 1979.

Kallós, Zoltán. "Gyűjtési élményeim Moldvában" (Fieldworker's experiences in Moldavia). In Anikó Péterbencze, ed., *Moldvának szíp tájaind születtem...*, 95-109. Jászberény: Jászberényi Múzeum, 1993.

Kotics, József. "Erkölcsi értékrend és társadalmi kontroll néhány moldvai csángó faluban" (Morality and social control in some Moldavian Csángó villages). In Ferenc Pozsony, ed., *Dolgozatok a moldvai csángók népi kultúrájáról*, 36–56. Kolozsvár: Kriza János Néprajzi Társaság, 1997.

Lükő, Gábor. *A moldvai csángók 1* (The Moldavian Csángós). Budapest: magánkiadás, 1936.

Magyar, Zoltán. "Vallás és etnikum kapcsolata egy moldvai csángó faluban" (The relationship between religion and ethnicity in a Moldavian Csángó village). *Néprajzi látóhatár*, 3 (1994): 75–88.

Mărtinaş, Dumitru. *Originea ceangăilor din Moldova.* Bucureşti, 1985.

Mikecs, László. *Csángók* (Csángós). Kolozsvár: Bolyai Akadémia, 1941.

Sándor, Klára. "*Apró Ábécé*-apró esély: A csángók nyelvélesztésének lehetőségei és esélyei" ("Little Alphabet"-little chance: Possibilities and chances of the revitalization of Csángó). In István Csernicskó and Tamás Váradi, eds., *Kisebbségi magyar iskolai nyelvhasználat*, 51-67. Budapest: Tinta Könyvkiadó és Kiadványszerkesztő Bt., 1996a.

——. "A nyelvcsere és a vallás összefüggése a csángóknál" (Language shift and religion among the Csángós). *Korunk* (November 1996) (1996b): 60–75.

Skutnabb-Kangas, Tove and Robert Phillipson, eds. *Linguistic Human Rights. Overcoming Linguistic Discrimination*. Berlin, New York: Mouton de Gruyter, 1994.

Tánczos, Vilmos. "Hányan vannak a moldvai csángók?" (How big is the Moldavian Csángó population?) *Magyar Kisebbség* 3 (1997): 370–390.

——. "A nyelvváltás jelensége a moldvai csángók egyéni imarepertoárjában" (Language shift in the individual prayer repertoire of the Moldavian Csángós). *Kétnyelvűség* 3/2 (1995): 51–68.

——. *Keletnek megnyílt kapuja* (The Gate of the East Opened Up). Kolozsvár: Korunk Baráti Társaság, 1996.

Trudgill, Peter. *Introducing Language and Society*. London: Penguin, 1992.

Index